WAR STORIES

The Men of the Airborne

TURNER PUBLISHING COMPANY
Paducah, Kentucky

"Thunder From Heaven"

The 17th Airborne Division insignia with the eagle's golden talon on the black background symbolizes the Airborne's wartime mission — a surprise strike from the darkness of the sky and the grasping of golden opportunities in the battle below.

TURNER PUBLISHING COMPANY
THE FRONT LINE OF MILITARY HISTORY BOOKS
P.O. Box 3101, 412 Broadway
Paducah, Kentucky 42001

Library of Congress Catalog Card No. 92-62338
ISBN: 1-56311-097-0

Printed in the U.S.A.
Limited Printing
Additional books may be purchased from the publisher.

DEDICATION

To those members of the 17th Airborne Division who, during World War II, died in the service of their country ... and, to those of the "survivors" who have since followed them in death.

PROLOGUE

When our troop train pulled into Hoffman, North Carolina, in mid-April of 1943, I looked out the window and saw a sign that read, "Home of the 17th Airborne Division." That was the first hint that I had that I was not heading for an assignment in the Army Air Corps.

During the two days and nights we had been confined in those hot, dirty railway coaches winding and back-tracking our way from the Reception Center, we had all speculated as to where we were bound and what type of unit we would join. With some 500 troops aboard, you had a wide selection of opinions to choose from.

I remember two things from the Reception Center. First, I remember how everyone laughed when they called for volunteers to join the paratroopers. Then, I remembered some interviewer had asked me if I objected to service in the "Air Forces." To this I quickly answered, "Absolutely not!"

Like many young men of my generation, I had always dreamed about flying. Those goggles and white scarfs looked dashing! My dreams, however, had all come crashing down when the local recruiter had turned me down for pilot training because of my faulty eyesight.

Even the Marines and the Navy didn't want me, so only the Army was left as an option. If I had to make the decision today, I wouldn't hesitate to go "Airborne, all the way!" But, on that day almost 50 years ago, I wasn't overjoyed to see those signs about something called "Glider Infantry." I thought what in the world had I done to myself!

My introduction to the 17th Airborne Division wasn't too unlike that of thousands of other young men that spring of 1943. Airborne was still a new concept in warfare and we were elated that we were going to be a part of it. Sure, it was different, but it was exciting and we were young and we rapidly got with the program! The skills and the espirit de corps began to build and we toughened to the task.

Caught up in the excitement of being "Airborne," and the idea that we were a notch above the rest of the Army, we were soon molded into an elite fighting force without our really being aware of it. Many a youth became a man in those hot, muggy days at Camp Mackall.

Now, as we mark the 50th Anniversary of the activation of the 17th Airborne Division, we have learned to appreciate the memories of those days. We now realize that those days we spent together and the deeds we did should not be lost to the ravages of time.

The combat history of the 17th Airborne Division has been chronicled elsewhere. This book gets to the heart of our history—the heroic and sometimes humorous incidents the individual soldiers experienced during those adventure-packed years of 1943-1945.

All the stories in this book are true. Although the passage of time may have dimmed the ability to pin-point some of the exact dates, some locales may be a little off and some names have long been forgotten, the events really happened. The stories are about real people in real places and in strange, but real times.

We did take the liberty of "cleaning up" some of the rough, barracks jargon that spiced our speech in those days! We wanted you to be able to show the book to your wife, your children, and your grandchildren.

I have rewritten most of the stories and put to words others gleaned from notes, letters or taped interviews. However, the final versions have all been checked with our "story tellers" to ensure their accuracy.

You may notice something else we have done throughout the book. Wherever the word "Airborne" appears, we have capitalized the word. In many cases this is contrary to the proper use of capital letters, but we felt that due to what that word has come to mean to all of us, it warranted that special recognition. I believe my past English teachers will forgive me!

My only regret is that every story sent to me could not be included. As with any publication, the author must adhere to certain space limitations. In addition, it is important to select a good "mix" of stories. I feel we have accomplished these goals, but I know it was at the expense of leaving out someone's favorite story. It just couldn't be helped.

A great number of people had a part in making this book. Without the wonderful guys who became our "story tellers" nothing would have been possible. Then, there were Ed Siergiej, our hard-working association secretary-treasurer and Joe Quade, our newsletter editor, both of whom channeled stories and "story tellers" to me.

Other association members called facts to my attention, put me in touch with those who had stories to tell, verified locations, names and faces and helped in hundreds of ways. I also received photos, many unpublished until now, from troopers who wanted to be a part of this project. It was, as always, a team effort.

I also appreciate the assistance and support I received from my beloved wife of 47 years, Georgeanna. For over a year I have had my material strung out all over the house, but she never complained and always encouraged me in this endeavor.

It is my hope that this book will live on long after all of us old soldiers are dead and gone. That's the real reason for the book. The zeal we had for the job we did must not be lost in time and forgotten. Whether we realize it or not, we blazed a trail and, I hope, set a standard for elite forces of the future.

AIRBORNE!

Bart Hagerman

CONTENTS

PART I

THE MAKING
OF
A DIVISION

"THE 17TH AIRBORNE IS BORN"

As told by Edward Dorrity 193 HQ 1

We were young.
  We were raw.
    We were green.
      We were scared.
The anxious young faces peering from the train windows were looking out at a strange parched land. Little dust devils danced across the space between the long passenger train and the line of army trucks that stood waiting. There were men in uniform stirring about with a certain impatience. We did not know for sure where we were, but it looked hot. Hot and dry.

The long passenger train came slowly to a stop. Just days before we had been civilians in places like upper New York State, Pennsylvania and Virginia. Our mothers and fathers had said goodbye and we went off into the Army. We had no idea what we were about to get into. We had been inducted into the Army, rushed through an induction center, standing for long periods totally naked. We had been prodded, poked and tested. All of us had scored rather well on certain portions of the Army AGCT test and now we were here, somewhere south of where we started several days ago. The train had barely stopped before orders were shouted and the young men started to gather their belongings and prepared to get off the train.

This is here we slowly began to learn procedure and to obey commands. Fall Out! Form a line alongside the train! Board the trucks! Willing to follow orders, scared of the soldiers who were giving the orders, eager to please we scrambled on the trucks as best we could. All that work made us hot and sweaty, especially in the dark brown, woolen O.D. uniforms. The convoy of trucks loaded with raw recruits started up and rumbled through the warm dust. No one had told us anything yet. All we did was follow orders. We were too much in awe of the situation to do anything else. Now we were about to learn several things.

The trucks had moved in through a development of new single story buildings. Down an asphalt road. It had started to turn dark when our truck stopped outside one of the buildings. The rear panel was pulled down and a voice shouted, "Fall out!" Gingerly and with a certain amount of care for our bodies and our possessions, one by one we got out of the truck.

"Holy Hell! Are we going to take all night, ladies?" The young recruits found themselves staring into the infuriated face of a menacing soldier, who seemed ready to take them all on, one at a time or all together, it didn't matter to him. It is strange, but at times like these, the people doing the yelling seem to grow to be nine feet tall. "Now, get back in that truck and when I say FALL OUT, I want you to come out of there and form a column of twos right here." He pointed to a spot in the dust.

Ed Dorrity owns a public relations firm in Memphis, Tennessee.

We memorized the spot so we'd be sure to be in the right place and not cause him to get any further upset. We started to get back in the truck when more fire was breathed in our direction. "Get back in the damn truck NOW! Shoving and pushing we scrambled over one another to get back in and took our places and waited.

"FALL OUT!" The command came again. The harried ex-civilians pushed and shoved and jumped out. It seems, however, that this was not fast enough for the sergeant. No one may remember just how many times we performed the FALL OUT maneuver before we finally satisfied our instructor. But we finally did manage to make one mad rush that made us appear to be a single lump of brown. Out of the truck, on to the ground and then lined up as ordered and only then were we marched into the building.

It was there that someone told us we were in the Airborne, whatever that was. This was where battalion and company assignments were made. Everything was a bit of blur. Somewhere in this series of events, we lined up in a column of twos (which seems to be the Army's favorite formation), and still wearing overcoats, were ordered to follow another sergeant at a trot. The reason we were wearing overcoats is that this seemed to be the best way to carry them. Besides, no one had told us to take them off. We had already learned that we could not do anything unless someone told us to do so. We learned fast and no one had even done a single push-up, yet. We sure had a lot of surprises coming.

So off we went. The sergeant was trotting with us grunting "Hut ... hut" each time his left foot hit the ground. The purpose of the "Hut ... Hut" we learned was to get us to trot along at the same pace. During the three or four block trot to the chapel, several couldn't hack it and fell out along the way. They were urged onward at whatever pace they could muster. The grinning Sergeant allowed as how he'd have them doing five miles and liking it in no time at all. I doubt that any of us really believed him.

In the chapel an officer welcomed the group to the 17th Airborne Division and gave a brief orientation of what would happen next. It all sounded strange. However, he could have spoken longer, the rest would have been welcome, because as soon as he was finished, the sergeant was there to Hut ... Hut us back to the reception area. Then we were told to gather up our duffel bags and start on the trek to the final destination, our new company.

The Division Road never looked so long. Stretched out before us was a staggering line of young boys and a few older men (guys at least 21 years old) hauling everything they owned on their backs. No one dared to stop or look back in fear that a sergeant may be there to breathe a little more fire to help us along at a better pace.

This was the Airborne. The 17th Airborne Division. It was newly formed and we were it. According to records, the average age of the men in the division at its inception was less than 20 years old. Considering the age of the officers and a number of the older recruits, such as Gil Egloff and Bob Chambers, that meant that more than 90% were 18 years old. That was just what we needed. Young, eager, fearless. Virtually a blank page on which the image of an Airborne infantryman could be drawn.

With great relief the sign we were looking for came into view. Headquarter Company, 1st Battalion, 193rd Glider Infantry. We turned into the area and once again were greeted by a sergeant. We got to know this one—his name was Mashburn. First Sergeant Herman Mashburn. In no time at all we'd learn to stand in awe of that man. He was the top-kick. Number one.

We had arrived, now the orientation and training were to begin.

The First Taste of Airborne Training Begins

Staggering under the weight of their belongings, the wide-eyed recruits arrived at their new home. It was Headquarters Company, 1st Battalion, 193rd Glider Infantry. The name had no real meaning at that time.

Our new home was a heavy weapons company. Mortars and machine guns, 81mm mortars, 30 caliber machine guns. Later we would come to know the true meaning of heavy weapons when it was discovered that these weapons would travel on our shoulders. The weapons would become a close and personal part of each soldier along with his own side arm. It was also the first time the word "Gliders" was mentioned.

There was so much to learn and no one was going to give us a lot of time to absorb all the new things. We began with each other's name. Chris Muoio, New York; Manley Gray, Colorado; Bruce Gardner, Pennsylvania; Maxie Gideon, Missouri; Adolph Schwab, Iowa; Mort Myers, Iowa; Cliff Stocksdale, Missouri; and Dale Strand from Florida. Just a few of those in our barracks. All new, all strange. Yet we instinctively knew that we were bound together by something stronger than any friendship we had ever had before.

In the barracks we were given a choice of an upper or a lower bunk. The "choice" was won by the first to arrive and take possession. We were also introduced to the footlocker. We learned quickly that one did not just dump everything into the footlocker and close the lid. In typical Army style there was a place for everything and a manner in which they should be displayed. Have you ever seen a row of socks come to attention? Why they put so much emphasis on how a bed should be made was beyond the young recruits. We watched with great interest as the sergeant showed us how to make "square corners" and how the sheet should be folded over the blanket at the top. There was even a prescribed amount of sheet that should be showing and there were specifics as to where the pillow went.

We had also been issued a rifle and told to memorize the serial number on the rifle as if it were our own name. The rifle was to be stored in the specific Army way as were shoes under the bunk. We also had to memorize our Army serial number. What's the expression? "The right way, the wrong way and the Army way!" On top of that you have to add "The Airborne Way," which seems to be the Army way only faster and better. We learned the Airborne Way to go to mess. We learned the Airborne Way to march, to fall out, to go to the rifle range and everything else. Every minute of every day we were learning to be "Airborne All The Way."

Now dressed in sensible khakis, we were ordered to fall out on the company street. There, assembled by platoons and squads, we met our captain for the first time. Captain Ben Miller looked like a hard, lean, no-nonsense warrior. We later nicknamed him "Black Diamond" in reference to his jet black head of hair and whiskers that made him look like he had 5 o'clock shadow at 6 a.m. Briefly and to the point he told us what we would become and how he would work us until we reached the level of excellence he wanted in his men. We knew the Army would be tough, but this Airborne was something else. Just how much tougher is what we were about to find out.

Among the other officers were Lieutenant Harry Sames, stern as he was, he was also funny. He was famous for his lectures on personal hygiene. Lieutenant William Ziegler, machine gun platoon leader, was a "by-the-book" leader. As "GI" as they came. He was also first to do any assignment before asking his men to do it. Lieutenant Ralph Vohs, tough, tall, and demanding. On the long marches, he was the one who ran up and down the column, picking up the laggers and energizing those who were tired.

Initially the training was physical, designed to build strength and stamina.

They were determined to make us as hard as nails. Before breakfast each morning there was the run, Airborne style, from the barracks area out on the Division Street and up the hill to the packing sheds. The same routine was followed each day before evening meal. Everywhere the recruits went, they went. "On The Double." Those three words became a way of life. "On The Double" to mess. "On The Double" to get shots, "On The Double" to the theater for indoctrination films. "On The Double" out to the parade grounds for calisthenics and close order drill. All of this in the broiling sun of North Carolina in the spring. What was it going to be like when summer hit? Those who couldn't cut it were weeded out and shipped to some other non-Airborne outfit. There were quite a few.

Then there was also the daily dose of side straddle hop, push-ups, and other arm and leg strengthening exercises that seemed to go on for hours on end. Bayonet drill, hand grenade throwing and hand-to-hand combat were given us in steady doses. Bayonet drill was serious. Because we were to be dropped among the enemy, we expected to have close quarter combat. We learned to use both ends of the M-1. The bayonet was like a spear and a sword, to be jabbed at some and slashed at others. Swing the M-1 and use the butt to knock someone's block off or disable him with a body blow. Hand grenade drill emphasized accuracy as well as distance. We tossed a grenade through a suspended car tire. We did it over and over until we were accurate more often than not.

Someone devised a devilish little exercise where one of us was blindfolded and stood in the middle of a circle of his fellow troopers. Initially they were armed with tent pegs and one of them was to slowly sneak up on the blindfolded one and "stab" him with the tent peg. It was the job of the one in the middle to "sense" the approach of the enemy and get him first. You are blindfolded. One of your senses has been blocked, you are in the dark, a black hole. Your ears and your mind worked to sort out the sounds around you. You begin to hear the sounds of distant commands drifting across the parade grounds. Your ears picked out vehicles moving far away. The sound of insects. Each of these sounds is cataloged and accepted. You are listening, trying to "feel" something different, something that doesn't belong. The sound of a boot on the sand. Breathing. Something that is not a part of the sounds you have cataloged and accepted. There it is! you turn to "face" the enemy and raise your weapon. You did it. You "felt" the approach of the enemy.

Once we became good at this "game" we switched from tent pegs to jump knives just to "make it more interesting." We were slowly getting the idea that our training was going to be tougher than most and we'd be required to be tougher, more alert and more resourceful and just plain better than other military. Friend or foe.

At the outset there were no parade grounds—just fields of scrub pine, rattlesnakes and the infinite variety of bugs that are an integral part of the southern habitat. It was the new trooper's job to clear the area and make it into

Troops of the 17th Airborne board the train at Hoffman, NC en route to Tennessee and the 1944 maneuvers. One year later and they would be fighting in Europe. (Photo by Albert Polinske, Abn. Hq.)

a smooth field. Clearing the area also removed all the trees and gave way to hard baked sand that reflected the sun and heat. Hardly perfect working conditions for a bunch of transplanted Yankees, Mid-Westerners and Western-ers. The immediate benefit of clearing the soon-to-be parade grounds was that the snakes disappeared. They were too smart to slither around on that stove-like sand.

It was here that we built the obstacle course with the high wall and ropes and other barriers that were to become a regular part of our training. Hauling our bodies up and over that 20-foot wall became a standard part of the tortuous physical regimen of toughening the young men to the point where we could be called Airborne.

Everyone learned the Airborne shuffle (today we'd call it jogging) and we did it everywhere we went while chanting those "sound-off" ditties that are a part of the memories. The cadre of sergeants and officers who were doing the training took great delight in seeing how far they could stretch the men. Double time some more. "Give me 50" became as common a phrase as "sound off." The "give me 50" phrase was demanded by the sergeants and it was the recruit who fell down and bounded off 50 push-ups.

Without warning we'd be commanded to "Hit The Dirt!" When the command "Hit The Dirt" came, you threw yourself at the ground with reckless abandon. The purpose was to get on the ground as fast as possible. Why? Well, later there could be in-coming enemy artillery, or rifle and machine gun fire or a diving Stuka bomber. Whatever, we did learn to "Hit The Dirt." We also learned not to keep perishables or sharp or hard things in certain pockets.

Because when you hit the dirt, the perishables perished and the hard and sharp things left their marks on your body.

The training was tough, and it was intended to be. It was physical and mental. We had to learn to respond to commands instantly. Learning to become resourceful was another vital part of the training. We had to improvise, turn any situation to our advantage. We had skilled teachers with able, eager students. Later these same men who bitched and complained about the severity of the training would be proudly bragging to civilians and other military what they could do. We were better than others and we were ready to prove it.

Training was briefly interrupted on April 15, 1943 so we could officially activate the 17th Airborne Division. This was the first time we had all seen the division assembled. It was quite a sight to see the entire parade grounds filled with troops and their equipment. A reviewing stand was set up. The division band filled the air with properly stirring march music. Our commanding general, W.M. Miley, a West Pointer, made appropriate remarks and we all passed in review. Our battalion was led by Lieutenant Colonel Robert Ashworth and Major Robert Rowan, the executive officer. We looked as good as any group with just a few weeks of training, but being Airborne gave us a certain jaunty attitude. One reason we looked better than most was because we had the benefit of the close order drill given by Lieutenant Ralph Vohs. He was the type who could give commands to send each squad in a separate direction, spread the company over the entire parade ground and bring us all back together in a column of twos. We loved it!

Back to the grind of basic training. This included going into the field to actually shoot the mortars. This was a bit scary at first, because most of us had little experience with exploding weapons and handling charges of powder. Each shell has a number of charges on it. By removing a proper number of charges you determined the distance the shell would fly. The explosions made by the mortar shells were very impressive to us. We were particularly impressed with our ability to hit the area where we aimed.

We also had to qualify as expert with our rifles. Some had been issued carbines, others fired M-1s while a few were given BARs and 03s so they could be used as rifle grenade launchers. We were introduced to the Drowning Swamp and the infiltration course. It was toss-up which was the most distressing. Drowning Swamp was a dark, dank, densely overgrown area which gave us the feeling we were in the jungle. This lead to rumors that we were getting ready to be shipped to the South Pacific.

Drowning Swamp had a turgid stream coursing through it that was coated with some kind of green muck. Water moccasins slid lazily through the murky water. We had to cross it as a part of the drill. This meant wading across, getting our boots filled with the mud and the slime that was on the bottom, while the rest of our clothes, packs and canteens got soaked with the watery green slime. That didn't matter too much, because we were already soaking with perspiration to start with and the water in the stream was cooler. Naturally we had to hold our rifles over our head to keep them dry. It didn't matter how wet we got. We damn well had to keep our rifles dry ... or else. On occasion one or more of us would slip and go under in the dark water. I don't think anyone actually did drown in Drowning Swamp, but several came mighty close. We did learn not to have our mouth open if we slipped beneath the water. It tasted like hell.

The infiltration course was another tester. We were supposed to work our way through the wooded area, always on the alert for the enemy. Wooden pop-up forms were rigged to surprise us as we worked our way, one by one through the area. As each form popped up we were supposed to shoot it, which we did reasonably well. However, making the forms easy to shoot was just a ploy to lull us into a sense of false security, because, at one point as we followed the trail, it went down an embankment to a small pond. The trail proceeded up the other side and actually led to the end of the course. Once again they caught us.

Just as we set foot at the bottom of the embankment and were about to jump over the pond, a shot rang out, a slug whistled into the mud next to our feet and someone yelled, "Hit The Dirt!" Some of our troopers actually did hit the dirt ... well not the dirt, but the muddy water of the pond and came up sputtering and gagging. This always gave the cadre a big laugh. The wiser ones made it across the pond and on to the embankment on the other side before flinging themselves to the ground and rolling over ready to fire their weapon. The sergeants and the lieutenant who were firing the M-1 found this all very amusing.

It seems that as the "basic" training progressed, the less basic it became and the more demanding it was. Just as we began to get used to the morning and evening five mile runs to the parachute packing sheds and back, they started a series of long marches. Long marches with full field equipment, which meant we had to carry those blamed mortars and machine guns. Keep in mind that this was in North Carolina and we are talking May and June, when it starts to really get hot. Trudging over the sand hills was not exactly a vacation in Bermuda.

It was amazing to see how these young troopers would steel themselves to keep moving at the pace that is set by Airborne troops. For instance, on a 26-mile march we'd start out doing the Airborne shuffle for three minutes and then our "normal" pace for two minutes. Remember, our pace is several beats faster than the regular "straight leg" infantry. We began to wonder, "If we are really Airborne, why do we have to be able to cover so much ground on foot in such a short time." The real truth, we learned, is that glider troopers and paratroopers are not always dropped exactly where they should be. So ... you double time to where you are supposed to be. Sounds simple doesn't it? Try it.

One of the marches was a grueling 26-mile forced march with water rationing. This was designed to really test our mettle. It was hot, dusty, and about as rugged an exercise we'd face. We started out with only a half canteen of water. We were not allowed to drink, except at specified stops and we were supposed to have water left at the end. Carrying heavy weapons in all the heat and dust really works up a thirst. Normal routine was for each squad member to take a turn carrying a piece of the mortar or machine gun. That worked pretty well. Every five or ten minutes you got relief and were able to march along with just your own equipment. Every once in while, because of frustration with the heat or the physical demands on our bodies, one of the guys would get mad and when it came his turn to give up a piece of the gun, he'd hold on to it and just keep moving forward. Tough? You bet.

The kicker to the whole exercise came when we marched back into camp. It had become routine that, as we approached camp, no matter how beat or hurting, we'd straighten up, get in step and come smartly down the Division Street to our barracks. When we lined up, waiting to be dismissed, we saw something different. The brass was so pleased with our performance they had a reward for us. A half dozen new, shiny garbage cans loaded with ice and beer! Plenty enough to go around. When the command "Fall Out!" was given, we attacked the cans. One after another the troopers downed the ice-cold beer, chug-a-lug. When the icy cold liquid hit the overheated innards the result was ... plop ... plop ... plop as they passed out from the impact on their bodies. Never fear. They did revive, took a shower, pulled on clean socks and shiny boots over blistered feet and in true Airborne style grabbed a week-end pass.

One day we were introduced to some boxes. These were simulated gliders. The boxes were firmly rooted on the ground, and they were designed to train the new glider infantrymen on how to get into them, load them, and get out of them. Most important was learning to firmly tie down the equipment. We'd discover later that when you are in the air, in the close quarters of a CG-4A, you don't want mortar equipment shifting about in a lurching glider, crashing up against your legs.

The getting out part reminded us of the first day at Camp Mackall when the sergeant had us scrambling out of that truck. The same routine applied in exiting a glider, whether the exit was from the oddly shaped side door or out through the raised nose section where the pilot sat, the exiting maneuver was done as fast as possible. Later we'd appreciate that being in a glider after it had landed in a combat zone was one of the most undesirable places in the world. The "thrill" of flying in a glider was to be reserved for a later date. The Airborne had it's timetable and the troopers had to take it one step at a time.

While the riflemen, machine gunners, artillery and other troops were learning their jobs, the mortar platoon was out on the same shadeless, frying-hot parade ground dealing with the intricacies of the 81mm mortar. The base plate and the barrel each weigh 40 pounds and the tripod weighs 36 pounds. Six rounds of ammo also weighs 36 pounds. These weights became more important when we started to carry these individual parts or wore a saddle-bag holding six rounds. That's how the mortar and its ammo got from place to place, on our shoulders ... whether it was from the barracks to the parade ground or a 26-mile march ... we picked them up and carried them.

Somewhere along the way during training, the Army supplied us with some little shoulder pads to protect our tender bones from the sharp edges of the base plate. These pitiful things which looked like a couple of dinner rolls on a string were useless. So were the little hand carts they came up with next. They worked perfectly fine marching down the Division Street, but once you started over sand and through brush and out into the swampy area surrounding camp, they were just something else you had to carry. They got the same treatment our gas masks got when we later went into combat. Deep six.

Part of the training for the mortar squads was to see how quickly we could get the gun into a firing position when needed. To train for this, we stood at a marked off position and, at a given signal, ran as fast as we could for about 10 to 15 yards and "hit the dirt" with the base plate as the barrel was jammed into it. The collar of the bipod was snapped over the barrel, the sight put in place, an aiming stake was put in place and the gun was ready to fire at a specific target. At the same time, another member of the squad had prepared a round of ammunition and was standing ready to drop it into the gun barrel. Determined, we did it over and over again in the heat, humidity and sand. We kept at it, each time trying to beat our fastest time. In a matter of seconds ... less than 20, we were prepared to start dropping mortar shells on the enemy. How much better could we get?

Then came the day when we actually loaded a glider and were pulled off the ground. The CG-4A may be better transportation than the camel, but that may be the only kind thing you can say about the CG-4A. It shivered and shook as it flew through the air on tow and it slewed from side to side. It dropped like a rock without warning. Not exactly the sort of thing that builds a lot of confidence. The glider's thin skin burned like a flash fire if hit by a bullet or touched by a cigarette. The erratic flight pattern of the glider induced air sickness in a number of the troops. The only place to toss the cookies was in the helmet. No barf bags on U.S. Gliders.

After several orientation flights with "Sunday afternoon in the park" landings, we were treated to a simulated mission with full scale combat-style flight and landing. We were in a double tow, which means that each C-47 was towing two gliders. They were on staggered tethers so that they would not sway into one another. To make it even better, we were blessed to have C-47 tow-plane pilots who had been through combat in an Airborne operation. Just to show off and to give us something to remember, along the way to the drop zone, they spotted a little lake and made a bit of a dive and skimmed the water with the gliders. We got our tails wet.

Once over the drop zone, gliders began to cut loose from tow planes. They swung silently in a lazy arc toward the landing zone. Some, however, dove in at sharper angles than others. There seemed to be a helter skelter race to get on the ground. Our landing was pretty much without incident. Unlike some of our buddies, our pilot did not shear off the wings as the glider slid between trees. Gliders have wheels, but the stop is rather sudden if the skids contact the ground. Giders have been known to do a somersault on landing. Or end up standing on their nose.

We quickly raised the nose and moved out of the glider with the speed we acquired in training. Just as we cleared our craft, another one came in and smashed the nose of our glider back down. Anyone trying to exit the glider at this point would be calling for medics. The other glider twisted in the air, hit the ground a bit sideways and spun crazily to a halt. A squad of groggy troopers spilled out and headed for the nearby trees.

Some gliders were just filled with troops. Others had some troops and a jeep, a trailer, artillery or other equipment. The landing field was filled with troops running for cover, gliders being bashed against trees or sliding into other gliders. Confusion seemed to be in charge. However, good training prevailed and the troops began to form fighting units and take up positions as had been planned. Now we were ready for combat well, not yet. More training coming up.

Our next exercise was a simulated glider drop in the pine woods of North Carolina. It was a bright and sunny day when they made the "drop" from trucks. We started off on our mission, a two-day trial. It turned out to be more of a trial than expected. As it began to turn to dusk, the clouds rolled in and with the clouds came the rain. At first a drizzle, then a gentle steady rain. As it rained the temperature began to drop. It got colder and colder. We were dressed for warmer weather and began to shiver as we carried our mortars to our designated area. The rain turned to sleet mixed with icy rain. We were freezing, especially when a halt was called. Huddling together we tried to keep warm. No fires. This was a secret mission. Rain and freezing began to take its toll. Our muscles cramped and ice formed on our backs.

At last the word came down. The simulated drop was called off. Fires could be started for warmth. We were a sorry lot. Our hands were so stiff with cold that it took two men to light a match. Frozen fingers were not working. No one could hold a little match to strike it. We were resourceful. One held the match between two hands and another held the book in the same manner. With teamwork they lit the match. Fortunately we were in the pine trees and the tar-rich wood caught fire easily. We soon had a merry blaze going. Troopers huddled around getting warm on the front, while their backs were coated with icy rain. Turn the back to the fire and the front froze. We toasted a lot of GI clothing just trying to keep warm that night. Finally the trucks arrived. A year later in December, we'd be in the snowy forests of Belgium suffering from frostbite.

In just a few months we had changed dramatically. We didn't realize how mentally and physically tough we had grown. Those who had been training us recognized it. Gradually the runs had become easier. The long marches were now taken in stride. Matter of fact, the long marches had become competitions. We were trying to beat our own times and we were competing with other companies to see who could do them the fastest.

On the long marches we put the shorter fellows in front. They set the pace. This also kept the guys with the longer legs from running away and leaving the shorter ones. At the beginning of the long marches we'd run three and walk two. As the miles wore on we ran two and walked three. The pace was determined by the weather and the condition of the men. We'd pick up some time at the outset by skipping a five minute break on the hour and go two hours without a break. Later in the march we took the breaks as they came up. We carried our heavy weapons, side arms, and a full pack. Our best time for 25 miles was six hours and 11 minutes and when we came marching down the Division Street, there was the band there to play us in. Boy, did we strut. Hut, Hut, Hut! "You had a good home but you left! Sound off!" Somehow you didn't feel tired anymore. We showered, dressed and took a pass to town. If our feet and legs hurt, we didn't let anyone know it. We were Airborne!

Our military skills were now rather good. We knew how to use our weapons, personal combat abilities had been acquired. We were just about ready to believe what our trainers had been telling us. We were "better than any six other guys who ever put on a pair of GI boots." Unfortunately for other troops in our area, it was a statement that some of us tried to prove on weekends. We did cock our cap jauntily on the side of our head. Cocky? You bet. And we were about to be given a chance to prove how good we were.

Tennessee Maneuvers

It was announced that we were going on maneuvers. Not only that, we'd be leaving Mackall for good. That idea sparked another flurry of rumors. "We're being shipped out right after maneuvers!" "The Tennessee maneuvers thing was a big fake and we were secretly going overseas." You name it, there was a rumor about it. We did go to Tennessee and we did go on maneuvers. We did not go overseas ... not yet.

Maneuvers tested us in many ways. On one occasion, we marched all night long, over rugged terrain in the rain to be on our objective ready to attack in the morning. We caught sleep when and where we could. There were times that night when some of us were actually marching in our sleep. One trooper walked off the side of hill because he missed a turn in his sleep. Fortunately, it was a small Tennessee hill. It did wake him up. The following morning when we showed up, combat ready, the "straight legs" were stunned. They could not understand how we had the ability to march so far, so fast and still be in shape to fight. No secret, it was just being Airborne.

At one point a glider mortar squad was surrounded by straight leg enemy. They thought they had captured a prize. They did not believe us when we told them we had carried the mortars on our shoulders. "That's a crock," they were sure our trucks had to be somewhere. No man could carry a mortar and the heavy ammunition plus his own side arms, food and other equipment. It took a truck. They had trucks to carry theirs and they knew it was not humanly possible to do what we said we did. An hour after they had become our prisoners when one of our rifle companies surrounded them. They still didn't believe us until we picked up our mortars, tossed them on our shoulders and walked off as they watched us go.

At the end of maneuvers most of the 17th Airborne Division was given a week-end pass to Nashville. After 30 tough days in the field, sometimes living off of rations, this sounded like heaven. One problem did arise, however, the local MPs requested that we supply our own MPs to look after our own troops. The regular MPs didn't want to tangle with Airborne troopers having a good time. Our company drew MP duty. Three of us patrolled as a team. It was easy. Any time we saw a trooper in trouble, we spoke quietly to him, told him he'd make us look bad if he caused a fuss. Most agreed to let us escort them to the truck to take them back to camp. If we had a troublesome trooper, he found himself surrounded and hustled off. Because troopers were helping troopers, Nashville became just about the only major city that was not put off limits to us.

We often got in trouble for fighting or helping some straight leg earn the jump boots he was wearing. We helped him earn his boots by tossing him out the second story window. We figured that if he wanted to wear jump boots, he should jump. Geronimo! Airborne troops knew how to have a good time, but they also knew how to fight when confronted. And they sure don't like to see anyone wearing jump boots who had not earned them.

When maneuvers were over on March 27, 1944, we were introduced to our new home, Camp Forrest, Tennessee. We were now almost a year old. Forrest was a big improvement over Mackall. The barracks were much nicer and had a look of permanence. Tennessee is a long, narrow, east-to-west state. Camp Forrest was near Tullahoma, just south of Nashville. We didn't know it at the time, but we were just a few miles north of Lynchburg, the home of the Jack Daniels Distillery. Camp Forrest was to be our last home in the States. But before we settled in at Forrest, we went home on furlough.

The cap with the glider and parachute patch, the gold and black Airborne insignia on our shoulders and the trousers bloused over the shiny boots made us stand out from the rest of the military who were home on leave. People were curious about us. They wanted to know what we did and how we did it. We were all pretty casual about it and, in some cases, folks doubted our abilities. One trooper in a chat with his favorite bartender allowed as how we were taught how to take a bayoneted rifle away from an enemy. The barkeep doubted that was possible and to prove it, he picked up a broom and challenged the trooper to take it away from him. He lunged forward using the broom handle as a bayonet. The next thing he knew, he was lying on his back staring up at the trooper holding the broom at his throat. Piece of cake. Not satisfied, the bartender tried it again. Same result.

Another trooper, fresh from his sessions in awareness and personal combat had an unfortunate experience. He was standing chatting with his girl friend's mother while his date was getting ready. Suddenly his date was on the floor at his feet. She had come up behind him and was about to pat him on the back. Reflex actions took over. He spent a long time trying to explain how he had been trained to sense someone coming at him. (Remember the bit with the tent pegs?) It was the truth and sounded reasonable to him. He never did see that girl again.

Back at camp the training began to intensify. Our division motto was "Vincit Qui Primum Gerit," which means, "He Who Strikes First Wins." We were preparing to be the one who struck first, descending from the sky in a surprise attack. Based on the fact that, in combat circumstances, we'd probably not have a ready source of supply, we were taken to the range and qualified on every side arm that the U.S. offered, the grease gun, the Thompson, the 45 pistol and anything else that was available. That was done so that we could remain combat-ready no matter what side arm we had to use. Later, in England, we'd also qualify on German side arms and mortars. The thinking was that if we ran out of our ammo, we could use theirs. The German machine pistol got off a magazine of shells in the blink of an eye. It made a sound like ripping canvas. The German mortar had a flip sight so that the Germans could be firing in an easterly direction, then simply flip the mortar and be ready to shoot to the west.

On July 22, 1944, orders were cut awarding officers and enlisted men the right to wear the Glider Badge at that time. Only the Parachute Badge brought in extra "hazard" pay. (Later glider troopers were given the same hazard pay as paratroopers.) Believe me, riding those gliders was just as hazardous as jumping out of an airplane. Some of our lads thought it was worse. Which is why they signed up for jump training when it was offered in May of 1944. Several troopers, including Bill Melrose, said they heard that landing in a parachute was no worse than a jump from a second story window ... about a 20 foot drop. So they headed for the parade grounds and the 20 foot wall. They pulled themselves up on the ropes that hung down the side. When they got on top and looked down, the 20 feet seemed a long way. But they were Airborne, so what the heck! They leaped off the top. It took only about a second to reach the sandy soil at the bottom, but that was long enough for them to think ..."This is stupid." Maybe so. But once they were safely on firm ground, they looked back up and said, "That wasn't so bad." The next day they signed up for jump school.

More than 2,500 elected to earn jump wings. Some may have hoped that they'd get out of the gliders, but it didn't work that way. We were greeted by a tough cadre who were determined to prove to us that we really didn't have the guts to jump. Fortunately we had been through the honing process and all the physical work and demanding training of the past several months came to our aid. The calisthenics were what we were used to, which is why we skipped a week of toughening. Jump School for us was only three weeks, not four. We were tough enough already.

Our trainers were rather fond of one exercise. You held your arms out to the side at right angles to the body and made a fist. Then you flexed your fingers straight out. Then make a fist. Flex. Thrusting your fingers out with a force that almost sent them off the ends of your hand. Fist. Flex. Fist. Flex. Do it to a rapid count for the longest time on earth and you think your arms are about to fall off. The double time runs were routine, but there were more of them. More push-ups, too. "Gimme 50," was quickly followed by "Gimme 50 more." No one really remembers how many thousand push-ups you had to do before you got to jump.

We started jump training, as we did with gliders, jumping from a land-based wooden platform, just a few feet off the ground. About this time the paratroops had abandoned their tumbling method of landing in favor of "crumbling." That meant instead of trying to go head-over-heels on landing, we just hit the ground with our feet and tried to land next on our thigh, then the hip, then our rear and finally the back. This was supposed to reduce the risk of broken collar bones. It didn't do our rumps any favor. We would go round and round. Jump and crumble. It wasn't too difficult jumping off those land-locked boxes. Landing from the jump tower on the move was a different story.

The trainers had rigged a tower, 40 feet or so in the air. A long wire angled down from it to the ground. As each would-be paratrooper reached the platform at the top, he was fitted into the T-5 harness. He was commanded to "Hook up, stand in the door" and then "Go." Out you went, sliding swiftly down the wire, your hands with a death grip on the risers above your head. It was better than a roller coaster. There was little time to think. The ground came up at you fast. React. Make believe you're jumping from the little platforms on the ground. And there you were. Falling in the dirt. Unhook and back up the tower again ... and again.

The toughest part was climbing that tall, seemingly endless wooden ladder. Typically, you didn't wait until it was your turn and then quickly ascend the ladder. No. You lined up and went up, one step at a time following the man just a step above you. Take one step up and wait. Take another. Wait. The ladder was a chain of humanity, hanging there in space. If ever you were going to be afraid of heights, now was the time. There you are, umpteen feet off the ground, feet on one rung, your hands firmly gripping another. You're just hanging around, so you've nothing else to do but look down, think about what you are going to have to do when you get to the top. You work up a sweat. Your arms get tired just holding on. Your knees get a little weak and then you move up a couple more rungs. Aha, finally you get to the top. Now all you have to do is hook up and stand in the door.

One day on one of our runs past the parachute packing sheds, we turned in and went inside ... Every paratrooper had to know how to pack a chute. You got to see how really big a chute is and how all of it gets neatly packed into such a small space. You learn to use the long canvas bags filled with lead shot to keep the billowy chute in place as you fold it. You also learn to respect parachute packers and understand why during a jump a shot bag might go down past you like a rifle shot. Someone forgot to remove the weight when packing the chute.

On our first jump we wore only the main chute and emergency chute. No other equipment. We also were dropped from a higher elevation than normal, about 1200 feet. In spite of all our training, there is a high feeling of tension as the plane loads up. You sit in silence, alone with your own thoughts and fears. Mostly you're afraid you won't jump and make a fool of yourself. You also wonder if any of the stories you've been told are really true. Does the jumpmaster really boot you out the door if you freeze? As you approach the drop zone the jumpmaster goes to work. "Is everybody gonna jump?" He gets a weak affirmative response. "I can't hear you!" This time we all yell at the top of our lungs. And we do it over and over again until he is satisfied.

The C-47 had two groups or "sticks" of men to jump, but only one door. This meant that the plane made one drop, then circled to make a second pass to drop the second stick. When you're the second stick out the door, you see the others go through their motions and then disappear out the door and the plane banks sharply to circle back for your turn. The only thing that remains of your buddies on the other side of the plane is their static lines hanging out the door. The jumpmaster goes to the door and starts to pull the static lines back in the plane. Then, just to loosen us up, he shouts, "Oh my gosh, someone is still on the end of the line" and he goes through some elaborate motions as he fakes pulling hard on the static lines as though there is a heavy weight on the end. There is no one on the end of the static lines. But he did catch our attention.

Then comes our signal to STAND UP! HOOK UP! CHECK YOUR STATIC LINE! CHECK YOUR EQUIPMENT! SOUND OFF FOR EQUIPMENT CHECK! STAND IN THE DOOR! We've all heard these words before, but never in a real airplane 'way up in the air. Hey, this is real. We're going to go over there, to that open door and just step out into the thin air with no net, nothing to hold us up but a thin layer of nylon. How did the first man to do it have the nerve? At the STAND IN THE DOOR command, one of us had the thrill of being first. That meant he had to have the top half of his body outside the C-47, with his hands outstretched, palms on the side of the plane. Nothing to hold on to. Just waiting for the slap on the leg as a signal to GO! Was that the slap or did I imagine it? If I don't jump when I should will we all end up in the trees? Then you KNOW you got slapped and you react just as you did on the ground, you go out the door.

There is that moment ... a very, very long moment ... when you think the chute won't open. You grab the ring of the emergency chute. You are grabbing it so tight that the metal ring might break. You count: one-one-thousand, two-one-thousand, three-one ... WHAP! The chute opens. What a beautiful sight. You get that sudden stop before you start down. If you did everything right as you left the door, you are in good shape. If not there are a lot of unpleasant things that can happen, most of which have to do with webbing scraping the skin off your chin or a buckle socking you hard. There you are just hanging there. Wow! Look at all those things down there. They are really men and jeeps. 'Way down there.

You're just limply hanging there looking down in wonderment. So pleased with yourself. Then you're snapped out of your reverie by someone yelling at you to reach up and grab your risers. Take control of the chute and not just drift along. That's the point where you also suddenly realize that you are falling toward the ground. It will be with you in a matter of seconds. THUMP! There it is. And you actually crumbled to a landing just the way you had been taught. Wow! This is great. Look at me. I made a parachute jump. A real one. Not on a wire out of a tower. A real jump-out-of-an-airplane, parachute jump!

There is nothing like the exhilaration of that first jump. No matter what you try to compare it with, the parachute jump wins. However, before you have the luxury of basking in your great accomplishment, they tell you when you get to take your next jumps. Each succeeding jump becomes increasingly more psychologically difficult. You begin to feel that your are bucking the odds each time you come away from a jump unscathed. To qualify as a paratrooper and get to wear those parachute wings you must take three more day jumps and one at night. The reason you make the night jump is that most previous parachute combat operations had been in the wee hours before dawn.

The night jump is an entirely different experience. In the daytime you get to see the ground, you know where you are going. At night, when you are first and stand in the door, the only sensation is the roaring wind. There is nothing below but black with the twinkling stars just above. You feel you are closer to the stars. And for just a moment you are lost in the stars. SLAP! And out you go. Into nothing. You hear the other chutes opening about you. Then you start to look for the lights. The soft, colored lights that are supposed to guide you to your area.

In combat, the pathfinder would have gone in early to prepare the way for you. Pathfinders jumped with the lights, found the proper drop zones and had their lights shining skyward as a beacon for the in-coming planes. Supposedly, none of the enemy are able to see the lights from ground level. For training, the lights come in by truck. You are supposed to land, gather up your chute and head for the lights. On this brightly lit moonlight night, as you prepare to land, you see what appear to be chutes littering the field. you mutter a few things under your breath about guys who leave their chutes and prepare to make your landing. You land OK, but around you you hear your friends uttering profanities as they hit the ground. You discover that what you thought were white chutes shining in the moonlight were really puddles of water left from an earlier rain storm.

There are lots of stories about what happens in training. There usually is someone who is star-crossed. In our case it was Andy Harkness. Harkness fell on misfortune almost every step along the way in jump training. On the last day we were to jump from the tower, he failed to tighten his harness about his legs. The result was that when he "went out the door," his harness was forcibly pulled into his crotch. Harkness got out of the hospital in time to make our first jump and he did. In subsequent jumps he managed to have a chute malfunction with a suspension line over the canopy in what is known as a Mae West. On the night jump he went out with the rest of us, but was among the missing when we made our rendezvous at our designated lights. We waited patiently. Finally, Harkness came limping up, dragging his chute. He had a rough jump, going out the door all wrong which made him swing in a wide arc as he approached the ground. He landed on his head and was dazed for several minutes. In spite of all his travails, he did get his wings.

We were proud that day they pinned those jump wings on us. Now we were qualified Glider Infantry and Parachute Infantry. We were truly AIR-BORNE! Regardless of how we may end up in combat—riding in, walking in, gliding in, or jumping—we knew we were ready.

We did remain as Glider Infantry and we continued our training at Camp Forrest. The Airborne was growing in respect and we were experimenting with a number of new things. They tried jumping from gliders. The thought was that gliders could be released very high in the air, a long way from the target, float silently in on the enemy and disgorge paratroopers. That proved impractical. They also experimented with picking up troops in a glider from the ground with a C-47. A braided glider tow rope was suspended between two poles. The C-47 swooped in low, caught the tow rope with a hook and jerked the glider off the ground and into the air. The method saw some use later on as a means of evacuating wounded, but as a regular procedure, it was judged not practical.

Now, however, we were eager for combat. Ready to join other Airborne troopers who had seen combat and gained fame. On August 14, 1944 we were given orders to prepare to leave Camp Forrest. Our gear was packed and we boarded the train to head north. Once aboard the train we were told to black out all the windows and remove all identifying patches. Our movements were to be secret. Our location at any time was classified. No one wanted to give Hitler any advance warning that more Airborne troops were headed his way. We arrived at Camp Miles Standish near Boston on August 16. We boarded the ship on August 20. Eight days later we landed in Liverpool, England. Moving to the trucks we trod on cobblestone roads built by the Romans. Our destination was a camp near Swindon.

We were tough, rugged, well-trained and confident. We were about to have the greatest adventure of our lives.

"GENERAL BUD MILEY: THE INNERMAN"

by Bart Hagerman, 193 D

Much has been written and said about our division commander. Most of us know he was an outstanding gymnast at West Point, organized and commanded the first parachute unit and helped devise many of the tactics that shaped Airborne operations of World War II. But what do you now of William "Bud" Miley, the man?

In the collection of stories for this book, a number of short incidents were reported that seemed to provide a window through which one could see and more fully appreciate General Miley—the innerman. As a division, we enjoyed exceptionally good leadership. And, it started at the top.

General Miley came from a military family. It was U.S. Army for five generations. Both his grandfathers, his father, brother, uncle, and son were graduates of West Point and spent their lives serving their country. Is it any wonder that molding our division into a tip-top fighting unit took high priority in his life?

In the beginning, from his staff down to the lowest private in the division, most viewed General Miley as a serious, unsmiling, aloof individual with much on his mind and generally too busy to be concerned with their personal problems. Many feared to approach him on ideas they might have had or certainly to take exception to his guidance. No general is often challenged on these matters and consequently, has difficulty getting feedback from the troops he commands.

To end this cycle, General Miley broke with tradition and was often to be seen out in the field, mingling with the troops and seeking to learn what worked and what didn't. The average trooper probably had more input in to how our division was run than he ever dreamed.

In those early days at Camp Mackall we shared the post facilities with the 11th Airborne. There may have been a few "misunderstandings" among the

Major General William M. "Bud" Miley

troops, but generally, things went well. The leadership each enjoyed, however, was quite different.

One instance involved the training of the glider regiments in the two divisions. Bear in mind that although the paratroopers had volunteered for parachute training, the glider troopers had not volunteered for duty in a glider unit. One look at the flimsy crafts was enough to understand why many were less than enthusiastic about going up in them.

When a 11th Airborne soldier refused to go up in a glider, General Joe Swing promptly had the soldier brought up on a court-martial. Then, when an entire company refused to go up, he had the men tied in the gliders and taken aloft. This rash action was not to happen in the 17th Airborne.

There was a case where a 17th Airborne glidertrooper refused to go up in a glider when so ordered. The story goes that the private was a farm boy and reportedly said he "didn't want to go lower than it took to plant potatoes or higher than it took to pull corn!"

He was then removed to the guardhouse while the brass determined what was to be done about the matter. If the private was excused and transferred, a dangerous precedence would have been set. With manpower limitations being experienced in all the armed forces, the division could not tolerate what actually amounted to a mutiny.

The situation soon came to the attention of General Miley. When he learned the private was otherwise a good soldier, he ordered his sedan and went to the guardhouse. He and the private drove around the post for awhile and the two talked about the problem.

The private admitted to just being afraid that the glider was not air worthy. He was afraid that it would crash and he would be killed. In some way General Miley convinced him it would be safe. Then they drove to the airport and the two men (General Miley and the private) took a glider ride.

The happy ending is that the private never had another problem going up in a glider and there were no instances of courts-martial in our division, and no mass mutinies. Score one for the cool, calm, reassuring, reasoning power of our general.

Long before he assumed the command of our division, General Miley seemed to know what motivated men. When the 501st Parachute Battalion, the first U.S. parachute unit, was being formed he sensed something was lacking. They needed something to set them apart from the regular infantry, something they could point to with pride for their unique achievement.

Accordingly, he had then Lieutenant William P. Yarborough design the jump wings that we wear today. He then dispatched him to Philadelphia to obtain 350 of them for the new troopers. Those wings remain today as one of the two most prestigious badges a soldier can obtain.

Sam Marks told us about the early days at Camp Mackall before the troops arrived and the cadre was being instructed as to how the rookies were to be toughened mentally. The Division Headquarters officers said the cadre should even go as far as to have the men dismount from the trucks with their heavy duffle bags and if they weren't fast enough, have them do it again and again.

General Miley said that they should also learn to obey all orders promptly. For example, he said, if they were late falling out for a formation, have them do 10 pushups in front of the whole company.

At this point, one of the division colonels reminded the General that he himself had been late to the present formation. General Miley immediately dropped and knocked out 25 pushups! There's an old axiom—you lead by example.

Another story appeared in our association newsletter several years ago that showed the way the General felt about his men. It seems a lone private (his name long forgotten) was walking along a main road on the post at Camp Mackall. It was late and it was raining. A bad night to be out.

As a "buttoned-up" jeep approached, the private held up his thumb to hitch a ride. The vehicle stopped and a door opened. Somehow the private never saw the stars on the vehicle's plate as he climbed into the back seat.

Asked where he was going he told the figure in the front seat the street where he was billeted. They continued to chat as they drove through the camp until suddenly the private saw the two stars on his cap of the man in the front seat. Immediately he froze.

Arriving at the private's street, the general then took him to his barracks, let him out and wished him well. The private stammered a "thank you" as he got out and saluted. I doubt if any of that private's buddies ever believed that story, but no doubt he will remember it forever.

I remember one near clash I personally had with the general. It was during a particularly bitter night while the division was on Tennessee Maneuvers. It either snowed or rained every night of our maneuvers, but on this night it was both snowing and raining and so cold we were all miserable.

It was my time to carry our 60mm mortar. I never could understand why it had to be carried in one piece instead of broken down into three lighter pieces. Accordingly, I was trudging up the road cussing the person or persons who thought up that order. That cussing branched off into every officer who passed down any order that led to our misery.

Passing through an intersection I spied a lone figure standing in the middle of the road, watching the troops file by. My cussing then turned to the MPs who had nothing else to do but stand in the road watching others suffer.

A split second before I came within earshot, I saw two silver stars on that rain-slick helmet. I recovered just in time to mumble, "Evening, general."

I think he said something but I have no idea what. It seemed pleasant enough under the circumstances. My only thought at that moment was getting farther down that road and fast! It did boost everyone's morale though as we saw the general was out there in the weather with us.

Brigadier General David Schorr provided another glimpse of our general and how he reacted. The scene here was during our Division Jump School at Camp Forrest, Tennessee. Select members of the 513th PIR were detailed to run the course and qualify some 2,200 glidertroopers as paratroopers.

Then a lieutenant colonel and executive officer of the 193rd GIR, Schorr was summoned to the general's office one day during the height of the training. General Miley said it had been called to his attention that the 513th "black hats" were being extra tough on the officer's class and asked Schorr what his opinion was.

Schorr replied that although the training was tough, it seemed to be in line with what he had been told the training was at the Ft. Benning Parachute School. In short, he said that he felt the officers were getting just what they had expected.

General Miley then said okay, but if the instructors got out of line, he wanted to know about it. He was not going to stand for these select NCOs taking advantage of their position and "riding" or "hazing" the officers.

Schorr said this, coming as it did from the Army's most ardent, experienced and Airborne-tough jumping general at the time, revealed a human touch not readily seen in his usual austere demeanor. It seemed plain: General Miley cared for his troops.

During the Bulge, a sergeant checking his squad's deployment was surprised to meet General Miley coming up from his rear. He asked how they were deployed and said "Very well," and moved on. He seemed to be everywhere.

Author Bill Breuer in his book Storming Hitler's *Rhine,* tells of the general's initial action after landing by parachute over the Rhine. Coming under fire from a nearby enemy strong point, General Miley enlisted the aid of two troopers in freeing a machine gun from a bundle and laying down a base of fire.

Colonel Lew Good tells of General Miley admitting he had made a grave mistake during Operation Varsity. It was a mistake in public relations, of all things, but it was to have repercussions that could never have been expected.

The then famous *Life* magazine journalist and photographer Robert Capra accompanied the 17th Airborne on the Rhine jump. In fact, Capra jumped just behind General Miley. After they had landed in the hot drop zone, Capra rushed up to the general and asked for a statement. General Miley, in the flush of the moment, reportedly replied, "Hell, I don't have time now for any damned reporter!"

Capra's story and pictures made the April 9, 1945 issue of the magazine but the 17th Airborne was barely mentioned. Capra himself is said not to have identified the 17th with any of his photographs.

Later, when the division was at Vittel, France, General Miley expressed his regrets that he had not taken the time to get some publicity when he could have for the division. Even today most people think of the 82nd and the 101st when they think of WWII Airborne. Many have never heard of the 17th Airborne.

In the Bulge the 17th was attached to General George Patton's 3rd Army and he was a tough taskmaster. In his diary Patton wrote of his displeasure with General Miley saying that the 17th had taken an unwarranted number of casualties. His displeasure was to the extent that he considered relieving General Miley. However, once the tenseness of the Bulge eased, General Patton thought better and no action was taken.

General Miley probably didn't help endear himself to General Patton after the Bulge was over. General Patton sent a case of whiskey to General Miley with a note indicating congratulations for a job well done. General Miley sent it right back saying, "We've got enough problems without everyone getting drunk!"

So, we'll leave it up to you as to what kind of a man General Miley really was. Caring? Brave? Tough? Principled? Concerned? We say he was all of these things. He was some kind of man and we were damn lucky to have had him as our commanding general. General "Bud" Miley truly was "Airborne All The Way!"

"TONY MORINELLI: AIRBORNE SOLDIER"

As told by William K. Tom, 194 C

If you think pre-induction physical exams were thorough and complete, don't you ever believe it! If you think that the Army selected the best men to serve as Airborne infantrymen, you can bet your life on it!

I had the pleasure of serving with Tony Morinelli in 194C and he was one hell of a soldier. The amazing part about it, however, was the fact that Tony only had one eye! A childhood accident at the age of three had left him completely blind in his right eye. What he was doing in the Army in the first place is a silent testimony to the Army's inefficiency and Tony's intestinal fortitude.

When Tony was sent up for his induction physical in 1942, he never mentioned his handicap. Without a word of complaint, he just did what they asked him to do and passed the physical without any problem. The blind eye became Tony's secret. He told no one about it. He was determined to be as good a soldier as the next guy.

Before he knew what was happening, Tony was at Ft. McCellan, Alabama, and taking basic training. On the rifle range one day the secret nearly came out. Trying to fire right-handed and sighting with the left eye, resulted in some loose teeth and black and blue bruises from the recoil of the M-1. The range officer solved that by teaching Tony to fire left-handed and he qualified as a sharpshooter.

He did so well in basic training, he was selected for cadre and served in that capacity for the next 18 months. He was then rotated and marked for overseas assignment. From Camp Miles Standish he sailed on the USS Wakefield to England and to a "repo-depot." A month later he joined the 17th Airborne and was assigned to Sergeant Joe Balum's rifle squad.

Tony served well in the Bulge, doing his job efficiently and quietly. His secret was still locked away and none of his fellow soldiers suspected that Tony was operating with only one eye.

Like so many, Tony became a frozen-foot victim. In fact, he darn near froze

Tony Morinelli perfected his left-eye shooting technique amid the bombed-out ruins in Germany.

his fingers and legs. He was evacuated and sent to a field hospital where he was treated. He remained there until a mortar shell hit the hospital and he barely escaped with his life.

Sent to a general hospital in Rheims, he received more treatment. Still the blind eye was Tony's secret. One day an order came to the hospital for all ambulatory Airborne soldiers to report to their units. Tony packed up and was shipped direct to the marshalling area and told to get ready to go to Germany!

From here it was "Operation Varsity" and Tony rode into combat in the glider with the other members of his squad. One Purple Heart and a Bronze Star later, the war was over and Tony had survived.

During the occupation, Tony decided to play on the regimental softball team. One day, as he played catcher, he was struck by a foul tip in his only good eye—the left one. The eye swelled shut and Tony, now temporarily completely blind, had to let the secret come out. He became known in the regiment as "the one-eyed soldier" and his fame spread rapidly.

Because he didn't have enough points for discharge, and his medical history was overlooked, Tony was then transferred to the 101st Airborne and marked for shipment to the Pacific. Fortunately, the war ended soon, the Pacific plans were canceled and Tony was returned to the States and discharged. Apparently, the Army still had made no record of his bad right eye.

Tony returned to civilian life, married and had a baby daughter. In 1950, with the Korean War starting, Tony was ordered to report for another physical. He passed this one, never mentioning his bad eye, and was enlisted in the inactive reserve. In only 48 hours his orders came to report for active duty.

If you think Tony failed to answer this second call for service to his country, you don't know Tony Morinelli. He reported as ordered and eventually was shipped to Japan and then on to Korea where he was assigned to the 710th Military Police Company.

It was business as usual for Tony Morinelli as he carried out his duties without a word of complaint. One day his bad eye became inflamed and infected and he had to report to the hospital. There the blind eye was discovered and it was determined that it would have to be removed. For this, Tony was returned to the States for the operation.

Tony tried to have his new plastic eye made with the American flag where the pupil belonged, but the VA turned down this request. Tony was disappointed as he was then working as a bartender and imagined he could have all kinds of fun with such a patriotic eye!

Well, that's the story of Tony Morinelli: a real Airborne soldier if ever there was one! Tony says he still has fun when some friend kids him about his eye. He waits until the friend isn't looking and then he slips his artificial eye out and drops it in the friend's drink! What a sense of humor! What a guy!

"THE PIGEONEER AND THE MISSING PIGEONS"

As told by Thomas Miller, 193 HQ 2

$\mathbf{D}$id you ever read about "Cher am mi," the pigeon that saved the "Lost Battalion" in WWI and was decorated for bravery? It was one of the great stories of that war. Of course that was that war. During our war we had radios, telephones, walkie-talkies and a lot of electronic equipment that made sending messages by pigeons completely obsolete. Or did it?

I understand pigeons were actually used by some units during WWII, but I probably helped kill the idea for the use of pigeons in the 17th Airborne. And, it really wasn't my fault! Let me tell you a weird tale.

I was a runner in 2nd Battalion Headquarters of the 193rd. When the radio went out, or radio silence was being observed, I was one of the guys who carried the messages. Due to the mission of Airborne troops, someone, somewhere, high up, got the idea pigeons would be of great help. As racing pigeons had been my hobby in civilian life, I found myself appointed as "Pigeoneer" for the 193rd!

I wasn't alone in this weird hobby. Lieutenant John Bailey of "D" Company, 193rd also had the hobby of racing pigeons. As a part-time duty, Bailey was appointed to supervise my pigeon activities, which were zero. Zero, that is, except for one fateful mission back at good old Camp Mackall!

One day I was given a crate containing six homing pigeons and instructed to accompany a group of soldiers that evening on a field exercise involving radio silence. I was taken to the airstrip at Camp Mackall where a C-47 awaited and I climbed aboard with a load of guys from one of the line companies.

I had no briefing on the exercise and to the best of my knowledge, there was no officer in charge of the group. We flew around for a couple of hours and just before dark, landed and taxied to a dark area at the end of the runway. We were told we were at Pope Field, which is part of Fort Bragg, but I was never sure of our location.

There seemed to be a great deal of confusion. No one seemed to be sure of where we were. I figured the exercise was screwed up and I just went along with the NCO in charge and didn't make waves. He led us to some deserted barracks where we broke in, lay down on the floor and tried to get some sleep.

The morning brought no news of what was going on. We seemed isolated and completely lost. I began to think that maybe we were the "Lost Battalion." When some 30 hours had gone by, I was almost sure of it!

We had no food and only the one canteen of water each man carried. Things were getting pretty grim. The men began kidding around that maybe they should eat the pigeons. I really was worried about the birds. Should I release them? If I didn't they would soon expire from lack of food and water.

I didn't have to make that decision, however. A sergeant came and took the crate with my six birds. As a private first class I couldn't object very strongly. That was the last I ever saw of the pigeons.

Soon a plane landed and picked us up and flew us back to Camp Mackall. From there a truck took us back to our area. While on the ride some of the guys told me to forget the birds as some "good ole mountain boy" had made a great meal of them!

I was really sweating out those birds. I just knew I was going to get a court-martial, but do you know, no one ever mentioned those pigeons! I never brought up the subject either and that was the end of it!

I think that exercise ended the idea of using pigeons in the 17th Airborne. I was never asked to practice my pigeon skills again and when we went on maneuvers, to Camp Forrest and finally overseas, apparently we left the idea behind. I, for one, am glad we did!

EDITOR'S POSTSCRIPT: *After the story by Tom Miller was written, more "Pigeoneers" continued to surface! All the stories told the same sad ending—pigeons weren't for the 17th Airborne!*

Over in the 513th PIR, Headquarters 2nd, Bob Bocchino was also designated as the unit "pigeoneer." Bob had an additional problem—he had to jump with the birds. The riggers made two tiny containers and Bob selected two beautiful homers and hooked the containers to the D-rings on his parachute harness. Bob jumped and executed a perfect PLF. He also executed his two little passengers. A real lover of the gentle birds, Bob refused to jump with them again and thereby lost his MOS.

Joe Hullihan in the 155th Airborne AA, told us of the experience they had using pigeons during Tennessee Maneuvers. They released their birds to send word of the position of the enemy force. The birds then proceeded to circle over Joe's position for 10 minutes while they got their "gyros" straight. After giving away the position of Joe's element, the birds finally left and Joe and his buddies were captured and spent the rest of the maneuver phase in a POW compound.

Finally, Bob Pattee wrote to us to clear up some of the facts. The 17th

Airborne Table of Organization and Equipment (TO&E) did in fact include a pigeoneer. And it was in the 517th Airborne Signal Company—where else?

When the division left for overseas, he was sent from Camp Crowder, Missouri as a professional pigeoneer to fill the slot. The 17th had no birds of its own—they were to be supplied by special Pigeon Companies who would support the line units. The birds would fly to their lofts and the messages would then be relayed to the proper headquarters.

Bob says the whole idea of pigeons was pretty well ignored and he served as a message center clerk most of his time. The only contact he had with a pigeon was when a division truck hit an English pigeon near Swindon and it was brought to Bob for nursing back to health!

There was talk about sending pigeons on the Varsity drop, Bob said, but he was hospitalized shortly before then and he never heard what happened. Our research ends here too.

Knowing how the Army works, it would appear to the writer that someone, high up in the chain of command, was unappreciative of the role the tiny birds could play and early-on nixed the whole idea. Then again, maybe Tom Miller was right—the pigeons just made too nice of a meal for a bunch of hungry troopers!

"ORDERS FOR P.O.E."

As told by Sam Marks, Div. HQ

A pall of tension hung over the Division Headquarters Adjutant General's Office. Instructions for our movements from Camp Forrest to our Port of Embarkation had recently been received, and our typists were preparing shipment orders. Though several typewriters were going full speed, there was none of the friendly conversation that used to dull their sound. Our colonel, normally quiet and composed, had just chewed us out in no uncertain terms. In a stern voice we had never heard him use, he had berated us for "gabbing all over town about when and where we were shipping out!" Weren't we aware of the familiar Army warning that "A Slip Of The Lip Can Sink A Ship?"

Sam Marks crossing the Rhine with the ground serial. Some troopers made the invasion by boat!

Back in my publication section of the office, surrounded by shelves of Army forms, manuals, and volumes of Army Regulations, I too, sat quiet and tense. It had seemed to me that the colonel had been looking directly at me when he spoke. In any event, I felt guilty. Only two days ago, while traveling from camp to Shelbyville where our wives were rooming, I had mentioned to my two passengers that I knew where the Division was headed for, since I had just received thousands of Army information booklets on "Paris and the cities of Northern France." The trouble was, I now realized, my passengers were two sergeants from our Counter Intelligence Detachment! I cursed them silently for the ungrateful wretches they were in reporting me. For weeks I had been providing them rides on a "share-the-gas" basis.

I looked up to find Major John Gray, the assistant adjutant general and my direct superior thumbing through my set of Army Regulations.

"Marks," he said, "I'm going to have to break you!"

My present rating was technician third grade, a staff sergeant's insignia with a "T" in it. This was an unusual rating in a combat division, and I was constantly being asked to identify it. I enjoyed the feeling of uniqueness. Besides, I had worked very hard for my promotions, and being "busted" to a lowly private was a humiliation I dreaded to contemplate!

I had been standing at attention, waiting for him to continue, but he walked out of my office with a volume of the Army Regulations.

I spent a restless hour trying to control my anger and my nerves. I had a lot of work piled up, but I simply could not operate.

I was roused from my thoughts by our head typist, who handed me a typed stencil.

"Run this off," he said, with what seemed to me a knowing smile.

I was also the office mimeographer. I had volunteered to take this additional job to free the former operator for much needed typing work. In fact, my promotion to Tech 3 had been my reward for taking over this additional duty. As I was scanning the stencil for possible spelling errors I caught sight of my name on the last line. My heart sank! My God, I thought, Army punishment sure is swift! But as I continued reading, the full line was, "Tech 3 Samuel R. Marks, ASN 35500214, promoted this date to staff sergeant, Division HQ, AGO."

I was flabbergasted! I quickly ran up to the desk of Mr. Joe Dear, a warrant officer and close friend, on whose recommendation I had gotten my job.

"What's all this?" I asked. "Major Gray just now said he would have to break me, and now I see this!"

Mr. Dear laughed.

"We had a staff sergeant rating open in our table of organization, and we wanted you to have it, since you are the only one in the office with field training. The major thought we would have to break you from Tech 3, but I pointed out to him that the rank of staff sergeant, being of field rank, is considered higher than a similar technical rank, so that we can promote you without 'busting' you!"

That evening, on the way from camp to Shelbyville, I treated two surprised counter intelligence sergeants to a couple of drinks. Little did they know how much these drinks helped to ease my conscience.

"MY MOST UNFORGETTABLE JUMP"

As told by Harold F. Green, 513 A

Jumping finally got me discharged from the Army, but I sure enjoyed it before the one where I got hurt. That jump probably should be considered my "worst" one, but one of our practice jumps before that has to take the cake.

We were at Camp Forrest and it was a daytime equipment jump. I only weighed about 175 pounds, but with the load I was carrying, I must have weighed at least 300 pounds. I could hardly move, much less walk.

It was a windy day and the plane was pitching and rolling all over the sky. I was the number six man in the first stick. Just after the command to "Stand in the Door," the plane swayed upward and the number one man went sprawling across the plane backwards.

Back it plunged and the other jumpers in front of me were gone. I staggered toward the open door and the plane pitched again. My feet went out from under me and I fell in the open door, half in and half out.

Harold Green loved to jump, but some were better than others! This one nearly killed him.

I began clawing and crawling on the outside of the plane with the idea that I'd fall out on the downward plunge of the plane. Then before anything could happen, I felt strong hands grab my boots.

Lieutenant Matthewson, our jumpmaster, had grabbed me as we had by this time passed over the drop zone and were then over a heavy pine forest. If I had gone out then, they'd never have found me in those pine trees.

Now, while I hung head down out of the plane, they began to try to pull me back in. Pull as they did, I didn't move one inch. I couldn't go out and I couldn't get back in.

Someone suggested that they push me out. The lieutenant nixed that idea, however, as my load shifted to the point where it would surely flop me over and some sort of a malfunction was bound to do me in. I'll always be grateful to him for that piece of thinking.

Finally, the lieutenant went forward to confer with the pilot. He removed his free fall chute and gave it to Lieutenant Matthewson so the lieutenant could lean way out of the plane and pull up on my backpack while the others pulled straight back.

In the meantime, the pilot began to gain altitude and to circle over the DZ. I was left to wonder what was going on back inside the aircraft and what they were going to do for me. And, the higher we got, the colder I got.

Little by little, inch by inch, they pulled me back inside. It seemed the lieutenant was two-thirds out of the plane himself as the guys hung on to him. When I got inside, they said I was as white as a ghost. I guess it was from being scared and from being half frozen.

Then the lieutenant took off the pilot's chute and put his own back on. He placed me in the number one position so that what had happened before couldn't happen again! Then we circled back over the DZ and after a few minutes we all jumped like nothing had ever happened.

My chute opened and I didn't even feel the opening shock. I floated down to earth without a care in the world. After my experience, I was so glad to be on the ground I didn't care how hard I hit. Yes, that was the most unforgettable jump I ever made!

"THE SEARCH FOR SOME GOOD HOME COOKING"

As told by Ben Scherer, 513 A

One thing a fellow sure misses in the Army is good home cooking. The cooks at the mess hall do the best they can, but when you're preparing for hundreds of hungry mouths, it just isn't the same as it is when Mom sets the family table.

Our guys seemed to always be looking for some good home cooking, and to that extent, we frequently got in some trouble. Not bad trouble, mind you, but trouble we could have well avoided and been better off without.

Anyone who experienced the Tennessee Maneuvers the division participated in has a pleasant memory of how wonderful the farmers in that area were to us soldiers. I can still remember the homemade biscuits and the ham and eggs they gave or sold to us at a price so low I still can't believe it.

When the maneuvers were over, we had a day or so to clean up our equipment and wait for the trucks that were to take us into Camp Forrest. Soldiers with nothing to do are bound to get into trouble.

A rumor had gone around that there were wild boars in the woods where we were camped and we should be careful. Indeed one day we spied one of these creatures. At least, that's what we thought it was. It looked more like just a boar hog, but it was running loose in the woods, far from any farmhouse.

The more we looked at the animal, the better it began to look and we felt it would taste even better. So, in search of some "good home cooking," we killed the critter! Next, we sent a truck in to Camp Forrest for some other delectables and an ample supply of beer. And, then the feast began!

To avoid any unnecessary problems, we called the meat "cheese" and the beer "coke." We ate "cheese" that night until we could eat no more. After all the "C" and "K" rations we had devoured on maneuvers, that was the best pork man ever enjoyed.

We never learned the end to this story until after the war at one of our reunions. Although there was no real secret about our feast and battalion headquarters (including Lieutenant Colonel Weikie) seemed to think it great sport, sometime later there was a change of attitude. Our CO, Captain John Spears, was called up on the carpet for our actions when some farmer went to the battalion CO about us killing one of his best boars.

Captain John must have figured that we deserved the pig roast because he coughed up the money to quiet the farmer and he never mentioned the matter to us. That's real leadership!

Our next clash with home cooking came while we were in England. We were housed (that's a poor choice of words) in tents atop a barren hill. It was appropriately called Windmill Hill and life there was Spartan to say the least. There weren't many pleasures there to keep us out of trouble—again.

Al West and I were walking in the nearby woods one day and we found a large iron kettle. It was all we could do, but we managed to drag it back to our tent. Our plan was to load it with charcoal from the mess hall, cover it with a grill of some sort, and get "some good home cooking!"

Things worked out great. The kettle, on its little short legs didn't seem to overheat the tent's wooden floor and the goodies we cooked there were the envy of the other fellows. We became very smug about our "grill" and probably a bit careless.

One day we had a surprise weapon inspection and were called to a company formation on the hillside near the tent area. Unfortunately, we had just started a good hot fire in the kettle and put some food on the grill. Nevertheless, we all grabbed our weapons and away we went to the formation.

The inspection dragged on and on as the sergeant looked for every speck of dirt or rust. We were standing at attention when I heard West whisper, "My God, look at that smoke coming out of our tent! The place is on fire!"

Sure enough, the smoke was pouring out of the tent. I didn't know what to do and I began sweating as I wondered if I should break the silence of the formation.

Finally, I decided that I could no longer hold it in. I blurted out, "Sergeant Gray, may I break ranks? Our tent seems to be on fire!"

Sergeant Gray looked up, saw the smoke and responded, "Everyone, in that tent, take off!"

In the mad rush that followed, we were able to extinguish the fire that the kettle had started in our floor. The food was long gone and we had a big hole in the floor, but at least, we were able to rescue all our belongings.

Later, Captain Spears came to our tent to view the mess we had made. He said we deserved credit for our ingenuity, but we were a fire hazard and the kettle had to go.

So, the kettle went, and so did our "good old home cooking." However, for a few short weeks we set a mighty fine table at our house.

"THE SUICIDAL GOOSE"

As told by Wayne Hyde, 513 I

Editor's Note: *This story is about two young officers and an incredible adventure they had in 1941 at Fort Benning. Both were West Point graduates, both later served in the 17th Airborne, both eventually became major generals and, regrettably both died of cancer a few years ago. Ward Ryan was the executive officer of the 513th Parachute Infantry Regiment and Lou Walsh was a member of the 517th Parachute Infantry Regiment when it was activated and later served in the 11th Airborne Division. We also have learned that the young captain identified as "Hank" in the story was actually known as "Dick". He was, in fact, Lt. Gen. Richard J. Seitz, one of the Airborne generals who reviewed this book and whose comments appear on the dust jacket.*

What had happened aboard that C-47 over Fort Benning, Georgia that early morning in 1941 wasn't at all funny; but the two men telling the story about 40 years later who had survived it, could then laugh about it.

They were Ward Ryan and Lou Walsh, then Airborne-qualified captains and both destined to have distinguished military careers and to wear two stars when they finally retired. But on that morning in 1941, it seemed they would have no careers at all.

They told me this story at a Saturday lunch hosted by Ward Ryan in a private dining room of a good restaurant in Fairfax, Virginia in 1981. In addition to the two retired major generals, also with us was a retired Airborne colonel and an retired Air Force lieutenant colonel who was a pilot. I was a former Airborne sergeant. I felt right at home and completely at ease. I was with good friends and rank didn't matter; we were all past-tense.

Ward, Lou, and another young captain (referred to only as "Hank") had been assigned to that gooney bird to "observe" a jump. Their aircraft was about 300 feet above the formations of paratrooper-loaded planes. Later, after the jump, they would all write reports and give verbal briefings on the jump.

That, as it turned out, was not what they wrote about or gave briefings about. But it's their story, so I'll let them tell it.

"We were in the pilot's cabin," Ward said. "There was a far better view from there and we could look down at the jump. There was no co-pilot. Lou Walsh was in the co-pilot's seat, and Hank and I were standing behind them. We were flying directly above the C-47s below us, a great vantage point to see the entire drop, but we never saw it!"

It was Lou Walsh's turn. "That's right," he said, with his big Irish grin. "We were about 10 minutes from the DZ. And then came this huge damned goose. We didn't know it was a goose then. Didn't even see it. It hit us head-on, smashed right through the pilot's side of the cabin, knocked the poor guy out cold, and then that goose just exploded! It must have been one helluva big bird, because its blood and guts covered the interior of the cabin—including us!"

"Yeah!" Ward said, "You know, come to think of it, that goose had more blood and guts that General Patton did!" And the small, private dining room got very loud with our laughter.

"Well, first thing we did was wipe all the mess off our faces so we could at least see," Ward went on.

Wayne "Raw" Hyde now lives in Paris. His wife, a former French nurse, made five combat jumps in Vietnam.

"Then we did the same thing with the lieutenant (the pilot). We tried the best way we could to revive him." Ward stopped talking and looked at the three of us who hadn't experienced that morning. "You must understand," he said then, "that we were all working much faster than the time it takes to tell you this. Trying to bring that pilot back to consciousness, was a pretty damned frightening situation."

"I thought the guy (the pilot) was dead," Lou Walsh said. "There was blood all over his face from where he'd been cut by pieces of the windshield. Turned out later these were minor cuts, but we didn't know it then. And we didn't know where to look for a first aid kit on the plane, though we were sure there must have been one—somewhere."

"All we could do was wipe the goose blood and guts off the pilot's face," Ward said. "My God, it was terrible! Nobody flying the plane. Lou was still in the co-pilot's seat trying to keep us on a steady course, and the entire cockpit smelled terrible!

"Smelled exactly like it was," Lou said. "an exploded goose, maybe about 45 pounds of it. Even the wind pouring into the cockpit through that blasted-out windshield couldn't take away the goose smell. And it was cold as hell in there!"

Then suddenly he laughed, "Oh, man, what a morning!" he said. So we all laughed, and then I seem to remember that an amber liquid called Chivas Regal Scotch was poured (rather liberally) into our respective glasses. It seemed to be a memory inducing potion. Or maybe not.

"Okay, where were we?" Ward said.

"In that busted-up C-47," Lou Walsh reminded him.

Ward pretended to ignore him. "I remember that Hank said he'd been checked out on single-engine aircraft—Piper Cubs or something like that. So he took over the co-pilot's seat."

"And I was damned glad to be out of there," Lou said "It was right after that, wasn't it, Ward, when we hauled the pilot out of his seat and took him back to the passenger compartment?"

Ward nodded. "We got him back there but the poor guy still hadn't come to. He'd taken one helluva shot. We got the blood cleaned off his face ..."

"Couldn't tell which was goose blood and which was the pilot's," Lou put in.

"... and found he wasn't bleeding much at all. Just surface cuts," Ward finished.

"So now what do we do?" he said. "Hank didn't really know how to fly that plane. He was just trying to keep it level. Doing okay at it, too, but for how long? So I ran foreword to the pilot's cabin ..."

"He didn't run, he sort of staggered," Lou said.

"... to tell Hank to try to gain some altitude and head for the swamp area. Told him I though we'd all have to jump, taking the pilot with us. Hank agreed to gaining altitude, but he didn't know where the swamp area was. He said, though, that maybe he'd see it from a higher altitude. Meanwhile, Lou had scrambled around and found some chutes."

"Yea. Back packs, they were the chutes jumpmasters used," Lou said. "No static lines. Found five of them. We'd decided by then to bail out. Nothing else to do. I'd put the pilot on my lap facing me while I was sitting in the open door (we had managed to get it open), then I'd tip out, hang onto the pilot, pull his rip cord and then my own, and start praying!"

Hank, meanwhile, was trying to gain altitude, trying to find that swamp area where the C-47 would go down in an uninhabited area once all four of them had cleared the plane. He didn't know if the C-47 had an automatic pilot control on it, or where to find it if there was one. And he knew nothing at all about the communication system or how to get in touch with Lawson Field at Benning to declare an emergency. Hank just did the best he could, trying to find that swamp area.

"You mean I gotta get out of this seat," he said to Ward, "let the plane go where it wants to, run back to the rear cabin, put on a parachute and be the last man out?" The question was lost in the drama of the moment.

Louis got the still unconscious pilot on his lap, helped by Ward Ryan. The prop blast was tremendous. The plane was flying fairly level now—altitude about 5,000 feet—and Hank came back to the rear cabin, struggled into the chute harness with Ward's help. Now they were ready to jump.

Then something happened. "Maybe it was the prop blast," Lou Walsh said. "Whatever it was, the pilot sort of came to and saw my ugly Irish face about six inches from his. He let out a yell and said, 'What the hell's going on here?' He looked down, saw nothing but about a 5,000 foot drop into what must have looked like a jungle. We were, I guess, over that swamp area then. He yelled, 'Get me back inside!' and we gladly hauled him in."

Lou laughed. "Then he wanted to know who was flying the plane. Nobody, we told him. His face froze in terror as he raced to the pilot's cabin. The plane was pitching and yawing and doing whatever a plane does without a pilot. But he got to the cabin, jumped into the co-pilot's seat (as I said it was freezing cold in there) grabbed the controls and got the plane leveled out and started to make a turn back to Lawson Field."

"I remember we all followed him into that icy cold pilot's cabin," Ward said. "The guy seemed to be the calmest one among us. He got on the radio (something we didn't know how to do), declared an emergency, but I don't remember exactly what he said, only that his windshield had been blown out. It was just as well—no one would have believed a goose had done it!"

"From there on it was a piece of cake," Ward said. "The landing was smooth as silk and the pilot taxied over and shut down the engines. There were two ambulances waiting and a bunch of medical personnel wondering what had happened.

"Ward stood in the open door," Lou added, "covered in goose blood and told them that everyone was okay but the pilot probably should go to the hospital to be checked out. I leaned out, laughed and yelled we did need a good dry cleaner!"

After that thrilling conclusion to their story I was dumbfounded. Everything else was anti-climatic. Seems the pilot was treated for facial cuts, kept overnight and then released. He had a minor concussion, was grounded for about ten days and then returned to flight status.

The three gory captains were driven to their quarters where they cleaned up and then reported to their offices. Their reports that day were not on the jump. They hadn't seen it. The reports centered on the emergency action they had taken when they met "the suicidal goose."

"THE WAR OF THE FLOORS"

by Bart Hagerman, 193 D

The 17th Airborne Division arrived in Liverpool, England on August 26, 1944 and closed on Camp Chisledon on the 30th. The area assigned to the 2nd Battalion, 193rd Glider Infantry Regiment, was largely undeveloped and obviously the first task for the companies was to make the area liveable.

The troops turned to, and in a short while, the area began to take shape. The company streets were gravelled, the electricity was hooked up, the water pipes were connected, a bulletin board was erected and the "honey buckets" installed.

After the necessities were provided, the troops began to think about some comfort items. One of the first things they looked to was some sort of

The author, Bart Hagerman, was with the division from activation until wounded Jan. 29, 1945 at the Our River.

flooring for the six-man tents. The cold English mornings only served to make it more miserable to hop out of bed onto dirt floors.

A vacant tent area immediately adjacent to Company "D" of the 193rd naturally attracted the glidertroopers's attention. This area they were told, had belonged to a unit of the 506th Parachute Infantry Regiment of the 101st Airborne Division. These brave troopers had parachuted into France on D-Day, June 6, 1944 and, as far as anyone knew at the time, were still fighting on the continent.

The area was completely deserted and there was no guard posted. The tents, however, all had nice wooden floors fashioned from empty packing cases and scrap lumber. It was unthinkable to leave those nice floors there where they would not be used and we needed them so badly. In minutes the floors were removed and installed in the "D" Company area.

Everything went smoothly for a week or so and then an unexpected move took place. The 101st was returned to England and unfortunately, they were returned to their old billets at Camp Chisledon. They needed only one look at their old floorless tents to realize what had happened.

Flush from 33 days in deadly combat, the 506th troopers came screaming and yelling into the 193rd area. All hell then broke out. "The War of the Floors" had started!

Many of the 506th troopers still had live ammunition and a lot of them had smoke grenades. They ran through the area firing their weapons in the air and tossing grenades into the tents.

In those days there never was much love lost between the paratroopers and glidertroopers and there was an intense sense of competition between the Airborne divisions. This all came to a head at this time as utter chaos reigned.

Fights broke out all over the area as the 506th troopers attempted to recover their stolen floors and the 193rd troopers attempted to defend their newly-aquired floors from an "armed" adversary. Officers from both regiments yelled and screamed and ran around like crazy as they attempted to restore order.

Finally, after about 15 or 20 minutes, things began to slow down and order was restored. Some floors were recovered and were taken back to the 506th area. Some of the floors were successfully defended and remained with their new owners. The 506th troopers departed but warned that they would be back to claim their property.

After that, the regular company area guard was beefed up both day and night to protect against the raid that everyone felt was coming sooner or later. In the days that followed, the 193rd area became an armed camp. Every man had a club, blackjack or knife beside his bed ready for the call to defend his floor.

The next great 506th/193rd battle never came about. On September 10, 1944, General Lewis H. Brereton, Commanding General of the newly-formed 1st Allied Airborne Army, alerted his forces for a new Airborne operation. By September 15, the 506th departed for their marshalling area and two days later they were jumping into Holland.

History records that because much of the 17th Airborne's equipment and records were still at sea en route to England, the division was not deemed operational and thus was not chosen to participate in the operation. There are a few, however, who maintain the brass didn't know for sure that the 506th and the 193rd wouldn't fight each other!

"The War of the Floors" probably served as a means for the 506th to "let off some steam." At the same time it demonstrated to all that the combat-untested 193rd could be counted on to stand their ground. And that they did.

"HASSENPHFEFFER"

As told by Eugene W. Bechtle, 193 F

On a typically gloomy, threatening day in November 1944, the 2nd Battalion, 193rd, was in the field running a series of tactical exercises in the area around Camp Chiseldon, England. My duties as "F" Company executive officer confined me to the company CP and at some time during the day, a corporal reported to me.

I do not recall what his message was, but we became engaged in a conversation which turned into a discussion of the great number of English hares which abounded in that area. I do not remember him telling me to which company he belonged, nor what importance the message had to do with our efforts of the day, but I shall never forget the discussion about those hares!

The corporal, whom I remember as Corporal Denmark, seemed to be a friendly, typical farm-boy type and he asked me if I had ever eaten stewed rabbit. I told him I had, but only prepared in the German style called "Sauerbraten" or "Hassenphfeffer." When I said I knew the recipe my grandmother always used, he promised to get me a rabbit if I would arrange to have it prepared by the battalion cook. I agreed and thought no more of it.

Then, this Corporal Denmark came to our "F" Company HQ one day with, you guessed it, a skinned English hare, ready for marinating and the rest. I took it to the mess sergeant at battalion and instructed him in marinating the beast in a mixture of vinegar, onions, spices etc. A week later I gave him the go-ahead to cook it and make the proper gravy.

It so happened I was duty officer the night that the rabbit was cooked, so it was delivered to the "F" Company tent along with some eating utensils. I sent for the corporal and we prepared to devour this succulent creature.

Man, that hare was as inedible as anything I have ever had placed before me! It had muscles on its muscles and no amount of marinating would have tenderized it. We offered the company commander, Lieutenant Joe Smith, and anyone else around to try their luck, but the hare finally wound up in the garbage untouched!

On Christmas Eve, as you will recall, we flew to France to begin a series of moves which brought us headlong into the Battle of the Bulge. After spending a few days in Charleville, we moved up to our jumping-off positions on the left of the 101st Airborne outside of Bastogne in Belgium.

Our first attack was scheduled for January 7, 1945, with Companies "D" and "E" leading and "F" in reserve. Lieutenant Smith had moved up with the lead companies to maintain better communications and I remained with "F" Company to bring them up later if they were called to assist in the effort.

While in reserve, I decided to do a little reconnoitering myself and walked toward our left flank and somewhat forward of our own reserve line. I heard an occasional rifle round go over my head and a few artillery shells exploded to my front, but nothing more exciting. I didn't feel I was in any danger.

Suddenly, as I walked through the snow, I noticed an American soldier lying face-down on the ground in front of me. Hurrying over to him hoping I could be of some help if he had been wounded, I called out to him. He did not respond, so I gently rolled him over. I found myself staring directly into the unseeing, lifeless eyes of a man I had known only as ... Corporal Denmark.

Shortly after returning to my company in their reserve position, I received orders to bring the company forward to relieve the pressure on Companies "D" and "E" that were having problems. Very soon thereafter I was hit by an 88 fragment and was evacuated. When I returned from the hospital, the 193rd no longer existed and I was assigned to the 194th.

I have told and retold this story several times to different members of our old company, but to my knowledge, have found no one who remembers a Corporal Denmark. Our division casualty list, however, carried a William N. Denmark as one of our KIAs.

I have harbored many thoughts and questions about this incident. I did learn later that Denmark was, indeed, carried on our Company "F" roster. We had received so many fillers while in England that we never did get to know everyone as well we would have liked. What had this man been doing when was killed? How had he been hit at this location? Did anyone see it happen? I know I'll never know the answers.

It is a sad thing to die in war. It is an even sadder thing to die and no one remembers you or anything about you. My only memory of this fine young man is the fact he liked stewed rabbit. It further points up the futility of war.

"THE HORSA GLIDER CRASH"

As told by Mel Therrien, 513 HQ 2

Some insist the deaths of 31 glidertroopers and two pilots, killed in England December 12, 1944, during a training flight were "hushed up." Others maintain that because the German's Ardennes offensive (The Battle of the Bulge) began the next day and the division was alerted the following day, the news just didn't have time to get around.

Regardless, many of the members of the division never heard of the tragedy that struck that Tuesday morning near Newbury, England. Today, as we study the operations and engagements in which our division took part, this day stands out as one of the dark episodes in our history.

We know that security was all-important during the war years. When several hundred American soldiers were killed off the coast of England in a training exercise designed to prepare them for the D-Day amphibious landing, they were quietly buried and no news of the mishap was ever publicized until after the war.

Also to be considered was the matter of morale. Many of the glidertroopers weren't too happy about flying in the motorless craft, but by this time they had pretty well accepted the fact that this was their lot and they were determined to make the best of it. News of a fatal crash at this point in time could have made a very bad impact on morale.

In any event, on that fateful day members of "C" Company, 194th Glider Infantry Regiment and selected members of Regimental Headquarters and their medical section were transported to Greenham Commons Airfield for a flight in the large British-made Horsa glider. It was a clear, bright day and most of the men were excited about riding in a glider other than the American CG-4A that they had grown accustomed to.

Not all of the troops, however, were happy to be going for the flight that day. There was some apprehension about flying in a strange craft. Some said they had heard that upon a hard landing the nose wheel would often penetrate the fuselage and emerge between the two pilots.

Rumor also had it that the Horsas to be used that day had been standing outside for at least a year and had had no first echelon maintenance for several months. They certainly appeared to be of older manufacture and not to have been used for some time.

The Horsa was constructed almost entirely of molded plywood and was bolted together by sections. The British had solved the problem of fast unloading by fixing a plastic charge on the rear section. Upon landing, the rear end was simply blown off and easy egress was attained. The live charge back there while the glider was in flight certainly was not a comforting thought for the troops inside.

Some of the troops were asking each other why were they making the flight in the first place. Chances were when they went into combat they would still ride the CG-4A. Some said it was a way of "getting acquainted with your ally" and the exercise was to promote a better understanding with the British Airborne. Others said it was necessary to make one glider flight every three months to qualify for their extra "Glider Pay" and these were the only gliders available at that time.

Because the Horsa gliders were huge, and they could carry more than twice the number of troops than the CG-4A, some theorized that the military was considering switching to the Horsa for all glider operations. It was very important for Airborne troops to maintain unit integrity in the airhead and to bring in with them as much equipment as possible.

Whatever the reason for the exercise, the troops turned to and things soon got underway. Major George R. Schnurr of 194SR had been designated as loadmaster for the exercise, and he remembers that glider number 12 was loaded with some men from each of the participating units.

Captain Roy Strang, company commander of 194C was supposed to fly on glider number 12, but upon request at the last moment gave us his place to Major James F. Klock, the regimental surgeon. That favor was to save Strang's life and cost Klock his.

Walt Wrzeszczynski, a medic with 194C who was waiting on the flight line for the next available Horsa, witnessed the accident as it took place in the sky.

"Everything looked fine," Walt said, "the glider was flying along smoothly when all of a sudden the tail section just came off. There was no explosion, it just fell off."

Walt shook his head sadly. The glider (what was left of it) swayed and flopped around at the end of the tow line and sank lower and lower. It seemed to be pulling the tow plane down. Suddenly it either cut loose or was cut loose and then it went almost straight down. It was all over in just a few seconds."

"We waited around for 15 or 20 minutes for one of the gliders to return and for our turn to go up, but I guess the brass thought better of it and they called off the whole operation at that point," Walt added.

Major Schnurr drew the dreaded task of supervising the gathering of the bodies and setting up a make shift morgue near the scene. Joe Vorsteg, a 194C medic, and two buddies had the unenviable detail of removing the personal effects from the remains.

The 33 victims of the crash (the 31 troopers and the two pilots) were buried in the Cambridge American Cemetery. Most of the bodies have since been returned to the United States for reburial upon requests by their families. However, six of our 17th Airborne comrades still rest there in that English cemetery.

To this day, the cause of the accident has not been determined and no doubt, it never will be. It remains one of those tragedies of war and those that perished that day are just as close and dear to us as those who later died on the battlefields.

"I REMEMBER LILLY"

by Bart Hagerman, 193 D

It was a cool, Sunday afternoon late in October 1944. My buddy, Ray Crabtree from West Virginia, and I were passing the day window shopping and girl watching in London. Soon it would be time to head for Paddington Station to catch the train back to Swindon and from there by bus or taxi to our camp. Another weekend of "R and R" was about to come to an end.

It was a four-hour trip from our tents outside Chiseldon to the big city, but the trip was always worth it. We never seemed to get free until noon on Saturday and by the time we got cleaned up, caught a ride into Swindon and then waited for the train, It was nearly dark when we arrived in London.

We would get something to eat first and then start hitting the pubs. Most of the time we'd "score." Somewhere there would be a couple of pretty, young English lasses who were attracted to two young paratroopers in shiny boots and cocked caps. Then, we tried to make Saturday night last as long as we could!

Most of the time, after we had spent a lot on them, we'd end up taking them home and it all ended there. Sometimes they'd even excuse themselves to go to the "WC" and then, when we weren't looking, they'd take off. However, frequently we would hit it lucky and they would take us home with them! Our average was just good enough to make us eager to come back to London every weekend that we could get a pass!

This trip to London wasn't one of our best efforts. We had "struck out" the night before. Ray and I had spent the night at the "Union Jack" Club. Actually, the place was like a USO Club, but only for members of "His Majesty's Forces." However, if you got there real late, the clerk on the desk was usually sleepy or drunk, or both, and he never looked at you too closely. It was the best and cheapest place in London to sleep and the breakfast was super.

Ray and I had ridden the Underground to Hyde Park. We liked to walk through there and listen to all the crackpots that came there to preach on their own special hate. Standing on their soapboxes, they were self-proclaimed experts on everything from weird religions to how the Americans were a pox on their soil. It was a real zoo.

We were on the escalator moving upward toward the street exit when I saw her. Lilly and a friend were on the down escalator heading for the lower level where the passengers could board the "tube." She was blond, with a "peaches and cream" complexion and moist lips that smiled when our eyes met.

I really don't know what got into me, but I felt that if I didn't act instantaneously, she would be gone out of my life forever, and I knew I couldn't let that happen. Without saying a word to Ray, I scrambled over the space separating the two escalators and onto the stairs heading down with them.

Lilly and her friend were quite surprised, as was everyone else in the immediate area. The British were hardly used to such goings on! But, I'm sure they must have tossed it off as "just another crazy American" and sighed at the price they had to pay in return for our help in beating the Hun.

When we reached the lower level, I was talking fast, trying to find out where they were going, and could we go with them. I knew I had to delay them until Ray reached the top of the stairs and could come back down to our level. This took a few minutes, but before too long, we had talked ourselves into a guided tour of London.

Although I guess this started out as just another pickup, it began to be something more than that almost immediately. At least it was for me. I was smitten by the beauty and sweet, gentle personality I found in Lilly. I really didn't know how genuinely lonely I had been until I met her.

We saw all the sights in London that Sunday. From Westminster Abbey to where the latest buzz bomb had landed. I could hardly take my eyes off Lilly. Her voice was soft and like music. Her British accent captivated me and I strained to hear every word she whispered.

We took them to dinner that evening and soon they said they had to go home as they had promised their "Mums" they would not be out late. These were definitely not the type of English girls we had been used to meeting on our trips to London!

Ray wasn't too excited about the date I had found for him. He had been looking for something—well, a little different. I had been too, but after seeing Lilly, I imagined that I was in love and I couldn't wait to see her the next weekend.

Several more weekends I came to London to see her and even met her mother. I would make arrangements to meet Lilly on Saturday night and then again all day Sunday. She fixed us picnic lunches and we walked in the parks. We ate fish and chips and we had dinner in different little restaurants she knew about where the GIs didn't go. We held hands and we kissed, but Lilly was a lady and I was well aware of the fact.

I was beginning to think of Lilly as "my girl" and I wondered what would happen if one day I took her back to the States as my wife. Of course, that was out of the question for now. We all knew it was only a matter of time until we would be alerted to go into combat and many of us would not survive. It was no time to take a wife.

It was turning colder by now. We had moved into December and Christmas was just around the corner. I had plans to spend Christmas weekend with Lilly. I had purchased a number of items from the PX that were in short supply to British civilians and I planned to take them to Lilly and her mother. As it turned out, I couldn't even call her that I wouldn't be coming.

Unfortunately, that weekend the situation on the continent went out of control. Von Rundsted's forces broke through in the Ardennes and the Battle of the Bulge was on. The 17th Airborne was alerted and moved to a nearby marshaling area where we began preparations for our entry into combat.

I never saw Lilly again. Even when I was wounded and sent back to England, I did not try to contact her. I was in a hospital in Wales and then in Scotland and I knew it was too far for her to travel to see me. To be truthful, I don't know if I wanted her to see me in the shape I was in.

Those days were the low spot in my life. I wasn't very good company I'm sure. After seeing your friends blown apart right before your eyes, I don't think anyone is ever quite the same. We all grew up fast. We had to.

Encased in plaster of paris from my neck to my waist, I had been told I was to be shipped back to the States. I envisioned a boring stay in more hospitals and then either a disability discharge or being shipped to the Pacific as more cannon fodder for that theatre. I was not a happy camper.

Then, lying in the hospital, a strange thing began to steal into my thoughts. I wondered what might have happened to the girl back in my home town that had broken up with me some two years before. We had been sweethearts since we were sophomores in high school, but we had had a bitter parting and had both said we never wanted to see the other again.

Well, I guess I should make a long story short. There was more hospital time when I got back, but I mended pretty well. I went home and I married my former girlfriend. We have been very happily married now for some 47 plus years. We have four successful, grown children and eight wonderful grandchildren.

Somehow, I was able to make the right decisions about my life as I stumbled through it and I am a happy man today. But, sometimes I think about the pretty, young English girl who showed me some affection at a time in my life when I needed a steadying influence. At a time when I had no anchor, she was a guiding light.

Yes, I will always remember Lilly.

"ENOUGH THRILLS FOR A LIFETIME!"

As told by James I. Mason, 139 Eng.

I had the honor of being the executive officer of the 139th Engineers and I assure you, there was never a dull moment during my service with that excellent unit! Like in all organizations, there were times you like to remember and times you just as soon forget.

I remember in particular, four times that still make me chuckle when I think of them. Maybe you would enjoy hearing about them too.

When the 139th Engineers arrived at our departure airfield for France, the battalion commander was pulled out and sent ahead as the advance party. He was then promptly flown to the wrong airfield.

About dark, as the XO, I was told by the base commander that the 139th

Major James Mason was XO of the 139th Engineers.

would provide protection for the base perimeter. We were to stop all perimeter traffic for inspection. It had been rumored that some German POWs interned nearby had escaped and were said to be planning to take over the base. Needless to say, our guys were pretty tense and keyed up.

Brush was laid across the perimeter road at critical points and the barriers were manned by riflemen and one light machine gun. We were ready for them!

The first vehicle that crashed our blockade was a British civilian sedan. The sedan was fired on and smashed into a ditch. The startled civilian driver received a minor head wound. He said he didn't want to stop because his passenger was his girl friend and she wasn't supposed to be in the barracks area.

The next vehicle which crashed our blockade was an Air Corps jeep driven by an airman. The jeep took a short burst from the machine gun, ran through the ditch and came to a halt in an open area. The driver suffered wounds in both legs. It developed that he had broken out of the base stockade and had stolen the jeep.

After arriving in France, the 139th Engineers settled into the Mourmelon barracks late in the evening. It was near a fighter base, but completely blacked out. The battalion commander was at Division Headquarters, so as the XO, about midnight I walked down our street to check on the companies.

I made out three forms approaching me through the dark. When within a few feet of these three forms, I saw it was three of our men walking side by side. I then saw the middle trooper was carrying an armload of champaign while the other two were supporting him and making sure he didn't fall and drop any of his precious cargo. Quickly, I stepped aside to let this strange example of teamwork pass. I could not identify the three troopers (naturally) but I certainly admired their initiative in finding their prizes in a strange area and under blackout conditions.

Later, after we had become involved in the Bulge, Sergeant Ralph Waterman, Company "A." was told to take his squad and replace a blown-out bridge to permit infantry to cross a stream. With chain saw, axes and other engineer equipment, Sergeant Waterman proceeded to the site, assembled timbers and the bridge was nearly complete when an armored unit colonel approached him and wanted to know how soon the bridge would be completed.

Sergeant Waterman told him it would be another 20 minutes. Then the colonel wanted to know if the bridge would support the three tanks he had with him. Unshaken by the colonel, Sergeant Waterman replied, "Probably, but if your first tank falls through, you can always get the other two over by using the first one as your bridge.

The colonel didn't look too pleased. Nevertheless, all three tanks crossed without incident. The infantry, for whom the bridge was originally built, crossed with dry feet.

Another interesting situation came up after we crossed the Rhine. After clearing his glider near Wesel, Sergeant Clifton Mingin of HQ Company, headed for his assembly area but stopped to offer what first aid he could to two wounded soldiers who lay in a ditch beside the road. Mingin got their names, but after proceeding to his assembly area apparently lost them.

Many years later at one of our division reunions, some of the old 139th Engineers were sitting around swapping stories of their war adventures. Mingin told the story and said he always had wondered what ever happened to the two troopers he had helped. John Huth spoke up to say that he was doing quite nicely in Frackville, PA!

For one, as the years pass, these memories grow dimmer and dimmer, but to those of us who lived them, we recall them with great amusement and wonder how we ever won the war! No doubt, it was only the quality of the individuals that brought us through.

PART II

THE BATTLE
OF
THE BULGE

"COMBAT DIARY"

As told by Dick Johnson, 194 F

December 18

"Give these Airborne people a ten minute break" was the order from a voice in the back of the room to the officer lecturing to the company on tank tactics. It was a statement that will long remain in our minds because it was the beginning of our entrance into combat.

The company had gone by truck to receive training in tank tactics by this particular unit of the 8th Armored Division, and a short while after we had arrived, word had followed us that our division had been alerted to move.

Back into the trucks we piled, every one under the impression that we were going into the field for practical work with tanks. To our amazement, we rode and rode, back in the direction of Ogbourne. As we did, tension began to mount and everyone became a bit uneasy as to the sudden, unscheduled return.

Recent news of the Ardennes breakthrough indicated that the war was not progressing too well. Someone had brought back rumors from town that the 17th was about to see action. Nobody had taken them seriously, but now as we rode back on trucks, some of us began to reconsider.

We were right, for as soon as we returned, the order was to pack up and prepare to move. With tremendous effort, the whole battalion worked all that day and night. In less than 24 hours, we were ready to move to the marshalling area near Romsbery. Here then, is the story of a glider infantry company, 194F, from their initial commitment to the end of the war with Germany.

December 19

English buses moved us to Romsbery. We carried everything on our backs, including duffel bags, rolls, ammunition, weapons, packs, belts, and gas masks. The day was so foggy that we couldn't see the C-47s lined up on the runways until we were close enough to throw our duffel bags at them. We loaded our equipment in the planes and prepared to leave, fully expecting the

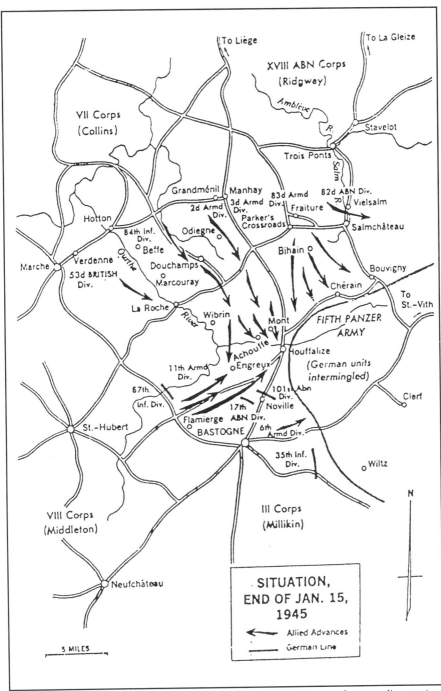

To Liège

To La Gleize

XVIII ABN Corps
(Ridgway)

Amblève R.

VII Corps
(Collins)

Stavelot

Trois Ponts

Salm R.

Grandménil   Manhay   83d Armd   82d ABN Div.
        2d Armd   3d Armd Div.Div.   Vielsalm
Hotton   Div.   Parker's Fraiture
84th Inf.   Odiegne   Crossroads   Salmchâteau
   Div.

Beffe

Marche   Verdenne   Ourthe   Bihain   Bouvigny
      53d BRITISH   Douchamps   Chérain   To
         Div.   Marcouray   St.-Vith
          La Roche   River   Wibrin   Mont   FIFTH PANZER
                                              ARMY
                              Achouffe Houffalize
          11th Armd   Engreux   (German units
             Div.   intermingled)
          67th.   101st Abn   Clerf
          Inf. Div.   17th   Div. Noville
               Flamierge ABN Div. 6th
                  BASTOGNE   Armd Div.
          St.-Hubert   35th Inf.   Wiltz
                                 Div.

                                               N

VIII Corps   III Corps
(Middleton)   (Millikin)

Neufchâteau

                SITUATION,
                END OF JAN. 15,
                1945

5 MILES
                ◀——— Allied Advances
                ····· German Line

By the end of January 1945, American forces had closed in on battered German forces, sending survivors eastward back to Germany. The Ardennes Campaign ended January 26th and the Rhineland Campaign began.

fog to lift during the day. However, it was the following Sunday before the weather finally cleared and we were able to take off.

At the marshalling area we slept in tents and enjoyed a lot of the comforts often given to men before they go into combat. The long chow lines were made up for by the excellent food that waited for us at the end. We saw movies during the day, including the outfits' favorite, *Two Girls and a Sailor*.

The Red Cross girls followed us that far with their club-mobile and we enjoyed the hot music and coffee with the sweet doughnuts and girls. The only real work here had been a detail to unload the planes so they might be used elsewhere. We later heard they were used to drop supplies to the 101st in Bastogne.

December 24

It was Sunday and the weather had finally cleared. The 2nd Battalion took off at 1500 for France, travelling over the English countryside, the White Cliffs of Dover, the channel, and finally arrived at the airfield A-68 near Snippes, France, at 1735. It was a cold, bitter, misplaced Christmas eve.

There was, as far as each individual knew, a battalion in the flight, but somehow this was all new and different and it forced upon each of us a lost, cold strange feeling.

Just less than a week before, everything had been moving toward a Christmas in England. Some of us were making plans for a pass to London for another mission with the Piccadilly Commandos. Others of a less social nature were figuring on extended periods in the sack, broken perhaps, by a movie in Swindon or something of that nature. Others had families or girl friends in Swindon where they planned to spend the holidays.

But now—this wasn't possible—were we really standing, nearly frozen, on some remote airfield in France on Christmas Eve? We were to wait here for three and a half hours. Three and a half hours of wondering: How near is the front? Where to now? Where are these trucks? They said this field was still strafed occasionally! This was all new to everybody, but somehow we all knew it was going to be a lot worse.

Finally, at 2109, we left airfield A-68. We rode open, slow trucks 30 some miles to Camp Mourmelon near Riems, France, where we arrived at 2400. This camp had been the base camp of the 101st Airborne Division. We moved into barracks there for the remainder of the night. Beyond that, we knew nothing!

December 25

This was no ordinary morning. We were painfully aware of that because to us it was still Christmas morning. However, there was no celebrating today, no church services, and who could possibly believe that we were really eating "C" rations for meals?

We had cleaned our new billets and arranged equipment and clothing neatly in all expectance of being here for a couple of days. Then word came down. We were alerted again. We hustled about preparing to move. By 1730 we were ready to go.

December 26

The alert held all that night and at 1030 on the 26th, we entrucked again. We moved 60 miles in six and a half hours to our forward area in Sedan, France. We arrived there at 1700 and were billeted in a vacant hotel.

This journey had been a very interesting one to us. The convoy moved along at a good clip as it approached more and more old World War I battlefields. Monuments all along the way reminded us of many famous battles of that last war. Signs by the roadside told us we were nearing the Ardennes. It was here that the last war came to a showdown.

Now in this war, U.S. forces had again pushed through the Ardennes, but the German drive in Belgium was headed straight for it again.

Even more noticeable were the French people. They were everywhere in yards, windows, along the roads, and in the fields. You could see the happiness and gratitude in their liberated eyes, and they threw bread, apples, pies, wines, and cognac into the passing trucks.

The company prepared positions in and around Sedan and along the Meuse River. These positions were all part of a line being established by Division along the river in case the German drive in Belgium should come that way.

Positions were prepared for all-around defense of the city in case it became necessary. Road blocks were manned, bridges over the Meuse were guarded, and patrols were active at all times.

These positions were held from December 26 through January 1 with no sign of enemy ground forces. A single Luftwaffe fighter, who flew by night to strafe our convoys, bridges, and road blocks, had bothered us four or five times. He was known as "Bed Check Charlie" and received his share of the discussions and jokes among us. "Charlie" had produced no casualties.

January 1

On the night of January 1, the company left its positions in Sedan and prepared to move to a new area. The streets in Sedan were strafed again at 2100, but no casualties were reported. Drucis had been sent to a hospital, sick.

January 2

We entrucked at 1830, January 2, for the front lines. No enemy had, as yet, been encountered.

January 3

The ride from Sedan to the front will be remembered by many in the company for a long time. For 20 hours the trucks crept along the snow-covered roads with the men in back huddled together in an effort to keep warm. During this ride, many of the frozen feet cases probably began.

We arrived at the front lines cold, stiff, hungry, and tired and made preparations to relieve elements of the 11th Armored Division. The Eleventh was new up here too. Just a few days previous to this, they had rolled through Sedan while we were there. They had attacked the town of Rechmont two days before we came up but had been severely beaten and forced to withdraw. It was a cold, snowy evening when we came up and crawled into their holes. They then made their way back to what they hoped would be a rest.

"There are Jerries just over the hill," they told us as they left.

It seemed pretty hard for us to believe this for there were certainly no signs of the enemy. Still, that night we kept an alert watch, just in case.

January 4 through 5

The following morning, after a night trying to sleep in ice-lined foxholes, we received orders to prepare to attack at 1830. "D" and "E" Companies were to lead with "F" Company in reserve. That made us feel better, yet no one was really worried about the attack. We had no idea of what we were facing and it was almost impossible to be afraid.

We started out in a formation straight from the field manual. The whole thing seemed like a problem. Our first objective was Hill 460 about 2,000 yards ahead. We began our way down the first snow-covered hill in that direction when suddenly there came a loud explosion. Everyone stopped and listened, and then there came another. Someone said we should it the ground for it was enemy artillery. Half believing, we crouched in the snow and listened. More shells came so we finally realized it was best to keep moving.

We came to a stream about two feet deep at the foot of the hill. Everyone had to wade across, and some even fell in doing so. This probably helped some of the frozen feet cases quite a bit. The artillery, although harassing, was not serious enough to cause much trouble. The only man wounded crossing the draw was Cecil W. Winburn, who later died of the wounds.

Up ahead, "D" and "E" Companies continued forward and advanced quite a distance up the hill until they were pinned down by enemy machine gun and rifle fire. Those who could, withdrew to behind a small bank for cover. A number of men from "E" Company were left stranded on the hill. It was then that "F" Company moved up close behind "E" Company and received the order to fix bayonets and charge the hill. Before the opportunity came, the order was changed, and "F" Company dug in.

During this advance, enemy sniper fire was a constant menace. Enemy artillery, ranging from mortars to 88s, although causing a few casualties in the company, did little damage other than give us a terrific scare. Most of it was going to outfits on our flank or to our rear. Our being on a reverse slope of a hill, protected us from direct tank and 88 fire. At one time, however, when our 60mm mortars fired, we received an answer from the German artillery.

The company dug in behind a several foot high embankment and pre-pared for a counter attack. Night began to spread over us, and as it did, the artillery began to get heavier and heavier with our own taking over the dominating role. With darkness came the possibility of saving the men pinned down on the hill. Several men volunteered to bring them back to our lines and during the night, they rescued all they could.

By midnight, the situation began to look more serious. They had told us the 87th Division would be on our left, but there we were with an unprotected left flank. Enemy tanks could be heard, and at times it seemed like they were just over the next hill and would soon be bearing down on our inadequate holes.

To our right, someone was taking a terrific shelling and a fire fight of some immensity was in progress. Riflemen kept a vigilant watch in case the enemy should come over the top of the hill about 200 yards to our front.

At 0500 on January 5, the order came to withdraw. The route of withdrawal was back over the attack route and then towards Houmont, Belgium.

The men, after the long night of bitter cold, were in poor shape for the long, hard march back over hills and through deep snow. Somehow, everyone started at the same time without ever being organized, and it was not long, with men and squads falling back, that the whole battalion was intermingled in complete disorder.

At one point, some of the officers stopped in a house to decide from the map the best way to withdraw. Everyone was grouped together, and an enemy shell landed close by. We did the natural thing, that is: spread out. As a matter of fact, we spread out so much that the battalion became separated into two groups. All of the officers were with one group. The other group had no officers. The former group made it back to Houmont with but little trouble. The other group, after a good bit of changing direction and discussion, finally made it to Houmont at 0900. First Sergeant Brauley received the Bronze Star in this action for organizing the latter group into companies and leading them back to their own lines.

On the way back, equipment of every description was dropped. Men put down their mortar and machine gun ammunition when the weight became too much for them. Parts of both 81 and 60mm mortars were also dropped.

Overcoats and raincoats that had become stiff were peeled off and left by the sides of the road.

To the uninformed enlisted men, the situation seemed even more desperate than it was, and his thoughts were solely to reach our own lines before the Germans caught up and attacked from the rear. As for those in the section split off from the officers there was even uncertainty as to the exact direction in which our lines could be found.

After we reached Houmont, we all agreed that all of the equipment could have and should have been carried all the way. However, the physical condition of the men had been severely beaten by the biting cold after spending a night in a hole in wet clothes with the thermometer as low as it was. This condition plus the fact that it had been the first day of combat for the men of Company "F" might explain the poor discipline during the march.

However, let it be noted here that this first attack and resulting withdrawal taught each and everyone a lesson: a lesson about cold and frozen feet, a lesson on hitting the ground in artillery zones, and a lesson of the value of every piece of equipment. But most of all, it taught us that war is hell.

Back in Houmont the company was crowded into a large barn. We started fires and thawed out. After we finally came to we realized the grueling experiences and by talking about them made them even worse. Artillery tried to zero in on the barn from the direction of Rochrival and forced most of us into the lowest floor among the cows and chickens who left upon request.

We gave the 11th Armored a hand in guarding their tanks, ducking occasional sniper fire on the way to and from the barn. Enemy snipers had taught us by now that all buildings must be cleared.

It will be well to make a break in the continuity of the story at this point to enumerate the casualties resulting from the attack. It was sad news to all of us to learn that Captain "Mike" Kyle, Headquarters Company Commander, had been killed in action. He had won the respect of all when he commanded "F" Company for a period at Camp Mackall, North Carolina.

Those actually wounded during the attack included riflemen Hall, Laughman, and Jordan; and runners, Bruno and Anderson. "Red" Stoneman stopped a sniper's bullet while standing in the barn doorway in Houmont. Art Baker and "Hutch" Hutchings were non-battle casualties. The long list of men evacuated with frozen feet reads as follows: Tech Sergeant Rome, Staff Sergeant McKinley, Staff Sergeant Young and Privates Boutt, Bagnelli, Buchanan, Fiorentino, Ramsey, Taylor, Thompson, Popp, Cagle, Stevenson, Acquilins, Munson, Belcher, Guerreso, Gipriani, DeMall, Davis, John Hughes, Schlee, Callahan, and Bert Miller. Some of these cases were very bad and a few of them later turned into serious trench foot.

January 7

On the morning of January 7, the entire division attacked, supported by tanks, T.D.'s and a great amount of artillery of the 11th Armored Division. Our company was in the lead this time along with "D" Company. The objective of the battalion was the high grounds and woods to our front. "F" Company advanced the farthest, to a town called Rechrival.

Rechrival was just a dot on the map, just a small place of perhaps 15 or so buildings in a bunch. Yet, it stands in our memories as the battle of Rechrival, one of the toughest spots we had ever been in.

The company went into attack formation from Houmont at 0815. The first platoon, under Lt. "Joe" Thompson, was the spearhead, with a mortar squad and the light machine guns attached. The second and third platoons were echeloned to the right rear.

The attack route leading up to the town was very hilly, up and down terrain which brought the attacking force over several ridge lines and then down again into a draw only to start up another hill. Excellently concealed enemy machine guns swept the top of the hills and down the ridges, and artillery covered everywhere you looked.

The first platoon swept down the last hill into the town without too much difficulty. They cleared out the buildings and then moved out beyond them.

The Jerry artillery increased steadily, and by noon, the number of casualties began to mount. At this point, Captain Dukes was stopped above a small wooded area on the side of the hill leading into the town. The snow-covered area was steadily becoming blackened by the bursting artillery. A "Yank" correspondent, travelling with the company, decided it was too hot for him to remain and made tracks for the rear.

After scanning the situation, Captain Dukes moved his CP into the village's largest building. Artillery had already wounded two of his runners, Kyte and Pielecha.

The 2nd Platoon, under Lieutenant Riechle, also found it tough going. Barely skirting the town, his boys had suddenly discovered themselves pinned down by the well-hidden Heine machine guns. Staff Sergeant Lassiter had caught a bullet through the chest. BAR man Wilbur Johonson had his arm badly hit. It was broken in four places below the elbow from shrapnel. Others wounded in the attack were the platoon sergeant, Tech Sergeant Irwin Goettache, Don Marsh, and Gardner. Marsh caught a sniper bullet in the back and Gardner, severely shell shocked, was later hit by shrapnel. Bob Young was also nicked.

"Joe" Thompson, pushing on past the town, also had part of his platoon pinned down by some of the Jerry guns. He became one of the casualties himself, when he was nicked in the shoulder by a bullet. Three 1st Platoon squad leaders were hit. Staff Sergeant Deem was killed instantly by concussion, Staff Sergeant Simoni caught a bullet in the arm and Sergeant "Matt" Beccio was hit in the foot. Gilbert, Karazsio, and Miscioscia were all slightly wounded.

The weapons platoon mortar section was too far to the rear and was receiving too much of an artillery barrage, to be used against the Heine machine guns. Casualties in the mortar section were weapons platoon sergeant, T/Sergeant Badertscher, Sergeant Cust, and three mortar men, Rickman, Zwycewicz, and Blair.

The mortars couldn't have done much against the guns anyway. It seemed impractical to fire on guns you can't even see.

Meanwhile, the 3rd Platoon under Lieutenant Jack Henry, attempted to advance far to the right rear. Crossing the crest of the hill, they were greeted with a hail of machine gun fire and artillery that sent them sprawling back. Both Lieutenant Henry and Platoon Sergeant Dall had been slightly wounded. Others wounded were T/4 Serbough and Sergeant Orvelius and Green.

Captain Dukes ordered the first and second platoons to withdraw as best they could. First Platoon BAR man Henry MacNulty, covered the withdrawal in fine order. He later received a Bronze Star for action here.

The covered withdrawal succeeded except for three men, Sergeant Paul Swartz, R.V. Young, and medic Art Freendlich. It was long after dark before they were able to crawl down off the fire-swept hill to safety.

With the platoons safely withdrawn, Captain Dukes set up a defense in Rechrival and prepared for a counterattack. This time we were sure it would come, but it never did.

This was the end of the day January 7. It had been truly a day of importance to the men of Company "F". The men still on line were aching with bad feet, but had seen others go back with even worse pains so they were to bear down through the days to come, defending their positions in the hollow called Rechrival.

January 8

This morning started our first full day of holding the positions in the village. The all- around defense Captain Dukes had set up included patrols to our rear to contact Lieutenant Jacobsen's 81mm mortar sections, and patrols to our left front to contact a line battalion of the 507th Parachute Infantry. Sergeant Schreck policed up 1,000 rounds of light machine gun ammo and a couple of 46 guns to add to our firepower.

This morning we got the story from Sergeant Paul Swartz of how he had been pinned down all day of the 7th. He was nearly frozen and very shaky as he gulped the hot coffee that was part of Mess Sergeant Dossett's first breakfast for us in Rechrival. R.V. Young, who had been glazed by a bullet and Art Fruendilich, a medic, had added a smoke screen of their own for cover, as they crawled off of the hill.

During the day of the 8th and also throughout the 9th, 10th, and 11th days of January, the company continued to hold at Rechrival, in a position that was 1,000 yards in front of the regiment.

All during the five day stay at Rechrival, artillery observers operating from the Company "F" CP, rained a constant adjusted fire on possible enemy position to the front. It was estimated that the enemy was only 400 yards away. A few times, American P-47 fighters strafed and dive-bombed targets in front of us. It gave everybody great boosts in morale to see the Air Corps operating in almost perfect conjunction with them.

On January 9, five officers had been awarded the Combat Infantry Badges. On the 10th, 167 enlisted men also received them.

January 12

On the night of January 12, the company sent a combat patrol led by Lieutenant Olson to Laval, about 500 yards to the front. No opposition was met and the patrol held its ground. On the morning of the 13th, the entire company moved up at 0430. They advanced northeast to Fossett where they went into an assembly area. From here they attacked at 0900 northeast and then on to Salle. In this movement, an 11th Armored Division tank destroyer outfit worked with us. Several TDs crawled over the hills, ahead of us, all the way. The distance from

Laval to Salle was five miles. No opposition had been encountered and one lone prisoner had been taken in the town.

George King and Lynn were evacuated here for frozen feet and Wilson went back as a non-battle casualty.

January 14

It was cold as usual on this morning, but the sun was out, shining brightly making the world seem more cheerful. The 2nd Battalion had the mission of occupying the town of Wigney. No opposition was expected, so we entered the town following the road, Colonel Stuart right up front with us.

At Wigney, we set up defenses on the forward slope of a huge hill where we could see the valley below and the rising ground on the other side. Deep snow and frozen ground made digging tough, but the bright sun continued to boost our spirits.

During the afternoon, the Air Corps gave us quite a show, British Spitfires dive-bombed a town up ahead and one Flying Fortress was shot down above us. Part of the crew bailed out at an extremely high altitude giving a few minutes of entertainment as we watched them slowly descend to earth some distance away.

Late in the afternoon, the report came that the Germans had withdrawn beyond the river which was below us in the valley. The company then made the long trek back to Salle to await transportation to another area.

January 15-16

The company remained in Salle in Corps Reserve.

January 17

We left Salle by truck. We rode part of the way then walked the rest to an area near Rochamps where the company relieved the 1st Battalion of the 506th Parachute Infantry. This regiment is part of the 101st Airborne Division.

It was just after dark when we took over their positions and it was so dark that not until the next morning was everyone oriented and able to fix his position permanently.

It was bitter cold all the time we were there, and we had all we could do to keep warm and eat. On the first day the enemy artillery caused us some worry but no casualties.

It was on the second day here, the 19th, that the Jerry mortars and artillery caused us grave troubles. The mortar section leader, Staff Sergeant Bucy, had been killed in action by shrapnel. Thirteen others were wounded, including Lieutenant Riechle, Staff Sergeant Burl Collins, Gerry Missimer, Joe Stepanik, John Layne, Barney Baxter, Oscar Thorp, Sergeant Wilton, "Mick" Micholson, Stan Halsapple, and Delbert Schain. Men who left with frozen feet at this time were "Sonny" Enstman, Ernie Jaroszewski, and Pete Foticoni.

During the stay in this area, Company "F" had established an outpost some 800 yards to the right flank of the company front. It was manned by a rifle and a machine gun squad.

On the 19th, the 1st Battalion started to move on the enemy across our left front. The outpost was to deliver small arms fire in conjunction with a 15 minute artillery barrage. The barrage, however, lasted only to the extent of four rounds of white phosphorous and all four of them landed short among the positions on the outpost. More trouble yet came when the Jerry artillery and mortars started answering the small arms fire. This enemy artillery went mostly overhead at the outpost and may have been some of the stuff that caused so many casualties in the company CP and 2nd Platoon areas.

Another interesting Jerry trick came into the picture here. At a time when all was quiet, several Jerry small arms began to bark. This was to arouse the men in our positions to get up and look around. Then, when the small arms stopped, what sounded like 50 voices, sounded off with a lot of yelling. The obvious purpose was to make our riflemen and machine gunners think a big attack was coming and cause them to return the fire. That was the Hiene motive, to get us to fire at nothing yet give away our positions. We didn't oblige.

January 20

On January 20, Lieutenant Gray, then the Battalion S-2, took a patrol to Tavigny to see if the enemy had pulled back that far. This patrol included Gray, three regimental I and R men, and from "F" Company, Tech Sergeant James D. Carter, Rohn, Spillman, R. Young, Sistek, and Hankins.

They moved forward all the way into Tavigny, through foot-deep snow. The march was slow and tiresome and they were all day in reaching Tavigny and returning. No enemy was found in the town. The Jerries had pulled out the night before; however, three prisoners were taken, one of them an SS man.

The patrol returned with its information, and we then knew for sure we would move up again.

January 21

Mess Sergeant Dossett brought hot chow up to the company and everyone ate a hardy breakfast. We had heard the rumor of moving but no one knew where. Certainly no one dreamed we were going to be on the road from dawn until dusk. The day was brisk, cold and clear with snow over a foot deep. Walking for short distances in snow is like walking three times as far on bare ground.

It was noon by the time we reached Tavigny, footsore, weary, and ready to put up for the night. Such was not to be our fate though, for after everyone had eaten a "K" ration, we received word to move again and we began the toil of trudging through deep snow once more.

After what seemed like many miles and hours later, we came to a small village where one of the civilians told us the Germans had left only the day before. Word began to spread that we were aiming for a town called Stienback, a few kilometers ahead of us. They were the longest kilometers we ever walked. After trudging through snow all day, it seemed doubtful that we could go on much further.

At about 1700, the company pulled into Stienback with a gruelling eight mile struggle behind us.

January 22-23

At Stienback, everyone found reasonably good billets where we could at least keep warm. We were in division reserve and the rest of the outfit and parts of other units moved through us up to the front.

Being so far behind the lines and in a fixed position allowed the kitchen to catch up to us. They began serving three "hots" a day, a great treat after a long period on K's and C's. We were beginning to get sore mouths from the lack of fresh fruits and vegetables.

Mail caught up with us and we even had a chance to answer some of it. Stars and Stripes came every day. We managed to remove the long growths of beards from our faces and began to look like human beings once more.

Everything seemed fine except for one very troubling item: our feet! Those of us who had not been evacuated previously because of them were beginning to wonder why. We stayed in a war room for a time and the blood began circulating causing our already swollen feet to ache and throb.

Captain "Doc" Ross, while inspecting feet, told us almost everyone in the regiment had a slight case of frozen feet. It was not too serious, however, and the pain could be reduced by soaking them in cold water. Yet to get better, they must be kept warm and dry.

Slightly confused by this, we continued to suffer regardless of what we did, but in the end, we found our feet would still carry us along, no matter how sore they seemed to be.

Steinback had been a great rest, but we knew it couldn't last. On the evening of the 24th, we left by trucks arriving at a small town about midnight where we hit the sack, well aware that in the morning it would be the same old story of chow at 0530, attack at 0830.

By dawn, we reached the line of departure. After waiting most of the morning, the company led off on the attack with the 1st Platoon riding on tanks. The Negro tankmen of the 2nd Armored Division were working with us this time and we all concluded, they were a good outfit.

That night we dug in and then moved into the town of Goldingen on our right to spend the night, leaving only a few men in the holes.

Jamuary 26

Rumors were hot by the 26th. We had heard about being relieved for the past week, and it seemed to be coming to a climax.

January 27

The next morning, we took off again back to the main road and went into an assembly area while "D" and "E" Companies were firing almost all their ammunition. No enemy was encountered. We spent the night in a woods, having learned that we were to be relieved the next morning. The next night we walked back to a small village where we again piled into trucks and travelled all night, a distance of 25 miles to Eschweiler, Luxembourg.

January 28

This morning, the company moved from Eschweiler into billets in Enscherange. We were to eventually stay here until February 5.

The days at Enscherange were far different from the forever moving, always cold days of the post. Here three hot meals a day were served. There was nothing to do but eat, sleep, read, and write. During the first two days there, everyone had been to a quartermaster unit for a shower. On February 2, several men in the company drew passes to a division rest camp near Virton, Belgium. This meant clean clothes, USO shows, movies, and perhaps even a chance to "hang one on."

This time spent here was only because the regiment was in reserve, but you could have sworn it was an official rest period especially when the first movie shown by battalion was *Two Girls and a Sailor*.

The weather had changed to a great extent. Fields were mostly bare of snow and warm breezes blew.

February 4-7

Word came down on Sunday that we were to get ready to move, which we did. We trucked a few miles forward to Consthum where the company was again billeted on February 5. We were in the regimental reserve until the 7th.

February 8

On February 8, the company, less mortar squads, went on a combat patrol. The situation was as follows: The division had a line set up along the Our River which separates Luxembourg from Germany. On the German side were the Jerries in position. this was the Siegfried Line. The mission of "F" Company was to get prisoners so the IPW team could get information from them.

Captain Dukes sent Lieutenant "Joe" Thompson and 20 men, armed to the teeth with automatic weapons, to a village on the river's edge.

Here they were to surprise the first Jerry patrol that came across the river, and get their prisoners from among it. If this didn't work, the patrol was to cross the river itself and get prisoners.

The whole thing was pulled off at night. The entire combat patrol with exception of the 20 men at the river, were put in position to deliver covering fire in case Lieutenant Thompson's men met trouble.

With the group at the river was Sergeant Frank of the IPW team, who knew the Jerry password until midnight.

Thompson and his men did not get across. Difficulties had proved too great to sacrifice the patrol in a suicidal attempt to probe the Siegfried Line. This night had been a wet one. The thaw that had been taking place here in Luxembourg was still offering resistence to movement and maneuvering.

The Our River was higher than its usual bed. Roads were muddy and slushy. To add to it all, this had been a rainy, black night, and communications between platoons and even within squads was difficult. The combat patrol returned to Consthum.

February 9-10-11

Through the 9th and 10th, the battalion was in regimental reserve in Consthum. The men rested. On the 11th, news came that the division had been relieved of front line duty.

The battalion moved in trucks in regimental column to Arlon, Belgium. We arrived there at 1100 then entrained in the familiar "40 'n 8s" at 1300 for the division base camp.

The entire regiment arrived at the base camp in Chalons, France, at 1800, on February 12. Trucks carried men, equipment, and all to a site outside of the city where they were to see their new home.

February 12

Chalons sur Narne seemed like a wonderful new world to us. Having arrived from the battle-scarred, shell-torn towns along the Our River in Luxembourg, it seemed wonderful to see a place with all of the buildings in good shape and no rubble in the streets.

At the beginning, our regiment was put into a tent city within view of Chalons. When we first arrived, the wind swept merrily through all the tents and rain could come down through the hole in the top center. We set up the stoves, pegged down the sides and began to settle down. It was going to be our home for a while. We wanted to make it secure.

Of course, strict discipline (we have another name for it) began to be part of the new world.

One day Sergeant Brouley called a company formation, and after some difficulty, remembering how it was done, we had the first look at ourselves in a long time.

Captain Robert J. Dukes and First Sergeant John P. Brouley were still up front. Lieutenant Joseph Thomson still had his first platoon with Tech Sergeant H.C. Schreck as Platoon Sergeant. Lieutenant Gray, who joined the company at Consthum, had taken over the 2nd Platoon in Lieutenant Riechlo's shoes. Staff Sergeant Haley was his platoon sergeant.

The 3rd Platoon was no longer existent, its remnants had been put in the other platoons as reinforcements.

Tech Sergeant Badertscher had returned as platoon sergeant in Lieutenant Elmore J. Olsen's weapons platoon.

All squads were under normal strength with a total of only 100 men in the entire company.

February 20

Just as our slicked up tent city was shaping up beautifully, we received orders to move to a different area about five miles away. Here we set up another camp, again starting from scratch.

This time it was to be more permanent. We knew that replacements would eventually arrive to fill up the company T/O. We did not know, however, that they were to come from our sister regiment, the 193rd.

March 1

On March 1, Company "F," like all other companies in the regiment, was reorganized according to a regular infantry T/O. Parts of the old 193rd were used to bring the companies roster up to 197 men.

We were now made up of three rifle platoons, each having three 12 men squads. The weapons platoon had three mortar squads (60 men), and two 30 caliber light machine gun squads. Two jeeps were permanently attached to the company.

We had a new officer now too. He was Lieutenant Hentz of the 193rd and he was leader of the 3rd Platoon. His platoon sergeant, also a 193rd man was Tech Sergeant Griesser.

Many other new men came into the company, and for a while, you very seldom saw a familiar face in the chow line.

After we had been in Chalons for a while, orders came down to sew on all stripes. We were able to see for ourselves who had been promoted. Walt James and Henry Schreck had become tech sergeants. Advances to staff sergeant had been made by Duncan, Frey, Shaw, Dodge, and Atkisson. Those who were made buck sergeants were Hammond, McNulty, Beal, Reed, Targerson, Haresnape, Lancaster, Ash and Statler.

Special Service was fast to get on the ball with outdoor movies every night. Despite the cold nights, great crowds sat on the ground to watch and cheer when the machine broke down.

The PX opened its doors nearby and sold us candy, Coca-Cola, French beer, and numerous other articles. There were even large stocks of perfume. Nearly everyone had a bottle of perfume sent home.

After several weeks, Special Service really did a swell job in bringing to us such stars as Marlene Dietrich, Mickey Rooney, and Bobby Breen. There were also smaller jeep shows which were nothing more than two or three GIs, musically inclined and very good showmen.

Our two biggest problems were light and heat. We solved the latter by going into the woods when official sources broke down. When we think of Chalons, we will always remember the constant swinging of axes and the flying chips. Some of the ambitious tents developed huge piles of wood which were soon swallowed by the hungry stoves on cold nights.

The lighting situation was always in need of improvement. It started by taking turns lighting matches. Batteries for flash lights were out of the question! Old fruit juice cans with legging lace wicks in gasoline or kerosene were common.

Gradually, the tents policed up lamps of many varieties. We heated water on our stoves and washed and shaved in our steel helmets. Every week or so, trucks took us to quartermaster shower units for a bath. We became more firmly attached to garrison life even though the garrison was a tent city. We waited patiently for warmer weather so we could enjoy our city.

During our life here, we followed a schedule which consisted mostly of fundamental training. Of the several problems we had, the one on setting up a defense on a river was by far the most important. It foretold our later actions in combat several weeks later although we never realized it.

March 20

The company, having been fully aware of a movement to come, boarded trucks for Chalons. Everyone had a full combat load including ammo and all.

In Chalons we boarded the "40 'n 8s" again and left that afternoon for ... no one knew!

March 21

We left the train at Mourmeliers, France, which is some 30 miles from Paris. Trucks took over again and moved us to our marshalling area on Airstrip A-58. It was 4:00 a.m. when we finally were assigned tents, fed hot coffee, and allowed to bed down.

March 21-23

On the morning of the 21st, all officers were taken to the war room for orientation. Company commanders had already been assigned their sectors and objectives. Now they were giving their platoon leaders the specific details of their part in the attack.

The orientations on this particular operation will never be forgotten by anyone who was there. It was all like a big game. This wasn't the usual type of unoriented attack. Everybody knew as much as the next group.

Sand tables had been prepared which were almost perfect duplicates of the area we were to land and fight in. Every road, fence, woods, house and all were right there. Company and battalion objectives were named in code. The bridges had names, the Issee River was tabbed, the canal too, had a code name. Routes of attack after assembly could hardly be missed.

As someone so appropriately put it, "The drop zones and plan of attack were tattooed on every brain."

Aerial photos from every angle were presented to the men. Flak, artillery, and mortar positions were brought out. Every trench in the whole area could be seen plainly.

All in all, the battalions success and each company's successes can be credited basically to orientation. For three days, every single man was in the war rooms of the 194 for the Wesel Airborne drop.

That covers plans and now to discuss equipment and supplies. The many showdowns at Chalons had a purpose. Slowly the already turned-in shortages came to us.

Clothing, ammo, individual weapons, trench knives, bug powder, air sickness pills, every bit of necessary first aid equipment, and many such articles.

Jeeps, trailers, A.T. guns, excess ammo, and other items, were tied into the gliders on March 23. All gliders in the tow were numbered, men met and became acquainted with their pilots, talk was of wines and kids, weather, how many automatic weapons each particular glider had, and in all, one could see that the next day, March 24, was "it."

By the afternoon of the 23rd, everything began to head for the same point. It was like a huge spring being wound tighter and tighter until finally it snaps and just flies in every direction. Tension began to mount.

Last minute enemy information came down. At exactly 10:00 p.m. the time when the British Commandos launched their Rhine crossing, we all prayed for them, for we knew that their success was important in that they were our linking force. Our minds never left the Commandos—we often thought and wondered how they were doing.

Supper on the 23rd was a class A meal again, like they all had been. Movers were again shown at night, as they had been on previous nights here.

Some men took their minds off of the whole deal by sitting through two and three movies, others spent several hours in the kitchen where steak, hamburgers, french fries, coffee, and many other eats, were at hand all night. Then there were others who slept, or sat and talked with buddies on "Gosh, what'll Mom think when she reads the papers?" Many were actually more worried about the folks at home than they were about themselves!

March 24

At 0330 on the 24th of March, the men awoke to a top notch breakfast. Plenty of time was allotted to the final adjustment of equipment and march to the glider. Press reporters of every denomination and many photographers were present.

The march to the huge herringbone formation of gliders and C-47s was a rough one. Men cursed and sweated under the weight of a combat airborne infantryman's initial combat load.

At approximately 0645, the men boarded the gliders, placed all equipment in the handiest possible places, attached safety belts, gobbled air sickness pills, and prepared for the take off.

At 0735, the first gliders were in the air. Long, circling formations were overhead while all of the planes and CG-4As were getting into line. Then at 0800, the complete train was formed and it started toward the rendezvous at

Brussels. Here similar trains from other airports joined in to make the longest train of airborne power the world had ever seen or heard of. From Brussels, the lead planes led toward Wesel, Germany, passing over Belgium, parts of Holland, a few rivers, and finally, the Rhine. Glider No. 22, with a mortar squad and a trailer, had broken loose over Belgium. It landed on a U.S. airstrip there.

In the gliders during the flight, men slept from the drowsiness caused by the dopey pills. What was a considerable rough ride bothered very few men. This was good because air sick infantrymen fighting on German soil against Germans aren't too effective.

The line of thought can easily be written for it was almost the same in every man's mind. We knew Wesel with its artillery, flak, and other positions had been bombed, strafed, and shelled ferociously by U.S. and British air power and by our immense British artillery support. We knew everything there was to know about the enemy, where all his positions were, and yet, we were wondering: "Wonder how everything is up ahead?"

From the gliders, we saw fighter planes buzzing around us like a spiral, war torn land below us, then further ahead we saw supply trains of trucks, tanks moving up, platoon bridges. Then we were close because we saw our C-46s returning after having released their jumpers. Practically at the same time we saw the Rhine and Wesel. Then came the flak and small arms. Machine guns were belching at us, the ground was a mess of haze and smoke where C-47s had been downed already.

Then we cut loose, a couple of sharp turns, a word or two from the pilot on the hazed smoke, and then on to a landing. Some landings were good, lots of them bad, a few serious crackups, and many caught hell in the air.

Gliders landed all over but where they were supposed to. Some came down on Jerry CPs, 88 positions, on roads, in among high tension wires, and even in woods. And in places, fierce opposition was met, snipers played havoc while men lay flat orienting themselves. The stories, hundreds of them can never all be put down. A conglomeration of them is what is really necessary in a company story, for to relate the many actions and doings of each glider load, of each squad, or to tell the innumerable tales of all that happened in such a short time, would take volumes. For in the case of each squad while moving toward assembly with platoon and company, never were so many pursued by so few with so much accomplished in so little time.

Had every glider landed on its proper drop zone, everything would have progressed perfectly. Men would have been oriented on the ground before leaving the glider. They would practically have known just where the other squads in their platoon were, where the other companies were, and which way to move. It would have all been ideal. As it was, gliders from every company in the battalion were all in together. The various squads were moving in every direction towards their particular company's objectives.

Here the perfect orientation of every individual paid big dividends. The men realized they were in the wrong D-Zs and quickly by high tension wires, a river, road, or bridges, recalled the sand table layout, found out where they were and moved swiftly down roads, through woods, across creeks, to get to their company's attack route as fast as they possibly could.

Everywhere squads fought immediate resistance. Men took 88 positions, CPs and bridges that were company objectives and were captured by squads. Small groups of men were taking bunches of prisoners five and ten times their size. Squads from different companies worked together to assault a defended house.

All of these things happened not only in one place, but all over the whole airborne drop zone. There was so much confusion to the Jerry soldiers and civilians that they just gave up in most cases.

The complete surprise of the drop, the "lead with lead-fast into action" policy of the men, and the initial, vast confusion caused so much surprise and amazement among the civilians in the D-Z, that women fainted, men were staring dazedly, children were crying and Heinie soldiers were running bewilderedly, hands high above their heads. In most cases they didn't even have guards on them. Company "F" fared about as well as anyone.

The reports show that every glider load or combined loads, that is, every small group that was moving towards our company objective, had met resistance, and taken all opposition, including many prisoners. In very little time, all had dug in on the company objectives, in their respective platoon areas, just across the three bridges that span the Issee Canal.

In action on leading up to the taking of these company objectives, three Jerry tanks were KO'd by "F" Company bazookas. These topnotch bazooka men were Weber, Giest, and Palamada.

At 1600, two enemy tanks attacked the positions of the 1st Platoon, driving them, in part, back across the canal, but they returned to their original positions shortly thereafter. At 1630, our supporting British artillery started answering directives from "F" Company's liaison officer. This fire neutralized another tank threat.

At 2100, "G" Company was forced to withdraw back across the canal, leaving our right flank open. British artillery again gave us a lift by keeping this area well-blasted with shrapnel. Again at 0300 on the 25th, tanks were heard and the artillery drove them off. Over 400 prisoners had been taken by Company "F" alone.

There was plenty of action all through the day of the 24th. Even after we were in position, B-24 Liberators caught plenty of flak as they parachuted supplies and ammo to us.

During the night of the 24th, Jerry planes buzzed over the British Commando's bridgehead at Wesel. Both Allied and Jerry flack guns burped all night long, filling the sky with red, yellow and orange tracers that were as beautiful as a big time July 4th celebration.

The linkup with the Rhine-crossing commandos had already been made now and everyone felt a lot better. The company rode tanks and trucks in the attack which was made along a road. Other companies cleared woods between attack routes.

March 25

Second Battalion moved ten miles cross-country on foot. The 3rd Battalion was in front as we advanced through the Wesel Forest.

From the time we arrived over Wesel until the night of the 24th, "F" Company suffered five men killed in action and 12 wounded.

Killed outright or fatally wounded and having died of wounds were J.B. Akin, who was a 1st Platoon scout; Cliff Emery who was killed in a glider crash and Putman, Rosenthal, and Shaw. All died of wounds received from action against the enemy. Wounded and evacuated were Sergeant Ash, Staff Sergeant Dodge, Staff Sergeant Leather, Bennis, Bice, Hankins, Knipland, Momrock, Staff Sergeant Lou Shaw, Woodall, Medic Frankie Ortez, and Jim Orb. On the 25th, George King was killed in an attack by Jerry tanks.

On the afternoon of the 25th, the 3rd Battalion attacked through "F" Company's positions. With the aid of thunderous British artillery, they drove some 500 yards in an effort to straighten out our lines so that they would be paralled to the River Rhine. It was during this attack that "F" Company mortars under Sergeant Lou Lancaster and the combined efforts of "F" Company's LMG section and four heavy MGs from the two battalions combined to rain murderous fire on more than 100 Jerries who made a break across the open ground to our front.

On the night of the 25th, the 2nd Battalion went into reserve.

March 26

We moved forward at 1930 to form a circular defense around the battalion CP at our new position.

March 27

With the battalion on line again, we moved forward against Wachtenbruck. No casualties were reported and six prisoners were taken.

March 29

On this day the company left Brosthausen at 1430 by truck with the 513th leading on British tanks. At 1845 we arrived at Bauschulinen where a defense line was set up to protect the highways and bridges in town.

March 30-31

The next afternoon we began the arduous task of clearing some woods. After we had been through many miles of German countryside, it was midnight when we finally stopped for the night at a barn into which we packed most of the company. On March 31 the company cleared woods again, capturing five prisoners.

April 1

We moved three kilometers northeast, capturing nine prisoners.

April 2-5

On the morning of April 2, we moved out at 0530 in the direction of Munster. After nine weary miles we at last came to a halt. However, instead of setting up a defense, the order came down to prepare to attack Munster.

It was late and we were tired and yet, we prepared as best we could, obtaining all the ammunition we needed and throwing away all excess equipment and souvenirs. We set off hopeful of no enemy resistance. We were still three or four miles from the center of the city.

The 6th Coldstream Guards advanced beside us and we concluded they were the best tank outfit we had ever seen. They seemed to use good tactics rushing across open spaces and advancing along wood lines whenever possible. We advanced slowly at first wondering if the artillery to our right was Heinie or not. Whenever we stopped because of a row of suspicious houses ahead the tanks would come up and blast them with heavy 50s. They acted as if it was a pleasure and asked us to point out more targets.

The Germans were in holes and their only weapons were rifles. After firing several times at us and receiving an answer, a whole group of them would give up. At one point the 2nd Platoon came to a large building used as a barracks. They won the prize for the day by bagging 564 prisoners at one time.

By 1800 all resistance stopped, but we were still a long way from our objective. It was midnight and we were footsore and weary when we reached the center of Munster.

April 3

The next morning we awoke to view the remains of Munster, once a great center of German culture, and in the war picture a highly important transportation hub. Around the outskirts there were a few scattered houses still intact. The rest of the city had been beaten and battered by Allied bombing. Even Munster's Gothic Cathedral had been wrecked.

April 5

We left Munster by truck after spending several days in houses. That night we found ourselves set up in a defense near a railroad track. It was cold and rainy and there was no place to stay nearby. We were guarding against an attempt by the Germans to break out of the Ruhr Pocket. That day we had cleared two small German towns with no difficulty.

April 6

The next morning a German tech sergeant surrendered his platoon to our company and we chalked up a score of 45 prisoners. We entrucked at noon for Altraruthen.

April 7

The next morning the battalion advanced from Altraruthen, capturing two towns. We set up a defense at Sultrop and prepared for a counterattack. We had heard the rumor that 30 German tanks were going to attempt to break out of the pocket and we were determined not to let them. The defense overlooked a huge valley and when the sun shone it created a marvelous view beside the advantage of offering excellent observation if the enemy did try to counterattack.

In Sultrop the 2nd Platoon was billeted in a nine-room house where they found a bathtub and although a lot of them had forgotten what such a thing was, after some simple explanations, they were able to remove a coat or two of dirt from themselves.

April 8

The following day we moved to Warstein and that night furnished protection for a field artillery unit CP.

April 9

On this day we received the word that we had the unpleasant task of clearing some more woods. We never realized there were quite so many as we seemed to cover in all of Germany. That day we walked from eight in the morning until six at night, covering 12 miles of wooded countryside. That night we were billeted under the stars thankful it didn't decide to rain.

April 10

We left our billet under the stars the morning of the 10th and launched an attack to high ground above Arusberg. At one point the company was halted by an enemy bazooka firing at those of us along the road. It was the 1st Platoon that advanced on the position. They captured four of the Germans and Sergeant James killed a fifth.

That night we dug in to prevent an enemy withdrawal in our direction. We heard that some other outfit was going to advance in the valley below us and attack Arnsberg. Shortly after dark an enemy 20mm flak wagon opened up on the battalion positions firing continuously. No one was hurt but the noise tended to keep us from sleeping well.

April 11

The division relieved us and we moved by truck a short distance and waited for further orders. We remained in the trucks all night, no one knowing our exact destination.

April 12

After breakfast in an open field we were ready to make up for the sleep lost the previous night. Instead we received orders to prepare for an attack. We were to advance along the Ruhr. No opposition was expected although it was possible that artillery and high velocity fire would be launched from across the Ruhr. All those who understood combat knew it was wrong, yet we had to follow orders.

We moved to the Ruhr and started slowly to advance along its bank. The company was well spread out on the open ground rising up from the river. Suddenly, all hell broke loose in the form of enemy machine guns and 20mm shells being fired at us from across the river. Almost the entire company was effectively pinned down by the outburst. Sergeant Statler, a machine gun squad leader, was killed instantly.

By cautiously creeping and crawling a lot of the company was able to return to covered positions. It was not long before the artillery went into action, silencing the enemy fire and permitting the company to withdraw. We did not know it them, but April 12 was our last day of actual combat in the war against Germany.

"THE BAYONET CHARGE"

As told by Don Scott, 513 I

On about January 23, 1945, in a snow-covered field just east of Houffalize between Limerle and Wattermal, Belgium, a bayonet charge occurred. Third Battalion (what was left of them), 513th Airborne Regiment, engaged in an ridiculous classic attack. Although the date and location may be subject to correction, the action took place just as described.

That no one was killed—was it pure luck or brilliant strategy?

It was an unusual formation trudging cross-country, as the remainder of the badly decimated "G," "H," and "I" Companies of the 3rd Battalion, 513th were all together in one force for a change, heading for a distant town. Major "Iron Man" Anderson led at a steady pace, followed by a bevy of lesser officers and assorted headquarters personnel, followed by the three parallel columns of the individual companies.

Normally a company would be hiking alone by itself, not in a battalion formation as they were now. There was less straggling than usual due to a general feeling of competition between the companies—no one wanted to look bad within sight of guys from the other companies. Also, with Major Anderson leading, no one wanted to call down the wrath of God upon himself. It was not unlike school kids on a playground who normally don't pay much attention to their teacher but snap to when the principal is nearby.

Suddenly a burst of enemy machine gun fire sent everyone scrambling for cover. The shots came from an emplacement 250 yards away right in front of a solitary little farmhouse and a larger barn.

"Yo, "I" Company, spread out to the right," shouted Lieutenant Crowley, "I" Company commander, waving arm signals from his prone position in the snow. "Move it, move it."

"G" Company did a similar maneuver out to the left, and "H" Company just bulked up in the middle behind Major Anderson's headquarters group.

With 200 men popping up and down like jack-in-the-boxes, running five steps and burrowing back into the snow, the flustered German machine gun team just fired an occasional burst, a sort of "don't come any closer" type warning. The range was too long to do much real damage except by luck.

It turned into a classic confrontation: the German machine gun set up in the front yard of the farmhouse, aimed across a wide, clear, snow-covered field towards a skirmish line of 200 troopers lying prone in the snow facing the gun.

"Company commanders assemble on Major Anderson," was the word passed on down the line.

"Hey lieutenant, hold it a minute," I hollered as I scrambled over to Lieutenant Crowley's position. "I can take a couple guys around to the right and come up behind those Krauts, easy as pie. It'd be a cinch."

Don Scott is a free-lance writer now living in Dubuque, Iowa. His favorite subject? Combat in the 17th Airborne.

"Yeah, sounds good," said Lieutenant Crowley, "but wait 'til I come back from the major's conference call. Pick out a couple guys and a bazooka in the meanwhile, but don't go until I get back." And the lieutenant slithered away through the snow to join the major in the center of the long extended line.

Thirty minutes later the lieutenant crawled back.

"It's like a Chinese fire drill down there," Lieutenant Crowley exclaimed, "everybody has a different idea but the major ain't listening to any of them. He's got his mind made up and nothing's gonna change it."

The lieutenant paused, catching his breath, then explained. "Here's what we're gon'na do; we're gon'na fix bayonets, and when the major yells charge, we're gon'na charge that damn machine gun nest."

There was a moment of stunned silence as the awesome stupidity of this development struck home.

"What in holy hell is he trying to do, get us all slaughtered?" was the consensus statement from the flabbergasted troops. "Holy Cow, he's lost his marbles. It'll be a massacre!"

"Yeah, yeah, quiet down, quiet down" Lieutenant Crowley ordered. "I told him we could take these Krauts from the rear, no problem, but he just ain't listening to nobody. He's the boss and when he says charge, we charge, Got it?"

There was more muttering and underbreath suggestions about what the major could do with his stupid idea, but gradually the guys with M1 rifles started affixing bayonets to them.

Sporadic rifle fire towards the Germans would occasionally be returned by a short machine gun burst, no harm being done, just a sort of "yeah, we're still here" pronouncement by both sides. Then word came down the line again to hold off firing, save ammo for the charge. A relative silence took over the field as dusk settled in. Evidently the major was waiting and counting on darkness being to his advantage.

Each soldier prepared for the 250 yard charge across the field by lightening his load. Off came the backpack to become the base of an individual pile of equipment with rations, entrenching tools, extra ammo, and any other gear that wasn't necessary for the fast dash.

Finally it was time to attack. The major jumped up, yelled, waved his carbine, and started running towards the German position. The rest of the troops rose as a mass and went plowing after him through the knee deep snow, screaming and firing weapons of all types toward the enemy position.

The sound and fury of 200 charging soldiers must have been overwhelmingly fear inspiring to the three-man machine gun team because the Germans didn't even return fire—they just disappeared. Amid all the rushing confusion no one even saw the gunners abandoning their position; all that was found was an empty space where they had been and a lot of fired cartridge shells.

"That Major Anderson is either the dumbest officer in the Army or the luckiest, damn if I know which," muttered First Sergeant Dean C. Swem of Buchanan, Michigan, as he started to assemble "I" Company into a specific area.

"At least he's got guts," said another voice. "He was the first one up, and he would've been the first one shot if the dumb Krauts hadn't taken off so fast."

At that moment Major Anderson suddenly appeared. No one knew how much he'd heard, and no one asked.

Don Scott (L) met his cousin, Lt. Keith Silver, a glider pilot, in London at Trafalga Square.

"Lieutenant Crowley, take your company and dig in for the

night along a line extending out that way," ordered the major pointing out to the right. "I'll make headquarters in the farmhouse, and "G" and "H" Companies will extend down to the left."

Fine. Headquarters got nice warm buildings with fireplaces to stay in, while the line companies got to dig foxholes in the snow again. The Army is not a democracy.

"Oh, and lieutenant, before you go, check out that barn, Make sure there's no Krauts in there," added the major.

"OK," Lieutenant Crowley snapped, "we'll rush some guys through there and shoot anything that moves."

"No, no," exclaimed Major Anderson emphaticly, "there's probably cows in there, and we don't want to shoot any cows."

Great. It's OK to shoot people, but don't shoot cows. The major definitely didn't have a full set of marbles.

"Hey Scott, c'mere," Lieutenant Crowley shouted. "Take a couple men and go clear out that barn. Make sure there's no Germans in there. And oh yeah, don't shoot any cows. We'll back you up from out here, OK?" And again the lieutenant had the grace to look a little shamefaced about passing this dumb order on to me.

It was darker now, and inside the barn it would be very dark. At the barn door I motioned my men back and explained, "you guys stay out here, I'm gon'na crawl in and if anything moves that isn't a cow I'm gon'na shoot hell out of it. Don't come in unless I call you."

If more than one person was inside the dark barn you could shoot friends in error. The guys were not unhappy about these orders; made more sense than charging a machine gun nest with a bayonet.

Crawling through the edged-open barn door was the most dangerous time, I figured. If anyone was going to take a shot at me that would be the logical place. So I scrambled low and tumbled through the door, fetching up banging my back with a hard thump against a pillar. After catching my breath and getting oriented, I could hear lots of cow noises—they were disturbed and very restless. There seemed to be about four of them milling around in one corner of the barn, and as my eyes adjusted to the darkness, I could see some stalls and another room.

Searching through the downstairs area turned up no Germans. That left only the hay lofts upstairs on each side of the central corridor. A ladder nailed to the wall led through a hatchway upstairs. By this time I figured that if there were any Germans in the barn, they weren't going to shoot me anyway because they knew they'd be slaughtered in retribution by the troops outside. At least that was a comforting thought as my head made a perfect target going through the opening at the top of the ladder.

After kicking through the small amount of hay in the lofts, I knew the Krauts were gone.

"Hey you guys, it's OK to come in now. No Krauts here, I don't think," I called.

Lieutenant Crowley and Sergeant Swem entered cautiously, followed by a half dozen others.

"How about it, lieutenant, we cleared it out—can't we keep this place for our headquarters?" I asked. "The cows keep it nice and warm."

"Yeah, I know," replied Lieutenant Crowley, "I already asked Anderson again and he said no. We got'ta dig in out there for protection purposes. Anderson thinks the Krauts may come back because now they know where we are, and he doesn't want all the troops huddled inside a couple of warm buildings. So we dig in out in the snow. Let's go, men."

We hated to leave the nice warm barn, but orders are orders.

"And hey guys," Lieutenant Crowley added, "Anderson thinks the Krauts may bring back tanks if they come. So dig deep!"

Nothing spurs a soldier digging a foxhole more than the thought of a huge tank rolling over him.

"NIGHT PATROL"

As told by Bob Richards, 194 E

"Lieutenant Robinson, you will take a combat patrol out tonight. You will cross the Our River in force, cut communications, locate enemy strong points, create confusion and cause casualities among the enemy and, most important of all, bring me back a couple of Jerry prisoners! Make your reconnaissance this afternoon and report back to me after you return from the patrol tonight. The S-2 will notify the 1st Battalion that you will be passing through their lines. Give him your plan and any help you need will be coordinated by him with other units. Any questions? That is all. Good hunting."

That was the order that Robby (my fellow officer, Lt. John Robinson) received from Colonel James R. Pierce—or "Fierce Pierce" as we secretly called him—our Regimental Commander. No excuses would be accepted because Colonel Pierce wanted his regiment to get across that river into Germany and hit the enemy. Nothing would please him more. Others had tried and failed. He had lost many good men during the Battle of the Bulge which had come to an end at the Our. Now was the time for revenge.

We were members of Company "E," 194th GIR and at the time we were in reserve near the Our River. We were billeted in the town of Costhum, Luxembourg, and dangerously close to the famed Siegfried Line. The plotted positions on the map which the S-2 handed to Robby looked like the enemy covered every possible avenue of approach down to and across the river. It looked like a jig-saw puzzle with guns.

"Well, orders are orders," said Robby as he slowly made his way to the company CP, "but dammit, they always told us at OCS that a patrol should be given only one mission and I have a half dozen! Wait until Frank hears about this. He'll blow his top."

Frank Erdman was a good company CO. He didn't appear to be too aggressive in combat as he was always trying to get the easy spots for his company. Many times he was misunderstood, as he was really trying to take care of his people, not to get a soft job for himself. I knew him better than that.

Robby didn't say much to Frank. He told him only a few of the things that his patrol was to accomplish and passed it off that way. He told Frank what men he needed and what equipment they should carry. He planned to take three squads of riflemen, each with two BARs. Then he notified the squad leaders that they would go with him on his reconnaissance that afternoon.

Few of the men actually wanted to go on the patrol, but none of them thought of letting Robby down. He had won their respect that first day of combat when he attacked a hill with a squad of men and was one of

Lt. Bob Richards on Jan. 2, 1945, in Belgium during the Bulge. Note the M-2 "grease gun" he carries.

only three who returned alive. He moved a little slowly, but when it came to just plain "guts," he had what it takes.

The company had rested now for two days and it didn't take them long to oil their weapons, dress warmly, blacken their faces and get ready to move. Then that old familiar look came to their faces. It was the look that tells you a man is sweating out a mission that might cost him his life.

I was particularly interested in this patrol because I knew the next one would be mine. Andy (Lt. John Anderson) had taken one out about three nights previously and didn't have much luck. My turn was coming and I was already sweating it out. Way down in the pit of my stomach was that "goose-pimply feeling" that never seemed to completely go away ever since our first contact with the enemy. I sort of admired Robby for the way he stayed calm and I wondered if I would be able to do that when the day came for my patrol.

Andy, Robby, the squad leaders and myself went on the recon that afternoon. We lieutenants always stuck together and anything we might do to help Robby was no more than our share. Besides, we were expecting to relieve the 1st Battalion any day and this way we would know what the terrain was like out in front.

So off we went, armed with maps, compasses, field glasses, and our always-present weapons. It was squish, splatter, squash, and splutter as we plowed through the snow and mud.

As we trudged along, it was plain that the Jerries had taken a beating from the Air Corps. Dead horses, cows, pigs, chickens, and enemy soldiers dotted the route. There were also remnants of what were once automobiles, trucks, wagons and busses which the Germans had been using for transportation when the planes had caught them in the open. These were all very real signs of war along the route we were taking.

The snow was still melting, but it was plenty cold, and it was not long until we began to feel the wind tearing at our throats. Our feet were getting wet for the "enth" time and some of the swelling was beginning to return. Walking became misery once again.

"Johnny" Johnson was not at his CP when we passed by his front line company, but one of his sergeants took us to the outpost position. From there we could pick up with our field glasses a few Jerries walking around on the other side of the river.

Our guys didn't fire at them as that would only give away the outpost position and invite an 88 barrage from the hill across the river. Our 81mm mortars had been trying to get at them for the last two days but all the good it did was to scare them a little. It was fun, however, to see them run for cover.

Robby decided it would be too dangerous at night not to keep to the beaten paths. He would take the patrol down the only available trail to a sharp bend where earlier he had tried to wade the river. The Jerries would not be able to spot him very easily at that point. From there on, he'd just have to trust to luck.

That's just how rough the plan was. The men would have to use their own initiative from there on. If Jerry spotted them crossing, they would catch hell. All I could do was offer a small inaudible prayer for Robby and his men. It looked like an impossible job and I didn't want any part of it.

We got back to the company in time for evening chow. Everyone ate in a rather disgusted silence because we naturally blamed the higher brass for all our troubles. The idea for this patrol was no exception.

Then I realized what I had to do. If Robby's patrol had something to cover their river crossing, they would have a much better chance of succeeding. A couple of light machine guns should be able to do the job. It would not be necessary for the machine gun squads to cross the river. They could wait for the patrol to recross after their mission was accomplished. Besides, I was getting nervous just sitting around and I couldn't see how Robby could do the job all by himself.

I talked to Sammy Weisman, my machine gun section leader, and asked him what he though of the idea. He was ready to go with me. I suggested that he talk to the men, but they decided that they would follow Sammy anywhere. Sammy hated Germans and he was ready to fight them every time he had the chance.

I didn't really ask the CO if we could go. I just told him Robby needed us and we were going. Robby never made much fuss and I think he felt better after that because now he knew he would have someone to back him up if he got in trouble. It's a hell of a feeling to be out there alone and not to have someone you can call on if things go sour.

L to R: Lts. Easterbrooks, John Anderson and Bob Richards in the marshalling area in England prior to the airlift to France. The canvas "holsters" were for the M-1 folding stock carbine.

It was therefore decided that Robby would take the three squads of riflemen and I'd take my machine gun section. That made a total of 45 men, a large number of men to handle on a night patrol. But, if we were to do the job, we believed we would need that many and probably would be wishing for a lot more.

Our plans for moving out were laid out carefully. Everyone had plenty of ammunition. They all memorized the signals to be used and asked questions until everyone knew the entire plan. Everyone knew what he was expected to do. They had learned long before that this was not a game of maneuvers anymore. It was a game of life and death.

At 1100 hours the patrol assembled outside the shacks in which we had been living. The night was pitch black, but the men were having a last smoke. They had developed that technique of smoking a cigarette without the enemy seeing the dim glow. Everyone was close together although little conversation could be heard. Every few minutes there was the audible crack of two rifle butts meeting. A thing like that could get you killed once we got closer to the enemy.

Robby led out with his riflemen and I took the rear with my machine guns. I was glad to be in the rear. There I felt a little safer. It was nice to know that someone was out there in front. Someone I could depend on.

Lt. John Robinson, already wounded in the finger, poses for photo on Jan. 5, 1945 while mortar fire lands nearby.

It was best that Robby and I were separated. If anything happened to him I could take over and vice versa. I knew his plans and besides, I wanted to be with that machine gun section which was my pride and joy.

All talking ceased as we moved out. It was difficult to see the man in front even with a piece of white rag tied to his rifle belt. White handkerchiefs had ceased to exist long before.

Although we were slipping and sliding some as we walked through the snow, there was very little noise. Everyone was thinking the same thing: Where were they? Even the cold didn't bother us now. Our blood warmed our bodies as we sweated under the loads we carried and from the excitement we were trying to control.

We passed by half-destroyed buildings and through a small village, but heard nor saw anything. If I had not known better I would have thought that no one was around for miles. I knew, however, there were troopers just like us out there in the shadows. I thought if one of them should decide we were a German patrol we'd be in for it. It was so quiet!

After almost an hour, the word came back that we were at the outpost. I wondered what surprises the terrain beyond held for us that night. My mind started racing. I knew what we should do if we ran into a German patrol or ambush, but would we be able to pull it off?

Slowly we moved down the road. Carefully we walked where the man in front had walked. We were afraid of mines. How we hated those mines! We placed every foot as though there were sharp needles everywhere. As we made progress, I checked landmarks that Robby and I had selected from the map. They were easy to pick up because the map was accurate.

There was still plenty of snow on the ground and it began to crunch under our feet. It was freezing again after the day's thaw. That crunching seemed to be like the tramping of a thousand boots. Otherwise, not a sound was heard with the exception of some heavy breathing from the men.

Swish, swish, swish and the wham, wham, wham as about a dozen artillery shells landed about a thousand yards in front of us. I wondered for a moment where the devil they came from! Then, I realized that it was our last artillery barrage being laid down on the enemy position. Our artillery was not going to fire near us after 2300 hours unless we called for it by radio. That 300 radio had become SOP with us and we never went anyplace without it.

"That's on the other side of the river where that stuff is landing," I said to myself. We were getting close and I knew it wouldn't be long now.

Then I heard it—the sound I had been listening for. Click! They had fired a flare! We all automatically hit the ground and froze motionless. A second later we heard another crack an the entire area lit up like a stage. The Germans had fired a flare and if they spotted us out in the open like we were, it would be rough.

We dared not look up for fear our faces would reflect the light. While I am sure all of us said a prayer, It finally burned itself out and the dark descended upon us again. Slowly the word came back and we got to our feet and moved on. Apparently, Jerry was satisfied as no shells came our way.

We rounded a hairpin curve in the road and there was the river. From where we stood it looked small, but I knew it would look wide and forboding when we got down to its bank.

The column suddenly stopped. I waited a few minutes and then the word came down for me to move to the head of the column. When I got there, there was Robby, cool as a cucumber. His back was against a cliff and there was a big hill down to the river in front of him. Both the cliff and the hill were too steep to climb, especially at night and with the noise that would surely announce our presence.

This was a terrible place to stop. There was no way out except by the road. With our backs to the wall we were ripe for an ambush.

Then we heard them. The sound of shovels grating against dirt and stone. A few guttural German words came faintly to our ears. We wondered if they had heard us. Then we realized if they had they wouldn't be digging, so we relaxed a bit.

The situation was bad. If another illuminating shell went up, we were dead. It was the time to make some decisions. We had to decide whether to go on or go back without accomplishing our mission.

Robby motioned to me and the two of us crawled to the edge of the road and listened. The digging was coming from a position less than a hundred yards below the road on which we were lying. On our right about 200 yards ahead was another hairpin turn in the road which would take us by the enemy position.

That enemy position had to be passed. The only way to do it was to kill the Jerries there. How to kill them without alerting the whole area was another problem.

Robby had a squad leader by the name of Worden. He was a full-blooded Indian. He liked to go on patrols and he had inherited the stealth talents of his ancestors and he had the eyes of a cat.

"I'll take Worden and we'll follow the road down into that position and see if we can take those Jerries," said Robby. "You stay here and cover that position below us as we move in. If we don't come back in 15 minutes, you get the guys out of here, fast!"

I knew we could lie on the road and blast the position below, but when we did, it would call attention to our own positions and they would let us have it from across the river. The Jerries had to be taken without any noise. It had to be done with knives.

Robby gave me ten minutes to set up the machine guns. I had one cover the road down which Robby and Worden would move and the other set to fire across the river. If we were discovered we would be like ducks in a shooting gallery with that steep cliff behind us.

I took one of the BARs and a couple of the riflemen and set up to cover the position down below us. We could also lob grenades down there if the alarm went up. How Robby and Worden would be able to get out, I didn't know.

Without a sound, Robby and Worden were gone into the darkness. If they were discovered, I didn't think they would have a chance to get out.

As I lay there in the snow I could feel myself becoming even more tense as my excitement continued to mount. I had never prayed much before, but with the idea that 45 men's lives might be in my hands, I lay my head in the snow and started praying for all I was worth.

I said to myself that I never should have let Robby and Worden go down there. Then I condemned myself for bringing the machine gun section without being ordered to. I could visualize the men trying to claw their way up that cliff if we were discovered and being ripped to pieces by machine gun fire and artillery.

As the seconds dragged by it seemed to get colder and darker. The digging had stopped now, but we could still hear the Germans talking. I figured Robby and Worden should be just about to the position by now an I expected the fireworks to start at any minute.

I was awakened from my worries by a gentle tap on my leg. I sucked in a breath and turned quickly. There was Robby and Worden. They were safe and sound and it was still as quiet as it could be.

Robby pressed his mouth near my ear and whispered that they had gotten about 150 feet down the road and ran into another German machine gun position. It was set up to cover the very road on which we lay. It was impossible to get close enough to knock it out without a lot of noise.

He asked me what I thought about the situation. That did it. I told Robby that his job now was to get all these men out of this no-win situation and back safely. A two or three man patrol might get across the river, but not this many.

Robby agreed and we laid plans for our withdrawal. We would go back the way we had come, doing an about-face with me leading the machine guns first and Robby bringing the rest behind us.

With Sergeant Weisman leading the column, we started back. It was slow enough at first, but soon the pace picked up as the men were anxious to get away from here. As the men passed I counted them. I didn't want to leave anyone here!

Soon Robby caught up with me and said the pace was too fast. We slowed it down and the column closed up. I never was so glad to be challenged by the sentries as we entered our friendly lines.

The walk had warmed our bodies and I knew there would be a hot cup of coffee waiting for us when we got back. It was a good feeling to be out of that potential killing ground. At this point it was great just to be alive. If we had been discovered on that road, most of us wouldn't have made it.

Sure, we failed to accomplish our assigned mission, but we did learn a lot about the enemy's defences and the cold truth that the Our could not be crossed via that road until the artillery had worked over the area. Only in the movies do things always go as planned. We brought all our people back and few days later when we were relieved and sent back to prepare for the Rhine crossing we were damn glad to have them.

"A REBEL AT THE OUR"

As told by Ray McNamara, 513 E

Many of the men in the 17th Airborne Division Association know and admire Hewlett E. Rainer. He is better known as "Reb," short for Rebel. They know him as one of the division's triple CIB winners, a retired colonel, an able speaker at several of our past reunions and an all-around good fellow.

It's unlikely, however, that many of them know Reb like I do. My name is Ray McNamara and I'm from Binghamton, New York. I was a scout in a rifle squad of Company "E" of the 513th Parachute Infantry that was lead by the then Sergeant Rainer from Birmingham, Alabama.

All of us guys from the North had a bit of trouble understanding Reb's deep southern drawl, but it didn't take us too long to realize Reb knew his business and he won our respect. That slow drawl could drip like honey sometimes and then, when the situation demanded, it could cut like a buzz saw. The men soon learned that when Reb spoke, it was the final word and you'd better get moving.

When the Division joined in the "Battle of the Bulge," Reb proved that he was equally talented in combat as he had been in training. It seemed he always knew the right thing to do and our squad, confident in Reb's leadership, performed well.

One day, late in the month of January 1945, the division closed on the Our River in the Eiffel Mountains. The river divided Germany from Luxemburg. The rain and snow-swollen river provided a formable barrier to the division's continued advance. The Germans, forced to retreat back into the Fatherland, were dug in near the Siegfried Line and the 17th Airborne was probing for a way across the Our to carry the battle to the enemy.

One cold, foggy night Reb was ordered to take a reconnaissance patrol out and look for a dry route across the river. Reb and seven of us set out to accomplish this mission.

Reb hand-picked me for the job and as I was scout, he sent me out in advance of the patrol to lead the way. I was up tight, there was no denying that.

In fact, all the men were scared as we picked our way through the snow and brush leading down to the river.

Suddenly, I heard a number of German voices and the sound of a large body of men advancing in our direction. Then, in the dim moonlight I saw them. There seemed to be dozens of them. I immediately signaled the patrol to halt and hurried back to report to Reb what I had seen and heard.

Reb listened intently to my highly-excited account of an estimated 100 enemy soldiers headed right toward us. He then listened for a moment and then calmly told me to go back to my observation point and lay low.

No sooner had I returned to my position when the darkness and quiet was shattered by the loudest,

Ray McNamara from Binghamton, NY. It took him awhile to learn about Southern soldiers!

most piercing, blood-curdling scream I had ever heard! The sound echoed across the river, up the valley, bounced off the hills and was loud enough to wake the dead!

"My God," I thought, "that's that crazy Reb doing that!" With my heart in my throat and almost wild with terror, sure the entire German Army would soon descend on me, I sprang to my feet and bolted back to where I had left Reb.

"What in the hell are you doing?" I stammered. "Are you trying to get us all killed?"

Reb, cool as he could be, smiled as he saw the fear that gripped me. "If you can't whip'em, scare em," he replied.

About that time I became aware of another racket. The Germans were crashing through the bushes and trees as they fled in complete disarray. They didn't stop until they were back in their bunkers on the German side of the river.

Reb shook his head at me and smiled as he said, "Mac, one of these days you damn Yankees will come to respect a good ole Rebel yell and what it can do for you!"

With my heart still beating like mad, I could only shake my head. That was not the first, nor would it be the last, of many adventures I was to have as a member of Reb Rainer's squad. I wouldn't have had it any other way.

"ACHTUNG MINEN!"

As told by J.R. Jones, 513 A

I guess it's not unusual for men who have seen combat to worry over things that happened and wish that they could do something to change them. The feeling that "it was not fair" can haunt you the rest of your life.

All of us would like to change the killing and wounding involved in combat, but that is history and we know that can't be changed. What is really frustrating is to see things that could easily be changed, but because of red tape or bureaucracy, are left undone. That hurts.

That's what happened in the handling of an incident that took place in early February 1945, to two members of "A" Company of the 513th. On a cold, miserable night near the banks of the Our River in Luxembourg, two sergeants, Nick Garcia and John Baines, performed an act of heroism that will go unchallenged in warfare, as far as I am concerned, and they received no recognition whatsoever. Here's what happened:

The Battle of the Bulge was drawing to a close and in our 17th Airborne sector, we had driven the Germans back across the Our River. They were back to the Siegfried Line and heading back into Germany. We then assumed a defensive position while we scouted and patrolled for a way to cross the flooded Our.

All the attack units of the division were critically short of personnel and equipment. It was cold and the men were tired and badly in need of rest and reorganization. To make it worse, our company was given the mission to defend the entire 1st Battalion front.

Because of the width of the defensive sector and the badly understrength status of the company, it was determined that the best way to do this would be to establish two strategically located observation posts in lieu of a main line of resistance. These OPs were designated as "A" and "B" and each overlooked the Our and provided observation of the battalion front.

A squad of troopers and supporting weapons would pull a shift and be relieved by another like force. The relieved force would then return to the company's rear for rest before going back up. Things went fine for a period of time. Then tragedy hit.

On the night of February 4-5, the force at Observation Post "A," consisting of approximately 10 troopers, had been relieved and were on their way to the rear. The route called for them to proceed back along a trail to a certain point and then cut right to hit a road leading down through a valley. This would lead them to the company's rear area CP.

Somehow, someway, the men turned right about 50 yards too soon and before they realized what had happened, found themselves in the middle of an German laid minefield. Suddenly the feared anti-personnel mines, called "Bouncing Bettys" by the GIs, were detonating everywhere and the troopers were taking casualties. Several were killed immediately and all the others went to the ground wounded.

Thinking he might not make it home, Lt. Jones had this portrait made in Tullahoma before shipping overseas.

One member of the group, T-5 Irving Byron who now lives in Tucson, AZ, despite incurring serious multiple injuries, drug himself out of the minefield and painfully made his way back to the company CP. He reported the incident to the CO, Captain John Spears, of Sierra Vista, AZ and was then evacuated.

On order, Sergeants Nick Garcia (now deceased, but whose widow resides in Miami, FL) and John Baines of Houston, TX, quickly organized a patrol and set out for the minefield to determine the situation and see if rescue was possible. Once on the scene they realized that several of the trapped troopers were still alive.

The big problem was how to get the men out without detonating any more of the mines. It was pitch dark, but if they waited until daylight, all the wounded would likely freeze or die of shock. It was now or never.

Garcia determined that it would be necessary to clear a path to the wounded and then the men could be dragged to safety. Crawling on their stomachs in the foot-deep snow, Garcia and Baines slowly felt for the indentations that marked where the mines had been buried. It was touch and feel from here on.

As Garcia and Baines located the mines, feeling with cold, numb fingers, they deactivated them and moved them to the side of the path they were clearing. The rest of the patrol lay huddled a short distance away holding their breath and fearing every moment one of the mines would go up.

Finally, about 10 of the mines were deactivated and the wounded were slowly removed from the minefield. The patrol then carried the men back to the company CP where they were evacuated through the Battalion Aid Station. The dead were recovered the next morning.

I was a platoon leader in "A" Company and had been wounded earlier and was not present when this event took place. When I rejoined the unit in the vicinity of Munster, I learned of this feat of heroism and was distressed to learn that although Sergeants Garcia and Baines had been recommended for an appropriate award, none had been forthcoming.

Later, when hostilities ceased, I tried to correct this injustice and see that these men received the recognition they were entitled to. I submitted documentation through channels again, but the results were the same: It was turned down.

Years later, still bugged by the injustice of this and figuring someway the recommendation failed to reach the proper authority, I tried again. This time I worked through the office of Senator Strom Thurmond. After 17 months of tracking the papers through various levels I was finally informed by the Secretary of the Army that "... time limitations for making recommendations for decorations that recognize service during World War II have expired."

So, this story must end here. Justice has not been done. I repeat my earlier statement that some things are "just not fair." Certainly these two sergeants did not receive the awards that they should have, but I know several guys who are damn glad that there were two brave men like Garcia and Baines around when they really needed a couple of heroes.

"MY BATTLE OF THE BULGE"

As told by James E. Costello, 507 HQ

Editor's Note: *Jim Costello was born in San Francisco in June of 1920. Soon after writing this account of his experiences in the Battle of the Bulge, he died in May of 1991. He never knew we were going to publish his story, but his widow has made it available to us. We dedicate it, and his poem, to his memory.*

The Autumn Leaves Have Fallen

The Autumn leaves have fallen
and the ground has chewed them up.
So now, we wait for springtime
when the roots of trees erupt.

They'll bring back to us new greenery,
to shade our Summer sun.
And then in Fall their colors change,
so soon their life is done.

But still there's joy for everyone
those different hues to see,
Joyce was right in saying
only God can make a tree.

The Autumn leaves have fallen ...

The life of the infantryman—even an Airborne infantryman is not a pretty one. You live in the dirt, you're unkempt, you get no baths and you risk your life every day. You're on duty 24 hours a day, seven days a week. There's no overtime pay, no holidays, not even Sundays. There is no breakfast, lunch or dinner time. Time to eat is a luxury and then it's out of a can—if you're lucky and have one.

Regardless, the infantryman must have the alertness of a deer, the patience

Near Mande St. Etienne during the Bulge. L to R: Wilbur Hadden, Don Neenan and Bill Shiver. These troopers were in 193 HQ 1, but the whole 17th Airborne sector was covered in deep snow.

of a spider and the stamina of a race horse. He must face artillery fire, mortars, land mines, booby traps, tanks, machine gun and rifle fire. You live and sleep with dead all around you, both friend and foe.

War is inhuman, vicious, and until victory—unrewarding.

I was in the demolition platoon of the 507th PIR Regimental Headquarters Company. It consisted of three sections of about 13 men each. When entering combat, each section was sent to one of the three battalions and became part of that battalion's headquarters company. My section joined the 2nd Battalion.

We were in England on the 17th of December 1944. It was the day after Von Rundstedt had started the counteroffensive through Belgium. The 17th Airborne was alerted and told to get ready to go to France and help halt the German drive.

On December 23 they served us our Christmas dinner. No one was much in the mood for Christmas about that time, but it was either eat the dinner then or miss it altogether. We ate, but I didn't hear anyone give out with a Merry Christmas.

On December 25 we flew to France and while being trucked to a place named Rocroi on the border of Belgium, we were strafed by the Luftwaffe. Everyone jumped off the trucks and headed for cover. Only then did I hear some joker yell out "Merry Christmas!"

Rocroi was a small coal mining town and we considered ourselves lucky to get to stay in a barn. Needing water for our canteens, I was elected to go get it, having in my possession a French-English pamphlet. It made me an expert in French!

Three of us collected canteens and crossed the street to a bakery. I whipped out my little book, looked up water and read what I thought it said: "Loo."

Everyone looked at me with a puzzled look. A woman called over another woman and I repeated the word again. Still no reaction. So I held up the canteens and their faces lit up. Laughing, they took us back to the kitchen.

We were than handed several bottles of beer and a loaf of French bread. It wasn't a bad translation although I knew my French had lacked something! Finally, a young man entered who spoke English and we got our water. After that trip I was in great demand as a negotiator.

The next day we moved up to the city of Fumay and were told to lay a mine field. They were expecting the Germans to counterattack in our direction. Arkie Davis drew up the diagram on a piece of brown paper and we laid out the mines in a criss-cross pattern, except for the road. I found out later that a jeep carrying our battalion doctor swerved off the road and hit one of our mines. The driver and the doctor were both killed.

On January 3, they trucked us into a wooded area northwest of Bastogne. We were close to the front now and it was time for passwords and guards at the perimeters. We were supposed to dig slit-trenches or foxholes for protection from artillery fire, but the ground was frozen solid. We formed four walls with logs and piled snow against them. It was the best we could do.

The next day we moved up to the front and while we were walking around the edge of the forest, the Germans threw a barrage of 88s at us. We also got some of those "screaming meemies" that were to drive us crazy all during the war. I remember looking off in this field where there were some horses. A barrage of those rockets came in and the horses just seemed to disappear.

We arrived at a road, crossed it and were told we were now in Mande Et. Etienne. I'll never forget that place. To welcome us was a sniper that we judged to be shooting from a church tower. We took cover from the screaming meemies and the sniper pinged away at us until he apparently ran out of ammunition and gave up.

Mande was more of a village than a town and what homes there were, had been heavily damaged. However, they all had cellars so we headed for them. On the way I saw an old woman covered with a blanket lying in a room. I spoke to her, but she didn't answer. She was frozen to death.

We crawled into a potato cellar for shelter. We then noticed that we had company—two dead Germans. We just ignored them and ate and slept there like they were not even there. It's amazing how hardened one gets in a few days of combat.

Having seen the sniper and now the two dead Germans had not been carrying gas masks, we threw ours away. If the enemy had no plans to use gas, we knew we didn't and that was just extra weight we couldn't afford to carry.

We had been issued sleeping bags, but we cut off the bottoms, made holes for our arms and put them on like coats. We also turned them inside out and the white lining made good camouflage while fighting in the snow. We were learning to adapt to our winter war.

Rudy and I were heading out on the perimeter to pull guard duty when we saw a dead German lying in the snow. I just happened to notice that his ring finger on one hand was missing. I guess someone hacked it off for a souvenir!

We took up a position in a small trench by the side of what would have been a road in the summertime. Rudy had to go to the toilet, but every time he got out to go, the Germans would fire at him. He tried four or five times and the situation was getting serious. I was worried too as I sure didn't want him to have to go in our hole! Finally, it got dark and he sneaked out.

The next day, the lieutenant (in the future I'll call him "Looie") had me put men out on guard to cover the area leading into the village of Flamierge. I went out at dusk to round them up, but couldn't find anyone. I thought they had all been captured.

I was standing on a slight rise trying to see some sign of activity when the Krauts must have used me as an aiming point as in came a salvo of mortar shells. a piece of shrapnel hit me on the head and thumped against my helmet as I hit the ground. Then I looked up and there was a sign, "Achtung, Minen." I was pinned down in a German minefield!

I laid low and finally the mortars stopped. I held my breath and very slowly, tippy-toed out of there. If I had known the wound on my hand would one day mean five points and the more points you had, the sooner you got to go home, I would have gone straight to the medics and had it recorded. But, I didn't and I went looking for my men again.

When I returned to our cellar, I found out that the Looie had pulled everyone back from their posts without informing me. I was pretty upset. That was point one against him. Point two: he never slept with us but stayed with the medics.

We were on the move again to the village of Flamierge. The weather was freezing cold and there was a real blizzard blowing. The snowflakes were pounding against your face and the visibility was very poor.

The town had been taken by the 513th, but the Germans had overrun their positions with a flanking attack and really beat them up bad. Our route was through a small valley and everywhere we looked lay dead troopers in the snow.

The distance from Mande to Flamierge was approximately two miles. It took us four hours to get there. The enemy threw screaming meemies on us all the way and we were always seeking shelter. When we finally reached Flamierge, the demolition section was sent in first to check for booby-traps and land mines. We expected some enemy resistance from snipers and small arms fire, but surprisingly, there was none.

There were many dead Germans and troopers lying about. Some were within ten feet of each other. We could see the combat had been intense. The enemy had set some booby-traps, but they were pretty crude and easy to see and disarm.

Point three against the Looie came in Flamierge. He sent two troopers into a basement to remove some booby-traps. Everyone who works with explosives knows only one man should be sent. Sure enough, one of the guys hit a booby-trap and instead of it killing only one man, it got both of them.

While in the village we built a fire to get warm and to dry off some. There was little danger in giving away our position to the enemy because the smoke would blend right in with the foggy weather. Gaeta tried to pull some branches off a dead tree and it was booby-trapped. We lost him, but not for long. He came back the next day and was out on point as our lead scout!

Our next orders found us moving toward Givry, about six miles to the northeast. We were not traveling on the roads now but plowing through the deep snow across the fields. We were also traveling at night. Although it was overcast, it was surprising how well you could see with all the snow on the ground. Unfortunately, we knew it was the same for the Germans.

We were all hoping that our scouts had gotten the right information and that the reports were all correct. In places the snow was hip deep and it was a real effort to move. If we were hit now, it would be rough.

Every now and then we would come to a small stream and the ice would break or it would not be completely frozen and in any event, we'd drop through over the top of our boots. It was impossible to keep dry and this was the way you could loose your feet if you didn't keep moving and get a change to some dry socks and shoes before morning.

We arrived in Givry early in the morning. We were dog-tired, wet all over, blistered and cold. We were badly in need of shelter and rest. As many of the houses in Givry were still intact, we had visions of some decent quarters for the night. We went in one house and there was a bed. Before we could get settled in, we were kicked out by the medics.

We finally found a nice barn that was reasonably comfortable. There was a cow sharing our quarters and Weehunt milked her. Boy, that milk tasted good!

Point four against the Looie: He rode the medic's jeep from Flamierge to Givry and arrived dry.

Our artillery had blasted the city before we arrived. A Belgian—the first live one we'd seen—told us it was unnecessary as the Germans had left 24 hours earlier. He was glad to see the Germans leave, but he didn't seem too happy at us for tearing up his town.

The Germans must have left in a hurry. There were no booby traps or mines placed in Givry. A celebration seemed in order. Someone shot a cow and the medics cut up the meat and we had steak.

Our boots had frozen from the icy water in the streams we had waded, so we tried to dry them out while we were stopped. We packed our arctics with straw meanwhile and found our feet were reasonably warm.

As we were in pretty bad shape, they trucked us back to Mande for a couple of day's rest. I guess we were actually in reserve, but we did get to relax for awhile and we needed it.

We got to discussing the hardships of marching in the snow and carrying all the demolition equipment we had to carry in our pockets and on our backs. The only advantage we had was the plastic explosive. You could break off a small piece, light it and it would burn. It was ideal to heat your rations or make coffee.

Someone else said it sure would be nice to have a jeep to carry all our gear. So, three of our guys caught a ride back to Bastogne and stole one! That really took a load off of our backs!

One day, Rudy and I were out taking pictures when a supply truck went by. It hit a rut and a carton of "C" rations fell off. You would have thought it was Christmas, we were so happy! We took it back to the section and cooked it all up. It was mostly hot dogs and beans. Everyone enjoyed a gourmet dinner followed by a bad case of the GIs.

The Germans had destroyed a bridge over a creek leading east to Houffalize, so we were ordered to build a new one. It took us most of the day, chopping down trees and hauling them to the creek. Trucks had been lined up for some time as this was the only road over the mountains. We finally got it up and the trucks began rolling.

There was a small farmhouse nearby so we went there to rest. We build a fire in the stove and Killingsworth put a can of "K" ration cheese on the stove to heat. The Looie was going on and on about our getting a medal for building the bridge. He never lifted a finger to help us.

Everyone but the Looie was watching that can of cheese as the can kept swelling as it heated up. The Looie had his back to the stove and couldn't see it. No one said a word and finally, the can burst with a loud bang and sprayed hot cheese on the Looie's neck! He now had a reason to ride in the medic's jeep!

From the farmhouse, we marched over another mountain and down into Houffalize. There we had to remove land mines. The Krauts had used a box type mine and we used mine detectors on the road surface but had to probe in other areas with bayonets. We heard a rumbling noise to our rear and all of a sudden, here came General Patton with his tanks. He was sitting on the top of the lead tank with his pearl-handled pistols waving to everyone. You'd think he was parading down Fifth Avenue!

The weather was still cold and miserable. We stayed in a German bunker with a fireplace and carpets. It even had a sewing machine. We got a fire going and were really getting comfy when the medics came and kicked us out again. Back we went into the snow. What a lousy war! They should have wars only in the spring or fall. Call a truce through the winter and summer.

It wasn't long before we were in Luxembourg ready to attack across the Our River into Germany. These approaches were guarded by the Siegfried Line and everyone knew the going was going to be tougher here than anything we had seen before. When the chaplain arrived to say mass and give everyone conditional absolution, we were sure of what we faced.

For almost two weeks we waited for the Air Corps to fly over and bomb the line so we could attack, but the weather was too bad and they never came.

We were so close, it was probably a good thing they didn't. We had to endure the shelling, the mortars and the tree bursts. One trooper had a mortar shell land in his slit trench. He was lucky it was a dud.

We spent our time crawling over the mountain and into a gully to view the enemy emplacements. Leading up to the pill boxes were rows and rows of accordion barbed wire and we were sure there were booby traps and land mines everywhere. The arrogant Krauts would stand on the roof of their cement palaces and smoke cigarettes, trying to draw our fire so they could pinpoint our positions and call in artillery on us.

On February 8, some big brass got the idea that we could attack without air support. Down the mountain we went for equipment which included wire cutters and beehives. The beehive was a shaped charge designed to be placed against a pill box and blow a large hole.

None of us commented on what we were about to do. I believe we all knew that we were going into a bloodbath. The demo men would be leading the way and we would be lucky to get past the first accordion of wire. If one man stepped on a mine, several of us would get it. And, with no artillery, it was just foolhardy.

By February 9 at 0300 hours, we were standing on the crest of the mountain waiting for the order to attack. The air was crisp and cold and it was as quiet as a graveyard (which it might have been in a short while). All of a sudden from our rear came the din of mess-kits banging in the thin air!

I wondered what in the world that racket was. Was someone trying to get us killed even before we got started? Just then the Krauts cut loose with flares, shells, mortars and tracer bullets. It looked like the 4th of July!

Our mission was promptly scrubbed. It took me awhile to realize what had happened. Apparently, someone had finally come to their senses and the mission was cancelled. Afraid that the front line troops would jump off before a message could reach us, the mess kit banging was an emergency method to stop us. Whatever it was, I'm sure it saved many lives that day.

The next day, February 10, we were relieved and they began trucking us back to Chalon Sur Marne in France. I didn't know it then, but the Rhine jump had been planned and they had decided they might need some Airborne types. There was no sense in throwing away a bunch of Airborne lives on some dumb mountainside. I was happy. The Bulge was over and I was still alive.

We had spent 47 days in the Bulge. We withstood the icy cold, the snow, mud, lack of sleep, monotonous cans of eggs, stew and cheese, the filth, screaming meemies, booby-traps, land mines and a tough enemy. My section had gone into battle with 13 men. Only four of us made it out in good shape.

"DOING AN ALASKAN!"

As told by Paul A. Reed, 513 H

It was early in January of 1945, and we were fighting somewhere in Luxembourg. The night was clear and cold. A full moon shone brightly on the snow-covered ground. Under any other circumstances, it would have been a beautiful night.

The Battle of the Bulge was reaching its climax and tonight our regiment was spearheading a night attack. There had already been a small skirmish, but now, when our squad stuck our noses over a white knoll, we were greeted with a torrent of machine gun tracers from a woods 200 yards to the front. Battle wise by this time, we automatically hit the ground and began to return fire. The platoon leader called for the squad's machine gun team to come forward and add to the fire.

My gunner buddy, John Greenlee from West Virginia, and I brought the .30 caliber, air cooled, bipod-mounted weapon to the brow of the hill. The German gun continued its steady fire from the woods, the tracers cutting a path above our heads.

John set up the gun, I inserted the ammunition belt and John cocked and pulled the trigger. Click! Again he cocked the gun and pulled the trigger. Again it went click! It was plain it wasn't going to fire. The firing mechanism was frozen tight! Fast, desperate action was needed.

I remember reading of the same thing happening during the fighting in Alaska. In desperation a quick-thinking GI had solved this problem by urinating on the gun. The salt in the warm urine melted the ice, freed the mechanism and the GI was able to fire the weapon.

Nothing ventured, nothing gained! Very carefully, I raised to my knees, opened my fly and did an "Alaskan!"

Just then, across the cold, clear, cloudless sky, with an orange flame trailing behind and chugging like a John Deere tractor at plowing time, came a German V-1, or as we called them, a buzz bomb. With our tracers from the German gun still popping over our heads, the voice of our company commander, Charles Martin, was heard above it all.

"There goes one of those damn buzz bombs," he shouted, "don't anybody fire at it!"

What a weird situation! The tracers arching through the clear, cold moonlit night, John trying to fire a machine gun dripping with urine, me trying to button my fly and our CO worrying about a buzz bomb at a time like this—it was too much! It seems funny now, but at the time no one was laughing!

We never did get the machine gun working that night, but on pure guts alone, we did take the woods and completed our mission successfully. I wouldn't recommend such "first echelon" maintenance on machine guns, but desperate men will sometimes go to desperate means to save their necks in battle. Even to becoming "Alaskans!"

"PRACTICING DENTISTRY IN THE ARDENNES"

As told by Dr. Doyle C. Ott, 193 MD

When we were in garrison, either Camp Mackall or Camp Forrest, the life of a dentist was a pretty routine lot. We went to the field ever so often just to get the feel of it, but most of our work was done at the dispensary or the post hospital. And, we kept the troops in pretty good shape with periodical dental examinations and needed procedures.

When we went to the continent and the Battle of the Bulge raged, things changed drastically for those of us tasked with this phase of the troops' health care. We found ourselves doing all types of of medical care, helping out wherever we could. Only occasionally did we practise dentistry and then it was under very crude conditions.

One cold, dark night in the Ardennes, I was asked to go examine a young soldier who reportedly was suffering from a terrible toothache. When I located him, I found the report was accurate. He had a tooth, his upper first molar, that had to come out.

The question then became how? We were in the front line, there were no buildings nearby and the only light available was a bright moon and a small flashlight I had. Yet, the tooth had to

Captain Doyle C. Ott, was the 193rd Regimental Dentist and he found himself practicing his skills under some adverse conditions.

come out. The trooper was game so I had him lay on the ground on his back and another soldier shielded my light with a poncho. I then straddled him, applied a shot of novocaine and went to work. Surprisingly enough, I was able to extract the ailing molar with little trouble. We packed it, gave him some advice on how to care for himself and that was the last we ever heard from our patient.

Fortunately, we were not pressed for dental supplies while we were in combat. Once while we were at Camp Forrest, the dispensary was badly in need of a new broom. In June 1944, we put in a requisition for one and never heard another word about it.

Then, one cold, bitter January night in the Ardennes four or five of us were huddled in an ambulance trying to keep warm. There was a knock at the rear door and we opened it a crack and peeped out.

A voice asked, "Is Captain Ott in there?"

I replied that indeed I was and the soldier then said, "Well, here's the broom you ordered!"

That delivery by our supply system was bad enough, but the mail service topped even that.

While we were in England we often would practice the art of dart throwing which seemed to be a royal pastime in the country. The dart board we had in the Officer's Quarters soon became rather battered and in pretty bad shape. I mentioned the fact in a letter to my wife in October and said we would soon have to purchase another one.

Wishing to send me some needed gift, my wife promptly went out and purchased a fine dart board and shipped it to me. When it arrived in mid-February of 1945, we were on the Our River and hardly in a setting fit for a game of darts!

After all this, let me say that our supply people and our mail people did a great job under terrible, almost impossible conditions. And, our combat troops must have suffered silently with some bad toothaches because no trooper ever sought to be evacuated because of dental problems. When we got to Germany and were on occupation duty, we found many cases that should have been evacuated and treated earlier.

"CAPTURED BY THE ENEMY!"

As told by Joe Pencek, 513 I

Editors Note: *This story is a condensed version of a detailed account written by Joe "Jake" Pencek of his four, long months as a Prisoner of War and the inhumane treatment he received at the hands of his captors. Our thanks to his widow, Mrs. Phyillis Pencek of Dunkirk, NY for sharing this with us.*

On January 7, 1945, the 513th PIR was heavily engaged in the vicinity of Flamierge, Belgium. The Germans were still determined not to be driven from the Bastogne area and this appeared to be one place where they were making a last stand. Our company had been in reserve, but were ordered up in an attempt to reinforce other elements of the regiment already committed.

It wasn't long until our third platoon was surrounded by seven Tiger tanks and supporting infantry. We were hopelessly outnumbered and it was a case of give up or die. Along with about 26 other troopers, I became a Prisoner of War. The four months that were to follow were the worst days of my life.

Before my capture, I had been wounded in the right foot by shrapnel from the 88 on one of the tanks. My boot was torn and blood from my wound left a bloody trail as I plodded along through the snow. To add to my misery, my ears and fingers were frost-bitten, I already had trench foot and a severe case of dysentery was slowly sapping my strength.

The Germans marched us back from Flamierge until we came to a large barn. There we were stripped of our jump boots and made to pick footwear from a pile of old shoes and overshoes. I knew the American rear echelon commandos all wanted a pair of jump boots, but this was something else! Apparently, the Germans all wanted a pair too!

Well, they could have mine. My feet were swollen and blue and my boots were now too little for me anyhow. I bandaged my right foot with part of my undershirt and selected an old pair of overshoes. They were cold and fit loosely, but they would have to do.

They put us on the march again—heading back toward Germany. I stumbled along, limping on my bad foot. I remember going through Luxembourg. Once I saw a big Pepsi Cola sign and later a Gulf Oil sign. They fed us one bowl of watery soup with a few noodles each day. Everyone was hungry. It was all like a dream. I couldn't believe it was happening to me.

After a few days of walking, we reached Limberg, Germany, and a prison camp I believed was called Stalag #12. Here they gave us a piece of blanket material that was only two by three feet in size! I would keep it until liberated! Some of the prisoners were given Dutch style wooded shoes. It was said that these shoes would keep them from trying to escape!

Later we were interrogated by a German officer who could speak as good English as I could. He said he had been a school teacher in Cleveland before the war! He also said that if he lived through the war, he was going back there. He tried to be a "buddy" to me, but I didn't tell him a damn thing except name, rank and serial number.

After my interrogation and refusal to give any information to them, they took me to a cramped windowless closet and locked me inside for the next two days. It was only about 20" x 20" and five feet high. With me being six feet one inch tall, I could not stand up, sit or lie down. I was miserable as I twisted and crouched trying to rest, but I never told them anything.

I don't remember when we left there. It took us several days and several cold, wet overnight stops until we arrived at a new camp. During the march, we got two thin slices of black bread each day. Day by day we were growing weaker.

The new camp was named Goilstine and it seemed to be a pretty big railroad center. Some POWs would go out every night to repair tracks that were hit each day by our bombers. They got extra rations for doing this. As hungry as I was, I did not have the strength to work.

By this time my feet bothered me a lot and the dysentery was no better. We lived on a cup of tea in the morning and a slice of black, sawdust bread at night.

Our building had bins in it three feet by three feet square and three feet high. They crammed two of us in each bin at night. I saw a guard shoot a prisoner in one of the bins. He probably had been too sick to move, so the German just pulled out his pistol and shot him to death.

One day they took us to a train and loaded us into a box car. We traveled for days, backing up and waiting, stopping and going. Several times we were strafed by our own aircraft. We couldn't get out—we just lay there and prayed we didn't get hit.

Finally, we reached a hospital where there were Russian and Italian prisoners. My good friend, Calvin Conte from New Haven, CT, made friends with some of the Italian prisoners and they gave us some chunks of bread. I was very grateful because at that time I was so sick I was convinced I was starving to death.

I was loosing weight rapidly now. My clothes were hanging on me and I hardly had the strength to walk. The dysentery still plagued me. I tried to crawl

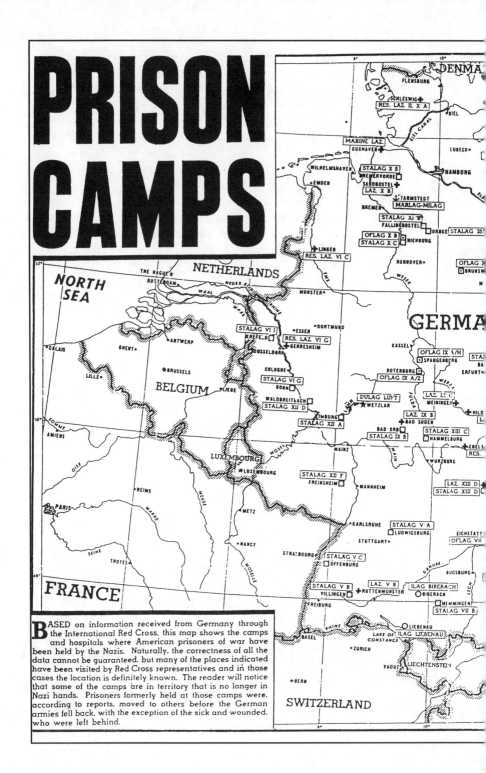

PRISON CAMPS

DENMA
FLENSBURG
SCHLESWIG
RES. LAZ. IL X A
KIEL
MARINE LAZ
CUXHAVEN
LUBECK
WILHELMSHAVEN
STALAG X B
BREMERVORDE
HAMBURG
EMDEN
SANDBOSTEL
LAZ. X B
TARMSTEDT
BREMEN
MARLAG-MILAG
STALAG XI B
FALLINGBOSTEL
ORBKE
STALAG 35
OFLAG X B
BIENBURG
LINGEN
STALAG X C
RES. LAZ. VI C
HANNOVER
OFLAG X
BRUNSW

NETHERLANDS
THE HAGUE
ROTTERDAM
NEDER R
MUNSTER
NORTH SEA
WAAL

GERMA
STALAG VI J
ESSEN
DORTMUND
KREFELD
RES. LAZ. VI G
GERRESHEIM
KASSEL
ANTWERP
DUSSELDORF
OFLAG IX A/H
STA
GHENT
SPANGENBERG
BA
CALAIS
COLOGNE
ROTENBURG
ERFURT
BRUSSELS
STALAG VI G
OFLAG IX A/Z
LILLE
BONN
WEBZA
BELGIUM
LIEGE
WALDBREITBACH
DULAG LUFT
LAZ. LE C
STALAG XII D
WETZLAR
MEININGE
LIMBURG
LAZ. IX B
MILD
SOMME
STALAG XII A
BAD SODEN
L
AMIENS
BAD ORB
STALAG XIII C
STALAG IX B
HAMMELBURG
MAINZ
EBELS
LUXEMBOURG
WURZBURG
RES.
OISE
LUXEMBOURG
MOSEL
STALAG XII F
REIMS
FREINSHEIM
MANNHEIM
LAZ. XIII D
PARIS
METZ
STALAG XIII D
MARNE
SEINE
KARLSRUHE
STALAG V A
NANCY
LUDWIGSBURG
EICHSTATT
STUTTGART
OFLAG VII
TROYES
STRASBOURG
STALAG V C
AUGSBURG
OFFENBURG
DANUBE
MOSELLE
STALAG V B
LAZ. V B
ILAG BIBERACH
FRANCE
VILLINGEN
ROTTENMUNSTER
BIBERACH
FREIBURG
MEMMINGE
STALAG VII B
LIEBENAU
RHINE
ILAG LIEBENAU
BASEL
LAKE OF
CONSTANCE
ZURICH
VADUZ
LIECHTENSTEIN
BERN
SWITZERLAND

BASED on information received from Germany through the International Red Cross, this map shows the camps and hospitals where American prisoners of war have been held by the Nazis. Naturally, the correctness of all the data cannot be guaranteed, but many of the places indicated have been visited by Red Cross representatives and in those cases the location is definitely known. The reader will notice that some of the camps are in territory that is no longer in Nazi hands. Prisoners formerly held at those camps were, according to reports, moved to others before the German armies fell back, with the exception of the sick and wounded, who were left behind.

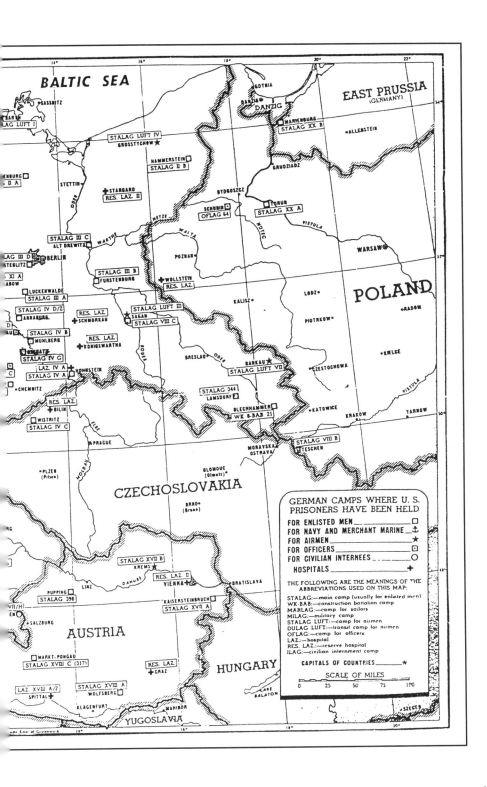

BALTIC SEA

EAST PRUSSIA
(GERMANY)

SASSNITZ

LAG LUFT I

GDYNIA
DANZIG
DANZIG

MARIENBURG
STALAG XX B

ALLENSTEIN

STALAG LUFT IV
GROSSTYCHOW ★

HAMMERSTEIN ☐
STALAG II B

GRUDZIADZ

ENBURG ☐
II A

STETTIN

STARGARD
RES. LAZ. II

BYDGOSZCZ

SCHUBIN ☐
OFLAG 64

TORUN ☐
STALAG XX A

VISTULA

WARSAW

POLAND

STALAG III C
ALT DREWITZ

BERLIN

POZNAN

LAG III D
TEGLITZ

XI A
ABOW

STALAG III B
FURSTENBURG

WOLLSTEIN
RES. LAZ.

LUCKENWALDE
STALAG III A

KALISZ

LODZ

RADOM

STALAG IV D/Z
ANNABURG

RES. LAZ.
SCHMORKAU

STALAG LUFT III
SAGAN
STALAG VIII C

PIOTRKOW

D

STALAG IV B
MUHLBERG

RES. LAZ.
KONIGSWARTNA

KELCE

GRAZ
STALAG IV G

BRESLAU

ODER

BANKAU ★
STALAG LUFT VII

CZESTOCHOWA

LAZ. IV A
STALAG IV A

HOHNSTEIN

CHEMNITZ

RES. LAZ.
BILIN

STALAG 344
LAMSDORF

KATOWICE

VISTULA

BLECHHAMMER
WK 8-BAB 21

KRAKOW

TARNOW

WISTRITZ
STALAG IV C

PRAGUE

ELBE

MORAVSKA
OSTRAVA

STALAG VIII B
TESCHEN

PLZEN
(Pilsen)

MOLDAU

OLOMOUC
(Olmetz)

CZECHOSLOVAKIA

BRNO
(Brunn)

GERMAN CAMPS WHERE U. S.
PRISONERS HAVE BEEN HELD

FOR ENLISTED MEN _____ ☐
FOR NAVY AND MERCHANT MARINE __ ⚓
FOR AIRMEN _____ ★
FOR OFFICERS _____ ⊡
FOR CIVILIAN INTERNEES _____ O

HOSPITALS _____ +

THE FOLLOWING ARE THE MEANINGS OF THE
ABBREVIATIONS USED ON THIS MAP:

STALAG:—main camp (usually for enlisted men)
WK-BAB:—construction battalion camp
MARLAG:—camp for sailors
MILAG:—military camp
STALAG LUFT:—camp for airmen
DULAG LUFT:—transit camp for airmen
OFLAG:—camp for officers
LAZ.:—hospital
RES. LAZ.:—reserve hospital
ILAG:—civilian internment camp

CAPITALS OF COUNTRIES _____ ★

SCALE OF MILES
0   25   50   75   100

STALAG XVII B
KREMS ★

RES. LAZ. II
VIENNA ★

BRATISLAVA

PUPPING ☐
STALAG 398

LINZ

DANUBE

KAISERSTEINBRUCH ☐
STALAG XVII A

VII/H
EN

SALZBURG

AUSTRIA

HUNGARY

MARKT-PONGAU
STALAG XVIII C (317)

RES. LAZ.
GRAZ

LAKE
BALATON

LAZ. XVIII A/Z
SPITTAL

STALAG XVIII A
WOLFSBERG ☐

KLAGENFURT

MARIBOR

SZEGED

YUGOSLAVIA

de East of Greenwich

away from the others to relieve myself, but I was weak and had little control. When we were on the march there was little choice but to soil one's self.

Moved again to another camp, we slept in an old barn. We wedged ourselves together to try to keep from freezing. If a man had to get up to relieve himself, when he returned, he found his space gone. He had to try and wedge himself into a new spot. One fellow I was wedged next to one night kept talking about his motorcycle and his home in Wisconsin. When we woke in the morning, he was dead.

Most of the men by this time had fever, pneumonia and dysentery. I had sores and scabs the size of silver dollars all over my body. I later found out that was because of the malnutrition. We were fed a cup of tea in the morning and water soup with potato peels in the evening. We figured the guards got the potatoes.

Before we left this place, they moved Conte away with some other seriously ill prisoners. Then, soon we were on the march again. This time we marched through the city of Bonn, Germany. Civilians lined the street spitting, yelling, and throwing stones at us. Several of the prisoners were beaten and the guards laughed and waited for awhile until they broke it up.

The POW camp they took us to was on a hilltop near the outskirts of Bonn. It had about 70,000 prisoners of all different nationalities. We were housed in a crowded, cement block building. We were sleeping like sardines again, body to body on the floor, trying to keep warm.

This is where I met an American officer. I can't remember his name, but he was a second lieutenant. Officers were supposed to have been separated from enlisted prisoners, so I don't know how he got mixed in with us. The Germans arranged us in groups of seven and the lieutenant was in our group of seven.

Each day the Germans would give us a loaf of bread to divide among the seven in each group. The lieutenant selected me to divide the bread. Then each day, a different man in the group would choose first as to the slice he wished. It would be the slice he thought was the biggest. I always waited until last as I was almost too sick to eat anyhow.

The lieutenant was a good guy. He was calm and encouraging. He would always say to me, "Cheer up kid, we're going to make it!"

Later, the camp was bombed and we were moved again. I was parted from the lieutenant and I missed him as he had renewed my will to survive this ordeal. I needed that.

We marched many days to the next camp. In the barracks we had one bucket of coal a night to keep warm. For a latrine we had a round barrel in the center of the barracks. Every morning someone had to clean up the mess that we sick men had made. Needless to say, our living conditions were horrible.

At this camp the German guards had those big German shepherds for guard dogs. They kept them on leashes and they were vicious. There were also some Russian prisoners in this camp and we learned one day that somehow they had got hold of one of those dogs, killed it, cooked it and ate it! They hid the head and hide under the flooring, but the guards found it.

Before we could find out what happened to the Russians (although I have a pretty good idea), they moved us out again. This time it was another long march to Hammerlburg. At least it was a little warmer by now and they would let us leave the building and lay on the ground in the sunshine.

Our chief pastime was picking lice off our clothes and body. At night the lice would drive you crazy running up and down your body. Adding to our discomfort were the malnutrition scabs.

One day we heard a lot of shooting and cannon firing around the camp. We were told it was General Patton's forces and they were trying to liberate the camp. That night the liberation took place—or at least, we thought it did. We saw American soldiers driving tanks around the camp and in celebration we broke into the kitchen and helped ourselves to the potatoes!

The next day we waited for someone to come and take most of us to an American hospital. However, toward evening the shooting and fighting outside the camp started all over again. By morning, we looked out and the Germans were back again. They had driven out our liberators and once again we were prisoners!

Quickly, the Germans got us ready to move again. Soon we were marching down the road. I don't know how I managed to make it, but supported by two men I didn't even know, I did. To fall out was sure death either by shooting or by the bayonet.

If a man fell, others would rush forward to pick him up and drag him on. I heard shots and screams but was too weak or too scared to look and see what had happened.

It was Easter Sunday when we came to a camp in Nurnberg. It was said it was a camp for Air Corps POWs only, but the Allies were closing in on the German forces and they were backing up too fast to stand on regulations. Here we got a British Red Cross food box before we moved on the next day.

Before we had gone very far, it happened to me. I was sick, I hurt all over and I couldn't go another step. I blacked out and fell on the roadside. I just didn't care anymore, live or die, I had given up. It was over for me.

The next thing I knew, I was laying on the ground at a railroad crossing looking up at a group of American POWs. One of them, an American officer, gave me a Hershey chocolate bar. I could see a train next to us and a open boxcar with some Red Cross food packages in the doorway.

This is where things changed for me. I was carried to the boxcar and put inside. It was full of British soldiers and when the train left, I was parted from any other Americans at this point. However, the Brits were very kind to me, probably saving my life.

They nursed my beat up feet, bandaging them and wiped my leaky malnutrition scabs. They tried to get me to eat, but my stomach ached constantly and I could force down very little.

At one time I was moved to another boxcar with other stretcher cases. The guards here were more lenient. They were Poles or Czechs, more or less pressed into the job and we were treated pretty well.

We ended up at a large camp near Mooseburg (?), about nine kilometers outside Munich. There were about 90,000 POWs here of all nationalities. On about April 1, I was checked over by British doctors and remained in the camp with British and Russian POWs. They were fine people and treated me well.

On April 12, we heard of President Roosevelt's death and then on Sunday, April 28 or 29, General Patton arrived. I actually saw the general with his pearl handled pistols standing in his Jeep. He stood at the entrance to the camp waving to us and watching us being carried out on stretchers.

Before Patton's troops arrived and we were freed that day, we heard some shooting going on right in the camp. We had laid low, but now we found out what had been going on. It seems the S.S. Colonel who was the camp commander, decided that before he surrendered the camp, he was going to kill as many of the POWs as he could.

The regular German Army soldiers, the Wehrmacht, rightfully figuring such action would only make things tougher for all when the Americans arrived, opposed this action. As a result, fighting broke out between the two fractions. The S.S. were shooting Russians and the Wehrmacht were shooting the S.S.

In the meantime, the S.S. Colonel packed up and tried to flee the scene. He was, however, captured by the approaching Americans. The camp was total confusion for awhile, but finally things got sorted out and once again we were free.

They took us to a large house and preparations were being made to move us back. As I lay there on the floor, over to me walks that same lieutenant I had met earlier and who had such a calming influence on me. He bent down and like he had said to me at Bonn, he grinned and said, "See kid, I told you we would make it!"

From Mooseburg, we went someplace to have all our hair cut and shaved off and to be deloused. Then they sent us back to Mourmelon, France, where we had started out on our Battle of the Bulge adventure. It was full circle for me, only I was now down to 116 pounds from my normal 175. And, I had my 21st birthday while I waited to go home.

"THE SECOND TIME AROUND"

by Bart Hagerman, 193 D

January 16, 1945 dawned cold, cloudy and overcast, but I was, neverthe-less, glad to be back with my buddies in "D" Company, 193rd. I wasn't, however, glad about the prospect of going back into combat.

It had been real comfortable back in the 101st Evac Hospital in Arlon, Belgium. It was warm, there was plenty to eat, and the thick stone walls of the old monastery made you feel safe and isolated from the war that raged on in the Ardennes. Once you had seen all-out war, seen your friends blown apart and known real terror yourself, you couldn't be too excited about going back into that nightmare.

I had been very lucky that January 7. A mortar or an 88 (I never knew for sure which) had landed dangerously close to me just as I began to get to my feet. Shrapnel had ripped a couple of places on the back of my jacket and one little piece nicked me on the tailend. It wasn't that that sent me to the hospital, however.

The concussion was something else. It really rang my bell. It left me temporarily deaf, apparently tossed me in the air and when I came down, I damn near bit the end of my tongue off. I was completely disoriented and more than a little frightened.

Some troopers from the 101st Airborne left their positions in the woods and came out and gathered me up. Soon a jeep arrived and they transported me to their battalion aid station. I was plenty scared by this time, but when a chaplain came over and began to pray over me, I really got worried.

They got no argument from me when they decided to evacuate me to the hospital. They gave me a sleeping pill they called a "blue 88" and that's all I remember for the next 24 hours.

Recuperating in Arlon was great. Movie star Mickey Rooney was a medic there, and one night he put on a show for the ambulatory patients. I was okay in a couple of days so they shipped me out and headed me back to my outfit via the "Repo-Depot" route. It had been set up in a part of the old Maginot Line.

The author, Bart Hagerman, qualified as a paratrooper at Camp Forrest before the Division left for overseas.

I had heard about those "Repo-Depots." It was where some rear echelon NCOs decided that anyone who came through the door belonged in an infantry outfit and they hated Airborne people. I was determined that I wasn't going anywhere but back to the 17th. There was no reason to sweat that as I soon learned that there was a real need for Airborne people to go to the 17th. They had suffered heavy loses and needed all the people they could get.

I salvaged my torn jacket for a warm, jeep driver's mackinaw and just barely missed getting a .45 pistol issued to me. Some enterprising trooper had convinced the issue clerk that all paratroopers were armed with a .45 in addition to their regular weapon! Unfortunately, they ran out a couple of troopers ahead of me. I was told to come back tomorrow and they would have some more in. I knew tomorrow was too late for me.

As I waited with a few other 17th men for the truck that would take us back to our companies, we watched an aerial sideshow. There were hundreds and hundreds of airplanes high in the sky and they weaved a never ending pattern of vapor trails that was fascinating to see. We were told that there was a big daylight bombing raid hitting Cologne. Never had this little Kentucky boy seen that many planes in the air at once and I was spellbound by the scene.

The hours ticked by and still we waited for our truck. As we waited we slowly became aware of two disturbing developments. First, earlier on we had been able to hear artillery firing in the distance. Then we had begun to hear machine gun fire. But now, we could hear the faint, unmistakable sound of enemy machine gun fire!

There was no mistaking the sound. Their weapons had a much higher cyclic rate of fire, so that once you had heard it you never forgot it. It was the reason the GIs had nicknamed them "burp guns." The rounds were so close together, you didn't hear each of them fire, you just heard one long "bur-r-r-r-p" as the rounds poured out of the weapon like one long steel rod.

If this wasn't enough, the other development that caught our attention was the fact that none of the cooks seemed to be preparing the evening meal.

Instead, they were packing the kitchen onto trucks and obviously, they weren't planning to even be here for the evening meal. This was really serious! If they were planning to bug out, the old hysteria that had accompanied the initial German breakthrough was back with us!

I wish I knew what happened next and how all this worked out. You could see panic in the eyes of the depot troops and you just knew it wasn't going to be a good situation. But, just when it was getting scary, our truck finally arrived and we were ordered to load on. Quickly, in a swirl of snow, we were on our way. I was just as glad that driver wanted to make tracks out of there.

Slowly we wound through the countryside on the snow covered, one-lane roads. Our first stop was in a small village that we guessed was somewhere near Corps Headquarters. There were big 240mm cannons set up nearby but idle at the time. It was dark and getting late, so we were told to fan out and find a place to sleep and we would continue on early the next morning.

Several of us headed for a large barn nearby. Barns were like motels in those days. They offered a windbreak from the cold wind, warm straw for sleeping, and if you were lucky, maybe an egg and some warm milk for breakfast.

There were some heavy, door-like shutters on some windows on one side of the barn and we tried to open them. I gave a mighty tug at them but, they refused to give. About that time, one of the other guys yelled that he had gotten some other doors open, so we ceased our efforts and walked around to the other entrance.

We each found a cozy spot, opened up some "C" rations and soon fell asleep for the night. With all the troops in the area we never gave a thought to security.

The next morning one of the guys who had been with me when we were trying to open that stuck door, asked me to come with him for a minute. He walked me over to the window and pointed up without saying a word.

There, wired to pull the pin if the door was opened was a German "potato masher" hand grenade. It was a crude but effective booby trap just waiting for some dummy to set it off. The one thing its designer hadn't taken into consideration was that the old warped door might not open easily. I felt like I had been saved by The Man upstairs.

We left it like we found it, although before we left the area we told some troops nearby and they said they would notify their CO and get him to ask the engineers to clear it. It's probably still there waiting for the Army chain of command to act.

The next stop was in a little village where I was dropped off at the 193rd rear echelon (the company kitchen and supply location). They were busy preparing a hot meal that they would take up to the company that night after dark. They would take another "hot" up before daylight and the troops would eat C's at noon. Not a bad deal for the troops but, of course, it was highly subject to change—both from the weather and the Germans.

I walked around the little village, but there wasn't much to see, so soon I returned to the barn where the kitchen was set up. I crawled up a ladder into the loft, found me a warm corner and went to sleep. You could never afford to pass up the opportunity to get some sleep when you knew you were safe.

A couple of hours later Joe Ritter, one of the cooks and a fellow Kentuckian from Glasgow, shook me awake and said they would be leaving shortly for the front and the company. I'd already given that move some thought.

"Joe, you guys go ahead without me," I said, "I'll sleep here tonight instead of in a cold foxhole and go up with you all when you take breakfast."

I guess this made good sense to Joe. It certainly did to me! He climbed back down the ladder, informed the others and away they went. I smiled smugly to myself, turned over and went back to sleep. After all, what help could I be to the company that one night and one more good night's sleep would only make me better prepared to what I might have to face the next day. At least, that's the way I rationalized my unwillingness to face up to what I knew I had to do.

It was in the early morning hours of January 16 when I finally rejoined the company. We were somewhere northeast of Houfallize occupying positions in one of those dense, Ardennes pine forests. None of us ever knew exactly where we were. The road signs that hadn't been destroyed in the fighting had usually been removed to confuse the enemy. As a result, both sides were often confused and everyone stayed lost most of the time.

Immediately I detected the change that had come over my comrades since I left them nine days before. To begin with company strength was now only about 100 officers and men. There were about 100 absent for one reason or another; killed, wounded, missing, or evacuated because of the sub-zero freezing weather.

Those that remained were quiet and to themselves. There was none of the usual joking that we had known back in training. Everything was literally dead serious now.

As I had been a gunner on the mortar in the first platoon, I expected to return to that job and I went looking for my squad. None of them were there. All six of them had been evacuated for one reason or another. The best news I got was that none of them had been killed. The mortar itself had been lost in that "strategic withdrawal" on January 7.

No one seemed glad to see me. One guy even told me that he had heard that I had been killed but, no one seemed to acknowledge that it was really me—maybe even back from the dead. A feeling of loneliness began to creep over me. I was back but no one cared.

Our CO, Captain Jerry Stuhrman, told me he had been sending my mail back marked "Missing in Action" as he had no idea what had happened to me. That added to my feeling of being in a no-win situation.

Captain Stuhrman told me to report to Staff Sergeant Leroy McCaslin who had the 1st Platoon. This is when I learned that Tech Sergeant Charles Pierre had been killed on January 7. That was a real blow because all of us thought he was indestructible. We had a real love-hate relationship with this man. We sometimes hated him because he was so tough on us, yet we knew underneath it was for our own good. We figured he would get us home alive.

To have this belief shattered was hard enough, but I also learned that we had lost our platoon leader, Second Lieutenant Bill Rudicel from Hutchinson, Kansas. We'd only had Rudicel for a few months as he'd been assigned to us while we were in England. Some of the guys said Rudicel was KIA as he had been badly wounded by artillery fire while a couple of others said he might have made it.

Bill Rudicel did in fact make it. He found out about the existence of a 17th Airborne Division Association a few months before our 1990 reunion in Washington, DC. He showed up there and surprised a number of those attending. It was like he had returned from the dead.

As directed, I reported to McCaslin and he filled me in on what had happened since I had left. He was still directing the first squad as well as the platoon. We didn't have an officer. All together, we had about 25 people and they were organized into two squads.

I began to really feel low. Once you've been wounded you figure you have "used up" all of your luck. You think that surely the next time will be for keeps. And, with the attrition running so high, you feel it won't be much longer. Up front with an understrength Airborne rifle company sure isn't a good, safe place for a person to be.

There was little time for me to bemoan my fate, however, as the company was preparing to move out. The word went around that we were going to pull back, load on trucks and be moved somewhere in Luxembourg for a few days rest.

For once the rumor mill had it right. After about a mile's march through the "Winter Wonderland" that was Belgium in those days, we came to the trucks and loaded on. Then came word that we were headed for the Wiltz area in Luxembourg. That was a good distance, so we hunkered down the best we could in the open "duce-and-a-halves" and tried to ward off the bitter weather.

We soon learned that Wiltz was near the Our River which formed the border between Luxembourg and Germany. This border was high in the Schnee Eifel—the mountain range that was known as "Skyline Drive." In other times it was a beautiful location affording a view of the valley that was a tourist's dream. To us, during that cold January 1945, it was just another obstacle, another cold place to die.

We stopped someplace near Wiltz in some deserted farm buildings. Here we got hot chow, some clean long johns and socks. We were told we would rest there that night and move on the next day. Then they passed out grenades and extra ammunition, and it was quite plain the next stop wouldn't be a rest stop.

The next day as our trucks rumbled through one little village, we came to a halt. Some GIs in the street told us the 17th Airborne Division Headquarters was located there.

I looked vacantly out of the truck as did my comrades around me. We stared without speaking as an officer approached our truck.

"Sergeant McCaslin!" the officer shouted to Mac in the rear of the truck.

"Hello, Lieutenant," Mac answered in a rather flat voice that carried little emotion.

I perked up then and looked hard at the officer that now stood at the tailgate. I was surprised to see it was First Lieutenant John Van Syckle who had been our platoon leader during most of our training and had left us to become the general's aide. I hadn't seen him since we arrived in England.

Lieutenant Van Syckle was a good officer, but for some reason I just never hit it off with him. Today I'm sure it was all my fault, but in those days I was a cocky kid and it seemed I was always trying to pull one on him and he was always trying to catch me screwing up. The battle of wits we were playing was no-contest. I was destined to lose everytime and I did.

After one of my better pranks while we were running problems in North Carolina, Van Syckle had caught me cold and busted me from PFC to private. After that, it was all-out war. I got my licks back at him in ways he never knew. It was the best thing that could have happened to me when he was selected to leave the company and become General Whitelaw's aide. At the rate I was going, I would have eventually earned myself a court-martial.

Now, as I looked at him talking to Mac, I felt a bit sorry for him. By this time we had come to regard anyone as far back as Division Headquarters as "rear echelon" and a little bit less than a real "combat soldier." Yet here he was with his .45 in its holster tied tight to his leg in the way of a cowboy for a "quick-draw." I wondered why anyone in the Division Headquarters area would have to make a "quick draw."

"Where's the 1st Platoon, Sergeant McCaslin?" asked Van Syckle.

"They're right here, lieutenant," Mac answered.

"I mean the rest of them," replied Van Syckle.

"Lieutenant, this is the rest of them," came back Mac, "The rest are dead, wounded, frozen, or missing in action."

A look of shock and disbelief came over Van Syckle's face and it was obvious he never thought that would ever happen to his old platoon. He was sad too as I know he liked us and was sad to see what had happened. He looked around in the truck and then slowly turned around and walked back into one of buildings.

He never showed any signs of recognizing me and I guess he didn't. It was the last time I ever saw him and I've always been sorry that to this good day he probably thinks I was the world's biggest screw-up. I'd like him to know that the smart alec kid he knew at Camp Mackall grew up fast in combat and became a responsible citizen. He'd probably have a hard time coming to grips with the fact Uncle Sam eventually saw fit to commission me a lieutenant colonel in Special Forces!

The trucks wound on through the snow-covered pine forests taking us closer to our destination. Once they called a break and let us get off and stretch our legs. It was near zero and was so cold we were getting stiff riding along.

The location where we stopped proved to be an interesting spot. A few yards away was the remains of a German convoy which evidently had been caught in the open by our planes. They had really done a number on that convoy.

There were at least a dozen armored vehicles and 10 to 15 trucks that were totally destroyed. Some were still smoking from the attack. There were a number of dead German bodies scattered about. And, there were several dead horses in the convoy. This bore out the word we had gotten that the Jerries were short on petrol and were using old-fashioned horsepower to get back to Germany.

Unknown to us at that time, January 26 officially marked the end of the Battle of the Bulge Campaign and opened the Rhineland Campaign. But no one felt we were any closer to the end of the war on that cold day. If Germany was near defeat, we didn't know it.

We strolled down the length of the convoy, looking at the destruction and probably looking for any souvenirs we could find. I came to a small Volkswagon that had been caught in the carnage and had been burned out. For a moment I thought about opening the glove compartment in the dash fantasizing it might have been the personal vehicle of some high-ranking officer. Then, I thought about that booby trapped barn door and decided to leave it alone.

A few moments later, after I had moved on down the line, some guy opened the door and instead of a grenade blast, he was rewarded with finding a small Italian automatic pistol. The clear plastic handle grips covered photos of nude female bodies! I was saddened by the "near-find" of this choice war souvenir. Like they say, "War is Hell!"

The trucks moved on and we sensed we were growing close to our final destination. Finally, we ground to a stop at the edge of a dark pine forest. It was the end of the line. We off-loaded, went into the forest a short distance, spread out and went to ground to await further orders. Soon the call went out for the non-coms to report to Captain Stuhrman and we knew we would soon get the word on our next move.

That word was soon forthcoming and it wasn't pretty to hear. We were to relieve a company of the 26th Division during the night hours. Now, a relief in place was a delicate maneuver and to do it at night in a strange place really complicated the difficulty. The location, we learned, was near a town called Hosingen and it was located on the Our River overlooking Germany.

Before we began the move up, Captain Stuhrman surprised me by assigning me to one of the machine gun squads in the weapons platoon. I guess that's where they needed some people. Maybe they just didn't know what to do with a mortarman without a mortar.

I wasn't too happy about the assignment although there was nothing I could do about it. Not only had I never fired the .30 caliber Browning machine gun, but I knew any automatic weapon drew fire and was a choice target for the enemy.

That night, January 26, when it was good and dark, we moved out. Things went unbelievably smooth. In no time at all we were moving into our area and the last of the 26th Division men were pulling back. We were on high alert, however, as the most dangerous maneuver a unit can make is the relief in place. It would sure be a bad time to run into a German combat patrol or worse still, an attack.

Fearing possible contact with the enemy during the move, everyone had their safeties off on their weapons. We were intently peering into the darkness watching for any suspicious movement. The only sound to be heard was the soft crunch of our boots in the crusty snow.

Suddenly, a shot rang out that shattered the silence and then there was the muffled cry of someone who had been hit. Everyone went to the ground and scrambled for cover. As we lay wondering what had happened, there was a thrashing in the bushes and we heard whispering and talking and then it went quiet.

When the shot was fired, I was on a narrow road near an armored vehicle of some type, maybe a tank destroyer. I immediately dove under it for cover. As I lay there, I could hear the crew coming awake inside. Then I heard a low whine as one of them evidently switched on the battery to "warm up" in the event they needed to move.

"My God, they're going to move the damn thing," I whispered to myself, "and I'm going to get run over by my own Army!"

I threw snow in every direction as I scrambled out from under the vehicle and into the trees. There I lay panting from the excitement of the moment.

Things soon quieted down and we found out what had happened. Mortarmen have canvas cases (like big pistol holsters) in which to stow their folding stock carbines when they need both hands free to carry the mortar. Casimir Stempkowski, from McKees Rock, Pennsylvania, failed to put the safety on when he put his carbine in his case. When jarred, it fired a round hitting him in the leg.

As the medic attended to Cas, the rest of us moved on up into the new positions without further incident. I really felt alone up there. I was a misfit in that machine gun squad for sure and I didn't even know the guys very well. They now had the new A-6 model with the bipod and it looked even stranger.

Then, I got a break. Staff Sergeant Earl Peck, the MG Section Sergeant, told me to share his hole with him that night and he'd give me a crash course in machine guns. I figured that might just save my neck, so it calmed me down a bit. I didn't even know how to load the weapon, much least clear misfires and change barrels.

That night Peck talked to me about deploying the weapon and servicing it. When morning came, he got a gun and we got into the mechanics of the weapon itself. By the time they called the NCOs to meet with the CO, I had calmed down a lot. I was an attentive student, rest assured.

Naturally, the meeting with our CO meant we were going on the attack.

The objective was Hosingen and the high ground beyond. H-hour was only a couple of hours away so there was little time to sweat it.

After a short, preparatory barrage during which our artillery rained on the village, we jumped off. The countryside was rolling and for the main part, wide open. Hosingen was some 800 to 1,000 yards away and except for an occasional ditch or swale, there was little cover.

We drew no grazing fire, but it wasn't long before mortar and 88 fire began falling on us. They were mostly firing in battery. You could hear them fire, then the whistle of the shells in the air, then a quiet period as they silently came in amongst us.

There seemed to be a few minutes between barrages and that's when we all rushed forward as fast as we could. Things seemed to be going pretty good. If we were taking any casualties, I couldn't tell it.

Struggling through the almost knee-deep snow, I began to warm up and was breathing hard. I saw a one lane road to my right and I made for it. It led to the village and I knew the footing would be easier. The rest of our three man squad, including the guy carrying our A-6 MG, was off to my left some 25 to 30 yards.

I was running on the road now, making better time and had about caught up to where I should have been when I heard another flight of shells incoming. Looking around for what shelter that might be handy, I saw a stack of crates off the side of the road and I dived in behind them.

The shells landed some distance away but close enough to send shrapnel into the cases above me. Then my eyes nearly popped out when I realized those were unopened, not empty, cases of 88 ammunition. The abandoned 88 artillery piece lay behind the stacks of cases. I had really picked a wonderful place to seek protection.

Before I could move out, I heard another flight of shells coming in. There was nothing to do but duck and hope my luck held out one more time. I realized if one of those shells hit in the cases, they would all go up like the 4th of July.

This flight of shells seemed closer. I heard shrapnel (or rocks) thump into the ammo cases, yet nothing happened. I also began counting those rounds that turned out to be duds. There were three of four out of about 12 rounds. I wondered if that was faulty assembly work back in some Berlin factory or if some blessed soul had sabotaged them and maybe saved my life.

After that flight had landed, still being in one piece, I rose and ran at top speed down the road packed hard with snow. I stopped only one more time before I made it to the first building in the village. As another flight of shells whistled in, I dived headfirst into a ditch and fought to catch my breath.

There were two other GIs in the ditch where I landed, but I quickly realized they were bodies and frozen still. Both wore the shoulder patch of the "Yankee" 26th Division and no doubt had been there a day or so.

One of the dead soldiers wore a wristwatch and as I looked at it, it was ticking merrily away. His eyes were open but glazed over with frozen moisture. He seemed to stare blindly toward the overcast sky. I thought to myself he was frozen in time and in years later, I would see his face in my dreams.

Once into the buildings on the edge of the village, I found my squad and rejoined them. They had taken shelter in one of those above ground cellars under a stone house. The sound of small arms fire was all around us, but seemed to be more intense about a block ahead of us. The street seemed to lead to the town center.

I asked if they had checked out the house above. They replied that they hadn't, so I climbed the stairs and entered the house. I looked in all the rooms on the first floor and then decided not to check the other floors. The proper way to do this dirty job is to throw a grenade into the room first and then look. I always had a fear of throwing a grenade in the room and then finding that some civilians had sought safety in there.

I returned to my squad in the cellar and sat down in the low window sill looking out on the street. The walls were at least 18 inches thick and the floor was covered with straw. The other members of the squad were sprawled on the floor resting and awaiting orders to move up.

Occasionally, a mortar or 88 shell landed in one of the buildings in this part of the town. I suddenly realized that sitting in the window was not so good an idea. If a shell was to land in the cobble stone street, shrapnel could sail in the window. I left the window and joined the rest of the squad on the floor.

It proved to be a wise move. Within the minute a shell hit in the street and shrapnel zinged in the window into the large wooded beams of the house. I gulped as I realized I had just missed getting my head taken off. It was beginning to be a very exciting day.

Soon we were ordered to move down the street, door-to-door, but still no order to commit our weapon to the fight. That seemed to be a little strange to me but, as I knew so little about machine gun tactics, I just went along without question.

We moved along slowly at first, but as the enemy pulled out of the village and retreated to the high ground beyond, things went faster. Soon we were moving quickly up the street and no one seemed to be checking the buildings.

Many of the buildings had a wall knocked down and all of them had been badly damaged. As I passed in front of one building where the front wall had been knocked out, I saw a large table facing the street and to my horror there was a German lying across it with his weapon in front of him.

I whirled quickly toward him, brought my carbine up and fired about five or six rounds as fast as I could. I'm not sure I hit him, but I know I hit the table. The German, meanwhile, slid slowly off the table and to the floor. The guy ahead of me turned and said to take it easy, he was already dead and had just fallen across the table.

I felt a bit stupid, but no one laughed or said anything, so I guess it was alright. That was the only time I ever fired my personal weapon in combat and that turned out to be needless.

We continued on down the street until we reached the open countryside. As we started up a steep hill leading to some woods, the artillery started coming down on us again. We really moved fast then and by the time we were in the woods, it quieted down again. Sometime, somehow during this hour or so, the Germans were able to get over the Our River and back into Germany.

We moved into the positions which the Germans had just vacated. Although we knew this was not a good idea, we really had little choice about the matter. The ground was frozen as solid as a rock and digging new positions was out of the question. We were exhausted by this time, and so were our German friends.

Our machine gun was placed on the far tip of the woods. There was about 200 yards of flat, open ground beyond as the slope steepened and then dropped off into the Our River Valley. Some 300 yards farther on was the river, swift and muddy and some four times its normal width.

It was late afternoon now and we were all spent from the day's activity. The Germans apparently had withdrawn across the river and neither of us seemed inclined to want further battle. We scooped the snow out of the holes we had found and tried to get some rest.

That was not to be, however. It wasn't long before the pounding started. They knew where we were and we didn't know where they were. They seemed to throw everything they had at us—mortars, 88s, and rockets, the famous "screaming meemies." For over an hour we lay flattened in the holes and praying they would stop.

Beyond us in the woods, they were getting tree bursts and we could hear the calls for a medic. Sometime during this period Captain Stuhrman was wounded and had to be evacuated. The XO, First Lieutenant Jim Logan, also was hit and we were left with only two officers.

The company was now commanded by First Lieutenant John Bailey. The other officer, Second Lieutenant Henry Webb, was sent over to "E" Company as they had lost all their officers.

Soon the shelling stopped and we were grateful. It was as if a truce had been obtained although we knew it hadn't. The calm was more like each side had had enough and they wouldn't fire at us if we wouldn't fire at them. Secretly each one of us hoped our artillery wouldn't fire because we had had enough.

With the respite, darkness began to creep in upon us. We began to think of our other enemies, the dark night and the freezing cold high in the Eifel Mountains.

The three of us decided on two hours guard duty each. We were practically all together, so one man awake could adequately safeguard the squad. Hopefully, we could all get some sleep.

We completely ignored an order to send out a guard every hour as a connecting link to check with the squad to our rear. We agreed to an arrangement that anyone out of his hole during the night was enemy. That saved us the dangerous job of stumbling around in the dark and making targets of ourselves. Although we thought the Germans might try to probe our lines during the night, all went well and it was a quiet night.

There was one thing we hadn't counted on. Due to the excertion we had expended during the attack, we were all wet with perspiration and during the cold night our wet clothes practically froze on our backs. The next morning one of our squad awoke with frozen feet. A medic came over, checked him out and promptly ordered him to be evacuated.

Almost as he hobbled back to the aid station, we got another man to bring us back to a three man squad. We had been forced to leave Lowell Kinnaman of Cedar Vale, Kansas, back in the hospital in England and now, at this moment, he had finally caught up with us and rejoined the company. Kinny had seen no combat up until this time and he was wide-eyed with excitement and not knowing what to expect.

About an hour after daylight, Lieutenant Bailey came around checking out the company's perimeter. I pointed out the German positions we had spotted on the other side of the river and a section of woods we suspected was a kitchen area. Secretly, I hoped they didn't decide to shell it as I dreaded the retaliation we were sure to receive.

Lieutenant Bailey told us our orders were to defend this west bank of the river until further notice. Little did I realize that the company would be here until February 10 when we would be relieved to make the jump over the Rhine.

Before he left, Lieutenant Bailey, almost offhandedly, said for me to assume the job as squad leader. I was astounded. I was the only one of the three who wasn't trained as a machine gunner and I thought he should appoint one of the other two.

"Lieutenant," I stammered, "I'm really a mortarman. I don't know anything about machine guns!"

"Well, now's a good time to learn," he answered, "besides, you're a PFC and they're both privates. Just keep calm, you'll do okay."

While I was thinking how I could wiggle out of that, he turned and walked away. I didn't know what to say to the other two guys, but they didn't say anything, so I didn't either. Little did I realize that my tour of duty as a machine gun squad leader was destined to end six hours later!

It was now January 29 and we occupied our time the rest of the morning improving our positions and watching the Germans move about on the other side of the river in Germany. The Germans, meanwhile, improved their positions and watched us watch them.

It wasn't so bad. We got out of our holes, relieved ourselves and enjoyed some of the sunshine that peeped out from the clouds every now and then. It was like a truce of sorts was in effect. We didn't bother them and they didn't bother us. It was a truce that was due to come to a screeching halt a short time later.

Sometime in the afternoon, I suggested to Kinny that we pull some of the small trees over the large hole that we planned to use for the MG. It would give us some protection from the cold and in case of another artillery attack, would give us some protection from tree bursts.

We shed our jackets so we wouldn't sweat so much and got about our task. We felt reasonably safe as we could see the Germans moving about also.

I guess we really got into that tree dragging as neither of us saw the approach of a combat patrol moving out of the woods to our rear and through our forward position. There were about 20 of them and in broad daylight they were heading toward the river and the German position.

I was standing in the hole, facing to the rear with my back to the river. Kinny was a few feet to my rear and about 10 feet to my left handing me one of the tree logs to place on the bunker.

I can still hear the loud "bur-r-r-p" of that M-42 machine gun as the Germans opened up on our position. The three of us apparently were not an attractive target, but the patrol changed that situation.

Kinny dived for a nearby hole and I either dropped or was knocked to the bottom of the bunker we were preparing. I felt no pain, but I noticed that my left arm was under me and bent in an unnatural position. I tried to move it without success and I could feel the ends of the bone in my upper arm rubbing together. I rolled over and looked and could see blood seeping through my wool knit sweater. My arm lay limp and my hand had gone numb. I knew I was in trouble. I also knew immediately that if I didn't go into shock, the war was over for me.

I yelled to Kinny that I was hit and he yelled back that he was too. I told him that it was in my left arm and asked where they got him. He replied that he apparently got a welt from a bullet under his left ear but he was okay.

We started yelling for a medic and it wasn't long before the medic with the patrol jumped in my hole. He stopped the bleeding, bandaged the wound and gave me a shot of morphine. Even before the shot I still had felt no pain, but I was worried about shock as I had a long way to go to get back to the aid station and I knew people died from shock.

Meanwhile, the German machine gun continued to fire on our little clump of woods. Small limbs and tree bark poured down in the hole, but as long as we stayed down, we were safe. There was nothing to do but wait them out. The patrol, meanwhile, hightailed it out of the area and that relieved the fire on our position.

The medic told me where I could find a medical jeep that would take me to the aid station and went on to rejoin the patrol. I took a deep breath and dived over the back of the bunker and began to crawl on my stomach through the snow into the woods and to the safety of the rear.

Years later Kinny and I talked about that day. Apparently, that burst from the German gun went right between where we were standing. As the rounds were so close together, we reckoned that one more on either end of the burst would have killed both of us. Me through the heart or Kinny through the neck. We were both left with a vision of that "steel rod" whirling through the air between us.

Once I got back in the woods, I stood up, tucked my flopping arm under my belt and headed for that jeep. Artillery started coming in now and after dropping a few times, I decided to hell with it and I got to that jeep without stopping. A short ride back to the aid station and I began to relax.

From here, it was two hospitals on the continent, a hospital ship to England, more hospitals and finally, I was "Z.I'.ed" (marked Zone of the Interior) and flown home to the States.

Just before my plane left Aires, Scotland on March 25, I heard the BBC broadcast the first news of the Airborne assault into Germany—Operation Varsity. I heard them say the 17th Airborne had lead the way.

I was happy to be going home and I was glad to be out of that snow and cold, but suddenly I was overcome with emotions I didn't even know I possessed. All these years preparing for an Airborne mission and now I had missed it. I thought about my buddies and I wished I was with them. I was surprised at myself and I cried.

"ALL IN A DAY'S WORK"

As told by Hank Parmelee, 193 SR

Being in a service company was just like getting up and going to work each day. We had truck drivers, mechanics, carpenters, all kinds of guys with civilian type job skills, so sometimes we forgot we were really soldiers. The main thing was to just get the job done, and I think we did that.

There are a gillion stories of how we learned to improvise and get the supplies to the troops under all kinds of trying conditions, but during Tennessee maneuvers and the Battle of the Bulge, we really pulled some good ones. I imagine we saved the day more than once for the troops on the front line, but most of those times they never knew it.

I remember one time I personally saved the skins of a whole truck load and they don't know it to this day. I'm not telling this because I

Hank Parmelee after the war, standing in the door of Gestapo Headquarters in Mulheim, Germany.

think I should have received a medal, it's just to show you what it was like "doing a day's work" in Service Company, 193rd.

It was about February 10, 1945 and the 193rd was in the vicinity of Hosingen on the Our River. We were being relieved and, although we didn't know it then, we were heading for Chalons-sur-Marne in France to prepare for Operation Varsity.

Our area was shaped like a horseshoe, about 200 yards across the open end and facing west. A light tank company occupied the center of the horseshoe and was poised as a mobile reserve. Our trucks and vehicles were traveling around that horseshoe and after picking up personnel at the front they were high tailing it back.

I was a first lieutenant and XO of our company, but that meant nothing in a service company. Everyone pitched in and helped get the job done. This particular day the job I drew was to stand at a turn in the road and direct traffic.

All of a sudden, I heard a loud explosion and directly across from my area I saw a 3/4 ton weapons carrier lifted high in the air. Apparently, it had hit a mine. Nearby personnel came to the rescue, however, so I kept my flow of traffic moving on down the road.

Although the thaw had started, there was still plenty of snow, ice and slush on the road and the trucks were slipping and sliding along. Someone yelled and I looked at the two and one half ton truck that was approaching me. I couldn't believe what I saw.

An American mine was caught under the front left wheel of the approaching truck and was being pushed along on the icy road. Since by this time the truck was only about 20 feet from me, I held up both arms and screamed "Stop! Halt!"

The driver slammed on the brakes and stopped. I eased the mine out from under the wheel, removed the "spider," took out the detonator and threw the parts as far as I could. I then rolled the mine into a ditch and motioned the truck to move on.

We got some GIs to search the road for other mines, but none were found. Where that one had come from was anyone's guess. I resumed directing traffic and we had no more trouble.

There were two amusing angles to this incident. One was the fact that what could have been a real tragic accident was never known to the load of troopers riding in the back of the truck. The three soldiers sitting in the cab probably figured out what had happened, judging from how big their eyes got, but they never said a word.

The other not-so-funny angle dawned on me after a few minutes. In a matter of seconds, I disassembled that mine like I knew what I was doing. I hadn't touched one since I was in OCS some two years earlier!

I guess it would have been nice if the guys in the cab had at least said "Thank you," but as I said, when you were in a service company, it was all in a day's work.

"THE DEATH OF AN ENEMY PATROL"

As told by Oliver A. Kirkconnell, 513 HQ 2

It was a bitter cold night: January 2, 1945. We were moving toward Mont, Belgium, some four kilometers southeast of Bastogne. Our mortar platoon had been ordered into this area to establish new positions. Our mission was to dig in our mortars during the next day and be ready to support the regiment's attack on the fourth.

It was about midnight as we moved through an open field where about 50 tanks of the 4th Armored Division stood silent and still. All of the tanks had been damaged in some way and the division's welders and repair mechanics were working feverishly to get them back in action before morning. They were shielding the flash of the welder's torches as best they could, but it was dangerous work and almost sure to draw enemy fire.

As we passed by them and our boots crunched through the snow, the repair men whispered "Good luck" to us. They knew we were going up to fight and some of us wouldn't make it. To me, it was like that last walk a condemned man makes as he walks to the electric chair and the other prisoners on death row wish him well!

When we reached Mont, as platoon sergeant, I took the two section sergeants and went up to look over the terrain to determine the locations for our mortars and our observation post. We returned to find the rest of the platoon bedded down in the lower story of a farmhouse. In Belgium, the people lived in the upper level and the livestock were kept on the ground level. We were right at home with the animals.

The troopers had found a small wood stove and had it going pretty good. It was bitter cold that January and the snow was deep. Fighting the weather was always on our minds. We picked out a place for our bedrolls on top of a rack of sugar beets and got a couple of hours of sleep.

Before light we were up and moving into the new area. By mid-morning, we had our mortars pretty well emplaced. We dug the four mortars in on the west side of Mont, behind a hill about 100 feet high where artillery fire could not reach them. Only German mortars could hurt us so tree bursts were our only worry.

We zeroed our mortars in and put out stakes for everything that could possibly be a target. We mainly concentrated on the two opposite ends of a wooded area about 600 yards to our front where we could see the Germans moving around. We stacked the mortar shells nearby with the proper amount of increments on each and as far as we could determine, we were ready.

The road through Mont on our right sector was also zeroed in as our right limits and we noticed that the 3rd Battalion was also dropping a few rounds on the road as it was their left limit. The rest of the day passed with us making improvements to our positions, but without any action from the enemy.

Our observation post was about 200 feet further forward at the brow of the hill. It could accommodate about six men and was just right for me, the two section sergeants and two others to help cover the night watch.

Lieutenant Walter Rydesky had briefed us earlier and warned us to be especially vigilant as we could expect the Germans to be probing our lines. They knew something was up and they would be trying to find out what we were doing.

As darkness approached, we checked our walkie-talkies with the four mortars. We adjusted the volume so there would be no surprising blaring during the night if we had to use them. In the quiet of the night, they could sure give your position away.

Oliver Kirkconnell (L) and Hall (gunner), sight the platoon mortar while on Tennessee Maneuvers.

During the night, I slept with "one eye open." At least I was aware of everything that went on. I heard Sergeant Bob Cox take the watch from Private Bobby Stevens and then Stevens turn the watch over to Private Tony Rozzi and he turn it over to Sergeant John Coltza. Finally, about two o'clock in the morning, Coltza nudged me and I began my watch.

It wasn't too hard for me to stay awake. The cramped position we were in and the biting cold kept you from getting comfortable. Every so often I also had to nudge Coltza who was inclined to snore. Add to that the fear of an enemy patrol coming up on us and the possibility of tree bursts and the situation had my attention.

About three o'clock I heard dragging sounds to my left front along a fence line which ran about half way between us and the wooded area to the front. All kinds of thoughts began running through my mind.

I realized my helmet would be a sharp, black outline against the snow-white background. To break up this outline we would pat snow on the net webbing, but after awhile, heat from your body would cause it to drop off and the process had to be repeated. Then I started to lift my rifle toward the area and it seemed to me to be as black and as big as a telephone pole. Surely the Germans would notice this movement!

When I finally brought my rifle to bear on the German patrol I had heard, I became aware of another dilemma. Due to the extreme cold, my fingers were swollen and split and bleeding.

They were stuck to the leather palm gloves I wore and I was unable to get my finger into the trigger guard to kick my safety off! I felt my heart beating as I put the gloved finger in my teeth and tugged at removing the glove.

As if I didn't already have enough trouble, my front partial plate slipped and about came out my mouth. The teeth had been knocked out by a parachute riser while I was at Fort Benning and so hectic had been our training, I had never gotten it fitted properly. It was clear to me that I was in a monumental mess.

I guess it was the loud beating of my heart that awakened the others, but soon everyone in the hole was alert and aware of the noise below us. With my safety now off, I was ready. As we waited for the perfect moment to open up on them, I pulled a grenade from my web harness and removed the tape. We wanted to be sure we could get every one of them because any German who got away could pinpoint our forward position.

Finally, the moment came. I lobbed the grenade and then all of us opened up with our rifles as we poured a murderous fire into the area where we had heard the patrol. We all agreed that no one could have lived through that curtain of fire.

Our fire caused a small war to break out in our sector of the front. Everyone who had been watching shadows and imagining they were enemy, but were afraid to fire for fear of revealing their position, now opened up with all they had! I can imagine the report that must have gone up the channel to generals miles away that an all-out attack was underway!

Things finally quieted down and by early morning we had calmed down enough to ease down the hill and investigate the result of our night time fire fight. I was certain we had wiped out a large German patrol and all of us were ready to carve some notches on our rifles and maybe pick up some fine German watches!

When we reached the area we could only find two bodies. They were the bodies of two black and white cows, badly torn with grenade and rifle fire.

Later, our mortars supported the regiment's attack on January 4, and the night infiltration of "the German patrol" was forgotten in the fighting that followed. Needless to say, those of us in that forward observation post were not too proud of the little war we had started, so we kept quiet about the details. Thus, it has only taken 50 years for the truth to come out!

"THE SEARCH"

As told by John F. Magill Jr. 466 HQ

This is a story of how I dealt with fear jumping into a fiery sky over Germany, and later, how I learned to deal with hatred which also threatened to consume me.

Since the war my wife and I have made three visits to Europe and I have written countless letters and followed up a number of leads, but all to no avail. You see, I have been trying to locate a German woman who, at the risk of her own life, chose to minister to me and 19 other wounded paratroopers and well could have saved my life.

To understand this tale of love and compassion and my search for peace of mind you must go back with me to March 1945, and the 17th Airborne's jump across the Rhine River.

We moved into the marshaling areas on March 20. The barbed-wire enclosure provided a secure billeting area for the Airborne troops. There would be no exit until the troopers departed for their planes. No chances would be taken for any breaches of security.

For three days we prepared equipment bundles, wrote emotional letters home that contained no information about the impending mission and attended briefings on what was to be maybe the biggest event of our young lives. It was code named Operation Varsity and the name made us feel good. It meant we were on the "first team!"

The briefings stimulated rumors among the troopers. The Germans were committed to hold or die in defense of "Der Fatherland! The Rhine had never been breached by an invading army since Napoleon in 1809! And, finally, old men, women and children had been trained to poison or maim wounded members of the invading Airborne force!

We tried to laugh these rumors off, but the almost continuous briefing about the massive and ever increasing concentrations of anti-aircraft guns in the drop zone added to our apprehension. We also knew there would be no friendly underground to help us as the troopers had had in Normandy. And,

John Magill in the Spring of 1943, following graduation from Jump School at Ft. Benning.

there was "Axis Sally" who broadcast that they knew we were coming. We tried not to show it, but fear was ever present.

We were awakened early on the morning of March 24, and treated to a heavy, somewhat unmilitary breakfast: steak and eggs and apple pie! We moved through the supply shed, picking up a main parachute and having the choice of taking a reserve or not. We were to jump so low, in the event the main failed there would hardly be time to deploy the reserve chute.

By the time we had moved through the line and picked up our individual equipment, we had a load of 80 to 100 pounds. Most everyone had to have help to climb the steps into the waiting C-47s and C-46s.

Using the new C-46s for the first time in combat seemed to be an ideal move. The wider fuselage and double doors meant more troopers could be carried and that they could all exit faster and land closer together on the drop zone. Unknown to most of us, the C-46s did not have self-sealing gas tanks and would prove to be a flaming death trap for many troopers.

After about an hour and a half of flight, we rendezvoused with the British 6th Airborne to form the largest single day Airborne invasion ever mounted to that time or since. Record setting was hardly on our minds, however, as we thought about what awaited us.

Soon we turned east toward the Rhine River and the pilot flashed the red warning light over the doorways of the C-46. We stood up, hooked up and checked our equipment. Then, as the Rhine became visible through the small windows, all hell broke loose.

The sheer concentration of anti-aircraft fire was far beyond all predictions. I watched in awesome disbelief as planes all around us burst into flames and plunged earthward, most with their precious human cargo aboard. The sound of shell fragments striking the wings and bottom of our plane was almost rhythmic!

At that same moment, the green light flashed on and the troopers surged forward to exit the open doors. Out we went into the inferno of exploding shells, tracer bullets and fire and smoke. We knew what awaited us below, but for now, we wanted to get away from that airplane as fast as we could!

For a few seconds, I was back at Fort Benning, counting "one thousand, two thousand ... opening shock, check your canopy ..." then I snapped back to reality and I was swinging in the sky east of the Rhine River, over enemy territory in flak thick enough to walk on.

I hauled down on my two front risers, literally collapsing half of my chute, to get down fast through the inferno and to the ground before I could be hit. Everywhere I glanced there seemed to be flaming airplanes crashing or lifeless forms hanging limp in their parachutes.

Looking down at the drop zone, I saw running cattle and horses and fleeing Germans. We had jumped right on top of the enemy! I caught a glimpse of our equipment bundle with its red canopy and I let up on those front risers as the ground came up fast.

I crashed into the ground, realized I was uninjured, and unbuckled my chute. Then I joined with others as we cleared the DZ of enemy. By sheer numbers we seemed to stun them and they began to surrender in great numbers.

By late afternoon we had linked up with the British paratroops and had seized all our objectives. We then formed a perimeter defense to throw back what we expected to be the inevitable German counterattack.

As night fell on March 24, my forward observer section gathered nylon parachutes for warmth. It seemed like an eternity since we had breakfasted in the marshaling area in France. We had seen lanes and gliders crash in flames; we had seen paratroopers lying limp and still in their chutes and we were still surrounded by enemy and expecting a counter-attack any moment.

However, we did feel confident of our own abilities at this time. After all, we had breached the Rhine and we had shown the enemy we were a tough force to deal with. And, we knew at that moment ground troops were streaming across the Rhine in barges. As Churchill had said, "the beginning of the end" was in sight!

We kept the Germans on the run as they fled back into Germany with us on their heels. Optimism rose as we approached the large German city of Munster on April 3. We moved into the outskirts of the city about 0900 that morning and occupied the large, elaborate Herman Goering Barracks.

In front of the huge building stood a large bronze statue of Adolf Hitler. One of our troopers decapitated it with a burst from his Thompson sub-machine gun. When the head hit with a thud, it seemed to symbolize the end to a horrible era.

By noon, despite the serious wounding of our commanding officer, we were in the center of the city. Just as my section was settling down to fry up some eggs we had "found," we were alerted to be ready to move up to provide some fire support. One of the parachute infantry companies had run up against some "die-hard" SS troops and we, along with an additional parachute infantry company were being sent to the rescue.

Arriving on the scene, we learned that the enemy troops were entrenched in a perimeter-type position supported by eight, 88mm artillery pieces and one captured Sherman tank. A quickly developed plan called for our section to move up, hopefully without detection, into a heavily wooded area some 200 yards from the enemy position. Once we "zeroed in" our artillery and gave them a good working over, the infantry ... waiting just behind us ... would rush in and polish them off.

Using our 610 radio, I quietly called in the coordinates of the enemy position to our Fire Direction Center. I asked for "one round of smoke," a white phosphorus shell that would enable me to adjust on the target in a hurry.

Moments after that first round landed, I was horrified to see some dumb guy stand up and fire his M-1 at one of the SS troopers that had revealed himself. His action gave away our position in the woods and the Germans reacted quickly as I knew they would.

The now alerted enemy immediately turned their attention to our positions, lowered the barrels of the 88s and we began to receive the most devastating shelling I had ever experienced. The shells hit in the trees, exploded and showered shrapnel down on the troopers. The explosions mixed with the cries of the wounded and the dying.

We were pinned down and couldn't withdraw. Pieces of shrapnel hit me in the forearm and upper arm as I struggled to radio back the corrections and adjust fire on the enemy. I was hurting, but I knew our only chance lay in getting fire on their position.

Seconds before my artillery barrage hit the SS position, another series of enemy 88s hit the tree tops. Shell fragments smashed our radio and some tore through the visor of my helmet and buried themselves in my nose, right eyebrow and cheeks.

Fortunately, the barrage was right on target and the 88s were silenced long enough for all of us to get out of the woods without further casualties. I teamed up with a trooper who had a leg wound. With his good eyes and my good legs, we moved back to the safety of a farmhouse.

There a number of us were treated by our medics, bandaged and given shots of morphine. We lay on the floor as we awaited evacuation. The medics moved off to help others and we were left pretty much on our own and unguarded.

Suddenly, out of nowhere, a young German Frau began to move among us, inquiring in broken English if we would like some coffee. The warning from the marshaling area about the danger of poisoning by enemy civilians was somehow lost in the morphine haze and trauma we had just experienced and we readily accepted her kind offer.

She continued to move among us, quietly rendering aid and comfort and the warming coffee. Some five hours later when we were at last being evacuated, she vanished just as suddenly and mysteriously as she had appeared.

As we were moved to the field hospital, I gave little thought to what she had done for us. Since then, however, I have had plenty of time to think about this event.

Although we had expected the worse from the civilians, this young lady had shown us compassion and loving care. She could have gone about a half mile and turned us all in to the SS troops. Or, of course, in our half-drugged state from the morphine shots, she could have easily poisoned us. Instead, she probably put her own life on the line by helping us.

Now, do you understand why "The Search" goes on? Do you see why I feel I must find her? I need to tell her that in the midst of war and hate she made love stronger than hate, stronger than evil, and in a sense, stronger than death. I need to tell her that the many blessings I have received in life were all held in the palm of her hand that fateful day in April 1945, when she "chose to minister unto her enemies."

This is not the end of my story. Despite my desire to locate the mysterious frau, during the years that passed after the war, I bore a deep hatred for the German people. I believe many soldiers did this as they could not find it in their hearts to forgive the people that they felt were responsible for the death of their buddies.

Hatred will eat a person up. You cannot live long with hatred in your heart. I knew this, but I couldn't shake it. A trip to Europe in 1969, did not help to ease the way I felt.

Finally, by 1979, my second trip back to Europe, I began to realize the difference between the cold-hearted Nazi SS soldier and the typical drafted soldier. I felt some better, but there was still a lot of hate in me.

It was not until 1983, when my wife and I made our third trip back to Europe that I was able to lay aside the burden I had carried all these years. We visited Wesel and I arranged a meeting with the mayor in hopes of locating the German frau.

My effort to locate her proved fruitless again, but an interesting thing happened that really turned my life around. The mayor took me to a cemetery where German soldiers were buried. As far as the eye could see there were line upon line of plain, gray crosses. Each one bore the names of four fallen German soldiers. Many had the date of their death as March 24 or 25 in 1945.

I began to think of all that artillery fire I had called for and adjusted. How many of those crosses was I responsible for? If I expected the Lord to forgive me for killing so many, then I had to willing to forgive also.

Then I saw an elderly German couple standing before one of the graves staring sadly at the grass and one of the crosses. We didn't speak or even get close to one another, but our eyes met. In my mind, they were visiting the grave of their son.

They saw me and the Disabled American Veterans jacket and hat I wore.

Someway, I feel we both knew. I felt something change inside me. It was a feeling of kindredship and understanding that took the last bit of hatred from my heart.

So, my search goes on. I am 69 years old now and I don't know how much longer I have to search for my "angel of mercy," but I will continue to search. Because, you see, I must find her. I need to thank her.

"HOOTON AND THE HAYSTACK"

As told by Jesse J. Hooton, 194 HQ

It was one of those bitter cold days in January near Rechrival, Belgium, while we were in the Bulge that "Mac" McNulty, our squad leader, told three of us to get ready to move. A line company was occupying a small village out in front of our lines and we had drawn the job of laying a couple of telephone lines to their position.

It wasn't going to be an easy task. The only way to get to their position was over a ridge, down a lone road that crossed a wide-open field, over a small stone bridge, then over more open field. We'd be exposed all the way so it would be a wild Jeep ride!

The job couldn't wait until nightfall, so we set out in the afternoon, determined to get there and back in one piece. The Jeep had two reels

Jess Hooton, home on furlough before the haystack adventure. Laying commo wire could be exciting!

mounted on the rear. One of us would tend each reel, feeding out and spreading the two wires apart as we rode. The idea of two lines was to guard against artillery cutting a single line and the job having to be repeated.

We crossed the ridge and then in full view of the German artillery observers, we raced down the hill toward the village. Then it began. Mortars or 88s started landing behind us and our driver really stomped on the gas and we were flying down that road!

We crossed the picturesque stone bridge and sped into the village. We had made it! Now if we could only be so lucky on the way back!

The CO of the line company wanted us to stay overnight, or at least until nightfall, but we decided against it. We were intent on accomplishing our mission by establishing the lines of communication. We tied in the two lines and took off for the ride back which we knew would be a dangerous one.

Across the field we went, playing out the two wires as far apart as possible. When we got to the bridge we were horrified to discover the Germans had effectively shelled it to the extent we would not be able to cross it.

Our driver didn't hesitate a second. He whipped the Jeep down into the small creek, we forded it and climbed up the bank on the other side. Then up the road we went toward the ridge and what would mean safety for us.

We were beginning to think we were home free when one of the reels jammed and we had to stop. There was a haystack nearby so we pulled in behind it in hopes the enemy artillery observers still hadn't seen us. We were wrong.

In came the first round. It was over and maybe 50 meters beyond the haystack. We were working frantically to free up the jammed reel, but in came another round. This one was short by about 50 meters. They were zeroing in on us!

Although we worked as hard as we could, we could not get the reel free before that third round was fired. We heard it coming in and we knew it should be on target. There was the sharp whistle, then the brief period of quiet that told you it was coming in on you. We braced ourselves. After all, how could they miss a darn haystack out in an open field!

Well, they couldn't miss. The round hit the haystack all right, but to our great relief, it was a dud! We heard it thump into the soft hay, but there was no explosion and we had been saved by a faulty round!

The reel was freed and before the Germans could fire another round we were roaring out of there and over the ridge. We had accomplished our mission—by the grace of God.

I've often wondered about that dud. Did it just happen to be of faulty manufacture or could some munitions worker have decided the war was lost and sabotaged that round? Or could I have been right the first time—it was by the grace of God?

"A CHAPLAIN IN COMBAT"

By Chaplain Clifford C. Cartee, 194 HQ

When my class was finishing our training at Chaplain School, we were told we could choose our assignments. I had heard of the formation of some new Airborne divisions and that's what I put in for. Everyone tried to talk me out of it saying those paratroopers are the meanest and toughest soldiers of all and that I should go elsewhere.

Regardless of what I asked for, I was assigned to units in Mississippi and then in Missouri for the next two months. Finally, I wrote a personal letter to the Chief of Chaplains asking for the Airborne assignment. In only three days I had a telegram ordering me to report to the 17th Airborne at Camp Forrest, Tennessee.

I was assigned to the 194th Glider Infantry Regiment and almost on arrival, Colonel Pearce, the regimental commander, told me to get ready to ship overseas in one week. Thus, I never really unpacked before we were on our way to England.

During the months we were in England, I performed what could be considered normal chaplain duties. We counseled with the troops, conducted church services and generally, tried to help keep up the morale. When the Bulge started and we were shipped to France, everything changed for the chaplains.

We were told we could choose where we served. Our Catholic Chaplain, for example, chose to assist the doctors at the Regimental Aid Station. I chose to assist the medics in the line companies as they gathered the wounded and brought them back to the battalion collecting points. We went where we felt we would be of help and could provide some degree of comfort to the troops.

I do not remember in which order were the towns that we fought through or our specific objectives. There was Millimont, Hubermont, Houmont and Recrival and many little small villages. I do remember how bitter cold it was and the many hardships the men had to endure.

During one of the first towns we attacked, the route carried us over some

In May 1945, Chaplain Cartee (L), held this baptismal service in the Rhine River for these 194th troopers.

open fields and we took casualties immediately. Even though the enemy could see us, we took the jeep out in the open to pick up the wounded. On the way back we came under artillery fire. The jeep driver made a run for it and got back safely. I dropped to the ground and although I was not wounded, I felt a piece of the spent shrapnel hit me on the back.

Another time we heard that there were wounded up on a hillside and they needed to be brought in for medical aid. There was a trail up there, but with the deep snow, it was hard to see. One trooper volunteered to sit on the fender of the jeep and guide the driver up the hill. Halfway up, the jeep hit a mine and we lost two brave men.

After we had cleared one town, I was at the aid station helping wherever I could. I was sitting beside one seriously injured man when the doctor came by to treat him. He could not find a vein in which to give him plasma. Finally, he gave up and said he probably had lost too much blood and was half-frozen anyhow.

I told the doctor that maybe I could warm him and that he could then find a vein. I asked him to come back when he had finished treating the others. I then wrapped the man in my coat and held him up against my body for added heat. And then I quietly began praying for him.

It was almost an hour before the doctor came back, but this time he was able to find a vein and to give him plasma. Another 30 minutes and he was conscious and even talking! I am sure the coat and the heat from my body helped, but no one will ever convince me that the good Lord wasn't there in that aid station that day.

Another town we attacked was located down in a valley. To get there, the men had to move up behind the protection of a large hedgerow and then dash across an open field to a wooded area. A truck, towing an anti-tank gun, pulled up and stopped. I could see it was too far out in front of the hedgerow and just as the colonel yelled for them to pull back, a tank fired a shell and hit the truck. A jeep went out and Lieutenant Ralph Epps and another trooper were loaded in and rushed to the rear.

A few minutes later, another medical jeep pulled up and the driver said he was told there were more wounded up here and did we know where they were. Someone told him they were out some distance in the field in a ditch, but if they went out there they might experience the same end the truck had.

I could tell the driver didn't like the idea of going down the hill and out here by himself. I asked him if I would walk ahead and show him the way, would he follow. He agreed and we reached the wounded without incident.

There were seven or eight wounded in the ditch so it was evident that the driver was going to have to make two trips. We loaded the jeep with wounded and back he went, bouncing, twisting and turning through the deep snow.

In about an hour he was back and we loaded the jeep with the rest of the wounded and he hauled them out. Remarkably, the Germans held their fire. Maybe they saw it was an errand of mercy.

After the jeep left, I began walking back up the hill to our positions. The Germans failed to show me the mercy they had the jeep as machine gun fire sprayed all around me. Someway, however, all of the bullets missed me. God reached out for me that day and I made it back safely.

As we pushed the Germans back, we were soon fighting in Luxembourg. During all this way, my chaplain's assistant, Laverne G. Bakeman, would drive me out to the aid stations, drop me off and then assist in moving the wounded back. I would stay with the medics until he returned whether it meant staying overnight or not.

One night I had just bunked down when a call came for someone to go out with a jeep and driver and try to locate a wounded man that had been left behind. I started to get up and go when one of the lightly wounded troopers said he knew where the man was and that he would go. Despite his wound, he went back out there and eventually they found the other wounded man and he was saved. I was touched by the compassion this man had shown for his comrade in spite of his own wounds.

It was not possible to hold "regular" Sunday chapel services during our time in combat. Wherever I was, regardless of what day it was, I tried to conduct some sort of Bible study. Sometimes only 10 or 12 attended. Sometimes we had as many as 100. We tried to see to it that at no time were the men too far from some sort of spiritual support.

"Operation Varsity" was another time when the men were severely tested and we tried to be with them as much as we could. Our entry into the battle was not without its thrills. Again, I feel we had divine help in the glider I rode into Germany.

We experienced severe turbulence and the pilot, looking out his cockpit window saw one of our wings bending back at a strange angle. Afraid it was breaking off, he cut loose from the tow plane and we made a forced landing.

When we had landed safely, he inspected the wing and found that a number of screws had come out of the two struts which held the wing to the fuselage. Had we continued on, the wing most surely would have come off before we reached our LZ and all of us would have been killed. As it was, it took us two days of bumming rides on trucks to catch up with the regiment.

Once again we seemed to move through a list of towns and cities. I remember after Wesel, passing through the towns of Dulmen, Applehulsen, Nienburg and finally, Munster. Our troops continued to drive on with the Germans giving ground reluctantly.

Near one of the towns our men passed through some woods, beyond a barn and started across a large pasture. Almost immediately three men were shot and fell to the ground. The sergeant leading the formation, quickly switched directions and directed the men into some woods in a flanking maneuver.

Meanwhile, the men who went down lay in the field. A medical jeep came forward and the driver was studying how to get to them. I jumped aboard and we went directly into the clearing, loaded the men in the jeep and headed back. As we returned, a shell (probably from a tank) hit a big tree behind us. It tore off the top of the tree, but failed to explode. Instead, we saw it bounce off, hit the ground and spin off harmlessly into the woods. Another shell landed so close to me, it splattered mud on me. It too was a dud. I was amazed that we were able to see them so plainly, but quite thankful that both had been duds.

After Munster, it was Ruthen, Kallenhardt, Warstein then Mulheim. The casualties during this campaign were lighter than before, but there were still troopers getting hurt and our work went on. Only on one occasion during this period did I have an experience out of the ordinary.

I was with one of the battalion commanders when a medical jeep approached through the bushes. "Where are those wounded you went for?" he asked the driver.

"I couldn't get to them, Sir," the driver replied. "The artillery fire is too heavy as you can still see."

With that the CO really got hot with the young trooper. "You go right back down there and get those men. I'm giving you a direct order to get to them!"

I saw a bad situation building, so I said to the driver, "Let me go with you, soldier, and I bet we can get to them, okay?"

"Yes sir!" he replied as he turned his jeep around.

The artillery continued to be heavy, but we went back and picked up the wounded men and drove out with them. Once we got back to our lines, I got out and stayed with the troops while the driver of the jeep took the wounded men on to the aid station.

That's how it went until the war was over. The duties I performed as a Chaplain were as varied as you can imagine. I tried to help the wounded as much as I could, I tried to set an example wherever I went, and I prayed and shared God's word with the men whenever I found the opportunity.

"ESCAPE"

As told by Horace Cathey, 513 HQ

After I finished high school in 1943, like a lot of boys my age in those days, I joined the Army. After basic training, I volunteered for the paratroops and following jump school at Fort Benning, I was assigned to the 513th Parachute Infantry Regiment.

I'd come from a little town in Arkansas called New Edinburg. It was a small town where just about everybody knew everybody else—or at least they knew their families. The nearest claim to fame for New Edinburg was that it was just down the road from Fordyce, Arkansas.

Now if that doesn't impress you, let me hasten to say that Fordyce was the home of Paul "Bear" Bryant, the famous football coach who was a legend at the Universities of Alabama and Kentucky. Still not impressed? Well, let me tell you how us boys from New Edinburg really got around during World War II!

I was in a .30 caliber light machine gun section and when we went into combat during the Bulge, they attached my section to "B" Company of the 513th. We became heavily engaged in the area around Flamierge. The Krauts had a strong force there and things went badly for us almost from the beginning.

My entire section was captured on January 4, and we were marched off to a POW compound behind the German lines. We felt badly about being captured, but it was either that or be killed. Later, we were to feel even worse as our captors were hardly able to care for us properly. We had little shelter and even less to eat. The Germans were only slightly better off than us.

A few days later, we were in a big building somewhere in Luxembourg. The Germans were shifting us around and we couldn't tell how the war was going. By this time we were mixed in with prisoners from several other divisions. This was typical of the Bulge as when the breakthrough began, all sorts of units were cut off and left to roam around in the Ardennes. Then as the Germans' offensive slowed, many of these isolated units were being rounded up and captured.

This building we were in was pretty dark and we couldn't see each other very clearly. I had decided that I wanted to keep a diary of my experiences and I was asking around if anyone had some blank paper in their gear. I asked one soldier and when he replied, his voice sounded sort of familiar. I picked up right away on his Arkansas accent!

"My name is Virgil Harris, and I'm from New Edinburg, Arkansas," he replied. "What in the world are you doing here, Horace?"

Well sir, my teeth like to have fallen out! I knew Virgil from back home and there he was in this lousy prisoner of war camp just like me! Virgil had been in another division, but I sure was glad to see him—although I was sorry both of us had to meet like this.

The Germans moved us around a lot. From one woods and one barn to another with damn little to eat between time. Finally, they got us to a railway and we reckoned we were about to be sent back deep into Germany—and we were right.

They packed us in like sardines and then we just sat there in the

Horace Cathey, a trooper who resisted the enemy all the way. He made good an escape opportunity!

boxcars on a rail siding. I guess we were waiting for an engine. It got real cold as we couldn't move around much. Our own body heat was about all we had to keep us from freezing.

Once again, it was dark inside that boxcar and we couldn't see each other very well. Out of boredom, we got to telling where we were from. Then I heard one soldier say his name was Charles Trammel and he was from New Edinburg, Arkansas!

Well, I just couldn't believe it! Here in the middle of nowhere, in the worst possible place I could imagine, was another guy from my hometown! Virgil and I lost no time in slapping him on the back and telling him how glad we were to see him—even if it wasn't the best of places.

Like Virgil, Charles had been in another division and had been rounded up in the prisoner bag. The three of us were a lot of comfort to each other and we spent countless hours talking about home and all our mutual friends. The Krauts eventually shipped us to Stalag IV near Muhlberg and put us to work clearing war damage. Life was hard and the food was skimpy. Many of the guys came down with some sort of sickness and all of us were weak and run down.

On April 13, the Germans came in our compound and rounded up all of the able-bodied prisoners and moved us out. Their plan was to send us to Leipzig where the bombing had all but blocked the entire road network. Long working days and equally poor treatment most certainly awaited us there.

Late that afternoon as they prepared to move us out, two of the other guys in my machine gun section, Vernon Cumberland and Bruce Waldo, were with me when we found ourselves unguarded and not a German in sight. We made good use of the opportunity and slipped off into the forest.

For the next two days and nights we toughed it out, moving by night and resting by day as we tried to put as much distance as possible between our captors and where we guessed the Allied lines were. Tired, hungry and half frozen, we finally came to a road and thanks to God, there were American tanks and armored vehicles moving toward the direction we had just come!

Things moved fast for us from here on. We were sent back to a hospital where we soon regained most of our strength. From there we were put aboard a ship and started back to the States. In mid-ocean, we got the word the war had ended.

The best of intentions sometimes never seem to work out. After the prison camp experience, I thought Virgil Harris and Charles Trammel would forever be my closest friends when we got home. After the war we each just seemed to go our own way, got jobs and moved away. We started families and we just seemed to drift apart. We never did get together.

I never saw Virgil again until October of 1991, and then he died the next April. I still haven't seen Charles, but I did hear he was in the VA Hospital in Little Rock. I guess I should go down one of these days and see him. It all seems so long ago, like a dream, a bad one.

"BAYONETS IN THE SNOW"

As told by Jim Baxter, 513 E

It was December 23, 1944, and I had just returned from a pass to London. Instead of finding a camp getting ready for Christmas, I found everyone packing and getting ready to go to war. The "Bulge" had broken out and the 17th Airborne had been ordered into the gap.

By the 24th we were in France, landing near Rhiems, and on our way to Mourmelo-le-Grande for a night and then on up on the line. On the way we were strafed by what we later learned was a jet aircraft. At the time we only knew it made a funny whistling noise as it flew and was way faster than any plane we had ever seen.

Soon we were on the banks of the Meuse River—or rather, in positions just behind the Meuse. My platoon crowded into a small, smoke-filled school house and tried to keep warm. Later, we moved to Stanay and another smoky room. It was an old paper mill and we bedded down on the cold, cold concrete floor.

We stayed here for a couple of days and took our turns guarding the road near the border of France and Belgium. We could hear the sound of gunfire, but we encountered no enemy.

By January 1, we had moved nearer Bastogne and I recall going sound asleep while leaning against a tree in Bois of Fragotte. Bastogne was a few miles away but the noise of gunfire could be heard about a mile from our positions.

Finally, on January 2, we went on the march north passing several snow covered bodies along the roadside. We came out of the woods and saw rolling hills topped with patches of trees. Just inside the tree lines were a number of American tanks, none of which seemed to be manned or in action.

Our stroll in the countryside ended abruptly as shell fire fell near us and we scooted for cover. When the firing ceased, our lines gradually reformed and we moved hurriedly through Monte and entered Mande St. Etienne with one file on either side of the street.

Mande was a mess. The town had been on the edge of the Bastogne battleground for some three weeks before we arrived and it had been shelled continually. As we edged past a cemetery, all eyes turned to gaze at the body of an American tanker. He had a hole the size of a watermelon where one hip should have been.

Near the center of the cemetery was a church. It had received heavy damage, but the steeple was still intact. We were ordered to halt and my squad halted near a tank crew doing routine maintenance work. As we had not been fed much for several days, we begged a case of rations from the tankers and split it up among our squad. Before I could eat a bite, Lt. Manning called me to select two others and go on patrol with him.

We walked about two blocks to the edge of town and entered a woods which I believe was the following day's first objective for our platoon. We penetrated about 100 yards coming across a booby-trapped rifle and bag which we left alone for the engineers to disarm.

We turned right and proceeded just inside the edge of the woods for about 300 yards without incident. To our right was an open field with the edge of Mande St. Etienne about 150 yards away. Then, without explanation, Lieutenant Manning halted the patrol and we retraced our steps to the tank. I really didn't see what, if anything, the patrol had accomplished.

We were sitting a few feet from the tank when we noticed the fins of an unexploded mortar shell sticking halfway into the ground. The crew had re-entered their tank and now they started the motor. As it started to back up, it was evident that one track was going to back over the shell. Yet, no one said anything or attempted to move. Inches from the shell, the tank spun on one tread and drove away leaving the shell in place.

Late in the afternoon, we were led back through town and told to dig in. We were in reserve and I believe our 1st and 2nd Platoon were being committed. We began to get artillery fire as shells fell along the hedge rows where we were digging in every 15 seconds.

Maybe digging in isn't the right term. Most of us had broken our entrenching tools earlier trying to dig in the frozen ground. We used our helmets, sticks and whatever we could find to get some cover from the artillery. Most found ditches of shell holes, but we did have a good field of fire as we waited for the battle to develop.

I dug a can of corned beef hash out of a pocket, used a bayonet to open it and scooped out a big spoonful. It was almost pure lard and I spat it out in the snow. The fat had congealed and it was impossible to eat. As it was cold or nothing, I threw the can away in disgust.

The only thing I had to eat that day was an old German biscuit I had found in the hedgerow. By then, I was so hungry I didn't care what I ate.

Shortly after dark, a Sherman tank pulled up behind us and proceeded to knock the top off a shed to clear its field of fire. We decided our position was too close to the tank which would be a prime target for the enemy, so we moved some 30 feet to the right and set up again.

Heavy fog began to roll in and soon visibility closed to about 100 feet to our front. In the next few hours, the troopers fired at any movement. As a result, we left several wounded cows stumbling around in the haze.

I passed up and down the line telling the men to hold their fire until they were sure of their targets. It was well that I did so as at about midnight a patrol approached and was halted. We asked for the password and they didn't know it. That was okay, however, as we didn't know it either!

I asked who played in the World Series that year and after a short consultation, one answered, "St Louis."

"Who did St. Louis play?" I yelled back.

There was another consultation and finally someone yelled, "St. Louis!"

By golly, they were right! Still not convinced, I asked who was playing in the Rose Bowl that year. There was another pause and then some yelled, "USC and Duke."

I was beginning to enjoy the game, so I tried them again. "Where are they playing?"

Several guys yelled, "Pasadena!"

One then spoke up loudly. "No! No! They played in Durham, North Carolina this year!"

That was enough. The patrol began cussing us and there was little doubt that it was an American patrol and they had had enough of the game. Turned out they were from the 101st in Bastogne. I escorted them to the company CP and then on to battalion.

When I returned, Lieutenant Manning called the non-coms together to brief us on the plan for the attack the next day. The division was to attack north on either side of the highway leading out of Mande. "B" Company was to be on the road with "F" Company to the left and "E" to the right. Our 3rd Platoon was to be in reserve.

We were to jump off at about 7:00 a.m. and with no resistance expected, we were hoping to cover about eight miles and meet the British at a river. That no resistance was a joke as we began receiving fire as soon as we started. We moved up closer and could see our guys dropping everywhere.

Lieutenant Dean, our CO, was dead and Lieutenant Hall, who was Lieutenant Manning's assistant, was shot in the chest. Sergeant Wright, a 3rd Platoon squad leader, was hit in the leg. It was plain that this would be no piece of cake.

Lieutenant Manning led me to a depression about 75 yards north of some farm buildings on the edge of town. To our front was an open field sloping up to our right front for about 200 yards. It was all open field. Immediately in front of us was a level stretch of about 80 yards with a barbed wire fence half way to a small finger of fir trees and a large woods stretching as far as we could see to the left.

I estimated it was a good 180 yards from the edge of town to the main section of woods. Our second platoon was pinned down between the depression and the woods with the first platoon pinned down in the open field to the right. "F" Company was fighting to get to the main section of woods. Heavy artillery and machine gun fire had halted the attack before it really got started.

Then we got our orders: Fix bayonets and get into those woods! Before we moved, we began to realize the artillery fire falling in the field was mostly our own 75s. Only one 88 seemed to be firing on the area. Lieutenant Manning went back to get the artillery fire lifted into the woods where the machine gun fire was coming from.

The next salvo was even worse. It was right on top of us. Lieutenant Manning, being an old mortar man, had gotten his "up 50" and "down 50" reversed and it had brought the fire in on us. He hurried back, made the correction and the artillery blew hell out of the woods.

We got ready for our bayonet charge. About 45 of us were to make the charge. We would move up under the artillery barrage and when we were in position, Lieutenant Manning would toss a smoke grenade as a signal for the artillery observer to life the fire. From there on it would be pure guts on our part.

Our first problem was that many of the men found their bayonets were frozen tight in their scabbards. They worked them free and attached them to their rifles. All the time that German machine gun hammered on the top of the depression where we lay. It was plain that unless something was done to silence it, not many of us would live to charge the woods. It would mow us down when we stood up.

Our artillery was firing white phosphorus now and it seemed they were right on target. Suddenly, the machine gun fell silent. I hoped the artillery had finally found it. I unbuckled my harness and bandoliers of ammunition and slipped out of my heavy overcoat. Damn if I was going to get shot because I couldn't move! Several others saw me and followed suit.

We crawled about 25 yards into the field and almost to the barbed wire fence. I shoved my weapon under the lower strand, but I couldn't crawl under it. I edged up parallel and pushed myself up and tried to jump between the next two strands. My trousers caught and I hung there for a moment before I jerked free. I was amazed that I had not been fired on.

Just as I was wondering if the time was right to rush the woods, Sanchez, our platoon runner, jumped up and shouted, "Let's go!" and rushed toward the woods.

We all rushed forward and in seconds were in the woods without a casualty. The machine gun that had been giving us all the trouble had indeed, been hit. A white phosphorus shell had found it and the bodies of the crew lay nearby with their clothing still smoking from the direct hit.

We tried to form a skirmish line to clear the finger of woods, but the artillery had left such a jumble of fallen trees, we couldn't move through the maze. We skirted the finger, reformed back on the main woods and began to move into them.

Almost immediately we ran into a series of bunkers. They must have been built during the siege on Bastogne as they were very well built with eight-inch timbers for roofs. Out of one of the bunkers emerged a German soldier, hands up, helmet on, dressed in an overcoat and with tears as big as nickels running down his face.

One of our guys poked an M-1 in his face, pulled the trigger and knocked him backwards into the bunker. You must understand that although this was a wrongful act, our men were highly excited at this time, they had just completed a bayonet charge, seen many of their comrades killed and were acting more on instinct than as rational human beings. War can make an animal out of you.

I threw grenades into two bunkers but they both failed to go off. I later realized that although I had pulled the pin, in my excitement I had failed to remove the tape I had put over the handle as a safety measure. I have always hoped that those grenades were not found by some innocent child or farmer.

The Germans were surrendering to us throughout the area. One surrendered and produced a "soldbook" showing he was a Belgian from Antwerp and claimed he had been impressed into the German army. We didn't believe him and passed him on back.

The road to Flamierge passed through the woods and this was the line along which the 513th was attacking. "F" Company was on the right bordering the road and "E" Company was to the right of them. The woods were "F" Company's objective and the high ground to the right of the woods was our first objective.

Although our platoon was in reserve again, we were committed one half hour into the attack. We had moved across the open ground, secured the finger of woods and were now operating on our own moving into "F" Company's territory.

Off to my left I heard my machine gunner, Bitting, shout that he had been hit. I wondered what he was doing over there as he should be behind us giving us supporting fire. Before I could move toward him, the same Kraut that had shot Bitting, fired a burst at me.

I ducked behind a tree and peeked around it. At first I saw no one, but then I saw someone crawling down a ditch about 60 feet away. I fired a couple of shots, but they hit nothing. I yelled to O'Berg who fired one shot and the body slumped over.

Then I saw the guy who had fired at me. He was standing in a bunker, exposed from the waist up and wearing an Afrika Corps hat. I figured he was the non-com in charge of the troops in this area. Every time I peeked a look at him he gave me a burst.

Now I found I had another problem. I was out of clips for my rifle. I had left my extra clips where I had dropped my gear. I yelled to Carter, our company sniper, to throw me a clip. He did, but it was a clip for a Springfield .03, not a M-1.

Now to fire, I had to extract a single round from the .03 clip and load it manually into my M-1. Not a good arrangement during a fire fight! I yelled to Carter to try to pick off the German.

In the midst of all this confusion, down the road came another German. This one was waving a white flag and wanted to surrender. When he saw he was in the middle of a fire fight, he jumped into a foxhole. Moments later, he crawled out and was motioned to the rear.

When I looked back at the German that had been firing at me, he was nowhere to be seen. Thinking he was gone, I waved the platoon forward and stepped forward myself. I took a couple of steps and then I heard a burst to my right. It felt like I had been hit by a 100 pound bag of sand. My helmet sailed off, my back straightened and I hit the ground.

I rolled into the ditch and landed by the body of the German O'Berg had nailed earlier. Then I looked up and right into the eyes of another German! His eyes were as big as saucers and were exaggerated by thick lensed glasses. I was helpless and I thought that this surely was the end for me.

As we stared at each other, I realized that he was just as scared as I was! He peeked over the edge of the ditch and seeing no one, he crawled about 15 feet to the road, then got up and ran some 500 yards to the next woods, his overcoat flapping in the wind! I was almost glad to see he made it.

I didn't know what shape I was in. I felt around in front and I couldn't find any place where the bullet may have exited. I got to my feet and although my back hurt, I found I could walk so I headed back to the rear and where I knew somewhere there was an aid station;

The medics were set up in an old barn. When I got there, they patched me up and I learned that it only grazed through the fleshy part of my back, missing my spine. Nevertheless, it was enough to preclude my returning to the squad and I was tagged for evacuation.

That aid station was a busy place. We had been taking a number of casualties and some were bad. I heard them say they were going up to the line to get Jim O'Grady. He had been hit bad by a piece of mortar shrapnel that ripped through his chest. They said he probably wouldn't make it, but I thought to myself it would take a lot to kill that Irishman. I was right. O'Grady made it okay. And, so did I.

"P.O.W."

As told by Edward W. Fitzgerald, 193 A

"Wo ist der Bahnhof?" The linguaphone lesson came floating up from a fog of pain and morphine to answer a voice asking "Sprechen sie Deutsch?" As the aid station officer in the barn turned away, I realized I was a prisoner. That tree burst had gotten my hip and I went down. Now I had been picked up by the enemy and now I was a POW.

I have spent most of a lifetime trying to forget that day and the following three months, but it will always stay with me. It was the worst days of my life, but I am very grateful to have survived and that makes every day of my life now, the best days of my life.

The German medics treated those of us that were wounded and then we were loaded onto boxcars for a memorable train ride to the rear and to Germany. The 88 tree burst that had taken a plug out of my hip, and chipped away part of the bone, left me in such a condition that I didn't much care what they did with me.

January 7, 1945 wasn't a good day for me. The division had attacked early that morning and within the first hour, I had been wounded by mortar fragments in the left leg, right arm, left thigh and little finger. Though painful, they were all flesh wounds so I got patched up and rejoined the company.

The second time I wasn't so lucky. The 88 really did a number on me. I sent Harold Konter of Coraopolis, PA, to signal my platoon to pull back and I tried to bandage my wound and took a morphine shot. I guess I must have passed out because they later told me my feet were half frozen when they picked me up.

Twice during the time we were on the train, we were strafed by American fighter planes. I guess if it hadn't been so foggy, they would have gotten the train for sure. In my boxcar we had no injuries from the strafing. I don't know about the other cars. We just pulled our blankets over our heads and prayed that the planes would miss us.

Our first stop was at a field hospital near Vallendar and we were there a

After his liberation, a thin, underweight Ed Fitzgerald (R) was sent to a hospital in England to regain his strength. He had gone from 135 lbs. to 90 lbs.

few weeks. It was run by German nuns. The medical treatment was good, but there was very little food for us. We were given water and a piece of black bread spread with Limburger cheese. We began to learn what hunger meant.

As our troops advanced, they moved us deeper into Germany. The next stop was to a hospital that was identified as SS Lazarette. Here American prisoners were being used as stretcher bearers and the soldier that carried me said he would place me next to another American who was there. Imagine my surprise when I found that other wounded prisoner had been a fraternity brother of mine at Fordham Law School!

My stay at SS Lazarette was the worst experience I have ever had. I was helpless, frustrated, weak and completely at the mercy of our enemy. I was also worried about my pregnant wife back home and how she would take the news that I was missing in action.

In addition to my other worries, we had a doctor who was impossible. He had lost his home and family in the bombing of Dresden, so he took his fury out on us. Each day he would rip the heavy adhesive from our tender parts, then, after dressing the wound, would slap us hard across the face.

After a couple of weeks of this, my Irish temper was getting hard to control. Weak as I was, I decided to fight back. After propping myself up in bed when he began making his rounds, I was ready to hit him back if he tried to slap me again. To my surprise, he passed me by. I figured I had signed my own death warrant, for two guards took me from the ward and down to a small cellar room.

Actually, along with many other prisoners in various stages of health, all malnourished and hungry, we were "marched," staggering, bleeding and stumbling some 25 miles to a prison camp near Wetzlar. I could barely stand and had to be supported by two other POWs all the way. Otherwise, I never would have made it.

The most vivid memory I have of that prison compound is of the vicious dogs growling and throwing their bodies against our barracks door. The camp commander was a visual model for the TV actor, "Colonel Klink." He would receive the morning report standing with his monocle and two dogs on leash and with a small bow, say: "Dank you vary much!"

The food at Wetzlar was only a little better. We got water, thin potato soup, black bread and more Limburger cheese. I continued to lose weight, down from my usual 135 to 90 pounds. My hip continued to ooze fluid and I knew it was not healing properly.

The days there drug on at a snail's pace. I was worried about our first child who was due about this time. I think most of us worried more about our families than we did ourselves.

One quiet night we heard distant artillery and we knew our armies were getting closer. We half expected to be moved again farther into Germany. To our surprise, as the armored vehicles approached, our guards surrendered and became our prisoners. We immediately locked them in the small cells which had been used for solitary confinement.

Then some of the more enterprising men "liberated" a nearby cognac factory and we had a "freedom party!" The effect of good cognac on our starving bodies was predictable. A troop of Boy Scouts could have recaptured us.

The 3rd Armored Division came rolling up, accompanied by a Pathe News cameraman. He seemed disappointed that we did not rush to greet them, so we re-enacted the "liberation" scene with yells and cheers for the camera. I saw the picture later in an English hospital, but my family never did see it. My wife was busy giving birth to our son the day it was taken.

It wasn't until after a week of processing and examining and being moved back into Allied control that I could get off a two page V-Mail letter to my wife. I found out later that when she got it, it was the first she knew that I had been "missing in action."

She received a notice from the War Department that I had been "slightly wounded in action," but that was from the wounds I got that morning. They lost track of me when I returned to the company and things were so screwed up, they failed to pick me up on the morning report. So, all my worrying during captivity was in vain—she never knew I was missing or captured.

I had a rough time getting back into the swing of civilian life. My experience as a POW left some scars, but time and a loving family have slowly healed the wounds, both mental and physical.

With my recovery also came forgiveness for the German people. In fact, I have heard from some of my German guards since my return. Otto A. Hoerig, who was a stretcher bearer at the German field hospital has written and I drop him a card every Christmas.

And, there was Ernst Schalck who used to smuggle out letters for us. He was an orchestra conductor who was drafted into the German army and worked at Vallendar. In 1945, he resumed his work as conductor of the Weisbaden "Sinfony and Kurorchestra." Yes, the war is over and long ago I put it to rest.

"ENEMY IN OUR RANKS"

As told by J.W. Peters, 155 Btry E

I've heard and read about German Lieutenant Colonel Otto Skorzeny and the special force he trained to infiltrate our lines during the Bulge. They wore American uniforms and were picked because they could speak perfect English. There has always been some question of how many of them actually succeeded. Well, I'm here to tell you I know some of them did!

My first day of combat was a day of high excitement for me. It all began early that morning of January 4, 1945, when our .50 caliber machine gun squad was attached to one of the line companies of the 194th Glider Infantry Regiment.

We were somewhere just northeast of Neufchateau and we apparently had the Germans on the run. At least, we hadn't been slowed down much by their withdrawal tactics. We maintained a steady advance receiving only occasional sniper fire and the infantry quickly eliminated that.

Suddenly, as we neared a small village (it probably was Flamierge) the picnic ended. Like a bad dream, we started taking heavy automatic fire from the hedgerows and some hay stacks. We seemed to be caught in a cross fire. Then the 88s started in on us. Private Frank Stoner, a close friend of mine who had enlisted with me, took a direct hit and was gone.

We struggled toward some buildings to gain protection from the murderous fire we were receiving. Once inside we could see German tanks and infantry advancing towards us. Our forward observer called for artillery support and pretty soon shells were sailing over our heads.

The artillery got some hits, but the enemy held their ground. To find out what was going on and hopefully, to get some flanking fire on them, two scout parties were formed and sent out to each of our flanks. The one I joined made it to a small wagon shed that had straw piled on one side.

The trooper next to me, gasping for breath, removed his helmet and wiped the sweat from his forehead. I saw him jerk suddenly and when he turned around, there was a small bullet hole almost between his eyes. He fell to the ground dead.

A couple more close calls and the NCO in charge decided that this location was untenable and it was decided that we would withdraw. As we started back, the ground under my feet was machine gunned and I dived down an embankment and into a hedgerow along a dirt lane.

As I looked around for the rest of the scout party, a bullet snapped off a twig near my ear. I dropped and scrambled away from the location. Crawling, dragging my M-1 behind me, I finally found the rest of the party.

Our radioman had been killed and another trooper was trying to work the damaged radio. We made our way from one building to another trying to get back to the main body of our troops. Sometime about here we caught on to the fact that our own troops, or at least what we thought were our troops, were firing on us!

Jim Peters, resting after his harrowing experience in the Bulge. He still hasn't forgotten the password and countersign!

We yelled at them but it was to no avail. We held our fire for awhile, but finally it was decided that these guys just couldn't be "our troops." Someone said that they were Germans in American uniforms and we opened up on them.

We dropped a couple of them and a quick check of the bodies revealed that none of them were wearing dog tags. There was no time to check further for identification, but every man in that party was convinced that they were Germans. I know I was.

Finally, we made it to a stone building that gave us some degree of protection. As I recall, there were nine of us that scrambled into that building. I didn't know any of them. I was the only guy from the 155th. The rest I assumed were infantry troopers. Darkness was descending and we were all wondering what we were going to do next. Would we make a fight of it here or would we try to break out before they came to get us?

From out in the woods surrounding the buildings came a voice in perfect English, "C" Company relief coming in!"

One of our guys answered by firing a shot back at them and with that, several machine guns opened up on us. We hunkered down and no one was hit during the barrage they threw at us. Then the same English voice ordered us to surrender and gave us until "a count of ten."

They might have pulled the ruse off if one of our guys hadn't fired that shot. By this time we had all heard about the "Malmedy Massacre" and no one was in the mood to surrender. It wasn't discussed, but the feeling was plain—we would fight to the death.

When we didn't come out, a tank fired at our building. It blew a big hole in the wall, but miraculously, no one was injured. Dazed, we looked around at one another, wondering what we could do next.

Suddenly, one of our guys pointed to two troopers crouched by themselves in one end of the big building. "Hey," he shouted, "who are you guys? There were only nine of us when we came in here! Where'd you come from?"

The rest of us were dumbfounded. Had two other troopers scrambled into the building unnoticed during the fire fight? Or had these two men been in the building when we entered?

"Let's see some dog tags!" the trooper yelled.

Without a word the two guys jumped to their feet and dived out one of the large windows into the snow. Several of us fired at them as they vanished into the dark, but we were all so taken by surprise, I'm not at all sure we hit either of them.

To this day, I'll always believe they were infiltrators. But how they ever joined us, I'll never know. There was so much confusion, I guess two of the enemy could have gotten in there, but why they never tried to shoot us before they were discovered, I'll never know.

Things outside had quieted down for awhile and it was decided that we had better try to get out of there before daylight. One by one we left. We climbed out one of the windows, crawled through the foot and a half deep snow to a fence and then crouched low, began to cross a field toward a road leading to the rear.

We were about 15 feet apart and crawling and running in a line. I was last and as I ran, my rifle slid from my shoulder and I tripped and fell heavily to the ground. Machine gun fire ripped over my head and I heard someone groaning ahead of me.

Jim Peters wasn't too happy this day when he was transferred from the 17th to the 82nd in Berlin.

I checked my rifle and discovered I had jammed the muzzle into the dirt and it was completely clogged up. I decided to slip out of my heavy overcoat and web equipment as it was slowing me down. I had a white phosphorus grenade and I thought maybe I could get near the machine gun and throw the grenade.

There was a farmhouse about

100 yards away and I headed for it. German artillery began peppering the field and then some American artillery answered. The field was smothered in fire. I could only hope our guys were able to get out of there. By now, I was completely by myself and I had no idea where the enemy was.

Continuing on toward the house, I was only about 60 yards away when I heard some voices. Listening closely, my heart sunk as I realized they were German voices! Then I saw some guards outside the house and I guessed that this was some kind of Kraut headquarters. It was a place to be avoided and I knew it.

Then, I had a stroke of good fortune. A lone farm horse, foraging in the snow and curious about my presence, approached me. He was real gentle and apparently not spooked by all the artillery fire. Just like in a cowboy movie, I arose behind him, grabbed his halter and walking behind his front legs slowly circled the house.

The trick worked perfectly. Some distance on the other side of the house I came to a fence and a road and I left the horse, slid down to the road and lay in a ditch to catch my breath.

In a few moments I heard a vehicle coming down the road toward me. A German recon car passed and stopped a short way beyond where I lay. I felt for my grenade but it was gone. I had apparently lost it. I had left my rifle back where I shed my overcoat so here I was in a nest of Germans and with only a combat knife left to defend myself.

A German officer got out of the car, barked some orders and a bunch of soldiers came out of the woods, loaded up in a truck and went roaring down the road. I don't think I moved a muscle as I lay in that ditch. I even worked to keep my breathing as quiet as possible.

It was beginning to break dawn as I made my way back the other way on the road. On the way I passed both German and American bodies that seemed to be locked in combat just as they had drawn their last breaths. I had been struggling for my life all night and I was pretty well spent.

Suddenly, I was challenged in English by two dark shadows on the edge of some woods. My throat locked as I had no idea what the password was. The events of the night had literally scared the password from my mind. I was completely blank!

I blurted out, "Oh Lord, don't kill me now—after all I've been through tonight!"

I guess my exhausted condition and my pleading words were good enough. The two 513th troopers that halted me didn't fire and they helped me into the woods and pointed out to me the way back to my unit.

To this good day I still remember what they told me. One of them said, "Best you remember, the password and counter-sign is Baltimore/Oriole."

"THE AFTER-ACTION REPORT"

Editor's Note: *As soon as possible after a combat action, military doctrine requires that the commanders of the units involved prepare an "After-Action Report." This document provides a record of the various actions taken and the results of same. As such, it is also a learning tool. Trends or mistakes of the friendly forces as well as those of the enemy are documented and often provide guidance for future battles.*

What follows are three examples of official "After-Action Reports" for the 193rd Glider Infantry Regiment. The first two detail the action taken by the two battalions in their first combat attack. The third report tells of the action of the 193rd during the period it was attached to the 11th Armored Division for the battle to capture Houffalize.

We are indebted to Gene Herrmann, 193rd HQ 2, for these copies taken from the U.S. archives in Washington, D.C. where they remain as a permanent record of our combat action. They are reproduced here in the style and language in which they were originally written.

193rd Regiment at the Bulge

(This material is from an interview with Colonel Maurice G. Stubbs and his Executive, Lieutenant Colonel David P. Schorr at Mabompre, Belgium on 20 January 1944. As we talked, the Journal was at hand and we constantly referred to it but found that the entries were invariably wrong as to time and the relation of one event to another. The interviews lasted all day. The two battalion commanders were called in and their reports of their separate experiences are included in the report.)

The 193rd did not actually move through 101st for its attack on 7 January (as reported by division commander) although that had been the plan. Battalion 2 moved up to its LD and launched the attack after taking a circuitous route forward, thereby avoiding the confusion which might have come from entry into 327th's sector. There was a 15 minute prep fire by division artillery and by some reinforcements, including 327th's CT artillery. That regiment also supported 193-2's advance on the right with small arms and mortar fire. The 327th also loaned them the support of the TDs from the 705th Battalion. The visibility

A patrol from the 17th Airborne Division, after a 20 mile march, meets men of the VII Corps, 24th Cavalry, near LaRoche – one of the first link-ups of the US First and Third Armies – on 14 January. (US Army photo)

was so bad that at the beginning "troops couldn't see accurately beyond 75 yards." (Stubbs) by 0745, the regiment forward CP was in Mande St. Etienne. Both battalions, 1st on the left and 2nd on the right, attacked with two companies abreast. They moved at 0800, but "B," the left company, came under fire before it had crossed the LD—artillery fire, and apparently from SP guns. "The fog was such that the men moved uncertainly." (Stubbs) (Compare with battalion commander statement.) The artillery barrage held from 0800 to 0815. There was one area N and slightly W of Mande which the enemy had consistently shelled since regiment first took over this ground. "B" was just to the W of this spot of woods (494602) and almost as soon as the American fire lifted, the enemy shells began to find "B" there. There were half a dozen or so casualties but the company moved on forward. At this time the right and center were having no trouble. At 0830 the regiment jumped off.

(The narrative at this point is taken up by the commander of Battalion 1, Lieutenant Colonel Robert L. Ashworth, the regiment commander and his staff being present.)

The battalion was disposed with "C" in the woods at 496-64, and the other companies moving up through Mande St. Etienne with "B" leading and "A" following. They were moving to a jump-off position to the right of the woods, this position being in slight defilade. The LD was the forward edge of the woods holding Company "C." The 81mm mortars were along the N edge of Mande. The HMG platoon was in the forward edge of the woods at 496-64. Both the mortars and the HMGs were in general support for the battalion.

At H plus 10, the 81s put down a WP screen in front on the initial objective. As a "screen" it met nothing; the "burning effect" was what the battalion hoped to get from it. (As to its success, Ashworth says: "We found a number of badly burned Krauts (perhaps 12 or 15) after we got into the woods and they said the WP had fallen directly on the position.") But the artillery fire (Ashworth) was not effective. The forward observers could not see anything; they did not know where their targets were clearly, and they could not observe the fire. (Subsequently the battalion learned from PWs that enemy SP positions had been set up along the Flamierge-Flamizoulle road and along the road running from Flamizoulle down to the main Bastogne highway. (There were also artillery positions in the two woods marked Al Caure and Gaimont on the 1/ 50,000 map. But these locations were unknown at the time and there was no counter-battery fire against them) (From Colonel Stubbs) The men couldn't see the shells hit because of the fog and therefore the psychological effect of their own artillery support was largely lost. (Ashworth) At 0815, the battalion jumped, with "B" on the left, "A" on the right, and "C" in the woods, supporting the advance with rifle and automatic fire. By 0845, both companies were on the No. 1 phase line. "A's" position being the narrow strip of woods (49567) which is about 300 yards forward from the LD and "B's" being the collection of little hills and woods at 49267. From this point the infantry could look SW down "Death Valley" (so named by the men) a deep ravine which the enemy covered with MG fire from the battalion's right flank. It was at this point that the company began to receive its heaviest casualties from automatic fire. "A" moved on and up a gradual rise. So far, it had received almost no enemy fire. It topped the rise and started down the reverse slope. About 75 yards from the crest, there is a line of woods. There had been no observation of this wood; the terrain hadn't been pictured. Therefore it could not have been foreseen as a possible enemy position. (Stubbs and Ashworth) "A" came over the hill in perfect silhouette. As its front element came to within 20-25 yards of the first trees, automatic and rifle fire, backed by mortars, poured out of the woods, and the line was knocked flat. Mortar and artillery shells were now falling all along the front, and "B" taking the worst of the artillery pounding. (Ashworth) Death Valley was so heavily pounded that when the day's action was over, the shell holes over-lapped all along this small ravine. The men of "A" who hadn't fallen from the first fusillade ducked for whatever cover the ridge at their rear afforded them. Some charged into the woods.

About 0930, both companies reported to Ashworth that they could not continue the advance. "A" had lost all but one squad leader; it had two officers left. "B" had three officers left but no squad leaders. Ashworth tried to retrieve his situation with tanks. Six mediums from the 707th Tank Battalion had been assigned for support. But the tank commandeer told Ashworth that the 88 fire was prohibitive and he dare not risk it in the "A" sector. In the "B" sector, at 1000, the tanks moved forward to a position behind "B," there remained in defilade and "didn't fire one damned shot." (Ashworth) At 1000 "B" reported that it was getting fire from friendly troops on its left flank—the 513th Regiment. Ashworth put in a call and at the same time PFC Paul Bogozelski of "B" crossed the fire-swept ground in a 35 yard run to tell the other infantry to lift its fire.

At 1045, the commander of "A," Captain Ralph H. Vohs, called Ashworth and said: "I want help. My losses are so heavy I can't hold my ground." Ashworth first gave him hell for saying in the clearing that he couldn't hold and was taking heavy losses, and then told him to pull back to a defensive position on No. 1 phase line.

At 1450, Stubbs told Ashworth to pull the whole battalion back to the woods position of "C." Stubbs: "It was obvious to me by that time that Flamizoulle could not be taken and the attack had failed."

At 1230, one plat of "C" under Lieutenant Franklin R. Morris moved up to protect "B's" left flank, which was receiving heavy fire. At 1115, another plat of "C," commanded by Lieutenant Walter B. Black, had made the attempt on Ashworth's order to reinforce "B," but couldn't get across Death Valley and had to fall back. By 1500, battalion was in a defensive position with "A" and "C" manning it, and "B" in reserve in the town.

In making the attack, the men had gone forward "boldly and aggressively" in fact "too damned fast" in that "in running so fast through the fog, they couldn't make use of fire and movement and they put no check on the enemy." (Ashworth) They left a covering force when they withdrew (the BARs and LMGs) and they came back by infiltration to the rear. "C," being in position, was able to cover them with fire to some extent. The attack had not been a wholly fruitless. Despite the withering effect of the first heavy fire against "A" from the surprise position the men who had gone on into the woods overran and captured the enemy position therein. With the Americans right on top of them, the Germans quit. Machine gunners who continued their fire until our troops were within 40 or so yards, crawled down into their holes and waited to be killed or taken prisoner. It was the common experience of "A" men on that day that the Germans showed no fight, once they had closed with them. (Ashworth) However, the capture of these woods positions was without important tactical effect as it was then put under intense shelling and "A" could not hold there.

Back at the CP, Ashworth had lost his HQ commander, Captain Benjamin F. Miller Jr., the battalion commander officer, Lieutenant William F. Leax and the artillery liaison officer, Captain White, in the first 15 minutes of the attack from artillery and mortar fire. Looking his troops over later in the day, Ashworth found that as a result of their losses and repulse this first time in battle they were "dazed and shocked, as if they didn't know what it was all about" but in talking with them, he found that they thought "the superiority of the enemy artillery and mortar fire and the foggy weather" had been responsible for most of their trouble. Stubbs himself traced it to another cause, saying "lack of previous reconnaissance was what did it. I had reported my belief that this was the strongest part of the enemy defensive sector and had been assured that there was no one in front of me." (This view had been passed down by Army to Corps to Division.) Stubbs had refused to pass it on to his men. He had told Ashworth to tell the men that they were for a "damned tough fight" and this was what was told them. (Ashworth) The battalion commander was so worried about the enemy strength that "it seemed doubtful whether the battalion would be able to get up to the LD."

During the morning, Battalion 1 drew artillery fire (principally 88) from both flanks, some of it coming apparently from Flammierge. The source of much of the enemy artillery fire seemed to be beyond 17th Division's flanks in both directions. (Stubbs)

How many men were lost by "A" in the fight around the woods is not fully known. but after the enemy had been cleared away in the withdrawal from the Bulge, "A" came back to this copse and looked it over. In it still were the bodies of 15 "A" men who up till then had been carried MIA.

2nd Battalion 193rd Infantry North of Mande St. Etienne

(The date of this interview was 20 January 1945. While most of the material was provided by Lieutenant Colonel Harry Balish, the battalion commander, the interviewing was done with the aid of the regimental and battalion records. As the work progressed, we found that the records were almost invariably in error especially when it came to the statement of time. These errors usually occurred because the record did not distinguish between the time when an action took place and the time when a message was received. The regimental commander and his S-2 and S-3 and executive and the other battalion commanders were also present during the Balish interview and were able to modify Balish's statements where necessary.)

The 2nd Battalion moved out through the little shrine at Fond de Laval which is a little to the north of Mande. Dog Company was on the left with the mission of attacking the woods at 503613. Easy Company was on the right and was to attack the woods at 508615. This whole terrain was blanketed under six or eight inches of snow on the level and the drifts were anywhere up to five feet in depth. In this whitened area the only cover which provided any security were the forest plantations. Any foxholes, trenches, or gun positions dug elsewhere were made wholly conspicuous by the snow, therefore, both sides turned to make the most use of wood patches and defensive areas wherever the terrain was favorable to such use. On this day and at the beginning of the action Fox Company was in reserve; there was a section of heavy machine guns in support of each company and the 81mm mortars were put on a reserve slope at 505598. The weather, according to Colonel Balish was "foggy." (The historical officer witnessed this attack. Foggy is an understatement of the case. The visibility was irregular and on the lower terrain one could not seem more than 25 or 50 yards ahead. Yet between ridges and areas of higher ground it was sometimes possible to see troops moving at distances of 20 to 300 yards.)

Fifteen minutes prior to the jump-off of Dog Company the 81 mortars fired for 15 minutes into the woods ahead of the company. How many rounds exactly were fired was not made of record but it is supposed to be somewhere between 40 or 50. Company "E" jumped off 10 minutes later, "D" having already gone on its way. The latter company got to within 200 yards of the woods and at that point came under artillery and mortar fire. This fire had not been ranging over the area up until that moment, but the first rounds coincided with the forward movements of the company and a few men fell from the fire. these causalities, however, did not make the other men go to ground. There was no cover immediately available. As the mortar and artillery shells continued to fall machine gun fire also came at the company but all of this was intermittent fire as if the enemy knew the approximate location of the target but could not see the effect of the fire. The evening prior to the company's advance and during the night the enemy had put some fire on a crossroads in this vicinity and the ground through which Company "E" passed was adjacent to this crossroads. However it was noted by the battalion commander that the first rounds coincided with the arrival of his men on this ground as if, despite the bad visibility, the enemy was somehow getting observation of the American force. (Large numbers of Germans dressed in American uniforms were apprehended along this front and it is a view held by many of the officers that the Germans were managing to get observation from within our lines. This view was expressed by G-3 and the battalion commander.) Captain Charles E. Juckes of Company "E" called Balish and said, "We are getting heavy fire. My right platoon is practically wiped out." (He had lost up to this time between 20 and 30 men.) He told Balish that he wanted help. Balish said, "What is your location?" but Juckes could not tell him exactly. All Juckes knew was that his men had pushed on into the edge of the wood and they were now under the trees. The radio was coming in very badly, Balish could hear the shells falling among the company and it seemed to him that one effect of the fire was that Juckes was speaking disconnectedly and could not give him a clear account of himself.

Because of these conditions Balish decided to put Company "F" in to help. He thought he would move Company "F" up to "E's" position and then bring Company "E' back into the support position. But "F" was on the left flank in support which put it behind Company "D" and confronting the woods which Company "D" was supposed to attack. He therefore decided that he would start Company "F" up to the woods where Company "D" was and from that point would have it swing right to relieve Company "E." The support company went on as ordered and then gained the woods. Balish got a message back from Lieutenant Joseph Smith of Company "F" at that point and then he learned for the first time that Company "E" had drifted left and all three of his companies were in the same woods. This drift was the consequence of fire in part and of some of the men of the company getting lost in the fog in part.

Juckes was ordered to stay where he was and let Company "F" go through him. Balish decided that instead of following his original plan he would forget about Company "E's" original objective and would try to send "F" and "D" Companies on to the far end of the woods where his whole battalion was lodged. It was well past noon by the time these decisions were reached. The battalion commander thinks that the hour was about 1300, when the advance began again. The fight through the woods was comparatively soft going. The Germans had held their ground while the battalion was coming through the open but as soon as it closed on their positions they showed that they wanted to quit. They would fire only a few rounds and they hold their fire as the companies closed to within 50 or 75 yards of them. Once it appeared certain to them they would be overwhelmed their main desire was to surrender.

Upon reaching the north end of the woods the two companies came under fire from a tank in the woods at 502617. This tank could be seen amid the trees at the front of the woods and was supported only by one machine gun. The men could see no enemy infantry around it but the machine gun fire and the range (the field between was perfectly barren) were such that the companies could not get their bazookas up close enough to fire. They put in a call for artillery and the area was shelled but our artillery could not find the tank. In the meantime the tank's 88 HE shells were taking heavy toll among the two companies and no counter within the battalion's means seemed to have any effect upon the enemy armor.

At 1430 Balish got up with the two companies. His arrival coincided with the terrific artillery and mortar shelling which seemed to be coming from the north around GIVRY and was so accurate that Balish was convinced the artillery was being directed by the tank. The visibility was better now and the men of the battalion could see the tank clearly but they could do nothing about it and as the field between the tank and the infantry was absolutely clear there seemed, to Balish, no way in which he could get his battalion forward. By 1600 he decided he was losing too many men. Not only was he unable to go forward but staying where he was had become very costly. He returned to his forward CP at 504605 and reported his situation to regiment. Colonel Stubbs told him that the 1st Battalion was giving over the Flamizoulle attack. Stubbs added that Balish should stay where he was until he got further orders. At 1630 he was told to fall back. In the meantime 101st Division had reported to Stubbs that two companies of enemy were moving down the road from Givry toward the wood which Balish was attacking. At just about the time the withdrawal was ordered large numbers of enemy began to debouch from the woods at 502618 to the north of the battalion. They were stopped for a short time only by our artillery fire. Then they came on around the right flank infiltrating through the woods with automatic weapons over ground where our rifle fire could no longer get at them. In the withdrawal, Company "E", which was in reserve, went out first;

Company "D," which was on the left and away from the flank which was infiltrated, went out next; and Company "F," on the right, set up to fight a rear guard action with Lieutenant Smith volunteering for this job. The enemy artillery and machine gun fire had continued and Smith lost five men while engaging in this covering action. He finally came out of the woods about 200 yards behind Company "D." But on the way out he ran into Lieutenant Arne C. Christiansen leading a small detachment of Company "E" men who hadn't been able to clear out of the woods with the body of the Company because of intervening enemy machine gun fire. This detachment of Company "E" men then covered Company "F's" withdrawal. Smith had lost his radio operator during the actions and he had strapped the radio on his own back and had maintained communications personally. Smith wanted to withdraw directly southward but Balish told him to pull out in a southeasterly direction. He had no particular reason for making this decision but it probably saved a large part of the company, for a German party was holding the northern end of the southwestern patch of woods. It was the belief of the battalion that this party had infiltrated into those woods in the late hours of the battalion action though it is a possibility that the party had been there all the time and had kept quiet when the Americans went forward. There were two automatic guns in this group and when Smith's company began their move southward from the woods they opened fire to the eastward directly across his rear. Private Rudolph Bailey of the communications section and a private from the AT Platoon (this man had not been identified by the battalion though a search is continuing to establish his identity) worked up to a position in rear of these woods and with a bazooka at extreme range knocked out one gun and forced a withdrawal of the remainder of the enemy party. (This was Bailey's second feat of the afternoon. The field where he and the AT man worked against the Germans had been under fire just a few minutes prior to withdrawal of the battalion. It is possible that this automatic fire came from the same German party in the lower woods. An American rifleman who had been coming back from the upper woods was hit and badly wounded as he crossed the field. One of his companions came on back and reported that he was lying in the field fully exposed to enemy view. Private Bailey, Sergeant Charles P. Jacobs Jr. of Regimental Headquarters Company and Private William M. Hall, another communications man, put their weapons down, ran forward into the field and pulled the wounded man out under fire.)

It was about 1645 when Christiansen, the last man, came out of the woods with his few men carrying the last of the American wounded back. In the meantime Balish had sent back for supply jeeps. The men made up improvised stretchers from blankets or rifles and branches of trees and carried the wounded up to the jeeps. Balish took the most fatigued of his men and put them on the jeeps to hold the wounded aboard. The battalion collected at its forward CP around dark. Balish formed an advance in rear guard and moved the battalion back to their defensive positions in the vicinity of 5059 where the battalion occupied high ground. Balish says of his men: "They were not only tired but they were well beaten down and many of them appeared to be dazed."

There are these further notes on the action from the command points of view. The fire of ten battalions had been put on the German-held woods that morning. This included direct support of the 2nd Battalion by the weapons which were normally in support of 327th Infantry of 101st Division, that is to say not only its artillery but its small arms and mortar and its TD support. Nevertheless the enemy artillery fire upon our positions was intense even back at the CP in Mande. According to Colonel Stubbs it was later ascertained from PWs that somewhere between 250 and 400 fresh enemy troops had come into the area along his front the night before. These were troops of the 104th Panzer Regiment and 108th Panzer Regiment. The enemy artillery positions along the flanking roads had also been strengthened that night Stubbs later discovered.

Advance to Houffalize

(Colonel Stubbs, his staff and the two battalion commanders were all present when this narrative was organized on 20 Janaury 1945. What was said was checked against the records at that time.)

At 1200 on 13 January, Major Green, assistant division G-2, notified Stubbs at Frenet that 193rd was to be attached to 11th Armored for the advance to the river and that if he, Stubbs, would get back to Mande Commodore 6 (Miley) would give him more particulars. First Battalion was then in the woods at 489627 and 2nd Battalion was in the woods at 506615. Stubbs went back to Mande and Schorr called the battalion commanders and told them to meet Stubbs there. Schorr then went back to 1st Battalion at about 1230 and a few minutes later Commodore 6-6 (Whitelaw) came by in a jeep. He told Schorr to send an officer to the road junction southwest of Bertogne (519667) and move the regiment to that point as quickly as possible. Schorr asked, "Is Colonel Stubbs likely to get any conflicting instructions?" Whitelaw replied, "No, go ahead." Schorr sent a platoon to the RJ and then instructed the executive of 1st Battalion to move out at once along the route Frenet-Givry-Gives and the RJ. Second Battalion was to go over a route which it had previously reconnoitered due north to Givry and follow in the rear of the headquarters group which was trailing 1st Battalion. Stubbs returned as this movement started and as his instructions were the same as Schorr had received he went on up to the RJ. The head of the column got there at 1415 and was directed into an assembly area in the woods at 523652. The regiment closed by 1600. At that time General Holbrook, who was present, said that transportation for one battalion in two and a half ton trucks would be coming up immediately and the battalion would go to a defensive position at 558653 where the 41st Cavalry Reconnaissance Squadron was already waiting. At 1645 ten trucks came in and Ashworth went forward with three of his rifle companies. At 1800 seven more trucks came in and the remainder of the battalion followed. They drew artillery fire all the way along as they moved up the road. At 1630 Stubbs went into Longchamps and reported to Holbrook at CCA Headquarters. He was told that he was being placed in command of Task Force Stubbs which would consist of 41st Cavalry Reconnaissance Squadron, 55th Armored Infantry Battalion, 492nd Field Artillery Battalion, one platoon of "C" Company, 56th Engineer Battalion, "C" Company of the 811 TD Battalion, Medium Company of 42nd Tank Battalion, Medical Company of the 22nd Tank Battalion, and 1st Battalion of 193rd Infantry.

Second Battalion of 193rd was to report to Task Force Bell commanded by Colonel Virgil Bell of CC Reserve. The battalion under Colonel Balish remained in the woods that night. Balish reported to Bell and was told to be prepared to attack the next morning at 1000, his mission being to attack and hold the Pied Du Mont woods.

There was a 15 minute preparatory artillery fire (the amount not known to the battalion commander) prior to the jump-off by the battalion at 1000 next day. The infantry followed behind ten tanks of the 42nd Tank Battalion lead by Lieutenant Colonel Joseph Aeheb. They took the east edge of the woods with Company "D" on left and Company "E" on right and Company "F" protecting the north flank. Then the whole battalion came under heavy mortar fire and the movement came in check. In the meantime the tanks had moved around to the east edge of the woods and had attracted the fire of some enemy 88s. However, these shells all went over the tanks and dropped into the woods along with the mortar fire. Balish lost 25 men. At 1300 the tanks and the armored infantry attacked the town of Compogne and had it by 1600. At 1700 Balish was ordered to move his battalion into a defensive position along high ground and to stride the road just east of Rastadt and Compogne. The following morning Bell went on to Houffalize. The battalion moved by truck to a point one mile east of Mabompre, detrucked there and marched to high ground at 6171 in the road bend. They continued to hold there as 1st Battalion of 193rd moved toward them.

At 1130 on 15 January Ashworth was directed to send a strong patrol through the woods to the northeast. (These are the woods which on the map are around the word Frazone.) The woods to the east of Compogne had been given as the objective of Force Stubbs. The mission of this first patrol was to move through the south end of the woods and determine whether the strength of the enemy therein was such that it would be feasible to attack through the woods toward the objective. Forty-five minutes later Ashworth was told to follow the patrol with his entire battalion. The patrol had gone half way into the woods and had met no resistance. This was taken as a sign that the enemy had probably vacated the woods. The 55th Armored Infantry was to move across in rear of the battalion through the woods Les Assins and support Ashworth's attack on the objective by fire from the lower woods. Provided the objective of the 193rd element was gained easily enough that evening the 55th was then to attack northeast toward the woods southwest of Wycort.

First Battalion moved out immediately but its progress was quite slow.

Unexpectedly there was a great deal of enemy small arms resistance from within the woods and though the enemy were few in number, they were in strong dug-in positions at the edges of the woods. The lower part of this forest was a plantation and the trees were perfectly checked in evenly spaced rows with fire breaks about every 12 or 15 rows of trees. Ashworth, not anticipating that he would meet much resistance in the woods, still approached it in the normally alerted position with his two companies spread out abreast as skirmishers and one company following in support. Even so the battalion line could not reach from end to end of the wood nor did it stretch to envelop the last few trees on either flank. This is what caused his difficulty for the remaining enemy had apparently anticipated just such a deployment and their fire positions were scattered through the trees beyond his flanks on both sides. They had sited their machine guns so that they could fire down the fire breaks and all the casualties which the battalion sustained on this occasion came from machine gun fire which hit them from the two flanks. After about half a dozen men were hit, it became clear to Ashworth that the line could not go forward in a sweep. In fact the men had already reacted instinctively to the fire and the line was breaking up as some of the men took cover. From that time on the battalion inched its way forward one man at a time going from cover to cover wherever it could be found. The whole movement therefore became painfully slow and Ashworth found it almost impossible to exercise any control. Further the radio communication between Ashworth and Lieutenant Colonel Hearn of 55th was almost totally lacking throughout the afternoon so that the two battalions were of little support to each other. Ashworth was further handicapped in that he had no forward observer.

Moving in this irregular fashion, the battalion reached the trail which runs from 566672 to 568668 just before dark and Ashworth that was as far as he could safely go that night. The woods engagement had been quite unsatisfactory; the battalion had done little hurt to the enemy which was playing a hit and run game. There was vigorous patrolling that night, Ashworth staggering his patrol so that he would keep abreast of his enemy situation through the hours of darkness. Lieutenant Edward E.A. Gillam of Company "B" captured eleven prisoners in the woods while taking a five-man patrol out at 1930. This patrol had been instructed to go all the way to the objective and probe it. But it did much better than that. Gillam went to the objective and then moved behind the woods where he made contact with 2nd Battalion. He notified Ashworth by radio that he would stay there until morning and he added that he had found the objective unoccupied. During the night Force Stubbs was ordered to complete the capture of the objective and then patrol northeast to secure crossing of the stream to the eastward, the Rah De Van. Stubbs told the engineers and the tanks to prepare to look the stream over for routes of possible crossing by tanks. At 0400 another patrol, consisting of three men under Lieutenant Jackson C. Roach went to the objective and reported to Ashworth that it was free of enemy.

At 0130 another patrol under Lieutenant Alex L. Atkinson of Company "C" with three men scouted the north half of the woods which the battalion was occupying and reported it clear. At 0755 Gillam took his five men back into the objective woods, captured the objective and fired 15 rifle shots. He had told Ashworth by radio that 15 shots would be the signal that the woods were clear; Ashworth felt that 15 shots was quite a waste of ammunition. At 0800 the objective was seized. Patrols were then put out to the river crossings and the regimental CP moved to Compogne at 1200. At 0745 Stubbs had reported to Holbrook and was told that after making certain of the crossings he was to stand ready for new missions to the east. All infantry troops were told to prepare their present positions for an offense. The TDs also were to assume defensive positions. At about 1200 orders were received for Force Stubbs less the 55th Infantry to proceed on the south side of the Houffalize-Bertogne road to seize the south half of the objective which was the high ground between the 68 and 71 grid lines south of Houffalize. From its position parallel to the main road 1st Battalion of 193rd moved in a northeast direction into the woods at Haut Sart and then went northeast towards Bois Merocay. Elements of 101st Division were observed at this time near Wycourt and to the south of this town and reports from Force Bell indicated that Mabompre had been taken and the infantry of that force was moving southeast to Abois Merocay. Second Battalion of 193rd reached a point 200 yards south of the road bend at 395690 and were there halted in the woods pending further instructions. This happened at 1330. Soon thereafter Stubbs was told that Forces Stubbs and Bell would be abolished within a few hours and the regiment would be together again (this order became effective at 2400). Second Battalion was moving to defensive lines on the objective from the southern edge of Houffalize to the bend in the road at 611777. First Battalion was to occupy the line from 2nd Battalion to and including Cowan. Here they would again come under command of 193rd Infantry. These movements were concluded without incident and the Regimental CP was established at Mabompre. Second Battalion closed by 2000 but 1st Battalion had to fight its way into the position on high ground west of Cowan and could not close until 0200 the next morning. The engineer platoon with force Stubbs had been directed to put up a road block at Cowan but could not do it because of enemy resistance. The tank battalion and the TDs moved in to support and the whole position was prepared for defense. On 18 January the division relief was accomplished and the whole regiment moved into a reserve position.

PART III

OPERATION VARSITY: OVER THE RHINE

"OPERATION VARSITY: A TIME FOR HISTORY"

by Bart Hagerman, 193 D

Editor's Note: This article first appeared in the February 1989 issue of Museum News, the monthly newsletter of the Silent Wings Museum Foundation in Terrell, Texas. Established by former glider pilots of World War II, the museum houses the most complete display of glider warfare equipment in the world.

"Operation Varsity" was the code name for the Airborne assault on March 24, 1945, over the Rhine River into Germany. It was made by the American 17th Airborne Division and the British 6th Airborne Division and it marked the beginning of the end for the German war machine.

The operation was a historic event for many reasons. It set many "firsts" and helped to shape tactics and standards for this country's Airborne operations of the future.

For one thing, it was the last combat glider assault ever made by the United States or any other country. Although the 11th Airborne Division landed seven gliders on an airstrip on Luzon on June 23, 1945, that landing was unopposed.

"Varsity" was the first glider assault into the homeland of an enemy force. It was also the largest air armada ever assembled for a single D-Day landing. Although during "Market Garden," the Airborne assault into Holland, more troops were committed, they were inserted over a period of several days.

There were 226 C-47s and 72 C-46s for the paratrooper elements and 906 gliders towed by 610 C-47s lifting the 17th Airborne. An additional 420 gliders, 42 C-54s and 752 C-47s formed the British lift.

The C-47 tug planes towed two CG-4A gliders each; another "first" for combat action. The double tows proved successful even with three incidents where the short tow fouled the long tow's line, shearing a wing and causing the gliders to crash.

In the marshalling area, the chaplain held prayer for the troopers before they departed for the airfield.

The first U.S. serial delivered 589 Wacos to the battle area despite the three towline mishaps. The second serial flew in 313 Wacos. Only one glider in this serial was forced to drop out—another record for successful flight completion for any nation.

Incidentally, this last serial, due to the stack-up of traffic over the LZ,

In the tent city marshalling area before Operation Varsity. L to R: Cpl. Floyd Pickering, S/Sgt. Miles S. Darnell, T/Sgt. William Jones and T/5 Sam Jonna.

was forced to climb to 2,500 feet to release their gliders. This resulted in another "first" as the record high combat release.

"Varsity" was also the first Airborne operation where glidertroops were landed on fields not previously secured by paratroops. The glidertroops were landed directly on their objectives and many found themselves facing point-blank into German artillery pieces. Frequently artillery and engineer units, along with their glider pilots, had to fight as infantry in a desperate battle to secure the LZ.

For the U.S. paratroopers it was their first time to jump a double-door

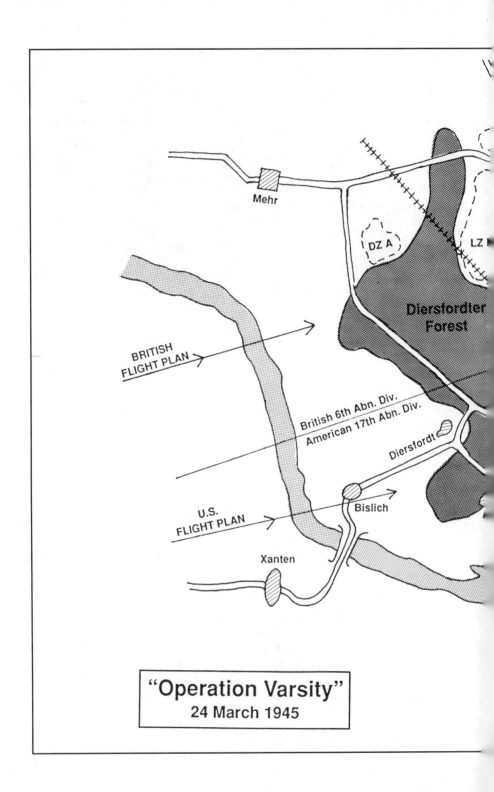

Mehr

DZ A

LZ

Diersfordter
Forest

BRITISH
FLIGHT PLAN

British 6th Abn. Div.
American 17th Abn. Div.

Diersfordt

U.S.
FLIGHT PLAN

Bislich

Xanten

"Operation Varsity"
24 March 1945

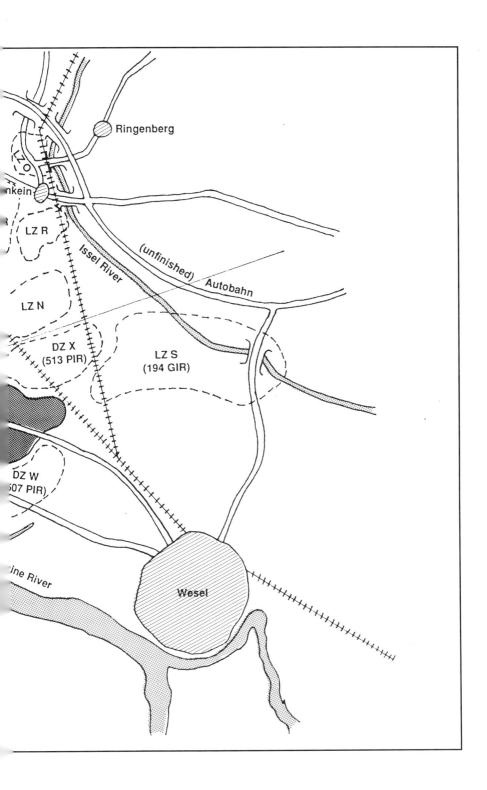

Ringenberg

LZ O

nkein

LZ R

Issel River

(unfinished) Autobahn

LZ N

DZ X
(513 PIR)

LZ S
(194 GIR)

DZ W
(507 PIR)

ine River

Wesel

aircraft in combat. The new C-46s, used here for the first time, carried about twice the number of paratroopers as did the C-47s. With two doors, the troopers could exit faster over the DZs and consequently, dispersion was not as great a problem as it was jumping C-47s.

Unfortunately, the C-46s had not been equipped with self-sealing fuel tanks. The thick German flak send many of the C-46s flaming down resulting in a heavy loss of troopers and air crews.

Another "first" was missed because of a last-minute decision. Twenty of

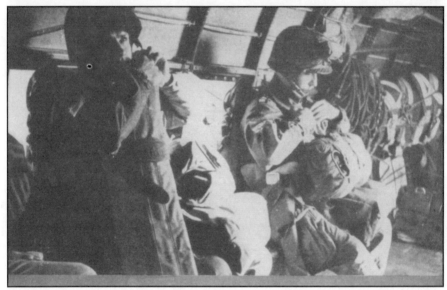

Fifteen minutes from the drop zone. It is a time for thought and a last minute check of equipment.

Troopers fill the air over the drop zone. "Operation Varsity" has begun.

C-47s and their CG-4A glider tows await the signal to take off for "Operation Varsity."

the new CG-13s (a glider capable of carrying twice the payload of the CG-4A) were ferried from England to France with the intention of using them during "Varsity." But, because it would have caused a major reworking of the flight schedule, it was decided not to use them.

Army planners probably were holding back a little on aircraft and pilots because unknown to most, another Airborne operation was taking shape. "Operation Choker," a drop at Worms some 160 miles south of "Varsity" at Wesel, was being planned for March 29, to support the U.S. 7th Army crossing of the Rhine. Due to the success of "Varsity" that mission was scrubbed.

German troops were warned as early as March 10, to expect an Airborne attack and their well-prepared positions showed they were ready. Our air reconnaissance revealed no "Rommel asparagus," but the LZs were criss-crossed with drainage ditches and wire fences.

Most of the four DZs and the six LZs were fields and meadows of 200 to 300 yards in length. The entire area was only about five miles wide by six miles long, making it the most congested airhead ever established by the Allies.

Nevertheless, most of the units were landed on or near their assigned DZs and LZs. The farthest off was the 1st Battalion of the 507th Parachute Infantry. The troopers were dropped nearly two miles away, but recovered quickly and within four hours had secured all their assigned objectives.

After landing at about 1000 hours, the 194th Glider Infantry Regiment was 73% assembled by noon and had all their objectives secured shortly thereafter. The 513th Parachute Infantry Regiment likewise quickly took all their objectives.

By the morning of the 25th, the 17th Airborne and the British 6th Airborne

This trailer is unloaded after its CG-4A glider has landed safely. Now if we only had a jeep!

were ready to pursue the enemy on into Germany. It was a drive that was to end in the defeat of Germany and ultimately, the end of World War II.

"Operation Varsity," despite the many successes and records set, was not without its cost in lives and equipment. By the end of D-Day, March 24th, the 17th Airborne alone had lost 393 KIA, 834 WIA and 165 MIA. British Airborne losses were equally heavy.

U.S. equipment losses included 22 jump aircraft, all C-46s, and 12 glider tow planes, all C-47s. Only 148 of the CG-4As were salvageable. Those that were not shot down or wrecked on landing, were vandalized by civilians for their clocks, compasses or other parts.

During the war the Waco Company, or their contracting firms, built 14,612 CG-4As at a cost to the government of about $20,000 each. After the war the government sold hundreds of them at surplus for $75 each, crated. Lumber was scarce in post-war America and it was the crating material that was needed. The gliders were discarded.

It seems like a sad end for these brave little crafts to be sold off for scrap lumber. Although they lacked something in the way of safety, they were a real bargain when compared to the price of troop helicopters today.

Safe or not, it is doubtful that World War II would have had such a successful conclusion had it not been for the CG-4A and the "go-for-broke," daring young men who flew them and rode in them.

"THE PART-TIME GLIDER DRIVERS"

As told by Bob Baldinger, 194 A

At one time or another, every glidertrooper probably wondered why the C-47s had a pilot and co-pilot, yet the CG-4A gliders only had one pilot. On occasions, a senior non-com would be permitted to set in the co-pilot seat, but he kept his hands off the steering mechanism and was strictly a passenger only.

None of us at that time recognized how short the supply was of glider pilots. They didn't have enough pilots to put two into every glider. So, if a glider pilot had a heart attack or some other serious problem at the time he was flying, likely the whole load would have gone down.

Recognizing this problem and knowing the increased chance of that happening in combat, the military finally took some action. Prior to "Operation Varsity," it was determined that some of the 17th Air-

Bob Baldinger, the glidertrooper who was hoping he didn't have to land the glider! Photo made May 25, 1945, in Hamborn, Germany.

borne senior non-coms would be given basic instruction in flying the CG-4A in the event they had to fill in due to the shortage of qualified pilots.

Thus it was that one of these senior non-coms, Tech Sergeant Bob Baldinger of 194A (formerly of 193B) was ordered to report one day to the airfield near Chalons for glider flight training. Bob and about a dozen other non-coms from the division reported but they weren't all that happy about the duty they had drawn.

It was only about two weeks before "Operation Varsity" and everyone knew something big was up. When they found out their assignment, a moan went up from the men. But, being good soldiers as they were, they quickly got down to business and set their minds to learn the best they could, how to bring one of the flimsy crafts to the ground.

The non-coms were given three days of instruction. This included ground training in wooden mockups of the CG-4A where they learned from the pilots how to coordinate the steering wheel with the foot pedals.

Then they went up for a flight. The first time they only observed the actions of the pilot and did not touch the controls. On the second time up, they laid their hands on the wheel and put their feet on the pedals, but only to feel the action of their pilot instructor.

The third time was crunch time! While in tow, Bob said he was told to take the controls and hold it steady. It bucked and weaved and Bob swallowed hard as he fought to keep it level.

Then it was cutaway time! The relative ease at which the glider then flew buoyed Bob's confidence until he began to realize he was coming down fast!

Before he knew it, there was the ground rushing up to meet him! At about 80 mph Bob slammed into the airport runway and the whole glider shuttered and rattled. Bob's teeth jarred as he bounced and slammed down again. It was

CG-4A gliders dot the LZ in the Wesel area. These brought in the 194th.

Containers for two equipment chutes lie next to this CG-4A glider east of the Rhine. The open nose of the glider suggests it brought in a jeep or trailer rather than personnel.

This glider crashed, but the troopers try to free the jeep inside which seems to be undamaged.

a rough landing, but he had actually landed the thing and it was still in one piece.

The training behind him, Bob then began to "sweat out" the Airborne operation itself. He not only had his own neck and that of his men to worry about, now he had to worry about if he had to land that glider under combat conditions.

On the big day, March 24, 1945, Bob was plenty "up tight" about how he would fare. Finally, he decided to put it all behind him and concentrate on his duty as platoon sergeant and trust in the good Lord to guide their pilot safely to the ground.

Apparently, that was a good decision as everything went smoothly that hectic day. The pilot had no heart attack and was not wounded during the flight and Bob was not called upon to demonstrate his flying skills. That's a fact, Bob says, that was also greatly appreciated by the men in his glider load.

"From the time we took off until the time the glider came to a stop, I prayed for that glider pilot's good health," Bob said. "With that much going for him, how could he have had anything happen to him?"

There must have been prayers going up from the other gliders that had the "part-time glider drivers" because as far as Bob knows, none of the other non-coms had to take over the controls. All made it to the DZs safely.

For his experience, Bob received a small pair of glider wings. There was, however, no documentation made in his personnel file and Bob assures all that he is not to be considered a competent glider pilot!

"A SLIGHT CASE OF SPAGHETTI"

As told by Harry Boyle, Div Recon

Sometimes combat can really be good for you. Now before you go to thinking that I've flipped out, let me tell you a story and how combat healed all my problems.

I had been in "D" Battery of the 466th Parachute Field Artillery Battalion while we were in England. When we went into the Bulge, our battery was detached and assigned to Division Headquarters to take missions of scouting and patrolling. Henceforth, we were designated as Division Recon Company.

After the Bulge, Division Recon was cut in size and about half of us went to various batteries in the 466th Parachute Field Artillery. Here we trained getting ready for the Wesel jump.

I was assigned to Headquarters Battery and being "the new guy," I did everything asked of me as I was anxious to make new friends and

Harry Boyle (L) and Ernesto Clemente caught a snake at Camp Blanding while the 464th Prcht. F.A. Bn. was on bivouac.

"be accepted." It was a good outfit and I was happy with things.

One day the cooks did us a good favor and cooked up a batch of spaghetti which I loved. The only thing wrong was they must have dumped in a bushel of pepper because that spaghetti was as hot as fire! But, liking spaghetti as I do, I plowed in and ate my fill.

The next day it caught up with me. I came down with the worse case of piles anyone ever had. I couldn't do anything. For days I couldn't sit down, I couldn't lie down and I couldn't walk. I was in a hell'uva shape.

About this time the rumors began flying about an Airborne operation somewhere and the tension began building. The whole thing was beyond me. All I could do was guzzle mineral oil and go on sick call.

Things began to heat up more until at last we found out that we were going over the Rhine and soon! I had a

Riding the 40 and 8s to Chalons-sur-Marne after being relieved in the Bulge.

terrible decision to make: I wanted to go, but in this shape I couldn't function and I would be a liability to my comrades.

This was the "big show" that we had all been training for and I certainly didn't want anyone to think I was trying to "chicken-out" and stay behind. I made up my mind that I was going regardless of how I felt and I limped and drug myself around the best I could.

That morning before we enplaned, they fed us a big breakfast of steak and eggs. I love steak too, so I stowed it away. Once on the plane and we had gotten underway, I could feel the adrenaline flowing and I guess I forgot about my sore tail.

The flight was long and bumpy. Some trooper across from me became airsick and lost his steak and eggs. Normally, that would trigger me to do likewise, but I gritted my teeth and made up my mind I had enough problems and I just wouldn't get sick. And, I didn't.

Flying along we looked down at the pock-marked countryside. We could see hundreds of shell holes but they were all greened over with grass. Someone said they were left over from World War I. Somebody else spoke up and said that they were from when the Germans came through here back in 1940.

Soon the Rhine came into view. We stood up and hooked up and got ready to go. I could hear flack and bullets hitting the aircraft and I wanted to get out. I knew the other guys did too. We pushed tight toward the open door.

Finally, the green light blinked on and away we went! The jumpmaster went number one this time and although I was about number 14 in the stick, I was out in less then 10 seconds at the most. That ground fire was a real incentive to hurry!

We had jumped real low. I later heard it was 500 feet. When my chute opened I then saw someone up there walking on my canopy. I was afraid he would spill my air out and I'd go rocketing down. And, there's also the chance he could land on top of me. Either alternative could ruin your day.

I slipped as hard as I could and finally the other trooper managed to slide off. Then, I realized that tracers from a machine gun were coming up all around me. Some Kraut was trying to zero in on me and in the air I was totally helpless.

I feigned being hit and went limp in my harness. I hoped he would think he hit me and direct his fire elsewhere. Apparently, my trick worked as I landed uninjured in the open field that was our drop zone.

Small arms and automatic fire laced over my head as I slipped out of my chute. Then I crawled to a drainage ditch about 60 feet away. For the moment I was safe.

I looked around for a target with my carbine at the ready. I saw someone and was just drawing a bead on him when he moved and I managed to see the chartreuse scarf he had on. It was a recognition precaution the 466th had decided to wear and probably saved that unknown trooper's life that day.

An officer then told me to go out in that open field and retrieve some field phones. The field was under fire and it was a touchy job. I dropped my equipment and ran, zig-zagging out there and back. I really flew and I could hear bullets snapping by my ears and kicking up dirt at my feet. I made the round trip without injury and I must add, in record time.

We were pretty busy the rest of the day and all that night getting set up, so I didn't have much time to mull over the day's activities. The next day, however, it suddenly dawned on me that I was having no pain from the bad case of piles that had troubled me so much.

I couldn't recall when I had been "cured." Was it the flight and the flak hitting us? Was it the guy on my canopy? Was it the fire I got on the way down? One thing is for certain: when I did that dash out in the field and back with those phones, I had already been cured! No one could have run that fast with what I had had when we left France!

Somehow, someway, combat cured me. That's why I say combat can be good for you. I don't, however, recommend combat as a cure-all for what ails you!

"TROUBLE OVER THE RHINE"

As told by Tom Funk, 513 B

I will never forget March 24, 1945, the day we jumped into Germany. I was a 19 year old man, I thought, but I sure aged rapidly that day. After we jumped over the Rhine and the next few days, I became a lot older in a short period of time.

It was pretty tough coming in as a replacement. It seemed like everyone knew each other but no one knew me or cared to. The 513th had just been relieved from combat in the Bulge and the guys seemed, to some extent, to be in shock after the violent combat they had seen.

I was assigned to Company "B," 1st Battalion, and I worked hard during those short days we trained before we were alerted. It didn't take long to make some good buddies once they found out I was willing and able to "carry my share of the load."

It wasn't long before the big day came. We were going in. I was nervous as I could be, but I worked hard at making sure none of my comrades could tell it. They did too, and many years later I was to learn that they were all putting on the same act. It really wasn't a bad thing either as we all took strength from each other.

We seemed to be a pretty "mean" bunch as we sat all jammed up in our plane and winged our way through the smoke en route to our drop zone. I remember one guy named Fox who was our platoon medic. He was leading us in singing. We sang "Over There! The Yanks are coming over there!" We also sang some Airborne songs and never seemed to realize the fact that it was all designed to keep our spirits up. But, it did and that was all that mattered.

We were having a pretty good time until we heard the flak exploding around our plane. It was hitting us like we were in a hailstorm. I looked out the open door of our plane and saw a nearby plane take a bad hit, sprout flames and head over and down. When it disappeared from my sight I had yet to see any troopers exit the doomed craft.

I looked over at Doug Lawson, one of my buddies in the mortar squad. "What's that noise I keep hearing?" I asked, acting like I really didn't know.

513th paratroopers await the signal to board their C-46s for the one-way trip across the Rhine River.

"Well, it isn't firecrackers," Doug grinned back weakly.

I tried to laugh, but it just wouldn't come out. I reached out to Doug, wished him good luck. I told him I'd see him on the ground with the leg bundle of mortar ammo I was carrying. He tried to smile but mainly we were all just hanging on now and talking was futile to attempt.

Finally, we got the word to get ready. We were loaded down like pack mules, but we managed to get to our feet and to stand in the door.

Tom Funk kneels in front of this jeep somewhere in Germany. That's Norval Lucas on the hood with the dog!

I was anxious to get out and to get away from this big target we rode in. I felt like it would be only minutes until we would be shot down.

I looked out the door and the ground seemed to be rushing by like I had never seen it. We were jumping at only 500 feet and it sure didn't look like 1,500 feet in jump school. Our jumpmaster was hanging out the door and I figured if we were too low, he'd know it. So, I just put my faith in him and hung on.

Having never jumped that low before, I reasoned that if a shell hit my canopy, I would really have to be quick to activate my reserve. So, I hooked my finger in the D-ring of my reserve to be ready. You probably know what

Heavily loaded, these 513th troopers board their C-46 to take off on Operation Varsity.

happened. The opening shock jerked my arm back and the reserve began to deploy.

I tried to hold the reserve in and then to pull it back, but with my main deploying, it was impossible. Then I thought about my leg bundle. I didn't want to land on that thing. I reached down and pulled the pin holding that to me and it dropped free. The rest of the way down (and it must have been only a couple of seconds) I fought that reserve. Fortunately, it didn't foul my main chute and I landed safely. Hard, but safely.

I never told anyone this before, but when I landed, looked around and couldn't see Doug Lawson with the mortar, I decided right then that I wasn't going to go running around with that bundle of mortar ammo. That DZ was hot and I wasn't going to go up like a Roman candle! I left it right where I landed and went looking for friendlies!

Try as I did, I couldn't find the assembly area. It just wasn't there. Years later, talking to guys in the 17th Association, I found out that we had been dropped approximately three miles from our intended drop zone. I've found out a lot of answers to questions that have nagged at me for years just by meeting with the guys at our reunions.

We got into a few fire fights with the Germans that were defending the DZ and the area around, but eventually, they were eliminated or pulled out. Some four hours later, I finally found Doug Lawson with the mortar. Doug had a badly sprained ankle but he was doing his job. We dug in and were cautioned about a counter attack, but it never came. I guess the Jerries had had all they wanted for that first day.

Early the next morning, our platoon leader, Lieutenant Arnold, came by my foxhole and asked me to volunteer for a patrol along with Sergeant Petre, Sergeant Story, Marvin Lampley, Frank Burton and one other man. I didn't want to go, but I also didn't want to be thought of as being afraid, so I agreed to go. It was a beautiful day, one like we would pick back home to go on a picnic. I knew, however, this was not going to be any picnic.

We were to check out and clear a large wooded area that was directly to our company front. Soon after we left, we spotted five or six Germans run into a house. We quickly headed for the house and almost immediately came under heavy grazing fire. Frank Burton was killed instantly.

We all hit the ground and started returning fire. Then I saw several Germans run from the house. One ran behind a crashed glider that lay behind the house. All I could see was his feet, but I started firing my M-1 through the glider at a height that I thought should be about belt high. After a few rounds I saw him topple over.

"That's for Burton," I said aloud to no one in particular.

Eventually, we captured one of the Germans who had been wounded and took into custody some suspicious looking older civilians. The area ahead looked clear after we we had routed the Germans left behind, so we headed back to our lines to make our report to the company.

We had been gone most of the day when we got back to our area. The company had moved out earlier to move toward an attack, so we hurried and caught up with them. I found Doug Lawson who had agreed to take care of my gear, but he didn't have it.

The ground crew hooks the nylon tow line to a CG-4A glider to ready it for the flight across the Rhine.

Doug told me had put the gear on a horse drawn cart and some trooper was driving it. Well, I then went looking for the horse and cart. When I located the cart it had broken down and they had turned the horse loose.

I learned 43 years later that a trooper named Novel Lucas had been driving the horse and cart, but the regimental commander, Colonel Coutts, had told Lucas to get rid of the horse and cart as it would draw fire and get him and some others killed. Lucas says he is grateful to the colonel for that advice, but at the time he certainly hated to loose his beast of burden!

I soon found my gear dumped beside the road. Lucas has become a close friend of mine, but on that day back in March of 1945, I thought the least he could have done was to carry my gear forward! Nevertheless, I've long since forgiven him!

It was hard to be mad at one of your own guys under those circumstances. We had to count on one another.

"CAPTURE THE FLAG!"

As told by Bill Consolvo, 507 G

There of you who attend the 17th Airborne Association reunions each year are well acquainted with our "War Room." There we have a unique collection of war souvenirs and mementoes of our service days both during training and in combat.

There is one item there about which you might be interested in learning some background information. It's the large red and black German flag which is usually used as a tablecloth for one of the display tables. To the men of "G" Company, 507th Parachute Infantry, it means much more than a tablecloth. It represents a trophy won in battle at the expense of the lives of some very good men. Let me tell you how it all came about.

Bill Consolvo died in March 1992, before his story was published. His wife, an Irish war-bride, sent us his photograph.

Our 3rd Battalion (call sign Blue) was at the airdrome in France getting ready for the Rhine drop. There was the usual amount of checking and re-checking, packing and repacking and the tension associated with an Airborne assault was in the air everywhere. Inside the barbed wire enclosure, the officers and noncoms were making sure all their people knew exactly what their duties were once we came down in Germany.

I had gone over and over the big plan with my squad and there had been several briefings by our officers. I thought we were pretty well prepared as long as everything went as planned. Time was getting short now. Tomorrow morning we go!

Troopers of the 507th march to their waiting C-47s full of confidence and ready to go!

In what turned out to be our last briefing, our company commander, Captain Bill Miller, went over the mission once more. Simply put, our battalion was to take a certain sector with "G" Company assigned a part of that sector. What made it interesting was the fact our portion of the sector contained historic old Diersfordt Castle which we knew would be strongly defended.

Then, before Captain Miller dismissed the company, he reached inside his jump jacket and pulled out a faded American Flag. He held it up over his head and announced to all, "Before the sun goes down tomorrow night, this flag will fly on high over Diersfordt Castle!"

It was an emotional moment for all of us. Without another word we

Bill Consolvo (R) and buddy, Lysek, wait to board for "Operaton Varsity."

all filed out returning to our billets hoping to get some sleep before the big day tomorrow. I thought as I closed my eyes that night, "Wouldn't it be a thrill to run that flag up the pole tomorrow!"

The next day things went smoothly as we chuted up and boarded the C-47s that would take us over the Rhine and into Hitler's Germany. As the planes rose into the morning sun we were quiet, but we were ready. I looked over at my buddy, Lysek, and he grinned back and winked.

Before long we were over the Rhine and things got a little more exciting.

The anti-aircraft fire picked up and we could see the flak bursts and machine gun tracers arching up at us. We began to anticipate our exit as we felt trapped in the confines of the airplane. It was too good a target.

Out the door I saw a couple of C-47s flame, peel off and head for the ground. A few more minutes and we reached our drop zone and the green light flashed. We were loaded down, but we cleared that door in record time!

Once out of the plane we immediately became aware of the machine gun fire directed toward our descending parachutes. It was like the fourth of July as the tracers laced through the air hitting the canopies of many troopers.

It seemed like it took forever, but finally we got down and started to return the enemy fire. Slowly, but surely, the men of "G" Company pushed the German resistance back, clearing the DZ and gaining cover in the wooded area.

Soon "G" Company reached the designated assembly area and began to organize for the push to their objective, Diersfordt Castle. Once communications were established with the supporting artillery, fires were directed on the castle and the company jumped off in the attack.

It was rugged for awhile, but progress was being made and the troopers pushed on. Fires from "H" Company on the flank lent support and soon the ground was dotted with the bodies of both friend and foe.

The word came down—Captain Miller had been wounded. He was hit bad enough that he had to turn the command of the company over to his XO. Word

A German armored vehicle is hit and burns as troopers attack a strongpoint shortly after landing.

also went around that the XO now was carrying the flag we were to erect once the castle was won.

Once the company reached the castle itself, it became a series of small individual battles. It seemed like there was a German under every block of stone and behind every bush. Finally, it all came down to one heavily fortified position. Here the defenders had chosen to make their last stand.

As the company poured fire into the building, one of the troopers, Robert Watson from Youngstown, Ohio, dashed from his position and managed to throw a white phosphorous grenade through an open window. When the grenade went off it severely burned the German colonel who was the commanding officer of the castle garrison. With their leader lost, there was little fight left in the troops and they quickly surrendered. The castle was ours!

Our XO turned to me and said, "Sergeant Consolvo, see if you can get that damn Kraut flag down and put this one up!"

Excitedly, I grabbed the flag and bolted up the stairs to the castle tower. In no time I hauled down the red and black Nazi flag and ran the "Stars and Stripes" up the pole. I sure got a warm feeling when I saw it fluttering in the breeze!

We lined up all the prisoners in a column of three's and started them toward the rear. There were almost 500 of them plus some tanks and a lot of weapons. Our 1st and 2nd Battalions did alright too, as they captured about 1,000 troops before dark that day.

We moved out soon after that and the rest is history. When I go to the reunions, however, and see that old Nazi flag laying there on the table, I can't help but think of that day and how excited I was when I hauled it down. And, then I think about how many good men fell that day just so we could accomplish our mission.

"DON'T I KNOW YOU FROM SOMEWHERE?"

As told by Paul Hartley, 513 E

A lot of weird situations occur during a war. I heard about one guy who was wounded and they sent him to a hospital where his brother operated on him. Another guy lost his Zippo lighter in England and a year later stopped a stranger on the street in New York and asked for a light and it was the guy who had found his lighter.

I saw a pretty weird thing take place myself. I was with "E" Company of the 513th and it was about a week after we had moved out of the Wesel area and were heading into the Ruhr Valley. We had been riding the British tanks, but this morning we were on the march. It was a beautiful day and we weren't running into any serious enemy opposition.

Earlier that day we had captured a German medic. He was a meek little guy and clearly he was not unhappy about being captured. As we were moving rather rapidly, we just brought him along with us thinking we would turn him over to some outfit on up ahead.

One of the guys in our squad, Ray McNamara, kept looking at our prisoner and whenever we halted, he'd come over, look in the guy's face and say, "Hey, don't I know you from somewhere?"

The guy would only shrug his shoulders and reply, "Nich Firstay," or something like that. He never gave any sign of having ever seen Mac before and we thought Mac was just harassing the guy.

This little game went on for an hour or two. Finally, Mac got right up in the German's face and demanded, "Don't I know you from someplace, Hans?"

Then, it was like a light had come on as Mac's jaw dropped and he gasped, "My God, you are named Hans! You're Hans Kruntzman from Binghamton, New York! What the hell are you doing here and in the German Army?"

Well, I guess the German knew that Mac had finally nailed him by then, so he decided to come clean and admit who he actually was. He seemed to breath a sigh of relief as he smiled weakly and said, "Yea, Mac, it's me, Hans!"

All of us guys were dumb-founded. How in the world could this happen? We still weren't 100 percent convinced, but Mac and Hans shook hands, grinned and laughed and began re-living old home week like any two old friends.

That German could speak as good English as any of us. He had understood everything that had been said to him. He was jabbering away with Mac while the rest of us stood around with complete disbelief this was happening. Naturally, we looked to Mac for some answers.

It seems that the German and Mac had worked together before the war in Binghamton at a company called General-Anihine Film Corporation. The company was a subsidiary of I.G. Farben Corporation, a German owned company.

Paul Hartley home on furlough in Ewing, Kentucky.

Hans had gone back to the Fatherland on a business trip and to visit some relatives. Hitler was rapidly nearing the bottom of his manpower bucket at about that time so the army had grabbed Hans and he had had no say-so about serving. Another victim of Selective Service!

Well, after that we took real good care of Hans. Mac's buddy was our buddy. When we finally had to turn him over to an MP who would route him back to a POW enclosure, we gave him some rations and made sure they understood that this prisoner was special and should be given special protection.

The story really doesn't end here. Once the war was over and we returned to the States, we were discharged and returned to our homes. Many of us took advantage of a law that said our pre-war employers had to give us our old jobs back.

Mac went back to work at General-Anihine and guess what? Right! There was our old POW buddy, Hans Kruntzman, back at his old job too! What's more, Hans was now Mac's boss!

Mac said he was the best boss he has ever had. Anytime Mac wanted off, all he had to do was ask Hans. He got the whole day—with pay! Don't try to tell me that German wasn't glad to have been captured!

Soon the company changed ownership and Mac says the new owners didn't think too highly of having an ex-German soldier as one of their key employees and poor Hans was fired. Mac left too for other employment about that time and he has since lost track of Hans.

Mac says now when something gets him upset he just thinks back on that day in Germany when his hatred for the enemy dissolved so quickly when he found out the enemy was really his old friend from back home. Yes sir, it's a strange old world.

"THE TROOP CARRIERS & THEIR GLIDER TOWS"

As told by David E. Mondt, 62nd TCS

Editor's Note: The average Airborne soldier usually saw the war only from his own unit's perspective. It was difficult to see the "big picture." Even after all their training, during "Operation Varsity," most of the troopers were astounded at the complexity and enormity of organizing an Airborne assault.

This story, submitted by a member of one of the Air Corps groups that carried the 17th Airborne into Germany, gives us a unique perspective into the organization of this mass operation. In it we see "Operation Varsity" through the eyes of the troop plane pilots, the tow plane pilots and the daring young men who flew the gliders.

The 314th Troop Carrier Group was composed of four squadrons: the 32nd, the 50th, the 61st, and the 62nd. For "Operation Varsity," the 62nd was designated to be the lead squadron of the group.

It would be the first and only time the 314th Group had pulled gliders in combat. At Sicily, Salerno and D-Day in France, the 314th had dropped paratroops of the 82nd Airborne. In Holland they had dropped British and Polish paratroops. For Varsity, they were tasked to deliver the 17th Airborne's medical personnel and equipment.

Although the 62nd Squadron was to lead the 314th Group, the group itself was scheduled to be "Tailend Charlie" in a 1,500 aircraft formation stretching 500 miles in length from airbases in England and France. When the first paratroopers began dropping at 0952 until 1304 hours (five hours and 12 minutes) men and equipment would continue to arrive at their respective DZs and LZs.

Being "Tailend Charlie" (last in the formation) was both a blessing and a curse. Airspeed became a big problem when it was necessary to slow down to keep from over-running the formations ahead. And, the turbulence from preceding formations caused great fatigue to the tow and glider pilots. The up side was that by the time the 62nd's planes arrived, most of the AAA and

The gliders landed everywhere. It was dangerous to be on the LZ for both men and beasts.

ground resistance had been neutralized by the troopers and the 1,000 fighters and bombers that had come before.

Let's pick up the story now as the 62nd lived and fought it as they carried the 17th Airborne across the Rhine River and into Hitler's Germany.

One month before Varsity, not much was going on in support of the front line troops on the continent of Europe. When the weather permitted we continued to fly group formations and some personal trips. On February 21, 1945, I returned to our base to find the word was out that we were moving to B-44 at Poix, France.

On March 1, our first trip to B-44 was aborted due to weather but on the 3rd it was possible to tow a glider to B-44, however, the return trip was through the fog and we developed ice on the wings. The second week of March was moving day with a stop at Greenham Common for a load of lumber from the glider crates. We needed a floor for the tent.

Then it happened, on or about the 19th of March, strange troops arrived and installed AA guns along the runway. MPs were placed at all exits.

The only way off of B-44 was by air. On the 22nd, we flew blood supplies to Paris and patients to England and went to Nottingham in the evening. We returned to B-44 on the 23rd and discovered a mission was scheduled.

Glider pilots had attended the mission briefing coordinated by Captain Harrison Loesch, and had been issued maps of the DZ and LZ areas, aerial photos and full combat equipment. The flight route was drawn and chalk numbers were assigned along with optimum landing spots for each glider. The briefing, however, was not without a bit of trepidation. A few days prior, Axis Sally announced the expected Airborne mission at Wesel, with the usual threats.

Finally, when March 24, 1945 arrived with clear skies, everyone scheduled was up, dressed and fed. In the tent of Lieutenants Roy Horning, Jack Hughes, Bill Johnson, and Chris Christianson, everyone was active except for Chris. Chris had been assigned and then removed when he returned late from a flight to Cannes. Chris bid goodbye from his bed and said he would come down to the flight line later and see them off!

At 0930 hours, Colonel Clayton Stiles and crew in chalk #1 was rolling with Majors Allen and Kenady flying the first glider tow. Using opposite sides of the runway, the next three followed and the first element was airborne.

The second element did not start off without a problem. The tow rope broke on the lead ship piloted by Captain Jack Downhill. There was a standby crew for just such an emergency but some of the assigned crew was off somewhere, perhaps taking pictures. Captain Grigsby who had not been assigned to the mission, recognized the problem and as he dashed to the standby aircraft, Chris Christianson was drafted to fill the right seat. Now they had a pilot and co-pilot, but neither had been briefed. They quickly hooked on to the glider and assumed a vacant position in the formation. In the glider were Bill Bowen and Tom Coleman, flight officers, on the way to the Rhine.

No other problems would occur during take off except Jack Downhill did not have a glider. He was determined to perform his assignment and returned, found a glider that needed a tow, hooked up and took off an hour and 20 minutes late to catch the formation at the IP.

Twenty-one serials departed air bases in England lifting the British 6th Airborne. The first six serials carried paratroopers and were from the 61st, 316th and 315th Troop Carrier Groups, a total of 243 aircraft. The next four serials were made up from the 46th Group, with 122 aircraft and followed by the 38th Group in 11 serials with 348 aircraft. The 46th and 38th Groups (British) flying Halifaxes and Sterlings, towed Horsa and Hamilcar gliders.

As the 713 aircraft of paratroopers and gliders passed south of Brussels, the Pathfinder Group of 46 aircraft joined the sky train followed by the 438th, 434th and 313th Troop Carrier Groups with 252 additional aircraft, all loaded with 17th Airborne paratroops. The 313th TCG had been converted to C-46 Commandos that carried a double load of paratroops that could jump from both sides of the aircraft.

The idea of a larger aircraft that could double the number of troops was a great idea except for the problem of a high pressure and leaky hydraulic system plus a design problem that allowed gasoline from a bullet hole to make it's way towards the engines. One or both problems caused the aircraft to become a ball of fire if hit just right.

The balance of the formation were serials A-8 through A-22, a total of 610 aircraft from the 437th, 436th, 435th, 439th, 440th, 441st, 442nd and the 314th Troop Carrier Groups. The 314th furnished 80 aircraft and crews. The 610 aircraft all towed CG-4A gliders, many as a double tow for the first time in combat history.

Three veteran aircraft of the 62nd participated in Varsity, all C-53D models that survived Sicily, Salerno, D-Day, June 6, 1944 and Market-Garden. Planes 42-68606, 42-68707, and 42-68716 had more battle stars than some of the pilots. Crew chiefs and radio operators were the exception. Two replacement aircraft for those lost during the Sicily invasion joined in the fray, 42-23929, better known as "The Empress of Wichita" and 42-24329 that Major Ray Roush called "The Young'un."

Chalk 1, with Colonel Stiles and Captain Evans, pilots, Lieutenant Welsh, Navigator, Tech Sergeant, Leo Rigard, crew chief, Joe Desnoyers, radio operator and Kieth Archie, radar, were listening to the chatter from other aircraft that were over the DZs and LZs. The three hour tow seemed to take forever. They had the problem of those double tows ahead and when one group had to slow down it was like a whiplash. The further back you were in the formation multiplied the problem. Take off at 0930, over the LZ at 1230, the glider cut off and as Col Stiles made his way out to the rope drop site they picked up a hole in the right wing.

Majors Allen and Kenady in their glider were on their way making a 90 degree turn for an approach through poor visibility due to smoke and receiving light flack. They deployed their pararester to get to the ground at a more rapid rate and landed without damage to the glider. They immediately started receiving sniper fire while unloading their jeep and personnel. They observed Captain Emil Crozier nearby and his efforts to save his passengers and later recommended an award for bravery while under fire.

Chalk 2 was towing Captain Emil Crozier, 62nd Glider Operations officer as pilot with Second Lieutenant Wesley J. Hare in the right seat. On board besides equipment were eight passengers. Captain Crozier had a vision problem and wore eye glasses that resembled the bottom of a coke bottle. The battle haze did not help his vision and as they approached their landing spot, Wes Hare was watching a farm house directly in their flight path.

Wes said, "Do you see that house?"

Crozier looked but could not determine the distance and dove the glider into the ground from 20 feet in the air at about 100 miles per hour.

The nose section was pushed into the cargo bay and all on board were injured. As the least injured attempted to help others from the glider, they were taking ground fire from three directions and mortars were falling within 75 feet of the glider.

Captain Crozier, seriously injured in the crash, was helping Wes Hare and passenger Private Alverex remove another injured trooper from the glider when enemy fire killed both Crozier and Alverez. Two hours later the Airborne cleared the area and medics treated the seven survivors and directed Lieutenant Hare to a field hospital.

Chalk 3 tow crew did not break as soon as the two preceding aircraft and maintained an on-course heading deeper into LZ "N". This gave Lieutenant Harry Andrews a better choice of landing sites plus he could land well into the LZ as instructed at the briefing.

They were taking some small arms fire but proceeded to make a good landing without damage to the glider. On board they had a jeep and two passengers, the commander of First Aid Section, an MD, and the driver, a medical corpsman. Harry and co-pilot, Flight Officer Dwight Orton, barely had time to crawl over the jeep when the driver put it in gear and drove through the nose section. So much for a perfect landing and undamaged glider.

Harry and Dwight went their separate ways while under small arms fire, dug in and waited for about two hours until the Airborne came through and cleared the area. Their immediate problems solved, they were assigned to guard some German POWs and that night served as guards once more on the perimeter of the area. Harry says he was in a frightful situation, dark, and dangerous.

Chalk 4 was in the air seconds behind the others in the 1st Element at about 0930 and circled B-44 for the first hour of the mission while the other 76 aircraft tows and gliders slowly caught up and formed serials A-21 and A-22.

Old 716 was performing well with Lieutenants John Peterson and Bill Hyden in the front seats while Sergeant Lawrence Vaughn was satisfied with the engine performance and Staff Sergeant Way Whitaker, radio operator, reflected that if he stayed with the Wings Headquarters, he would be safer flying a desk. The 716th still had a few grains of sand from Berguent and Kairouan tucked away in its hard-to-reach areas.

It also had a future as the presidential aircraft in Cuba after a post war interior modification. Flight Officers Warren Page and Joseph L. "Cannonball" Bowler found the air turbulent, as did the six medics in the back with a 1/4 ton trailer. As they crossed the Rhine River with two airsick medics, they were met by light but accurate automatic weapons fire. Shortly they recognized the LZ through the haze and smoke of battle. They cut off and followed Chalk 2 that would crash on the LZ.

They landed between two farm houses. They were close to the crashed glider of Captain Crozier. The hard jar of landing caused the trailer leg rest to go through the floor of the glider, but this was the least of their problems as they began to receive crossfire from both the farm houses.

Cannonball and Page, along with the six medics, were out of the glider immediately and flat on the ground digging holes. During his efforts to dig in, Cannonball received a flesh wound in the back of his knee. During the next two hours, Warren Page and two medics were wounded before being rescued by paratroopers and receiving first aid. Flight Officer Warren Page died two days later of his wounds.

Some confusion now enters the sequence; the flight assignment lists Chalk 5 was towed by Jack Downhill but they had the broken tow rope on take off. Grigsby stepped in, hooked on to the glider that was piloted by Bill Bowen who reports a broken tow rope, but he is listed as Chalk 6. We may never know who delivered glider Chalk 5, but it was flown by Lieutenant Bill Pospisil and Flight Officer Burl Cook. They don't know who flew the tow plane, but they got there!

It appears from the After Action Reports that where you landed the glider and the time had a lot to do with your problems. Both Pospisil and Cook reported the same problem following touchdown with no damage to the glider in spite of taking out two fences. They were out of the glider and under fire until the paratroops moved through, then returned to the glider to assist in removing the Jeep and supplies.

Next they assisted in removing a trailer from another glider. Burl Cook took some medics and supplies to a house where he had helped set up a first aid station, while Bill Pospisil helped Lieutenant Coleman organize the glider pilots in the LZ "N" assembly area.

The night was spent on guard duty prior to delivering POWs to the rear area. The last act by Bill Pospisil, before leaving the LZ, was to help identify Captain Crozier's body.

Chalk 6 was in the air after about a ten minute delay due to the tow rope break. Flight Officer William Bowen with the able assist of Flight Officer Thomas Coleman, found the flight normal for the conditions and ended up in position 8 rather than number 6 as assigned.

Tow C-53D was one of the veteran planes that had departed the USA for North Africa, and had on March 23 returned from the French Riviera with a happy crew. Plane 42-68707, "Daughter D-Dog," was assigned as standby for Varsity the following day. We don't know who was assigned as standby pilots since they did not stand by. They wandered off and when the tow rope broke, Stephen Grigsby grabbed Christian Christianson and with the assigned crew chief, Corporal Jim Valentine and radio operator, Ted Langdon, quickly moved into position as the replacement tug.

No one expected to need the standby aircraft so it had not been prepared for battle with a little iron under the seats nor was there any flak jackets aboard. As mentioned before, the crew had not been briefed, had no maps or other instructions. The glider cut off and during the 180 degree turn old "Daughter D-Dog" started receiving hits from AA and other smaller arms, Crew Chief Jim Valentine counted about 18 holes after landing and admits to being scared as hell while the bullets were hitting.

Co-pilot Christianson was unprepared for the flight as well as the next few moments of his life. The first explosion went off somewhere behind his seat, followed by a second shell that passed between his feet before exploding. He felt the concussion in the cockpit but did not realize he was wounded until feeling the warm blood running down his leg. Chris moved to the rear of the plane where crew members treated his wound and radioed a message to B-44, "wounded aboard."

Jim Valentine, with a bit of guilt, because he enjoyed the ride home in the co-pilots seat, proved to be a capable crew chief watching the instruments and operating the flaps and landing gear.

Meanwhile, Bill Bowen and Tom Coleman were having trouble finding a landing area until they spotted a small area in the LZ and put the glider and seven passengers down without damage. As with the others, they were taking a lot of small arms fire and all nine ran or crawled to a ditch about 30 yards distant. From their hiding place they watched the glider with cargo destroyed by fire.

After 30 to 40 minutes, paratroopers arrived and they joined the medics in setting up an aid station with German POWs as litter bearers. POWs were also put to work digging ditches for the wounded. The GPs spent the night on guard duty.

Chalk 7 was towed by First Lieutenant Ward Jones who had been subjected to the rigors of combat during the Market Garden flights in Holland. Lieutenant Roy Horning was a little nervous and excited at the prospect of his first combat mission, and having the best seat in the house watched the GIs on the ground scrambling about among the many gliders.

Three hundred feet behind was Flight Officers John Murphy and Wendell Ericson, as the saying goes, "being roped in." Pilot Murphy cut the tow and headed for a clear lane at an indicated 100 MPH, deployed the chute at about 100 feet and released it at about 20 feet. He pulled the spoilers and hit the ground and proceeded through two fences losing the right landing gear on the last fence.

John Murphy broke out the window and hit the ground and rolled to his feet, took off at high speed for a nearby ditch, where some minutes later he observed a glider cartwheel over a farm house. Sending his medic passengers to help the people in the glider he instructed other troopers to give them covering fire on the farm house the glider had hit.

This same house contained Germans firing on them as well as other glider personnel and passengers. Murphy's Irish dander was up and with covering fire from the Airborne troops, he gathered other paratroopers and they took the house and six prisoners. More help arrived and searched the Germans for weapons and Murphy marched the POWs to the GP assembly area and then across the railroad tracks.

While keeping his eyes on the Germans, he saw an Airborne officer shot, and he determined the fire had come from a culvert under the railroad. Murphy spotted him and promptly killed the sniper.

Flight Officer Wendell Ericson followed much the same pattern from the glider to a ditch but found himself up to his hips in mud and water. With rifle fire and mortars landing nearby and a paratrooper next to him shot in the neck, Ericson decided it was time to move. He made his way along the ditch to a point where he observed a single German sniper. Ericson shot and killed him.

These two GPs later proceeded to the assembly point, dug in for the night, but found sleep impossible with the continuous fire.

Chalk 8 had a 35 year old second lieutenant at its controls. James Cox was not old except when compared to the kids in their early 20s that usually flew the gliders. Jim arrived at the LZ and put the glider down without damage.

Flight Officer Harvey Caldwell found himself in the same predicament as Cox and six medics, on the ground and under fire from a house. During the next 90 minutes two of the medics were killed and four wounded, Caldwell

The paratroopers and gliders turned the DZs and LZs into a crowded and dangerous place to be.

was wounded in the back by shrapnel that also set the glider on fire with the loss of all equipment. Later they moved to the assembly area, guarded some POWs and pulled their time on the perimeter.

Chalk 9 tow plane led the 3rd Element with Captain Robert McDonald, Lieutenant Clem Howard, pilots, Flight Officer Owen Ulmer, navigator, Crew Chief George Bessert and Herb Caldwell, radio operator. The glider was piloted by Second Lieutenant Donald V. Peterson with co-pilot Flight Officer Lenden Flaming. Both were later KIA.

The Chalk 10 crew, led by tow pilot, Second Lieutenant John Manion, had time to visit with glider pilots, Flight Officers George Goyette and Joe Shropshire, while the gliders were being loaded. In the glider was a jeep and two airborne troopers, Sergeant Twitty and Corporal Helms.

The take off, circling the field while forming, and the flight to the Rhine was normal with the problem of airspeed variation from 90 to 130. The term normal is a misnomer when applied to a large formation of tugs and gliders, normal in this case was more like an out of control rat race. The flight was completed, the glider released and John Manion was looking for air space that did not have other aircraft using the same chunk of sky.

The rope drop area was just back across the Rhine River, a large field with a big windmill. This John recalls, as "the big tow-rope caper." No doubt the first aircraft with tow rope trailing, spotted the windmill and decided to play bomber with the windmill as the target. Some one managed to drape his rope over the windmill and everyone else had a go at it.

Later a report was heard that the windmill had been selected as a VIP observation post. Some high brass were mad as hell when they became a target for 300 feet of nylon with big iron rings.

GPs Goyette and Shropshire had volunteered for the mission. They flipped a coin for the left seat and George Goyette now found himself on the approach for LZ "N." The perfect landing was the last good thing that would happen to them until they found themselves back at B-44, two days later.

At the end of the landing roll, everything went from bad to worse. Like the others when they landed they became under fire, made a fast exit and started to dig in.

Along with two medics on board, they returned fire on the Jerries who were on the railroad tracks. Joe Shropshire positioned himself at the tail of the glider and fired off a burst when his Thompson jammed. They were outnumbered and for each shot they fired, it was returned five fold.

All around them gliders were landing, burning and the glider forward and to their left took a direct hit from artillery. They later learned it was Peterson and Flaming plus two medics. All were killed.

Medic Helms, hoping to save the group, waved a white surrender cloth. Sergeant Twitty, the other medic, yelled at him and said if he did that again he would shoot him.

Sergeant Twitty who had taken Joe Shropshire's place at the tail of the glider, while Joe was attempting to clear his gun jam, was then hit, the bullet going in his side and out his back. They moved him to his fox hole that was four or five yards in front of the glider, later he called for help and Joe Shrophire crawled out to him to administer a shot of morphine.

Corporal Helms, regaining his composure, got up and entered the glider to get the radio and call for help. His only answer was from a person with a very commanding voice that told him to get off the radio.

With everything else going on, the B-24s began arriving with their supply drop. One passed directly overhead and crashed just beyond the railroad tracks. The only thing visable to our people on the LZ was the propellers flying in the air.

After three and a half hours the area was cleared and the troops could move around. They checked the glider to the front and right that had burned. This was Lou Zeiden's.

They went to the glider that received the direct hit and confirmed the death of Peterson, Flaming and the two medics. Told that Captain Crozier had been killed, they went to check the report and found the dedicated glider operations officer dead with the same worried look he always wore.

Chalk 11 with Flight Officers John W. Heffner and Bruce C. Merryman, didn't know they were destined to make history, with the most spectacular landing on LZ "N." Medic Wallace E. Thompson was not happy to be in the drivers seat of the Jeep, on board a CG-4A, and expressed his opinion of the merits of parachute entry into combat as opposed to riding a glider.

Prior to take off, Heffner and Merryman discussed with Medic Thompson as to what they could expect over and on the LZ. They repeated the message from Axis Sally to the effect that the 17th Airborne could leave their parachutes at home and walk down on the flak. It was suggested that on the approach, Trooper Thompson should start the jeep engine and as soon as they completed the landing roll, they would release the nose latches and he could drive out.

Trooper Thompson was still venting his opinion on glider transportation when the "88" shell arrived as they made their landing approach. The "88" exploded in the cargo area, cut the ropes that held the jeep to the floor and Trooper Thompson and the jeep moved forward.

The latches broke. The nose section, complete with pilots, flipped up and locked.

The jeep with Thompson at the controls was now airborne! The first in history to solo a jeep, Thompson made a perfect four-wheel-landing and beat the glider to the ground!

When the nose section went up, the control column was pulled forward and then back towards the pilots, striking Merryman in the nose and breaking it.

It was about this time the pilots think they lost control and the glider made a "straight in" approach and landed in a vertical position.

The German "88" gunner fired again and took off the left wing-tip. This prompted Heffner and Merryman to break out of the cockpit and dash for a ditch. The Germans continued to fire at them so they crawled along the ditch hoping to avoid the shrapnel. Heffner was hit in the hand and Merryman received two hits in his right thigh to go along with his badly sprained ankle.

They crawled on and came upon a man lying in the ditch. It was Trooper Thompson and until that moment they had no idea what had happened to him. Thompson's first question was, "What the hell happened? One minute I'm sitting in the jeep inside of the glider, starting the engine, the next minute I'm sitting in the jeep out in the open."

Dazed from his landing, Thompson was brought back to reality when a German defender used the white cross on his helmet as a target. The bullet crease in his helmet prompted Thompson to leave the jeep and dash into the ditch.

Things are never so bad that you cannot find a little humor in a given situation. Merryman explained that as they had mentioned before take off, the Germans were waiting for us and we had to unload sooner than planned.

Trooper Thompson failed to see anything amusing about his glider ride, the unexpected landing, and most of all, Merryman's explanation. With profanity that reached hitherto unknown heights, Thompson expressed his opinion of the Glider Program in general and the one he had just made an exit from in particular. His last words were that he had just taken his last glider ride, they could shoot him and put him in one, but that would be the only way!

The unhappy medic decided he was not doing his job. After treating their wounds and giving Heffner a shot of morphine, he advised his ditch mates that he would return and take them to a first aid station. Merryman and Heffner remained in the ditch. Merryman could not walk and Heffner was woozy from the effects of the morphine. Medic Thompson departed to pick up and treat wounded, delivering them to the first aid station.

During their two hour wait for Thompson, Bruce Merryman decided to look over the edge of the ditch, to see what was going on. He found himself eye-ball to eye-ball with a burning B-24. No doubt the same B-24 that passed over Goyette and Shropshire who were some distance away in the middle of the LZ. Bruce was certain that the end was near but the pilot pulled enough to clear the railroad tracks.

True to his word, Medic Thompson returned and drove Bruce and John to the aid station. There they met the crew of the B-24, the pilot told them he thought he was going to hit them and the railroad tracks but managed to clear everything by a few feet.

After they bellied in they started to exit the burning plane and the first crew member out the door was killed by the Germans and the rest were taken prisoner. They were taken to the cellar of a farm house, given some cognac and held while the Germans decided who was winning.

A little later the Germans realized they were losing and surrendered their weapons and themselves to the bomber crew. The Germans were turned over to the Airborne and the bomber crew was delivered to the aid station.

John Heffner and Bruce Merryman were placed in a farm house for the night. Bruce needed John as a crutch if he was to walk and John had been given another shot of morphine and was now in a higher orbit.

During the night, Bruce woke up and John was gone. Unable to go find him, Bruce was concerned until a paratrooper brought John into the house and asked it if he belonged there. Bruce said yes and the paratrooper suggested that John be tied up, he had been found outside leaning against a tree watching a fire fight. John, of course, did not know where he was and didn't really care.

The following morning, John and Bruce were evacuated across the Rhine to a field hospital, from there to separate hospitals and a couple of weeks later they met at B-44.

Bruce noted that the squadron records show that they were wounded by small arms fire. If the German "88" is small arms fire he says he is glad they didn't run up against any big stuff.

Chalk 12 was on the outside of Element 3 and that may have had something to do with their reaching LZ "N." Second Lieutenant Charles Hancuff and Flight Officer Lucian Cade were too far south and elected to land in DZ "X." There they encountered the same problem of intense ground fire. Other gliders were burning in the same area as in LZ "N."

Along with the Airborne lieutenant and the jeep driver, they took refuge in the ditch just west of the railroad that bisected both DZ "X" and LZ "N." After the shooting eased up, they helped to unload the jeep and made their way to the assembly point. There they spent the night on guard duty and hiked out the next day.

Chalk 13 tow pilot was Captain James R. Hamilton, better known as

"Hambone." He was leading the 4th Element. At the end of the rope was Second Lieutenant Newton H. Foster who was living on borrowed time since ending up in the Mediterranean and keeping his head above water for half a night and half a day.

Co-pilot for Newt Foster was a recently assigned power pilot that had been one of several hundred pilots who were sent for additional training in gliders following graduation from flight school. Flight Officer James M. McCloskey, like most of us, had visions during flight training of boring through the sky in P-51s and shooting holes in Messerschmitts. On his arrival at the 62nd he did not mention his glider training, but unfortunately, there it was in his 201 File.

Always short of glider pilots, McCloskey was offered the choice of volunteering or being ordered to make the mission as a GP. We are glad to say he volunteered as any good soldier is inclined to do.

Newt Foster at age 28 was an experienced glider pilot. A little older than the average, he had confidence in himself and as a veteran of other battles, he was calm in his approach to another mission. On the other hand, co-pilot McCloskey was not pleased with his assignment and had no idea what was about to happen or what to expect.

As the glider was loaded with a jeep, stretchers, and two medics, McCloskey was a bit apprehensive at the site of a fully-loaded glider that required the pilots to enter the cockpit by way of the emergency hatch. Never saw anything like this in training, he thought. We used sand bags to get the feel of a fully loaded glider.

As they approached the LZ, McCloskey did not see a big open field, rather a postage stamp-sized area cluttered with gliders, some wrecked, some burning. Newt called for spoilers and the nose of the glider pointed at the ground. Newt called for the arrester chute and McCloskey found himself dropping like a rock until Newt called for the chute release. The nose came up, they landed taking out a fence and a fence post that tore off the left landing gear. McCloskey thought, it works, just like in training.

As the glider skidded to a halt, Newt Foster yelled, "Everybody out," and dove through the emergency door. McClosey tried to follow but could not move, he had forgot to release the safety belt. The next moment he was outside looking around for his pilot and discovered Newt, flat on his back next to the glider. At first he thought Newt had been hit but then discovered him calmly lighting a cigarette.

Forty minutes later the firing let up enough to unload the jeep and proceed to the assembly area where they spent the night. On the 25th they and other glider pilots marched a few thousand German POWs to the Rhine.

Chalk 14 glider was piloted by Flight Officer Robert H. Salyer and his debriefing report was short and sweet. His report to Captain Harrison Loesch, Interrogator read, "Everything OK, was pinned down after landing for about one and a half hours. No damage to jeep or men. Landed on LZ "N." Went to glider pilots assembly area and was evacuated to home base."

Co-pilot Martin T. Laffey gave a few more details but his main point was that the evacuation of the glider pilots was smooth and efficient. "All personnel involved in the evacuation should be commended for their efficiency and consideration," he concluded.

Chalk 15 crew, Flight Officers Herbert Muncy and Walter Phillips were selected for the mission, attended the briefings, inspected their glider and discovered someone had chalked, "Shoot Kraut, you're faded," on the bird's nose.

Flying the third glider in echelon to the right, of the 4th Element, Muncy and Phillips were boxed in between tow planes and gliders. There was no room for error but a lot of work that at times required both to be on the controls to maintain their position.

Soon after take off, it was obvious that the sun was going to bake them in the greenhouse. Herb Muncy had taken precautions against being cold and dressed in his Class A uniform, complete with tie, and over this he wore the green combat uniform. During the flight and the hard work of keeping the glider in position, being cold was the least of his problems. While dressing that morning, he was asked by tentmate John Murphy why he was wearing Class A's? Herb replied, "Who knows, I may be selected to represent the squadron at Adolph Hitler's funeral."

First Lieutenant Hoyt McNatt and crew held a steady course as they entered the south end of LZ "N." Muncy and Phillips were busy looking for any opening to land the glider. On the north end were several gliders on fire that apparently severed the high voltage lines. Muncy made a quick decision and continued his left turn rather than argue with Wesel Power and Light. With the help of the drogue chute while continuing his turn they approached the LZ and the ground at a rapid rate, jettisoned the drogue and forced the glider to make contact with Deutchland.

The second choice for landing put them close to an apple orchard. The gear was sheared, followed by the loss of the left and right outer wing panels to the apple trees and they came to rest nuzzled against another apple tree. Thirty yards away was a two-story brick farm house from which they began receiving small arms fire.

Phillips and the two troopers made a quick exit from the glider. Muncy dove under the jeep but decided he would be safer outside and cut a hole in the fabric. Outside they were digging in, but Phillips found himself and one trooper on the farm house side of the glider and they crawled to the "safe" side.

The farm house had come under attack by the 17th Airborne as they landed. In a short time the Germans were observed coming out of the house with their hands up. This gave the pilots and passengers an opportunity to unload the glider and the troopers drove away to perform their mission.

A sleepless night without additional contact with the enemy, was enhanced by a night-long engagement, known then, as now, as the Battle of Burp Gun Corner.

They joined the rest of the GPs in herding the German POWs over a ten mile stretch to the Rhine. The roads and ditches on both sides of the Rhine were filled with burned out shells of German tanks and armored vehicles.

Chalk 16 had at its controls, Second Lieutenant Louis H. Zeidenschneider. Lou and co-pilot Flight Officer Edison F. Best suffered the same flight problems as the other GPs to the LZ: air speed from 95 to 150 MPH, towed too far south to reach LZ "N." They elected to land on DZ "X" putting the glider down without damage only to be welcomed with rifle, mortar and machine gun fire.

After about a half hour, Trooper Mann was wounded in the leg. Lou tossed his first aid kit to Mann and he treated his injury. A little later the two Airborne men would make a dash for the ditch next to the railroad. Seeing the Airborne troopers make it safely to the ditch, Lou and Best were considering the prospects. Lou crawled to the front of the glider and as he reached the pilots compartment, it was hit by an incendiary just above his head.

Lou was attempting to beat out the fire with his bare hands and losing the battle when he received a jolt in his tail. This was not from a medic but from a well-aimed German rifle. Ed Best did not know how serious the wound was so he moved out of his foxhole to assist.

In a few minutes Lou realized that it was only a flesh wound but a greater danger was from the glider that was now burning furiously and setting off the ammunition and grenades. They dug deeper, hoping to survive till dark. By 4:00 p.m. the field started to fill with Airborne troops. Their glider destroyed, they helped unload other gliders after they moved on to LZ "N."

On return to the squadron, Lieutenant Lou Zeiden is reported to have refused the award of the Purple Heart, "don't want to explain where I was shot," he said.

Chalk 17 tow plane was flown by squadron commander, Lieutenant Colonel Oral W. Lee, leading the 5th Element with Flight Officer Myron Norman as pilot and First Lieutenant John L. Coleman as co-pilot. We don't know if this decision was made by Coleman, or if they like many other crews, flipped a coin to decide who flew the left seat.

The glider had a heavy right wing that would not respond to the trim tabs and increased the work load for the entire flight. Like most of the gliders, the intercom between the tow and glider went out and they were dependent on visual signals. From the south end of the LZ they made a 270 degree approach, Coleman watched for other aircraft as Flight Officer Norman selected a landing area and put the bird down without damage.

Crew and passengers hit the ground and were pinned down for the next 15 minutes. Coleman felt that the Airborne needed the jeep and led the others back to the glider. Still under fire they raised the nose and started to remove the jeep when the locks failed. An Airborne officer was recruited to help hold up the nose as the jeep was removed.

Coleman and Norman took cover in the woods near the railroad track and worked their way towards the GP assembly area. They arrived at about 1530 hours and found no other GPs present. Their next move was to join up with some Airborne troops and capture some Germans in a nearby farmhouse. Coleman and Norman stayed in the fight for an hour and a half during which they routed other Germans from the woods.

Returning to the assembly area at 1700 hours they found other glider pilots from the 314th Group as well as the 62nd. When advised that Captain Crozier had been killed, Coleman took command of the 62nd Glider Pilots and had a roll call.

Reporting to a Captain Scott, acting Group Glider Officer, he was ordered to have the 62nd dig in for the night and set up a guard schedule. Coleman's roster still had a number of MIAs listed and he found some people at the aid station.

The following day the 62nd departed for the Rhine in two groups with the German POWs under their watchful eyes. Lieutenant Coleman with his ever present roster, found others that he was carrying as MIA. They were transported across the Rhine in DUKWs (Ducks) where they were welcomed by the British with a cup of tea. Later trucked to B-86 (Helmond) they returned to Poix by a 32nd TCS aircraft.

Chalk 18 Glider Pilots, Flight Officers Paul M. Johnson and Thomas E. King mentioned something in their debriefing that has not been brought up by the glider gang before. That is the inevitable stacking of close formations. They cut off at 950 feet that left them exposed to enemy fire for a longer period than those in the 1st and 2nd Elements that cut off at 600 feet or lower.

Landing with no damage to the glider, they spent the next 30 minutes under fire but felt that it was light enough to allow them to unload the jeep. They had trouble with the nose lifting mechanism and noted that it worked well when loading under excellent conditions, and definitely was a problem when they were exposed in combat.

Taking cover with the Airborne in the woods, they were directed to a temporary command post and from there made their way to the Division Command Post. There they met Major Allen, pilot of Chalk 1, and spent the night. The next day they were evacuated to the POW area and assisted in moving the German prisoners.

Chalk 19 may have been next to last but Flight Officers Truman Hyde and Thomas Farquhar were in for excitement. When they cut off from the tow ship, they dived some 200 feet to clear the tow ropes. Leveling off, they received a hit in the tail section that caused the glider to stand on its nose allowing the jeep to move forward and affect the CG. The airspeed increased to 140 MPH before they recovered level flight and their planned 270 degree approach was abandoned for what became a 450 degree approach. The original plan was to land on LZ "N," however, the hit in the tail section removed the arrestor chute and they landed in the adjacent DZ.

Pilots and medics made their way to a small building that was being used by paratroopers. There were a lot of wounded around so they made the decision to get the jeep from the glider and its load of medical supplies. The nose lift would not work so they went back to the house for additional help. Two paratroopers joined in lifting the nose and the slightly wounded jeep was driven away.

Hyde and Farquhar were pinned down for the next two hours and when the firing let up they decided to make a break and find the GP assembly area. Hyde and a paratrooper made the first break and drew a lot of fire so Farquhar and the rest of the paratroopers took off in another direction.

Hyde could not find the Division CP and spent the night in a house. He located the CP the following morning and was evacuated to the assembly area. Meanwhile, Farquhar met another GP and they followed a road until they found a 105 Howitzer Unit with whom they spent the night. Both were directed to and arrived by separate routes at the site of the German POWs.

Chalk 20 is listed as being towed by First Lieutenant James Sullivan. This may be the aircraft and crew that was displaced by Flight Leader Captain Jack Dowhhill after the broken tow rope. Captain Grigsby stepped in and replaced Downhill at the time of the broken tow rope.

The last glider to land at Wesel from the 62nd was piloted by Second Lieutenant Lewis Johnston with Flight Officer Gerald Buist on his right. They landed in DZ "X" where four other gliders, unable to make LZ "N," had arrived, plus a lot of paratroopers. Johnston and Buist were in the wrong place at the wrong time. They were pinned down for three hours while the "88s" destroyed the other four gliders. The jeep they carried received a hole in the gas tank and radiator. The glider had a lot of holes from small arms plus a missing wing tip and a pole through the floor.

Finally they were able to make a break for safety with the Airborne, and assisted in the capture of five Germans in a house. They spent the night with an artillery battalion before making their way to the Rhine crossing to return to B-44.

The tow crew of Jack Downhill, Second Lieutenant Earle Hopkins, Navigator Dalton Watts, Crew Chief Albert Jimro and Radio Operator John Albin, as mentioned earlier, used the space between B-44 and the IP to close the gap between them and the squadron.

When the tow rope broke, Dalton Watts' main concern was that he could miss his first, and maybe only, combat mission. He also wondered if they were unable to catch the formation, would Jack Downhill take them in solo to the LZ. At this late date, Dalton thinks Jack would have made a single run and he would have approved.

For a period of 30 minutes or more during the flight, they listened to the conversations of the preceding formations over the target area. They reported heavy flak, injuries, engines out, fire, and crash landings. When they arrived the flak was all around them, some close enough to shake the airplane, yet they escaped without a single hit.

Tow crews had little to do except deliver the glider and hope they could survive the flight. This is not to say their expertise was not necessary, but compared to the glider pilot, from the moment of cut off to landing and his survival on the ground, the tow pilot's duties paled in comparison.

Tow number 19 had on board Second Lieutenant William L. Johnson Sr. On the release of the glider they made a climbing right turn and when additional power was applied, the engine sputtered. Their first reaction was to think they had been hit, but the engine picked up and all seemed to be normal.

In his excitement, Bill Johnson forgot about the rope drop and some time later during the return flight, a message was received: "Zero Niner Three, you still have your rope!"

Without thinking, and with an expletive, Bill cut the rope. After all these years, Captain Walter Stark, Flight Leader, reminds Bill of the lost tow rope and threatens him with a statement of charges. Three hundred feet of nylon at a buck a foot, 1945 prices!

Nearing B-44, Bill Johnson heard the radio call from Steve Grigsby of "wounded aboard." The tower requested a name and the reply was "Christianson."

Hey! wait a minute, that can't be," exclaimed Bill, "we left him in bed this morning."

On this last mission for gliders, the one request most often mentioned, was doors on the pilot's cockpit. It is not hard to appreciate the need.

As I studied the mission, I was amazed at the number of gliders scheduled to land in LZ "N." There were 234 ahead of the 314th Group, our pilots and glider pilots remarked about the congestion of gliders on the LZ, the 62nd arrived with 20 more gliders, most of which found a spot to land and yet there were 60 more gliders to arrive from the 32nd, 50th, and 61st Squadrons.

Conclusion: This account of the 62nd's role in Operation Varsity is not unlike that which might be compiled from the other squadrons and groups. It was the largest Airborne operation ever mounted and no doubt will be the largest ever.

No longer a part of the inventory, the CG-4A glider has passed into history. Although paratroopers continue to be used in modern warfare, it is unlikely they will ever be used again in these numbers and in this type of situation.

One thing, however, will never cease to be of premium value. That is the courage and daring of the young men who fly into battle. Whether they fly themselves or are flown in, it takes a special kind of person. Our country will always have a need for these types of individuals.

"A WELCOME FROM AXIS SALLY"

As told by John Baines, 513 A

Just before we moved to the isolation area for "Operation Varsity," Nick Garcia and I got a weekend pass to Paris. We separated when we got there and each went his own way.

I was sitting in a small bar having a beer when suddenly I became aware of English being spoken over the radio. I realized it was the English babe who had been broadcasting for the Germans and trying to damage our morale. We called her "Axis Sally." We paid no attention to the junk she put out, but listened to the Nazi station because it played good American music.

Then I heard her say, "Welcome to the 17th Airborne Division! We know you are going to jump over the Rhine River soon, and we want you to know we will be waiting to greet you!"

I then realized that everyone in the bar had turned and was looking at me. I was the only paratrooper in the place and they obviously were waiting to see what I would do.

"You won't need your parachute," she went on, "the flak will be so thick you can walk down!"

Secretly, I gulped a bit then raised my beer in a toast gesture and uttered a curse to the old girl. But, you know what? She was right. They did know we were coming and the flak was so thick that we could have walked down.

"JUMPING WITH GENERAL GAVIN"

As told by Ken Kasse, 513 I

It was late in February of 1945 and we were just beginning to feel comfortable at Chalons, our new rest camp in France. We knew it couldn't last long as we just recently had been introduced to our new means of insertion into the combat zone—the C-46. An Airborne operation loomed and we knew it.

Then came the word that we were to have a practice jump from the new plane. It was larger than the old C-47s and would carry more jumpers and a bigger equipment load. We were anxious to get back to jumping after the bitter days of the Bulge.

Ken Kasse at Ft. Bragg in early 1946.

For the first time ever, I found myself jumping the number one spot in the left door stick. I was looking forward to the jump, but a little anxious about the number one spot. Whoever that man was had to do his job right or else he could lead the rest of the stick out at the wrong time.

We loaded in and I was thinking that I was going to make damn sure I went when the jumpmaster gave the signal and not a second before. That way we'd get all the guys on the drop zone and the last ones wouldn't be in the trees.

Shortly before takeoff, I looked out the open door and saw another trooper climbing in the door. When he looked up at me, I saw two big stars on his helmet and I recognized him immediately as Major General James M. Gavin, the commanding general of the 82nd Airborne Division.

"What the devil was he doing here," I thought, "he isn't in the 17th Airborne—or was he?" Stranger things had happened since we had entered combat!

The general looked me right in the eye and said, "Soldier, would you mind if I jumped ahead of you in your stick?"

Well, that was certainly an easy question for a private to answer and I replied, "No sir, General, be my guest!"

I guess I was struck dumb because what kind of a conversation could a private carry on with a two-star general? If I said anything, I can't remember it.

I do remember the general took a good door position and made a vigorous exit when the jumpmaster shouted "Go!"

I didn't hesitate a heartbeat. I was right on the general's back when he went out the door. The jump was rather routine. None of us had any problem with other jumpers in the air and no one was injured in landing. I looked around for the general when we were on the ground, but I never saw him again.

Well, I never forgot that incident and I was proud to have jumped with him. I always had tremendous respect for that man and history has proven me correct.

Back in 1983, I was moved to write him a letter. I recalled the day he climbed aboard our plane and jumped in my original position and asked him if he remembered it. I was surprised when, a few days later, I received a reply from him.

His reply was short and to the point. Here's what he said:

"Many thanks for your letter of April 11. It has been good to hear from you again.

I remember very well the practice jump in France. We had had an accident in the morning. I wanted to jump from the same plane in the same formation. You may recall we had a good jump.

I hope all goes well with you.

James M. Gavin"

I do remember now that the story had gone around that some jumper had been killed earlier that day, but we didn't pay much attention to it, thinking it was the usual rumor that was always going around. I guess it was the truth and there was the general, putting his own neck on the line to make sure all was okay for his men.

Yes sir, I always had a lot of respect for old "Slim Jim," he was one hell'uva man. He was certainly "Airborne all the way!"

"YOU SAVED MY LIFE!"

As told by Jerry Davis, 513 A

After we jumped across the Rhine, several of the troopers in our battalion landed in the woods. Hanging from the trees they were sitting ducks for the German gunners. I saw at least two who were hanging limp in their harness.

I landed just short of the woods, freed myself and ran to try and help those who were in the trees. There was one guy whom I helped get down. I recognized him as Sergeant Joe Carter, the first sergeant in 1st Battalion Headquarters Company. He was completely helpless and there was a German machine gun nearby making the woods a pretty hot place to be.

Once he was freed, he went running off and I went my way and that was

The gliders landed right in the face of the enemy artillery.

the end of it. He thanked me of course, but that was no time to stand around talking about it.

Forty-five years later while I was at the big affair in Washington, DC, celebrating 50 years of USA Airborne, I saw this guy that looked very familiar. I asked a friend who he was and was told he was Joe Carter and that he had been in Headquarters Company, 1st Battalion.

I began to suspect who he was, so I went over to him and asked him if he had landed in a tree on the Rhine jump and had been trapped there. He said he had and asked how I had known. "Because I'm the guy who helped you get down," I replied.

Well, with that he dang near went into orbit! He grabbed me and hugged me and with tears in his eyes, he said over and over, "You saved my life—God bless you!"

He told me how he had thought of that day so often and had told his family of the trooper who had saved his life. He said the family had always regarded me as their hero. It was pretty heady stuff for me.

I never had thought of it as a courageous act or anything like that, but I was always glad that I had been there to help him. I guess I'm getting tender hearted in my old age as it sure gave me a warm feeling to see him and know that if I hadn't gotten him down when I did, all of this would never have happened.

"MY LONGEST DAY"

As told by Jack Trovato, 155 A

Jim Murphy and I met in an infantry replacement depot in France. Both of us were 18 years old and we soon discovered that we had a lot in common. For one thing, we were both eager volunteers for the 17th Airborne Division.

We were assigned to the 1st Squad, "A" Battery of the 155th Airborne Anti-Aircraft Battalion then located at Chalon-sur-Marne, France. They had been in the Battle of the Bulge and everyone in our squad had either been killed, wounded or half frozen except the squad leader.

After two weeks of torturous physical training interdispursed with piling in and out of airplanes and gliders, we received our glider wings and a very welcome raise in pay. Within three days, however, we were in a marshalling area looking over maps of some town named Wesel and a bridge over the Rhine into Germany.

On March 24, we squeezed into one of the egg crates and prepared for our introduction to combat. The view through the tiny window was both awesome and spectacular. The sky was filled with airplanes and gliders as far as the eye could see. I was now committed; I was into it up to my neck. Strangely, I felt more like a spectator.

The ride got bumpy and I could feel my stomach churning. I fought the feeling off until I saw Murphy throwing up. That triggered the rest of the squad and then finally I followed suite. That glider was one big stinking mess. A hell of way to ride into what might well be the most important day of your life!

I was in a state of disgust with myself, but was shaken out of it in seconds when I became aware of the big, black puffs of smoke all around us. I realized that this was flak from German AA fire and someone was trying to kill me!

Soon, we touched down. We bounded hard and ran across a field that rattled our teeth with holes and bumps. We swerved and came to a stop in a cloud of dust. In what seemed to me to be only a split second, we all piled out and tried to get our bearings.

For the next two hours we were in the landing zone area, mostly trying to

Jack Trovato had a rude awakening as a replacement to the Airborne.

find out where to go. It was both confusing and chaotic. As I look back on it now, the events flash through my mind like a kaleidoscope. It's a wonder we didn't all get killed.

The squad was spread out all over the place; crawling on our bellies trying to get together. Enemy small arms fire was picking off anyone who dared to raise to his knees or stand up. Mortar shells were opening up the ground here and there. All this time gliders were landing in all directions, crashing into houses, telephone poles, power lines and trees. We were all afraid we would be run over.

I saw C-47s being shot down like sitting ducks as they exposed their underbellies when they banked after dropping their cargoes. A B-24 roared in only about 100 feet above my head with its wings aflame. I could see a guy in the door still pushing bundles out as it it disappeared over the treeline. Seconds later I heard a thunderous crash and a big fireball roared up into the sky.

Before that day was over, I was to see many men get killed or wounded. I saw one trooper who had had his cheek torn open by small arms fire. He stood there, his helmet at his feet and blood pouring down his face and body. With a boiling anger in his eyes, legs spread apart, he began pumping rounds from a grease gun into a house some 100 feet away. Within a few seconds he was blown away by small arms fire. I have no idea who he was, but I'll always remember his courage.

After I had been on the ground for about two hours, all I could think about was survival and finding someone to give me orders and directions. Finally, our squad leader got us together and we moved out of the landing zone. I had been hearing a snapping and popping sound in my ears. I asked Sam Strain, a veteran trooper, about the noise. He calmly informed me they were shots and that some sniper probably had me in his sights.

Ever so often a shell would come lobbing in with deadly accuracy, hitting a jeep or a piece of artillery. I learned to keep my distance from any potential target. I loved trees too, but I learned to keep away from them too. A shell

The Germans resisted but then surrendered as the troopers kept coming at them.

hitting a tree would splinter it into a multitude of fragments, showering death all around.

Within hours, we began taking prisoners. The unwritten word was that the Germans were taking no airborne prisoners. I'm not sure about it, but it seemed to me all of the prisoners we took were never sent back to the POW cages. The guys who were detailed to take them back weren't gone but for a few minutes and they were back.

I tried to help a trooper who had been hit by a tree burst. The right side of his body had been slashed open and part of the tree was still lodged in him. I yelled for a medic and I guess I became a little hysterical as he was hurt bad. Corporal Gillespie grabbed me and told me to keep moving.

Having grown to fear trees, I soon learned to fear crossing open fields. We came upon an open field and began crossing it when we were introduced to the fury of German artillery fire. The air bursts were about 50 feet overhead and shrapnel rained down on us.

I saw Murphy jump into an abandoned German foxhole and I decided to do the same. I then felt the butt of Sergeant Strudsky's rifle on my helmet and heard his order to "Get out and keep moving!"

That was the last order that Sergeant Strudsky ever gave me. Ten minutes later he was killed along with two other members of our squad.

Corporal Gillespie was now my squad leader. We had stopped for a minute to catch our breaths, but soon Corporal Gillespie shouted, "Okay you guys, on your feet. Let's go!"

I soon realized that this was going to be a special mission as only our squad and Lieutenant Mandrell moved out. Out of the woods and across a big open field we went. I knew this wasn't going to be any picnic.

Lieutenant Mandrell was affectionally called "Mandy" by the men and I was soon to come to both love him and hate him. He had volunteered our squad to move across that field, which seemed like it was about two miles across. The idea was to test the strength of the enemy whom we knew held the other side.

The plan seemed a little dumb to me and I couldn't understand why he picked our squad. We were understrength, had lost two veterans, our squad leader and had Murphy and me, both rookies. Oh well, the Army wasn't paying me to figure out things like this. I got up and moved out.

We walked out into the field at a slow pace. I could see a farmhouse which was close to the tree line at the opposite side of the field. Mandy headed us in a direct line toward it.

We were midway between our lines and the farmhouse when all hell broke loose. Mortar shells came lobbing in from the German side of the field from behind the farmhouse. Seeing Murphy and Tom Burnard jump into a shell crater, I jumped in behind them. Within seconds, the rest of the squad was lying on top of us. Mandy yelled at us to get up and spread out.

Corporal Gillespie asked, "Can't we wait for our people to give us some covering fire?"

Sam Strain came back saying, "The Krauts have probably taken off by now, seeing us coming to get them!"

The mortar shell bursts were getting closer and closer to our crater. I realized that it wouldn't be long before they zeroed in on us. Without saying a word, Sam Strain crawled out of the crater with a bazooka, knelt and took aim at the enemy treeline. Boom! It fired and Corporal Gillespie fed in two more rounds. Boom! Boom! He must have hit something as the shelling stopped.

We all crawled out of the crater. Sam Strain had saved all of our lives though his heroic action. I thought to myself, "It's going to be a long run back to our lines."

My heart then jumped to my throat and then sunk like a rock when Mandy started running toward the farmhouse and shouting for us to follow him. That wasn't the direction I wanted to go, but we all got up and ran after him.

My lungs were bursting as I tried to keep up with him. A glider, which had landed miles from the landing zone lay close to the farmhouse. It had taken a direct hit in the nose and had been all but demolished. We never stopped, but ran on into the farmhouse.

There were no Germans there, only a farmer and his daughter. They were tending the wounds of a trooper who had crawled there from the glider. The trooper said he thought there may be some others still alive in the glider.

Immediately, Sam Strain grabbed his carbine and took off toward the glider. He had gone only about 100 feet when the Germans opened fire on him. He knelt down and returned the fire. About this time, Mandy yelled for us to cover him and we all began to fire in the direction of the enemy fire.

Despite our efforts, a round hit Sam in the head. I saw his head jerk back and his helmet flew off behind him. We all knew it immediately—Sam was dead.

I had really come to admire Sam. Because of his cool actions that day, he had become a role model for me. I joined the rest of the squad in a cry of vengeance as we fired clip after clip at the German positions. It was all I could do to fire I was trembling so with excitement.

I peered over a windowsill into the trees and I could see figures pop up and then disappear. I followed one figure and kept him in my sights and squeezed off three rounds. I could tell I hit him as he jerked and went down. I had been firing at treelines all day, but this was the first time I had knowingly killed or wounded a human being.

Gillespie had seen the German soldier fall as he watched with his binoculars. He leaned over and said, "Nice shooting, trooper!"

He was the first veteran of the outfit to call me, or Murphy, "trooper." Up until now they had referred to us as "hey you" or "new guy." It felt good.

Mandy gathered us together and said, "We have to get back to our lines. We'll start out together, but we may have to split up and it will be every man for himself."

Some of the men started grumbling. "How about the wounded trooper in the house? How about Sam Strain's body? We can't leave them here!"

When Gillespie asked for volunteers to carry them, the grumbling stopped. The sun had set and if we were going to make it back to our lines, we were going to have to travel fast. We needed to get back while it was still light enough to see, but not light enough for the Jerries to zero in on us in that open field.

Gillespie looked at me and said, "Okay, I'm going to take off. You count to 10 and then take off after me. The rest of you guys follow Jack the same way."

I could hear the Germans open fire as Gillespie ran and I could see the bullets kicking up the ground at his heels. I counted to five and froze. Mandy gave me shove and said, "Go kid, Go!"

Someway I got started and the rest of the squad came sprinting after us. We were halfway across the field when Gillespie stopped and waved us down. We were in a little depression and the machine gun bullets were passing over our heads. They were so low we couldn't stand up.

We laid there as darkness began to fall. The moon, however, was pretty bright. There were some clouds and when they rolled past the moon, we figured it was dark enough to move. Before we could, tracers arched over us from another direction. We were caught in a crossfire!

We lay there for what seemed like an eternity. The German gunners were spraying us and our guys were spraying them. We dug in and sweated it out. We were safe as long as we didn't stand up and get caught in the tracers.

It was close to midnight when the firing stopped. Mandy stood up and walked about 50 feet toward our lines and then signaled us to follow him. Each time the moon came out from behind a cloud, we'd hit the ground and stay motionless until another cloud rolled by.

We were making pretty good progress when flares suddenly lit up the area. We hit the ground again as our own troops opened up on us. We all started shouting obscenities in no uncertain terms! Our guys got the message and the firing stopped.

Mandy told us to stand up and hold our rifles over our heads and start walking on in. We found out that our outfit had come under heavy shelling and had suffered high casualties. As a result, they had to pull back and regroup.

About an hour later, another unit took over the positions. They had been informed that the Germans were expected to counter-attack from across the field at anytime with infantry and armor.

Later we learned that the Germans had been ready to jump off when we appeared in the field. Apparently, they postponed the attack until they could determine what we were doing out there. By doing so, they lost the daylight hours they needed for the attack.

We rested for awhile until about 0300 hours when Mandy gave the order to move out again. We had a hard night ahead of us if we were to find our battery before morning.

We wandered throughout the forrest all night. All the units were bedded down for the night and we were challenged by sentries at least six or seven times. It was close to dawn when we finally found our battery.

Sergeant Fred Bell and Corporal Charlie Knight were the first to greet us. "We had given you idiots up for dead," he said.

He couldn't have been closer to the truth.

The sun was just coming up as Murphy and I sat down and looked at each other. His face was caked with dirt and there were streaks down from his eyes where tears had trailed. I'm sure I didn't look any better. We just had time to freshen up before we were on the go again.

It took about 10 days of fighting until the rest of the Army and some armored units arrived to relieve us. Or, at least I thought that was what they would do. Wrong! Instead of them relieving us as I thought they were supposed to do, to save an Airborne asset, we went right on chasing the enemy and taking casualties.

We continued to fight for the next three months until the Germans surrendered. By that time our squad was reduced to only four members; Corporal Gillespie, Murphy, Burnard and myself. All the others had either been killed or wounded.

After being on the cutting edge of combat like this, we had all been hardened to killing and the horrors of war. It's a wonder any of us ever returned to normal. But time has a way of mending broken bones and broken men.

Recently I visited with Tom Burnard and Charlie Knight and we talked over old times. I am happy to report that these two old heavily-bearded killers are now nothing but pussy cats! And, with the passing of the years, time has healed the pain I felt in those days. It's not bad being a pussy cat and it's a damn sight safer!

"IT'S A SMALL WORLD"

As told by Alfred West 513 A

Like so many of the guys, I was real excited when I jumped across the Rhine in "Operation Varsity." I guess I imagined all the bad things that could happen to me. I worried that if I was killed, I'd never see my family again and that made me sad.

I had my usual "spread eagle" landing, struggled out of my chute and went looking for members of my company. I was glad to be alive at this point, but I knew I still faced some rough times.

As I looked around for some of my buddies, I saw two guys talking to each other and both looked strangely familiar. I came up to them and then I knew.

Al West (center, rear) with buddies. L to R: James Simms, Leo Pinder, Trigg and Denson in early April, 1945 after Munster.

It was two of my uncles: Robert Sitzenstock (Stock) a member of the 507th Parachute Infantry Regiment and Robert Pioch, a glider pilot. Fate had put all three of us into that tiny DZ. It sure was good to see those guys and it had a calming effect on me.

We chatted a bit, wished each other good luck and then went our own ways. All three of us survived the operation without injury.

Yes sir! Old Walt Disney knew what he was talking about when he said, "It's a small world!"

"JUST IN TIME FOR THE BIG SHOW"

As told by Kendall Eyers, 513 A

On my 22nd birthday, February 6, 1945, our troopship landed at Le Harve, France and I began my trek up front. There I was to join the 513th in their positions on the Our River just opposite the German border. As one of a group of new replacements, I hardly knew what to expect, but I was eager to be assigned to a unit and to do my part.

However, before we could join them, we learned the regiment was being relieved. They then began a trip by "40 and 8" railcars until the full 17th Airborne Division closed in their new area at Chalons-sur-Marne. It was here that I finally became a member of "A" Company, 1st Platoon.

Sergeant Jerry Davis was my squad leader and he quickly helped me to fit in as a member of the squad. Time passed swiftly and after only one practice jump, we found ourselves getting ready to make a combat jump into Germany.

I know everyone, including myself, was really scared when it came time to board our C-46 and take off. At that time we didn't know how easily the C-46s would catch fire. Had we known, I suspect we would have gone anyhow. Morale was high at that time, and we were eager to prove ourselves in an Airborne operation.

I was to jump from the left door and I was sitting where I could see out. It was a piece of cake until we got to the Rhine. Then there was smoke and flak—lots of flak. We could hear it hitting the plane.

By this time we were standing up and had hooked up. We were anxious to go. Then suddenly, the guy in front of me (I believe his name was Donald Erb) said he was hit. A piece of shrapnel apparently had sailed in and hit him in the right arm.

I helped him unhook and lie down. He decided to take his chances in getting back to the airbase in the plane. He made it alright and later rejoined the unit in Germany.

Seconds later the green light came on and out we went. I was loaded down

Kendall Eyers home on leave in Wisconsin in November 1944, after graduation from jump school.

to include a bag of rifle grenades on my leg. I just fell out the door and went spinning head over heels.

My bad body position gave me twists in my risers and I had to kick and turn before I could get my head up to check my canopy. Fortunately, the chute had opened properly and I hardly had time to gather my wits when I was on the ground. I rode that leg bundle in but wasn't hurt by it.

At first, I couldn't free myself from the harness. I lay there in an open field and struggled with my canteen which had become hooked over the webbing of the parachute. It seemed like every German in the area was shooting at me. Finally, I got free and I headed for the nearest woods where I saw some other troopers.

As we formed up and headed through an orchard, one of our gliders came in near us. It bounced off the roof of a farm house and crashed into the ground on the other side. Bits of the glider and its passengers were scattered for 30-50 yards. All I could think was how glad I was that I jumped. No gliders for me.

We began to take considerable small arms, artillery and mortar fire about this time. We also spotted a tank behind a barn that would poke out every now and then and fire at the troops coming in. It was here that we learned how accurate the German fire was.

We saw a British Horsa Glider land and a small, two-man tank came roaring out. It hadn't gone 100 yards when the German tank peaked out, fired one round and set the small tank afire. Amazingly enough, the two Brits escaped.

Then we got to see one of our new Airborne weapons in action. The new 57mm recoilless rifle that we had received in France really lived up to its reputation right here. The next time the German tank peaked out one of our gunners nailed it with the 57mm and that was the end of that threat.

Our next problem was a farmhouse that was on the edge of our drop zone. Some Jerries were holed up inside and they had already killed several Company "A" troopers who had landed nearby. We had dived in a ditch half filled with water so we were anxious to get going.

Some officer shouted we were to rush the house and as he leaped out to lead the charge, he was immediately hit in the ear. He quickly leaped back into the ditch and the charge faltered. He was preparing to go again, but someone stopped him. He was hit too badly to continue.

Then Lieutenant William MacFarlane, who now lives in Crofton, Maryland, stepped up and led the charge on the house. He and three or four troopers reached the house. I had headed for a tree but when I got there there was already a trooper there.

As I was wondering how he beat me there, I realized he was dead. I waited a few moments then I thought that quite possibly the Kraut that shot him was now taking aim at me. I arose and in one motion dived headfirst over a low fence and scrambled into a foxhole. As I did, I heard bullets whizzing around me.

From the house, the Krauts hurled a rainstorm of hand grenades at us. The lieutenant yelled at the rest of us to get back so I dashed back to the ditch. It was then that I realized that my right leg pocket was shredded, either from shrapnel or bullets I never knew.

Then I did what I should have done before. I had a grenade launcher and grenades, so I set up and fired some into the house. Finally, the firing stopped and the Krauts gave up and were taken prisoners.

When we entered the house we heard some commotion in the basement. Some of the guys investigated and of all things, there was some woman in there about to give birth! That was too much for me. I got out of there! One of our guys went for help, but I never did hear how that situation was resolved.

We continued taking the fight to the Krauts and soon we were chasing them deep into Germany. Things would go good for awhile and then we'd hit a hot spot where they would give us quite a fight before withdrawing. One of those tough spots took place when we came to the Autobahn.

The DZ was a busy place. Here troopers tow a British 6-pounder anti-tank gun.

Digging in at the assembly point after the jump across the Rhine.

We moved up to the famous road during the night and dug in. Things were quiet during the night, but the next morning they threw everything they had at us. Mortars and artillery kept us in our holes, praying mostly.

One mortar round hit our radio operator's hole dead center and several others were wounded and had to be evacuated. One weird thing I remember is a mortar round that came in almost at the feet of Lieutenant MacFarland. He was lying flat on his stomach at the time and I guess that's what saved him. He didn't get a scratch, but it sure shook him up!

Later we crawled aboard the tanks of the British Guards Armored and that was good duty. We really made time, dismounting only when we hit a strong point. The Brits were a good bunch, always sharing a cup of hot tea with us whenever we stopped. They'd have it ready in about three or four minutes.

One day (I think we were near Haltern) we got word that our kitchen truck had caught up to us and we were going to get some hot chow. After weeks on K-Rations that sounded good to us. I really loaded up and found a place nearby to sit down and eat.

For some reason, however, I was uncomfortable. Something was wrong. I couldn't eat. And then it came to me: Don't bunch up; one round can get you all. That old reminder from training was nagging at me.

I said to myself it was silly to move, but I gathered up my chow and walked around the corner of the building where we were seated and found myself another spot. No sooner had I got settled good when, "WHAM!"

A German .88 had come in directly on the kitchen area. Evidently, the area was under observation by the Krauts and they had zeroed in on it. Two of our cooks were killed and several other troopers were wounded. I decided right then that I would not go back for seconds.

Apparently we didn't learn our lesson from this because a short time later a number of us bunched up by one of the British tanks and in came another .88 round. We all scrambled for cover and I was the third man in a one-man foxhole.

A young, 18-year old trooper named Taylor was knocked flat by the blast and then discovered he had two new dings in his helmet. He already had two or three small holes in it from other close calls. Needless to say, Taylor always kept his helmet on his head. He didn't have anymore problems, however, and never got more than a scratch.

I had one experience I'll not soon forget. We were moving into Munster and I was lead scout for the company. At one point I stopped beside a brick wall to look the area over. All of a sudden a bullet hit the wall just by my head.

I dropped to one knee and looked to see where the shot had come from. Then there was a second shot that would have surely got me if I hadn't dropped to my knee.

After that, I went flat. A third shot banged into the wall right where I would have been on my knee. By this time I was throwing up bricks trying to get even lower. Fortunately for me, someone had located the sniper by this time and brought enough fire on him that he scooted out.

Life was like this as our company pushed on through Germany. We all had a lot of close calls but most of us made it—in one condition or another. I remember that after five weeks of combat we had only 17 men left in our first platoon out of an original 43 or more. About 26 had been killed or wounded. It was not a fun time but my time as a paratrooper during the war remains my proudest achievement.

"THE 400-YARD DASH!"

As told by Walt Holland, 517 Sig.

One night during the week following the Rhine crossing, my partner, Slim Connors of Girardville, Pennsylvania, and I were told to set up our radio truck in a small cluster of trees at the edge of a field. On the other side of the field, about four or five hundred yards away, was a road leading toward the outskirts of the German town of Haltern.

About mid-morning the next day, I set out on foot toward Division Headquarters to find and repair a break in the telephone line that we had laid between our radio and the message center. These breaks were a frequent occurrence, and, in daylight, usually took less than an hour to fix. On this day, however, for reasons I can't remember, the task took considerably longer, and it was sometime after noon that I arrived back at the edge of the field across from the radio.

Ed Carey, also from Girardville, and, incidentally a cousin of Connors, was there operating a Jeep radio behind a wall near the road. He told me that the Germans were intermittently shelling the field with .88mm air bursts. He said the shelling seemed to have no pattern, but some had come close enough to cause him to dig a slit trench next to the wall.

Just then, a cluster of three shells exploded near enough to send us both diving into his trench. When we climbed out, Carey said he had been told the Germans were firing from a wooded ridge to our left from which they commanded a view of the entire field. This was disturbing news as this was the field I had to cross to get back to Connors and our radio. Carey didn't know whether shells were also exploding in the trees that concealed our radio.

As I huddled near the Jeep, I realized that I had to make a move. I couldn't stay here. Carey hadn't complained about sharing his slit trench, but, obviously, it wasn't intended for double occupancy. Besides, my conscience was really bothering me about having left Connors alone for so long. My imagination had conjured this vision of him, wounded and bleeding, and unable to call for help.

My plan to get across the field was based on two premises: one, I would zig-zag as I ran, just as they had taught us in basic training; two, I told myself that, at this stage of the war, the Germans surely would not waste .88 shells on a single person. This last thought shows the extent of my rationalization. I completely ignored the fact that the Germans were already wasting ammunition by shelling an empty field. In fact, they might find a live, moving target kind of exciting.

However, having convinced myself, I started running across the field. Right away both my premises fell apart. First, I forgot all about zig-zagging and ran straight as an arrow; secondly, the Germans were indeed willing to waste shells on a single person. Fortunately, the shells were exploding behind me. I could hear them but I couldn't see them. If they had been in front of me I don't know what I would have done. One thing I'm sure of, though, is that if someone had been timing me with a stop watch that day, I would have set a record for the 400 yard dash that would still be unbroken.

When I reached the woods, I saw that the radio truck had not been hit. The whole area looked as secure and untouched as when I'd left hours before. Nevertheless, I knew that Connors would be glad to see me. He would have been able to hear the shelling, and knowing how little you could see from inside the radio truck, I knew how concerned he would be, wondering what was going on.

I will never forget what he said to me as exhausted and gasping for breath, I finally climbed into the truck. That phrase, those memorable words, are forever etched in my memory. He said, "Was there any mail?"

"I WAS A PRISONER OF WAR"

As told by Bill Whalen, 194 C

Maybe it was the training we had received to prepare us for this day— it had all been very professional and highly organized. And, maybe it was the realization that after the Battle of the Bulge and its freezing snow and fog, we knew nothing could be that bad. In any event, as our Company "C" of the 194th loaded our gliders that morning for "Operation Varsity," I was not afraid or nervous.

We all knew we were not going on a picnic and that the Krauts would be waiting for us, but now we were confident in our own abilities. It was different than it was last December when we were hurriedly thrown into the chaos of the Bulge.

We were all trying to keep loose with a joke here or there, but we were serious about the impending mission. I remember that only the weapons platoon leader, Lieutenant Claussen, seemed to very up-tight. A deep frown curled across his forehead and he was obviously worried about the task at hand. Years later I learned that he was killed in action that day.

It was a beautiful morning and things seemed to be going just as planned. We had a smooth take-off and our tow took its place in the vast armada that was circling the Chalons-sur-Marne area. Then we headed east and each of us craned our necks to peak out the small windows and retreated into our own thoughts.

It wasn't long until we spotted the wide Rhine River below us. Beyond it we could see nothing but smoke. It had the advantage of covering our approach, but at the same time, it screened the LZ and we knew it would force our glider pilot to make a near-blind landing.

As he tried to spot an opening in the smoke, the anti-aircraft fire rose up to meet us. The other glider in our double tow cut loose and was gone. Still we plowed on as the tow ship maintained a straight-ahead flight.

Finally, I heard our pilot say, "Well, we're not doing any good up here, we might as well go on down!"

Billy Whalen was captured after his glider missed the LZ.

With that he reached up, pulled the lever overhead, and we started our trip down through the smoke and fire. We broke out into the clear in a few seconds and found ourselves a few hundred feet above the ground.

There was plenty of open field for our landing and that was no problem. Rough maybe, but no one was hurt. We piled out and headed for some nearby woods where we stopped and tried to get our bearings.

I remember how quiet it was. We couldn't hear any firing—not even the artillery and anti-aircraft guns. It was like we were alone in the middle of Germany.

Lieutenant Glasser, our platoon leader, poured over his map as he tried to locate our position. As his runner, I stayed close to him and awaited his orders which I would pass on the squad that comprised our glider load.

Finally, it was determined that we had come down some seven to eight miles from our intended landing zone. We were deep into enemy territory and we were definitely "on our own."

I carried the small 300 radio (the "walky-talky") but with a range of two to three miles, it was useless. The only option we had was to move out in a southwesterly direction and by stealth and evasion, try to reach the area of the main landing and marry up with our own troops.

Everything was so quiet at this time, we thought we may have been able to have landed undetected. Later we learned how foolish this was. Apparently, we had been observed from the very beginning. The Germans were just waiting the most opportune time to jump us.

That time wasn't long in coming. After we had gone a few hundred yards through the woods, we came under fire. Snipers dropped a couple of our guys and we all hit the ground and spread out. We later found out it was a German parachute unit that had hurriedly set up an ambush when they saw our lone glider descending.

Lieutenant Glasser told me how to disperse the men and I scrambled into the brush to find the squad leader and pass on the order. It amazed me but all of a sudden our guys had seemingly vanished. I couldn't find anyone!

I could see fire coming from the trees across a wide gully from our woods. I began to shout at the top of my voice, "Spray the trees! Spray the trees!"

The guys heard me because I heard Dick Maurey, the BAR man, open up and many of the squad armed with M1s started ripping the trees. I saw one German fall from a tree—my first glimpse of the enemy that had us pinned down.

According to Lieutenant Glasser's orders, I placed one of our new replacements (I never really knew his name) at the edge of our woods. I got a good view of things then and I could see we were up against a sizable force.

I hurried back to the lieutenant and we were trying to decide what to do when suddenly he was struck in the side of the head by a bullet. It was a bad wound and at first I thought it had killed him.

The round had also destroyed his first aid packet attached to his helmet, so I opened mine, doused his wound with sulfur, applied a bandage, and gave him a shot of morphine. He was alive with his eyes wide open, but apparently he couldn't speak.

The firing at us continued and I scrambled into the brush trying to locate Staff Sergeant Standridge, the squad leader. It was a hell of a spot for me, a lowly private first class, and I needed some help fast!

I never found the sergeant, but later I heard he was dead. The fire from across the gully had found him. I then started hunting for Sergeant Gabriel Renzi, the assistant squad leader, but I couldn't locate him either.

I found another of our men, but he had been hit and he was dead. By this time, our return fire had tapered off drastically. I wondered how many of the other guys had been hit and if we could continue to resist. I fought the idea of surrender, but subconsciously I knew we were approaching that decision.

I went back to the edge of the woods and tried to see what was happening. Strangely enough, I realized that I was not afraid. Mostly I was mad at the level of responsibility that I was beginning to feel had been placed on me. As a private first class, I wasn't supposed to have to make big decisions like I saw looming before me!

The Germans then threw the book at us. We received machine gun fire, rockets, mortars—everything they had. The woods thundered and tree limbs showered down on us. After five minutes my ears were ringing and my head swam with the concussion of the barrage they loosed at us.

I looked over at Maurey and he had been riddled. Another of our best had been killed. Things were not looking good for us and I guess I knew then that it was futile to continue to resist.

Then I saw the most incredible thing. Across the gully, a German officer stepped out in the open, completely exposed. He called out in English for us to surrender before he called in another barrage.

In the quiet of that moment I could see Germans all around us. We were surrounded on at least three sides and our ability to resist was completely gone. It was time to save the few of us that were left. One more barrage like the last one and it would be over for all of us.

I looked around and I could only see Renzi, a commo man named Miller, one other guy and myself. Renzi nodded and it was agreed. We lay down our weapons, raised our hands and stepped out of the woods. It was all over.

The German officer advanced and said to us, "The war is over for you. Don't be afraid."

The soldiers behind him emerged from the woods and we could plainly see we had been greatly outnumbered. It would have only been a matter of minutes until they had wiped us out.

One of the Germans had suffered a bad leg wound and he threatened us. The officer spoke to him harshly and he immediately shut up. The officer then turned to us and said, "He has a bad wound and could lose that leg. He has already lost a brother in the war, so he can't be blamed for being a little mad."

I then told the officer that our officer had been wounded and could we go and get him and take him with us. He agreed and two German soldiers accompanied us back to the spot where we had left Lieutenant Glasser.

We made a litter from limbs and field jackets, gently loaded Lieutenant Glasser aboard and started our trip to the POW camp that we knew awaited us somewhere. He was still alive, but could not communicate with us.

We carried him nearly 23 miles as we wound our way back through Germany. We were about to drop when we reached a pretty good sized town and identified a hospital a distance off the road. Our captors told us to put the lieutenant down there.

They sent some civilians to the hospital for them to come get him and told us we would have to move on. Although we didn't like the idea of leaving him beside the road like that, we realized we were near the end of our endurance and that he had to have medical aid or he would die.

I took his hand and looked into his eyes and told him he was going to be okay. I think he understood me, but he did not speak. Although I have never seen Lieutenant Glasser since that moment, I did hear he survived the war. For that I am grateful.

From that time on, time meant little. We walked on through dozens of small villages and towns. We were not mistreated, but we were given very little to eat and we were terribly tired at the end of each day.

As we were shuttled from one group of Volkstrum to another, we were joined by other allied prisoners—mostly English glidertroopers. We were headed for a railyard where transportation was supposed to be waiting to evacuate us to a POW camp. However, when we arrived, we were told "our friends" had been over and bombed out the yard!

One day as we trudged down the road we were strafed by our own P-47 fighter planes. We scattered as did our guards, but there was no chance of escaping. I think some of the prisoners were wounded, but none were killed. The four of us made it without harm. Believe me, that was a very frightening experience and made us appreciate what the Germans were getting every day.

Later a captured P-47 pilot joined our prisoner column and he said we wouldn't have to fear being strafed anymore as the squadrons had been alerted to the fact POWs are on the roads. He was right. The planes completely ignored us from then on even though we saw German combat units moving up on the same roads.

The long trek back into Germany became a blur to us. I remember passing through a large city. I think it was Frankfurt or maybe Hanover. We headed northeast sleeping in barns, trying to find a rutabaga or anything that we could eat. Our guards were not much better off than we were.

One day we reached a POW camp called Falingbastal, or something like that. It was packed, however, and we were made to move on. It was lucky for us as most of the prisoners there were Polish and they were very poorly treated.

We walked on until finally we came to the coastal city of Bremerhaven. There we were delivered to a camp called Melag 10, which stands for Maritime Internment Lager. Here the prisoners were primarily merchant seamen who had been torpedoed in the North Sea making the dangerous Marmask run carrying arms to Russia.

Most of the sailors here had been imprisoned for two to three years and they had pretty well adjusted to the routine. Many of them went out daily on work details and they brought back food and news of the war. They really took care of us and we owe a lot to them.

I got to be friends with an older sailor who had been captured in the same way during World War I! His name was Bill something and he was of Russian descent and lived in the Baltimore area. I'll never forget how good that cigar tasted that Bill gave me one day!

Life dragged on at Melag. We had a secret radio in the compound and we eagerly listened to the BBC broadcasts and waited and prayed for the end of the war. Our German guards did not mistreat us, but they did little to help us get through the long days of confinement.

We would get a half loaf of black bread every now and then and maybe a little cheese. Our hosts also served us what we learned to call "skilly." It was a broth of some sort. It wasn't tasty, but it was warm and it kept us alive.

One of the best things was the Red Cross parcels. We didn't get any, but the sailors had received a number of them before we arrived and they were very good about sharing them with us.

We slept in wooden bunks the men had built. We had blankets and kept warm enough and we learned to live with the lice that infected both. If you did what the Germans required you to do and mostly kept your mouth shut, you got along okay. The Germans knew the war was lost and they didn't want any more trouble from us.

One day we could hear firing off in the distance and we knew the war was getting close. All day long it went on and by that evening it was really loud. No one could sleep that night as we sensed our liberation was eminent.

Sometime in the night a British patrol actually reached the fences of our compound. They told us the area was not completely clear as yet and that we should stay where we were for now. They expected to be able to free us the next day, but didn't want a bunch of unarmed ex-POWs running around loose on their battlefield!

The next day we were treated to a ringside seat of a tank battle. The Brits and the Germans banged away at each other from one hill to the other and we watched like spectators at a bowl game! It was like we were not even involved in the war.

Soon the Germans turned tail and fled and our rescuers threw open the gates and we were once again free men! We later learned that our guards had bugged out the night before and we could have walked out then. But, no one was that eager to get in the crossfire.

It had been a long six weeks for the four of us "C" Company troopers. We had walked farther than we had thought we could and we had eaten less than we thought we could get by on. Before we left the area, the prisoners butchered a cow and we had a real feast. That was the best steak I have ever eaten!

"THE BRONZE STAR"

A story about Arthur P. Bronzo, 507 I

Bravery comes in many different packages. Some brag about their deeds. Others downplay their actions and are reluctant to talk about it. Many who display bravery say they thought little about it at the time, and that they were only doing their duty. Sometimes doing your duty means laying your life on the line.

Arthur Bronzo was only a 19 year old youngster when early one April morning he laid his life on the line. While under fire, he made his way across a collapsed bridge and firing his M-1 as he went, charged head on into a machine gun position 100 yards away. Although wounded in the hand and face by shrapnel, he certainly didn't hesitate to do his duty.

Arthur Bronzo, winner of the Bronze Star for valor.

In addition to the Purple Heart, Art Bronzo won the Bronze Star for his actions that morning. To get the feel of the action and courage it demanded from the young trooper, read the exact words of the citation as it was written in 1945:

"ARTHUR P. BRONZO, Private First Class, 42130710, for heroic conduct against the enemy in combat at Bottrop, Germany on April 7, 1945. Private First Class Bronzo, a lead scout, when his platoon was assigned the mission of establishing a bridgehead across the Rhine-Herne Canal, led off with the utmost courage and aggressiveness. The only route of approach was a collapsed bridge which was under heavy enemy artillery, machine gun, and small arms fire. Private First Class Bronzo continued his advance in the face of heavy fire from a house directly across the canal. The remainder of the platoon, following in single file, was pinned down by this machine gun and its supporting rifle fire. Private First Class Bronzo, without a moment's hesitation, charged the house, entered it, herded ten civilians into one room, and then preceded down to the cellar where the machine gun was located, firing his rifle and shouting as he went. Nine of the enemy bolted out the rear entrance and 11 threw down their arms and surrendered to him. Private First Class Bronzo's heroic actions enabled his platoon to proceed and successfully accomplish it's mission, and is in keeping with the highest traditions of the United States Airborne Forces."

"JUMPING INTO GERMANY"

As told by Robert "Lendy" McDonald, 513 A

"**A**" Company, 513 Parachute Infantry Regiment came out of the Bulge with only 45 men ready for duty. And, that's out of approximately 200 troopers who were originally committed to combat. The worst part about it is the fact we were one of the largest companies left in the regiment.

When we arrived at Chalons-sur-Marne, we were in bad need of rebuilding and refitting. Soon we began to get some of our wounded back from the hospitals and then the replacements began to pour in. Finally, we got a new CO and even a new battalion commander.

We were issued new equipment and after resting up, we began training again. Most of the veteran members of the company got passes to Paris and some even got furloughs home to the States. Slowly life returned to almost normal.

We made a practice jump using a new airplane, a C-46. It looked a lot like the old familiar C-47 except it was a little larger and it had two doors (one on each side) from which to jump. This meant that more troopers could jump together, empty the plane faster and land in a tighter pattern on the ground.

What we didn't know then was that this new plane did not have self-sealing gas tanks. In combat, when they were hit, gasoline poured back along the fuselage and likely as not, ignited and turned the C-46 into a flying torch. This was to send many a trooper to his death in the coming operation.

The big day (March 24, 1945) finally came for us. We started loading for "Operation Varsity" before dawn and we circled some three or four hours while the vast air armada formed for the thrust into Germany.

They told us we would never be over 50 air miles from our drop zone. As it was the largest airborne assault ever mounted, it took that long just to get everyone airborne and into their proper position before heading over the Rhine.

Another thing I remember they told us: We would have a fighter escort but they expected the new German jet planes (whatever a jet plane was) to run them off. That was a comforting thought.

I was next to last in my stick, so I was near the crew compartment. I saw the navigator's seat was unoccupied so I helped myself. There was a large plastic observation bubble over the seat and it provided a wonderful view of the invasion fleet.

In every direction, except to the front, there was a continuous stream of airplanes and gliders as far as I could see. I had never seen so many! There were literally thousands and my confidence grew by leaps and bounds!

It was about 0945 now and we were given the order to "stand up and hook up!" No sooner had we done so than we began to hear the sharp crack of German anti-aircraft fire. We were crossing the Rhine and the war was heating up again!

Suddenly the area where we were standing was showered with plastic. I looked back at Bill Trigg,

Robert "Lendy" McDonald ready to board for a practice jump. It was easy when no one was shooting at you!

the trooper who was standing behind me, to see if he was okay. He was fine so I looked up and saw that the observation bubble was gone with just a few jagged pieces left.

Then I looked down at the metal seat in which I had been sitting moments before. The seat was practically gone with just a mass of sharp, jagged metal fingers pointing up. We had taken an ack-ack round straight up through the plane. Luckily it didn't explode. Even more luckily for me, I wasn't still sitting in that seat.

We were coming in low and they had us in their sights, I know. I could hear the shrapnel and machine gun rounds popping through the plane. I wanted to get out of there!

The green light was on and I heard someone yell, "Go, go, go!" The line of troopers in front of me began to empty out. I could feel Trigg pressing behind me as we moved toward the door.

When I got to the door, there was a wall of fire outside. I turned to Trigg and yelled, "Jump the other door!"

Fire covered that door too and Trigg yelled back, "No time! Go on, jump!"

Someway I figured that the fire would melt my nylon chute, but I had no choice. This baby was going down and I had to take my chances jumping. So out I went with Trigg right on my tail!

We were to jump at 600 feet, but when we went out, we couldn't have been more than 300 feet off the ground. The chute opened with a shock and before I could do anything, I slammed into the ground.

I rolled over in time to see our flaming plane go over a treeline and a huge ball of flame and smoke go up when it hit the ground. The pilot and co-pilot never got out. They held the plane level until all of us jumped and then they were killed. They should have received the Medal of Honor.

I got out of my chute and was cutting out a large section of the canopy to use as a blanket when I heard a swishing sound. At first I thought it was a mortar round and I looked up just in time to see some poor trooper come sailing in with a streamer. Someway the chute had failed and he had had no time to pull his emergency. He hit with a sickening thud and the war was over for him in a hurry.

With four or five other troopers I ran to a ditch on the side of the field. We crouched low and followed that ditch down toward some houses. We began to take automatic fire from one of the houses so we went to the ground in the ditch.

A British officer came running down the road and dived into the ditch beside us. He asked who was in charge and what the situation was. As a staff sergeant, I told him I guess I was and that apparently there was a German machine gun firing at us from one of the houses.

With that, he abruptly stood up and said, "Well, let's go and get them blokes!"

It was his last words as he fell back in the ditch almost cut in half by a burst from the machine gun.

We crawled on down the ditch to within about 10 yards of the house and began throwing grenades inside. When the dust had settled all was quiet in the house. I felt bad about the Brit. If he had just waited a minute. He was brave but very foolish.

It was early afternoon before I found Captain Anderson, our new company commander. He had injured his leg badly on the jump, but he was dragging along trying to get the company organized. We had missed our DZ by a couple of miles so we had a way to go to accomplish our assigned mission.

There were railroad tracks that ran through the woods that were our objective, so we were hunting for those tracks. After a few hours we found them and soon were involved in a fire fight with the Germans defending the area.

By this time we had gathered a pretty good sized little force. We had Pinder, Graan, Kidulich, Dennison, Trigg, Segner, Wernz, Leathers, Lieutenant Beckett and some others. There were some 30 other troopers pinned down behind the railroad tracks. A Kraut machine gun kept anyone from advancing.

We learned the group had started to advance across the tracks and an open field when the machine gun had opened up on them. All had made it back to the tracks except one and he now lay in the open field and no one could get to him.

While the entire body of men brought a heavy concentration of covering

Parachutes draped over the power lines marked the route of the troopers' advance.

fire on the machine gun, Graan and I ran out, grabbed the injured man and ran back across the tracks. We fell to the ground exhausted, but uninjured.

Captain Anderson said that he had seen us do this and he was going to put us both in for Silver Stars. A few hours later he had to be evacuated because of his leg injury and that was the last we ever heard of the Silver Star stuff.

Somebody finally got a bazooka round on the machine gun and that problem was eliminated. After that, it was fire a few rounds and then they would give up. I guess they realized we were there in force now and there was no reason to die in vain. In any event, our POW bag really began to mount up.

When night came we were pretty well beat. I joined Kenny Segner and Kenny Graan as we dug in under the wing of a crashed glider. We wrapped up in parachute canopy, munched on some "K" rations and agreed, that compared to the Bulge and winter in the Ardennes, this was sheer luxury.

All the next day, we moved further into Germany meeting with mild resistance and taking more and more prisoners. It began to look like we might get out of this operation alive.

Late that evening, after we had cleared a large wooded area, we came to a large open field with woods on the other side. We radioed back for orders and were told to move out and clear these woods too.

It was getting dark fast and we told Lieutenant Beckett with no more visibility than we had, we were afraid we would be shooting at each other. Not knowing what we might run into, we suggested it would be smarter to wait until morning.

Lieutenant Beckett agreed and had the radioman radio back our decision. We got an immediate reply to that telling us to get our tails up and clear the woods.

I have to admire Lieutenant Beckett. He grabbed that radio, identified himself and said, "You tell General Miley that if he wants those woods cleared tonight, he'd better hurry on down here!" That's all we ever heard on that matter.

Early the next morning we moved across the field and into the wooded area. After several hundred yards, we came to another clearing and could see bunkers and activity in the woods beyond. We brought fire on them and started across one or two at a time.

I was watching one of our guys named Clawson running hard when I saw something in the air heading toward him. It was a Panzerfaust round, the equivalent of our bazooka. It hit the ground, seemingly right at his feet, and exploded in a cloud of dirt and smoke. Clawson kept on coming, not missing a step and not getting a scratch.

We had now reached the German Autobahn, the superhighway, so we were told. We couldn't really tell at that time as it was still in the ground stage of construction. Anyway, it was one of our main objectives and we had made it there and we were still in one piece.

Later when the regular forces broke through and caught up with us, we were attached to the British and rode their tanks as we pushed on into the Ruhr Valley. We would ride until we met opposition, then dismount and wipe them up and then ride some more.

Things were going pretty good for me until the tank I was riding was hit by one those Panzerfaust rounds. I was blown off the tank, wounded, and knocked unconscious. When I finally came to, I was paralyzed in both legs and my right arm, and I couldn't speak. My buddies all figured I had been killed and wrote me off.

Years later when Ken Graan visited me at my home, he told me in the presence of my mother, that they had felt so sorry for me that they had drug my body off the road so the tanks wouldn't run over me and mess me up. Poor Mom nearly fainted. I made Ken swear he wouldn't tell her any more war stories.

"LONG ROAD TO MUNSTER"

As told by Dean Swem, 513 I

The drop over the Rhine had been made on March 24, 1945, at 1000 hours on a bright, sunny morning. The initial objective to "establish islands of defense" had been completed.

The next phase, to cross the German Autobahn and secure the high ground beyond, had been accomplished by the classic infantry school tactic of "marching fire" preceded by an artillery bombardment. The troopers were hard to control when they finally reached the ridge at the top and realized they had accomplished their Airborne mission.

Now it was time to wait for the arrival of the British tanks. The tanks were to pick up the troopers and carry them on a swift salient

Dean Swem. After the shooting, on pass in Paris!

to the Ruhr. Operated by the Scots and Coldstream Guards, the tanks had crossed the Rhine earlier and were to "marry up" with the troopers here at the Autobahn.

The troopers eagerly mounted the tanks when they arrived as they thought they would have an easy ride the rest of the way. To any infantryman, the chance to ride instead of walking was a welcome opportunity. Those tanks were big, their guns were big and the tankers themselves were big and mean looking.

Strangely, the tanks were all named after birds! Cygnet, Swan, Lark, etc. However, those tough, veteran tankers who had fought Rommel in Africa were anything but birdlike, unless you thought of a flock of mean, nasty old fighting cocks!

When the column moved out, the troopers clinging to the tops of the tanks soon began to realize something they had never thought about before. Those big, powerful engines generated a lot of heat and in no time, the decks of the tanks were like a frying pan! So hot, in fact, a Jerry-can of water carried on the deck was ready for brewing tea whenever a halt was called.

Except for the tea breaks and when heavy resistance was encountered, the column never stopped. Snipers were everywhere and frequently a trooper was picked off as the tanks roared through the countryside. Seems like anyone, kids, old men, males and females, anyone who could aim and fire a Mauser rifle-was a potential sniper. The "meat wagons" followed the tanks and picked up those who were hit and we roared on.

Soon, things really began to get rough. The white flags of surrender became fewer and fewer and the resistance got meaner. They were not giving up anymore as we got deeper and deeper into Germany. The troopers had to dismount and clear every house and every little village.

It finally dawned on the troopers that after they had cleared a strongpoint and sent the prisoners to the rear, the tankers were getting even for the damage done by the Germans to Britain. Also, those tankers had not been able to get home for some four years and they were just plain mean. Few of those prisoners ever reached the safety of the POW enclosures.

So it went, village after village, town after town, day and night the salient rolled on. The names ran together; Haltern, Baldern, Dulmen, etc., but each one got harder and harder to take.

The 3rd Battalion of the 513th was assigned to clear the left sector of a rather large town and then to move to the high ground beyond. Our company,

I Company 513th awaits the order to load their plane for "Operation Varsity." Dean Swem is the fifth seated jumper from the left.

I Company, 513th PIR bails out over the Rhine, note the smoke.

Company "I," was given the left portion of that sector. Our new company commander called the platoon leaders in to issue the attack order.

As platoon leader of the 3rd Platoon, I was given responsibility for the extreme left of our sector. I gave it a real hard look. I formerly had been the first sergeant of the company and had received a battlefield commission during our action in the

513th I takes prisoners after the Rhine Jump.

Bulge. I was on to a lot of the tricks that the Germans were apt to pull and I didn't want to get our guys zapped by going off half-cocked.

On the other hand, the captain who was now our company commander had only recently arrived overseas and had been assigned to us during the time we were at Chalons. He was totally combat untested. In fact, he had already given me some cause to doubt his ability to command a combat unit.

There was an open common to our front that apparently was used by the village to graze their livestock. To the left of this open area that we would have to cross was a series of large buildings that appeared to include a school and

Glider troopers of the 194th take a break along the road to Haltern, Germany.

a hospital. The Germans were known to use schools and hospitals as ammunition dumps and troop cover and these buildings worried me.

I asked the captain who had responsibility for reconnoitering and clearing that extreme flank and securing all these buildings. When I didn't get a satisfactory answer, I told him I wanted to take a detail and clear them before we started across the common. As any good infantryman knows, you should know who and what is on your flanks at all times. If you get caught in the open, flanking fire will wipe out a whole unit.

The captain refused my suggestion saying that "battalion was responsible" and told me again to get going. When I asked "who in battalion," he really got hot. I wanted to check myself to be sure, but he screamed at me to get going before he had me court-martialed.

I could see that I wasn't going to get anywhere arguing with him, so I shrugged and called my platoon sergeant, Marvin Earl Rice, over and clued him in on what was coming down. I told him we would move out but every man should be very, very alert to that flank. In the event we drew fire, we would head for a small barn just to the left and take cover.

When we had advanced far enough that we were committed and couldn't turn back, they opened up on us. Withering small arms and automatic weapons fire poured in on us from those very buildings on our flank that had been my concern. We took several casualties but the rest of were lucky enough to make it to the barn and what protection it afforded.

Inside we took cover and I began to try to figure out a way to get my men out of this mess. There was a half door affording a good view of the enemy position and I would take a quick look out and then pace back and forth cussing myself for letting the captain talk me into this dumb situation.

I said I should have disobeyed the captain's order and gone ahead and checked out that flank. I knew I was right and now here I was in trouble over my head. I paced back and forth stopping only to look out the door at the Germans who now had us trapped. It was only a matter of time and I knew I had to do something and fast!

Sergeant Melvin Grant from Troy, New York had been assigned to us a replacement just before the drop. He was a good squad leader, an experienced non-com despite not having any combat time prior to this. A solid, no-nonsense guy who was respected by the men.

Grant spoke up saying, "What's the deal, lieutenant? Are we bogged down here? We oughta keep moving."

I told him it sure didn't look good for now and I was going to have to quit kicking myself and do something that would probably get some more of us hurt. I said the only thing I knew to do was to take some of our number and rush those buildings head on. Otherwise, they'd just keep picking us off one a time. It was a hell'uva decision to have to make.

Grant then replied, "Well, then you won't mind if I have a look too, will you?"

He rose and went to the half-door and looked out. I guess he looked too long. A round that probably was intended for me the next time I walked to the door, struck Grant in the heart and he fell dead on the barn floor.

17th troopers linked up with British tankers after jumping in at Wesel.

This was a terrible thing and I was quite disturbed, but all of us were in imminent danger and I had to think about the others and not mourn this brave man. I quickly told Sergeant Dan Acosta, our machine gunner Paul Dunlap, and a young kid who was long on guts that I called Harry "The Horse" Deaton, to get ready because we were going to rush the enemy position.

Rush them we did, yelling, cussing, screaming and firing as we went. Across that open space and into the buildings Dunlap carried that .30 caliber machine gun and fired it from his hip just like in the Hollywood movies!

On the road to Munster, the troopers rode atop the British tanks.

We were damn lucky again. We got across without mishap and quickly built up a base of fire that allowed the others to leave the barn and move up to our positions. The remainder of the platoon soon joined us and the defending enemy was either killed, wounded, captured or bugged out.

Of course, we then had to clear the flank, just as it should have been done in the beginning. And, we also found the suspected arms cache in the hospital. The school had been used to house the German troops.

The way I felt about it was some good men had paid the price of not following good infantry tactics at the very beginning. I resolved right then and there I wouldn't let the fear of a court-martial keep me from taking the necessary action if I was ever faced with that situation again in the future. Unfortunately, that time was soon to come.

As our column of British tanks approached the large, German city of Munster, we halted and were given the order to dismount and to locate and secure all bridges in our respective areas. We were closing in on the enemy in his own backyard and we knew the going was going to be rough from here on out.

My platoon was given the point for the battalion. We moved out with scouts Harry "The Horse" Deaton and Sergeant Cecil Deal to my left and right. Sergeant Rice followed with the platoon dispersed to his rear.

Things went smoothly and finally we topped a rise and there in plain view were three bridges over a good-sized canal. Two of the bridges had already been dropped, but the third one was in good shape and seemed to be just waiting for us!

There was a small problem, however. There were two guards on the bridge. One was on the end nearest us and appeared to be on the alert with his Schmeizer pointed in our direction. On the other end was another guard and we could see that he had a detonating device, a small black box with a plunger. He was ready to blow the bridge as soon as we showed ourselves.

I sent "The Horse" back to get the captain and bring him forward so we could formulate a plan. We needed that bridge so the tanks could follow us on into Munster and provide us with some support as we cleared the city.

My idea was to take a detail to creep along the riverbank until we could get close enough to pick off both of the guards at the same instance. We could then disarm the charges and the bridge would be ours.

The captain agreed and we set a time of one and a half hours. I took Deaton, Sergeant Deal and Sergeant Rice with me to get the guards. The captain was to wait with the rest of the company until the deed was done. We hacked our watches and moved out.

There were scrubby little trees and lots of brush along the river bank and the going was slow, but we were making good progress and as yet, were undetected. Finally, after about 45 minutes, we had reached a point almost directly under the bridge. In another minute we would be ready to fire.

I was surprised to see the guard on the friendly side of the bridge, turn and run like the devil for the far end. Knowing something was wrong, we fired in vain, but it was too late. We were not in a good position then and the guards were alerted and able to avoid our fire.

Then it happened. There was this terrible explosion and the bridge went up in a roar! Stones, some as large as your body and support timbers began to rain down on us. Our ears rang and dust choked our lungs. I still don't know why it didn't kill us all, but surprisingly enough, we escaped serious injury.

We climbed up the bank to the road surface to see what had happened that had blown this perfect opportunity to capture intact this much-needed bridge. We couldn't believe what we saw.

Here came the entire company with the captain leading them down the road like it was a parade. I was completely puzzled. What could have happened to our time schedule? Only 45 minutes and here came the whole company! Why didn't they give us the time we had agreed upon? What went wrong?

I really blew my top. I screamed at the captain, calling him names I hadn't uttered since my days as a first sergeant! I demanded to know why he had moved out early, alerting the guards and almost getting us killed.

Imagine my amazement when he said, "The more I looked, the more those guys on the bridge looked like friendlies, so I moved the company out."

I couldn't believe it. I got right up in his face and screamed, "With those long gray overcoats, jack-boots and peaked caps, they looked like friendlies? If you don't get with it, you're going to get us all killed!"

Well, it was over. We had to wade the canal and the tanks had to wait until the engineers could throw a Bailey Bridge across it. We had missed a good chance to charge on into Munster, but that was the way it was.

There never was any mention of a court-martial and that wasn't the last boner our CO pulled. After that, however, I never trusted him again. Someway, most of us made it and came home in one piece. I guess the good Lord must love paratroopers.

"MY BROTHER AND I WERE AIRBORNE"

As told by Vitautas Thomas, 194 HQ 2

This was to be our first Airborne mission and at that time we had no idea it would be our last. In fact, it was to be the last Airborne mission of the war; but to us, it just seemed the war would go on and on and God only knew how many times we would have to go through this routine.

I faced the mission with grim determination to come out of it alive. The war had already claimed my brother who had been a trooper in our sister regiment, the 193rd. He had been a scout in "D" Company and had been killed in the Bulge. I was determined to do my duty, but to take no unnecessary chances. I didn't want to be another dead hero.

There were six of us in our glider. Most of the room was taken up with a Jeep loaded with ammunition. I was going to sit in the Jeep and I knew I'd have a spectacular view of the landing through the nose windows. If the Germans put a round in the glider and hit that ammo, I also knew it would all be over in a hurry.

We circled around Brussels, Belgium several times as our formations got organized and then we headed east for the Rhine. I never saw so many planes and gliders in the air at once. It was a sight to behold!

When we reached the Rhine, things began to get real serious. We no longer joked among ourselves. We just held on and prayed under our breath that we would be able to get down safely.

Our landing was rough, but we were all okay and in one piece. The jolt had sent my helmet and my rifle flying over the hood of the Jeep and just behind the pilots' seats. As soon as we gathered our wits, we realized we were getting fire from somewhere. We grabbed a .30 caliber machine gun, piled out of the glider and scrambled into a slight depression a short distance away.

We couldn't tell where the fire was coming from, but there was a house across the field and we guessed that was the location. My buddy set the gun up toward the house and we laid low for awhile.

Things got quiet after a few minutes, so I decided I had better go back to

Troopers of 155th await to board their glider for the trip over the Rhine. L to R: J. Landreth, L. Dunkowski, A. Damico, J. Maliko, unidentified.

the glider and get my helmet and rifle. I felt naked there in enemy territory without them!

I reached the glider without trouble and was about to climb over the Jeep to retrieve my equipment when I stopped and thought again. If we were being observed, they'd have a great view and could pick me off easy. Then, I wondered how accurate could they be from the distance where that house was? Then I decided there was no reason to test them. I'd play it safe and crawl to the front of the glider, squeezing between the wheels of the Jeep and the sides of the glider.

Well, I guess they could see me or maybe they were just making it too hot for anyone to recover that Jeep, but when my head was just beside the wheel of the Jeep, a round hit the tire. If it had blown with a loud bang, I probably would have had a heart attack, but it just made a hissing sound and went flat. That, however, was enough for me. I got out of there!

I scrambled back to the others and found that my buddy, a guy named Whelan from Watertown, New York, had taken a bullet through his cheek and another in the arm. I tried to give him some first aid and in the process, I got pretty well soaked in his blood.

We were pinned down and there wasn't much we could do. After awhile some British came through the woods and that took the pressure off of us at last. We were able to get Whelan to the medics and I was able to go back to the glider to get my helmet and rifle.

That's when I saw it. One of the rounds had gone through my helmet leaving one neat hole and one gapping one. Luckily, it hadn't been on my head at the time!

Later on, when the other guys in the company saw me with the holes in my helmet and my jacket covered with Whelan's blood, their jaws really dropped open! It was like they were seeing a ghost!

We had a few more adventures before the war finally wound down. We were in Mulheilm when we heard that President Roosevelt had died. And, then there was occupational duty and the longing for the orders to go home. But, I had made it. I was going home. My brother would have to wait until later.

"YOU ARE MY PRISONER!"

As told by Robert Vannatter, 507 HQ1

It was the Rhine jump. We still had about an hour to go to our drop zone, just outside Wesel, Germany. Quietness had settled in throughout the plane. Each was with their own thoughts. It could be expected that some will die.

It's hard to maintain even an air of calmness to hide the buildup of fear as the time approaches. I had seen it before: faces without expression, eyes unfocussed. Perhaps recounting their last goodbyes with a loved one, praying, or visualizing what their encounter may be when they hit the ground.

I fought to overcome the emotions. I wanted to be cool. I wouldn't dwell on a thought. If I made a nervous gesture, I turned it into a deliberate one. Yet I wouldn't let myself become too nonchalant. Pleased, and at times amused, at my own success, it gave me strength. I wondered if those in my view were seeing me as I saw myself. After all, I was the ranking NCO in the plane, and would be their kick-out man.

The crew chief exited the cabin. Ten minutes, he advised the major, our stick leader. Everyone stirred to a new sense of alertness. We made last minute checks of our equipment: harness straps, weapon, reserve chute, chin strap, ammo pouches, all secure.

Almost immediately the major stood in the door. It seemed like two minutes, then, in quite rapid succession, "stand up and hook up, stand in the door, go!" I had hooked up behind the major's static line. It would be my position as the kick-man (an affectionate term mostly) to stand by the door and take care of mishaps, or urge hesitant jumpers. I would be the last man out. Someone said, "good luck sergeant," as the stick filed quickly past me and out the door.

I reminded myself that our C-47 is the front, right-most plane in the entire formation. We, myself particularly, will land on the extreme outskirts of the drop zone. Counting the seconds, I disconnected and reconnected my static line forward of those which had stacked up in front of me, nodded to the crew chief as he gave me a thumbs-up, then out the door. How long? Three seconds?

Four seconds? You know what that can mean in ground distance.

A lot of chutes were already in the air as others continued to stream out. Below them I glimpsed the broad open space where they would land. I oriented myself to that, knowing it's where I will make my way to. Below me? Trees! A carpet of trees.

Apprehensive that I was already awfully close to the ground, why hadn't my chute opened? Then the pronounced awakening, accentuated by the impact of my steel helmet against the bridge of my nose, then disappearing below me. Scanning the area for Germans, as well as I could through the trees, and for the brief moment I had, I saw no one.

Robert Vannatter in East Berlin in 1945, in front of the Russian headquarters.

No more time! Resigned to a tree landing, crossing my arms in front of my face, I slithered through the outer limber branches of two adjacent tall trees. It hardly broke my fall as far as my body descent was concerned. The chute had snagged on an upper branch, however, and brought me to a soft spongy stop with my feet about twenty feet above the ground. "Damn it," was my natural thought of disappointment when things aren't perfect, but I was not overly concerned since I had continued to scan the immediate area and seemed to be quite alone.

It looked as if a single shroud line was snagged on a willowy twig, bending downward under the weight of my body. Thinking I might break it loose, I lifted my body by the shroud straps and let it drop several times. It didn't work. No reason for panic-right! I could open my reserve chute and use it to lower myself to the ground. Expressing more surprise than fear at this point, how can it happen? My reserve chute had disappeared.

Instinctively examining the D-rings where it had been fastened, it took a second to realize it was still connected to the right ring only, pivoted down and hanging to my knees. Not dwelling on how that can happen, I would have to work with what I've got. I probably still could have opened my reserve, and I am not sure why I didn't try, but, lucky or not, someone else seemed to be calling the shots. Making rapid decisions, good or bad, I would release myself from the harness, hang down as far as I can, and drop to the ground. The height was scary, and I didn't really need a broken leg, but weighing scary against fear, I decided to do it.

Grasping an upper strap with my left hand so I wouldn't have an uncontrolled fall when my leg straps suddenly released, I twisted the strap release buckle and hit it hard with the side of my fist. The straps should spring out much as a seat belt release in an automobile, but they didn't. More twisting and pounding and pulling didn't do any good. Threading my left arm through an upper strap so I could hold on, reaching down, then, with both hands, pressed, wiggled and pounded, but it was no use. I told myself, "there's a lot of irony going on here." Feeling the frustration, I think back to the time in the plane: calm, cool. But this is in real time. Still, knowing I had my knife strapped to my leg, I would cut my harness straps and hang down as I had planned before. Then, oh boy!

As I lifted my leg, and reached for the knife, I made another star-

Many troopers landed in the trees. Some were shot before they could free themselves.

tling discovery. The end fastener of my carbine sling was caught in the left fastener of the reserve chute. The carbine extended below my feet. Knowing that the sling had been threaded through the same D-ring that had held my reserve chute, it was just another near-impossible happening that I would think about later.

The realization hit me, if my leg straps had released as they should have, I would have been on the ground looking up at my unretrievable weapon.

It was easy enough to retrieve my carbine. Safely in my hands, and as I reattached the sling strap (I couldn't believe it) no clip in my carbine. Shaking my head in disbelief, yet awed and shaken by its reality, I conceded.

I could only hope that my pouch of spare clips is intact. No matter what else, my first priority had to be to get a clip in my weapon. Figuratively and literally, I was not out of the woods yet.

The pouch was there; I saw it, I felt it, and I could feel the clips inside. The top flap holding the clips in place was tied with a shoestring like cord. I knew the cord was tied in a hard knot, as I always did, to keep from losing the clips in the opening shock.

Not that I had been just loitering about enjoying the view of the lush green forest, but the feeling of helplessness, not having a loaded weapon, aroused a new sense of urgency. I didn't waste any time deciding to cut the cord instead of trying to untie it. I knew my knife was there, for I had seen it when I reached for my dangling carbine.

Reaching again for my knife, I froze. Whether my body rotated slightly, or if he had made a slight movement that attracted my attention, there he was; a German soldier. Five more seconds and I could have had a clip in my carbine.

Facing the direction where the main body of troops had landed, he didn't see me. He was kneeling on his right knee, his left arm resting on the other. The butt of his rifle rested on the ground with his right hand grasping its barrel. There was a small white patch on his left ear. The scene is burned in my memory.

I thought, "am I to believe this character hasn't heard or seen me?" Flashing back in my mind, I realized it had been extremely quiet. No snapping of brittle branches, nor metal-to-metal contact. Even the pounding of my buckle had been a subdued sound. I guess my oaths had been uttered under my breath. Whatever, I could be thankful for that much.

Very slowly, I straightened up and readied my empty carbine in his direction, knowing that if he saw me, I would have to try one of the biggest bluffs of the war.

Troopers of the 507th clear a roadblock on the way to Duisburg.

I was reminded if I had opened my reserve chute earlier, as I might have, it would have drawn his attention before I even knew he was there. The outcome, whatever it was to be, could be quite different.

He was not more than 30 feet away. I was to his left, and seemed to be within the range of his peripheral vision. It helped that I was 20 feet up, but still, quick moves would likely attract his attention. The eeriness of mounting circumstances, and the evil crafts working against me, had shaken my confidence. The right now situation was shaking my body. I surely was not ready for a showdown.

Once more my hand creeped toward my knife with my eyes still fixed on his face. He hadn't moved a muscle. Could he be dead and frozen in that position? I have heard of such things. I noticed his head was slightly bowed. As I continued to watch, I felt sure he was praying.

I could feel the snap fastener which held the knife in its scabbard. Restraining it with my thumb while prying outward with my fingers, trying to muffle the sound, as well as the motion, suddenly it gave way with more force than I had hoped. My arm jerked outward—this is it! Suddenly the chute broke loose then caught again, holding me about five feet up. The grand finale had begun.

He turned with the startled look of a cartoon cat. Pivoting as he did, and losing his balance, he rolled awkwardly on to his left side. Simultaneously, in my roughest and best German, "hands up," I ordered, as I thrust my empty carbine toward him in the most threatening way possible, concealing the open slot where my clip should be. To him, he had no chance. But I expect he realized that if I meant to shoot him I would have done so immediately.

Carefully, as if not to incite me, he raised one hand, and cautiously placed his rifle on the ground with the other. "Comrade," he said-sure! He was scared, and I knew the bluff was working.

With both hands stretched above his head now, I motioned for him to move away from his rifle. There were no other weapons that I could see. Still about 30 feet away, it would give me enough time to respond to any sudden notions he might have, while I rid myself of that damned parachute harness.

I felt sure I would have enough time to cut the cord on the pouch and insert a clip before he knew what was going on. Forgiving the paranoia, what if it is damaged and won't fit? It would tip him off that I don't have a clip in my gun—then what? I waited.

I had to try my strap release buckle one more time. My tentative prisoner watched with curiosity as I tensed my muscles and pounded the buckle against my stomach to no avail. Relieved to have my knife in hand, I began to saw away at my leg straps. The straps are tough and the knife was dull; being more for stabbing than for slicing. The double edged blade working between the tight straps and my leg was not doing my leg any good either. I struggled with one hand while I held my carbine with the other. German artillery was coming in close.

My prisoner lowered one arm and extended it toward me—"Comrade," he said again. I knew he was offering to help. I rationalized, if I don't get out of here soon the troops will move out without me. The thought of running around in the woods guarding my prisoner and dodging other Germans urged me to consider his offer.

Judging his height and my distance off the ground, he could barely reach the straps. If he choose to, he could only cut my legs. I would take a chance that he wouldn't try that.

More artillery! This time he hit the ground, then sprung back immediately, shrugging his shoulders apologetically. I nodded okay, having a full appreciation for a soldier's reflexes to do that. Yet I was hanging totally exposed.

I motioned for him to come close. Raising my carbine above his reach, but still pointed at him, I tossed my knife to the ground. He didn't have much choice but to cut me free. Anything else, I would simply shoot him, or so he believed.

With both hands to work with, instead of my one, he began to cut through the straps with relative ease. As he was nearly through the last strap I ordered him to stop, to give me the knife, and return to where he had been. I wasn't about to let myself fall down into his arms. The fear he had shown before was gone; relieved perhaps that he had earned a reprieve from any violent intentions I might have had. For him the war was over. He seemed resigned to being my prisoner.

My body filled with a new vigor and confidence, having severed the last thread of my straps, and swung to the ground. Still, I was not yet willing to let him see me cut the cord, and try a clip that might not insert. Murphy had earned my respect.

I had to contrive a way, so I directed him to move to a new location as I followed behind. I hoped he would look back for instructions, which he did. Then with a harsh "No," I was pretty sure I could do what I had in mind before he would turn again. It worked well. After one hard slice of the cord, I had quietly inserted a clip into my carbine. It fit!

After those agonizing moments of anxiety, frustration, and fear, and having reclaimed my cool, I needed a display of paratrooper arrogance to hone my wit and courage.

I immediately withdrew the clip and placed it back in the pouch, making sure it was on the end so I would get the same one back. A different one might not fit! Then I ordered him to stop and face me.

Conspicuous as a billboard, I lifted the clip from the pouch as if it were the first time, fit it into the slot, and slammed it home with the heel of my hand. Thinking I should have a bigger audience, I stared at him paused for effect, and slapped a round into the chamber.

I waited for his reaction. "You idiot," I thought, "don't you realize that, to this point, I had no ammo in my weapon?" Maybe that was the puzzled look on his face. But more than that, fear had returned to his eyes. Certainly he saw no logic to my forcing him to march 50 feet opposite to the direction of my own

Artillery men load up as the war moves out of the drop zone area. The yellow scarves worn by some of the men were for instant identification purposes.

troops. Or was it to find a better place to leave his body? His head darted left and right as if to make a desperate attempt to escape. The arrogance faded. I couldn't shoot a sitting duck anyway after coaxing it to feed from my hand.

I dwelled on my thoughts. We are soldiers cast in circumstances not of our own choosing, doing what we have to do for our own survival. Because we are on opposite sides, we are enemies. The only control of our destiny is the control of our immediate circumstances. One will lose. It's good to win this way.

No doubt he was relieved to see me sling my weapon over my shoulder. I had to do that momentarily in order to disable his rifle. That being done, we were ready to head for my troops.

Pointing the direction, I signaled for him to move out ahead of me, observant as we moved along, that other Germans may be near. As if I were their primary target, artillery shells kept exploding at our heels. After hitting the ground each time, he would wait for my signal before moving forward. We weren't moving fast enough to suit me. Taking the lead, I motioned for him to follow, being more concerned about escaping the shelling than of losing my prisoner. Nevertheless, he maintained a proper distance behind me; not too close to appear threatening; not to far back that he might escape.

Surprised, we came to a two-lane rural highway that I had not noticed from the air. It would be a good place for German mechanized units coming from my right to engage in battle, or from my left, fleeing the scene. Several small arms engagements were going on near by. Logically, and judging by the sound of the weapons, Germans were on my side of the road and GIs on the other. Studying the situation for a moment, I theorized if we run across the road, one behind the other, the first one will draw attention, and the second one will be the target. I would go first.

On the other hand, if I raced across and into the trees, my prisoner, if he chose not to follow, would have an excellent opportunity to escape back into the woods. To lessen that chance, I drew him to about five or six feet of me. Gesturing to him what we would do, he nodded that he understood. When I was sure no Germans were in sight, I darted across, glancing back to make sure he followed.

"Sergeant! Look out behind you," came the warning shout. It was Martin from my own platoon, already raising his rifle to fire. He had been lying concealed in a ditch on the other side of the road. I quickly waved him off, letting him know that the guy was my prisoner. "Damn!" he said, "I thought he was chasing you." He asked me what happened to my nose and I explained about the helmet.

Everything was uneventful as we continued together to our assembly area to seek out members of my section. Martin was amused as I related the events of my experience. More with humor, now that the seriousness of it had passed.

I turned my prisoner over to a medic with a broken leg who sat atop what had been a German foxhole. We were not concerned that he didn't have a weapon. He was surrounded with plenty of rear echelon troops who would not be moving out right away, and who wouldn't abandon him in any case. I lit out to find my own men.

Sometime later, as a column of troops crossed our path on the way to take up new positions, I caught a glance of a prisoner with a white patch on his ear. Wouldn't you know it! He was toting a twin pack of mortar rounds. The mortar platoon welcomed prisoners just to do that.

When I did a double take, I saw that he was already staring at me. He easily recognized me as the one without the helmet. We focused on each other for a moment, then both of us gave a faint smile and nod of recognition.

Reflecting back, I wondered what would have happened if I had landed squarely on the ground from the onset. What I see is each of us reacting quickly and vigorously to protect our own lives. With an empty carbine, and not knowing it, either dragged by a chute whose straps wouldn't release, or tangled in the web of its silk and shroud lines, I expect a German soldier would be telling his children a story somewhat different than my own. It adds up to a strange happening, beset with mysterious circumstances that rendered me helpless to take his life, and seemingly saved mine.

Something else I thought about: My prisoner's first awareness of my presence is when I dropped from the tree's 20-foot level to the 5-foot level. He had to believe that the drop was my initial landing. The planes had long since come and gone. I expect he is still trying to figure out where I came from.

"FIRST DAY OVER THE RHINE"

Editor's Note: Among the archives of the 17th Airborne Division Association is a handwritten account of "Operation Varsity" written by an unknown author in Headquarters, 507 Parachute Infantry Regiment. Dated March 26, 1945, only two days after the airborne assault, it was scribbled in pencil while the facts were still fresh in mind and while the combat still raged. It is reproduced here exactly as it was written that day east of the Rhine.

As no doubt you know by this time this last operation was a jump across the Rhine in Westphalia in order to establish a bridgehead. The point chosen was important because it was in a sense the northern extremity of the German defensive positions. From here the line turns to the W to follow the Rhine to the Dutch coast.

The caserne at Chalons-sur-Marne where the 17th rested and refitted after the Bulge and prepared for the Rhine operation.

Hence a crossing here would leave our left flank free for maneuver, a matter of considerable importance to the military. We had an unhoped for success, the causes of which I am not yet sure of, but it may partly be because the fighting spirit of the German army is finally breaking down. I hope so.

Here are the details. We were, or at least I was, briefed a couple of weeks before the jump and everyone was favorably impressed with the plan. The principal town of the region was a place called Wesel. A British unit was to cross the Rhine and attack Wesel directly during the night before the jump. Five or six miles further down the river and also before dawn another British unit was to cross.

About ten o'clock in the morning our 17th A/B Div. and a British parachute division were to jump between the two crossings, prevent the Germans in our area from interfering in the crossings, and assist the northern British crossing. This plan had the advantage of not leaving (the airborne troops) exposed alone to the Germans for any length of time, which is a matter of considerable importance to us. At the same time by good coordination we could still surprise the enemy and deal a heavy and unexpected blow.

The jump field for the regiment was a couple of miles from Wesel. It was roughly oblong, about 1,500 yards long from east to west and 1,000 yards from north to south. To the south it was bounded by swamps along the river, to the north there was a forest. According to our intelligence there were defensive works throughout the field, and along the edge of the forest, and there were supposed to be quite a few troops in them, quite enough to make us nervous.

Four days before the operation we went to the marshalling area and were sealed in, as tightly as if we had been convicts. But we didn't mind it because the process was much more like a religious knight fasting before an important ceremony. As a matter of fact, like monks we couldn't afford to think of anything but what we had before us and during the whole time there was a general studying of maps, sharpening of knives, cleaning of guns and fitting of parachutes. The whole thing was well organized and went off very easily.

The units were briefed and re-briefed until every man knew his job as well as everyone's in his squad.

Before we knew it, it was 0830 of D-Day, March 24 and we were taxing down the runway. The flight was easy

513th troopers arrive from the marshalling area and wait to board their C-46s.

269

The hour before departure from the marshalling area near the Achiet, France airfield, these troopers sweat it out.

since we were over friendly territory almost all the way. It was not until we got the warning signal to jump that we began to hear flak bursting in the air. Four more minutes that meant.

We stood up and hooked our chutes to the anchor line in the plane, listened to the flak crackle, and wished from the bottom of our hearts that the jump signal would come on so we could move out of there. No matter how many Jerries were on the ground, it seemed a lot easier to face them than to stand around in mid-air as a living but passive target.

The signal came and those of

513th troopers move to the doors of the C-46 and await the green light to jump over the Rhine.

us who hadn't yet been shot down rushed for the door and instantly found ourselves dangling in mid-air a good thousand feet up, much too high to be reassuring.

Now the formation the planes were using was a "V of V's." That is nine planes wide plus the intervals between them. Thus, either because the formation was too big for the field, or because of a slight miscalcuation on the part of the chief aviator, the left wing planes were behind the edge of the woods and dropped their men in the forest. That was inadvertently the key to the problem.

The Germans, for some reason or other, had failed to man their positions in the field itself, but they were at their guns along the edge of the woods from which they could sweep most of the field with fire. As we dangled there, a thousand feet up, they opened up with a dreadful crackle of MG and rifle fire.

Bullets whistled in all directions, but the air over a field 1500 x 1000 yards is tremendous even when it is full of men and Jerry quickly turned his attention to those of us who had hit the ground. These men being right under the German guns and unable to fight until they got out of their chutes were pretty exposed, and in fact the enemy inflicted some casualties. He had coordinated automatic fires along the edge of the woods.

Our men made for the woods as soon as they were out of their harness partly for the concealment they offered and partly because the unit assembly areas were there, and Jerry knocked over numbers of them as they got there. But before he could warm up to the fight the men in the left flank planes who had fallen in the woods behind the position were out of their chutes and attacking.

Troopers clear the drop zone between the Isel River and Diersfordter Forrest. It was a kill zone for the first serials.

These troopers take shelter in the ditch while others clear a wooded area of enemy snipers.

They distracted the German's position, broke up the organization of his fires and drove him out of his holes. In an hour it was all over, except for a diehard German who had dug himself in in the middle of the field with a MG and announced his patriotism and Fascist faith by means of bursts of fire for several hours. This field was supposed to be the drop zone for all three battalions. But in any plan there is always a mistake in execution, and so far we hadn't had our share. The aviators of the 1st Battalion however missed the DZ en-

These Germans were captured near the "Operation Varsity" drop zone by troopers of 513th I Company.

tirely and dropped their men 1,500 (yards) too far north. This mistake which might have been disastrous turned out to be a Godsend, because the battalion landed right on top of the German artillery supporting their position on the main DZ.

These poor artillerymen, surrounded before they were attacked, confused by the speed of the event and ineffectively armed to resist, took to their heels without firing a shot. Thanks to the lucky mistake of the aviators and to the energy of Major P.F. Smith of Boston, Massachusetts, battalion command, no shot of artillery fell on the Airborne all that day. In spite of jumping on the wrong DZ, the 1st Battalion was still close enough at hand to move to its objective without any appreciable delay.

The Germans were not only beaten but thoroughly demoralized. By eleven o'clock, all three battalions were moving toward their objectives and by 1330 the objectives were taken. The 1st Battalion was a little slower getting into the reserve position assigned to it because of the mistake in the drop. In the course of this movement the Germans made no opposition but surrendered in droves.

"THE CAPTURE OF A WAR CRIMINAL!"

by Bart Hagerman, 193 D

Editor's Note: *Our thanks go to Thomas McKinley and Herb Stuebner for the photographs and newspaper clippings they provided for this story and for the interview with McKinley. Both troopers were members of Company I, 194th and participated in the capture of Baron Franz Von Papen as described here.*

By early April 1945, the Germans were withdrawing rapidly into the heart of Germany. As they pulled out they left numerous roadblocks, each defended by a few soldiers to impede the advance of the Allied Forces. After firing a few shots and possibly causing several causalities, they would surrender and the Allies moved on.

When word came through civilian channels that there was a concentration of troops in the Neheim-Arnsberg area, it was decided to go after them. Task Force Faith was formed mainly from elements of the 95th Infantry Division which was in the immediate area. The 194th Glider Infantry Regiment was also attached to this task force effective 2130 hours on April 7th.

Early that morning, the 194th had crossed south over the Moehne River and had attacked some three miles into the Task Force Faith zone. By the next day, the 377th Infantry, a unit of the 95th Division, moved to the left flank of the 194th and joined in the push.

Both regiments advanced against light resistance until, by the end of the day, the zone had been cleared east of a line from Allagen on the north to Hirschberg in the center to Meschede in the south. By 1550 on April 8, the 194th had made contact with elements of the 9th Infantry Division that had reached the south bank of the Ruhr River in the vicinity of Meschede.

On April 9, beginning their attack at 0800, both regiments advanced against light opposition. By the end of the day the task force had advanced some six miles west. The 194th, operating in the southern section of the zone, had made contact about noon with the 5th Infantry Division at the south bank of the Ruhr River.

Both regiments resumed the attack the next morning of April 10. The

Members of the patrol who captured Franz Von Papen. L to R: Tony Guinti, Hugh Fredricks, Herb Stuebner, Charles Elder, Denver Terrel. Not shown were: Thomas McKinley, Jesse Leonard and Steve Witchiko.

roadblocks continued to slow the advance as hundreds of trees had been felled by the German engineers. The delays encountered had the effect of exposing the 194th's flank so their advance was held up until the line could be reformed.

Lieutenant Thomas McKinley's 1st Platoon of "I" Company moved in and occupied positions along the Ruhr River near a place designated as Stockhausen. There they found a number of displaced and very frightened Polish workers who were huddled together trying to escape the shelling that poured in on the advancing Americans.

One of his sergeants, Steve Witchiko of McKees Rock, Pennsylvania, struck up a conversation in Polish with some of the DPs. He asked who owned the big estate they could see up ahead and they replied it was the home of Colonel Max Von Stockhausen, the son-in-law of Baron Franz Von Papen.

When Witchiko passed this information on to Lieutenant McKinley, the officer immediately recognized the importance of the intelligence. He recalled from his history studies back in college that Von Papen had been chancellor of Germany back in 1933 and at one time had been one of Hitler's top diplomats. In fact, he knew that he had been a leading statesman in Germany as far back as WWI and had played a leading role in the events leading to WWII.

McKinley went to the task force G-2 and reported that Von Papen might be in the area. The G-2 had never heard of the man, but McKinley quickly filled him in. Von Papen had been an advisor to the senile Marshall Von Hindenburg during WWI and had deceived him to pave the way for Hitler's rise to power.

Before the United States entered the war against Germany, Von Papen had been the ambassador to the United States but had been deported for suspicion of running a German spy network in Washington. More recently, he had been Hitler's ambassador to Austria and had delivered that country into the Nazi camp. Then later, as ambassador to Turkey he had fought to the last to turn that nation away from the side of the Allies.

Before further action could be taken, another break came to "I" Company. Checking out the estate,

Baron Franz Von Papen, in his natty attire, was captured and returned to the Task Force HQ for interrogation.

Sergeant Witchiko came upon a German who spoke perfect English. Further investigation proved him to be Baron Von Papen's son, Captain George Von Papen. Witchiko immediately took him prisoner.

A SS Captain and battalion reconnaissance officer in the 5th Panzer Division, Captain Von Papen had been wounded on the Russian front and was convalescing from a broken hip. He had only been released from a hospital in Berlin some three weeks prior. He wore civilian clothes claiming his status as on leave from the hospital did not require him to wear a uniform.

The young Von Papen readily revealed that his father was presently residing at a small hunting lodge in the hills a few miles away. He insisted that his father, as a statesman, had nothing to hide and thus no reason to flee from the Americans. The troopers thought otherwise and plans were made to go after the elder statesman early the next morning.

Company "I" drew the assignment to go after Von Papen and they left on the mission with McKinley's first platoon as point. Climbing almost five miles into the thick forests and lush meadows, they came upon the hunting lodge and were surprised to see that apparently it was completely unguarded. The first squad, comprised of seven men along with Lieutenant McKinley, were given the job of advancing to the lodge to scout out the situation. The

Interrogating Von Papen on April 15, 1945 at Warstein, Germany. L to R: Lt. Ferguson, Sgt. Frank, Franz Von Papen, Sgt. Anderson, Sgt. Shayne and Capt. George Von Papen.

remainder of the company, took positions in the wooden area about 200 yards away to provide fire support if the squad ran into trouble.

Near the lodge the squad saw someone sitting on the porch with a rifle across his lap. Otherwise, all was calm and quiet and no other armed individuals were in view. The squad continued their advance, apparently still undetected when they reached the building.

At a signal from McKinley, the squad rushed the lodge, covering every door and window and completely surprising the man on the porch. Sergeant Hugh Fredricks of Adamsville, Alabama, disarmed him before he was hardly aware of what was happening. He turned out to be Von Papen's son-in-law, Max Von Stockhausen.

McKinley rushed in the lodge and to his amazement, there was the "Old Fox," Baron Franz Von Papen himself, seated at the dinner table. McKinley pulled out a photograph of Von Papen that he had picked up at the Stockhausen estate and asked the Baron if he was the Baron Franz Von Papen. When he replied that indeed he was, McKinley then told him he was his prisoner.

"There are no Germans here," he replied, "and I don't know what the Americans would want with an old man of 65 like me!"

McKinley told him nevertheless, they did and that he could answer to his superiors about that. Then, as the rest of the squad gathered in the lodge, McKinley joined the Baron in a few bites of the meal that was destined never to be eaten.

Any German guards in the area had long ago fled. Von Stockhausen's wife and five children were the only others in the lodge. They were also taken into custody and returned to Stockhausen and Task Force Faith headquarters by the troopers.

"I wish this war was over," remarked Von Papen as the troopers moved them out.

"So do 11 million other guys," commented Sergeant Fredericks.

At that time, Franz Von Papen was the only war criminal of major status who actually had been captured by the Allies. The only other one then being held was Rudolph Hess who had parachuted out of his fighter plane over England.

After the war, Von Papen was put on trial by the International Military Tribunal in October 1945, at Nurnberg. He was, however, acquitted by that body. He was then charged and brought to trial in February 1946, before the German Denazification Court and sentenced to eight years at hard labor.

Perhaps the saddest note to this whole affair is the fact that the eight troopers who stormed that hunting lodge, not knowing what kind of resistance they would face, were completely ignored when the awards were passed out. Top brass at the task force level received awards and they weren't within five miles of the action. Meanwhile, the eight men who laid it on the line were completely overlooked and forgotten.

Forgotten, that is, except by their comrades.

"MEDIC! MEDIC!"

As told by Franklin E. Dentz, 194 C

Ask any combat soldier who they had the most respect for and chances are they'll tell you it was the medic that accompanied their unit. Those guys were subject to the same fire and danger that we were and they carried no weapon! I know I wouldn't have been up there without something to defend myself with!

I had good opportunity to observe our medic, Walt Wrzeszesynski, during our days in combat and let me assure you

Medic Walt Wrzeszesynski (on bike) and his buddy, Frank Dentz, in Duisburg after the shooting was over.

he was a dedicated professional, a credit to the Airborne and the medical branch. I remember some hectic times we had after the Rhine crossing and they show the mettle of the guy.

It was shortly after we had landed near Wesel on March 24. We were in a foxhole together and we were taking a heavy shelling. A cry went up, "Medic! Medic!" It was the dreaded call we all hated to hear as it signaled that someone had been hit and needed help—fast.

I hunkered down in that hole and began to dig deeper with my entrenching tool. I wanted to get as low as I could to avoid that hot shrapnel that I knew was whipping around out there in the open.

But Walt didn't hesitate a moment. He grabbed his little pack of first aid supplies and piled out of that hole and like 911 and went to the rescue! There was old Walt, out there in the open giving the wounded man attention and the shells landing all around them. Turned out it was our forward observer that had been hit and the aid that Walt gave him probably saved his life.

The medics used any conveyance they could find to bring the wounded in.

Later on during the attack on Munster, we moved out and headed across an open field, a maneuver that will almost always get you some very unfriendly fire. I was carrying the SCR300 radio and walking just behind Captain Roy Strang, our CO, and Lieutenant Clausen, the XO. Walt was behind me.

Unexpectedly, a Panzerfaust rocket came in and struck a tree near us and exploded. Lieutenant Clausen was the only one hit, but he got it bad. I saw his eyes roll back in his head and almost immediately he went into shock.

Before I could clear my head as to what had happened, Walt was there. Together we dragged Clausen to a ditch for some protection from the fire we were receiving. Walt worked feverishly, but it was not to be for Clausen. He lost him. I saw the look in Walt's eyes as Clausen died and it was a look of utter despair.

After awhile, we started on across the field. This time Walt was about 30 yards in front of me. I was still lugging the radio. Right in front of me, and behind Walt, all of a sudden I saw the camouflaged cover of a small foxhole lift up and a German infantryman raise up. He had a rifle in his hands and never seeing me, he cooly took aim at Walt's back.

I lunged at him, slapping at the rifle as we both crashed to the ground. I also yelled loudly to Walt to come help me and he hurried back. The German never got off a shot or old Walt would have been a goner.

I took the German's rifle and smashed it against the ground. By this time he had his hands up and was screaming, "Kamerad!"

There were more troops coming up behind us, so we pointed him to the rear and Walt gave him a swift kick to help him on his way!

There was a funny thing about this incident. Somehow, someway, the Army came up with a press release on it. No one ever interviewed me and Walt says no one ever asked him about it. All I know is that the press release was written and it went to my hometown newspaper and was published.

Even stranger, it had changed a bit by the time my Dad got a copy of the Army's press release. Here's how it came out:

HEADQUARTERS
EUROPEAN THEATER OF OPERATIONS
UNITED STATES ARMY
NUMBER 70014 (CENSORED)
AIRBORNE DUO WORKS "ONE-TWO" ON NAZI
WITH THE 17TH AIRBORNE DIVISION IN GERMANY

One Wehrmacht soldier might have suffered a little damage to his German "superman" pride when two 194th Glider Infantry Regiment soldiers strolled up to his foxhole. Private First Class Franklin Dentz, of Middlesex, New Jersey, hauled him out by the scruff of his neck and took over his weapon. Corporal Walter Wrzeszczynski, of Philadelphia, Pennsylvania turned him around in the direction of the rear lines and the prisoner inclosure and started him off.

One thing for sure, we didn't just stroll up to his hole! I hit him like a ton of bricks! It wasn't as easy as that Army writer made it sound. But he was right on one thing, Walt certainly started him off in fine fashion!

Another thing about medics: they never got as much rest as the other guys. They always had hurt and sick men to look after whenever we stopped. And, every patrol wanted a medic to accompany them, day or night. Medics were few in number, but long in providing service.

Once, just after the Munster battle, we were going into a small town. Walt was in front of me again and we came down a hill running from some .88 shelling and machine gun fire that was coming our way. We crossed a railroad and jumped over a fence into the backyard of a small house.

Walt ran up the back stairs with me on his coat tails. Entering the house, we found ourselves in the kitchen. Apparently, the homeowners had fled to the safety of the cellar as no one seemed to be around. There on the table was food, evidently set for the noon meal.

Well, you know soldiers. Our zest for the attack bogged down right there. We were always hungry, so we made ourselves scrambled egg sandwiches and started eating. Then, there came that cry again: "Medic! Medic!"

Walt dropped the food and out the door he went. Someone was hurt somewhere and Walt knew he was needed. He knew he could make a difference in life or death. It is no small wonder to me that Walt later received the Bronze Star for his devotion to duty. I think all medics warranted one.

"A LETTER TO MOTHER"

As told by Walter Burdick, 139 Eng.

Editor's Note: *The following account of "Operation Varsity" is an exact quote of a letter written by Walter Burdick in April of 1945, to his mother, Mrs. R.S. Burdick of Hudson Falls, New York.*

Dear Mother:

I don't know if it was good or bad luck, but the engineers were turned into glider riders for the operation.

I'd never seen the inside of a glider until the morning I piled into one with the rest of the squad for the Rhine bound take-off. It looked like a reinforced egg crate and I admit I had my doubts.

When we finally started rolling, the old glider took to the air like a ruptured crow, trembling, rolling and pitching all the way. We eventually hit the right altitude and fell into formation with the rest.

About all we could do then was to make ourselves as comfortable as possible for the rest of the three and a half hour ride (France to Rhine). We lit up cigarettes and talked for awhile, despite the fact you had to scream to make yourself heard above the wind that was blasting all sides of the glider.

We settled down to gazing out the small port windows, down on the sun-drenched fields, farms and towns below. About a half hour from the Rhine, we began spotting a few C-46s and C-47s that had dropped their load of troopers and were heading back to France.

On the ground, well pocked with shell craters, we spotted one or two C-47s with comet-like trails in the earth behind them. They'd apparently been shot down and crashed landed in.

Finally the Rhine loomed up ahead of us and we began to think to ourselves "It won't be long now." Having come abreast of the Rhine and crossed it, our glider took on a fourth motion. Our tail would jump a couple of feet with the concussion of flak shells when they burst close to our ship. By that time we were all doing some sweating but we finally came over our drop zone when our glider pilot cut loose from the C-47.

We banked pretty steep and headed down in a slow arc.

Peeking through the port windows yet, I spotted three or four different gliders on the ground, smashed to a wood and fabric pulp, a couple more in flames. Then I really began to sweat. But the ground came up pretty fast and the glider kissed it with a thump.

Before it had stopped rolling we had the emergency doors knocked out and were grabbing our rifles and taking out the doors as fast as possible.

That night after we'd taken our positions and were more or less settled safe in our foxholes, I began thinking. I recalled those gliders I had seen smashed to bits and then a couple of parachutes all covered with blood and the I couldn't figure out, "Was I, or wasn't I lucky to have come in on a glider?"

Thank goodness I am able to tell the tale anyhow.

Love,

Walt.

PART IV

AFTER THE FIGHTING

"THE OCCUPATION OF GERMANY"

As told by Jim Costello, 507 HQ

So the war is over; we are now a peacetime Army; conquerors of the great Nazi war machine which had destroyed most of the cities in Europe and brought destruction to their own country because one man thought he was a God.

We are housed in a doctor's home on the outskirts of Essen, an area of mansions and they are all intact. Strange how the war never hurt the rich, just the middle and poor classes.

The house is a three-story mansion with a full basement, bedrooms galore and the basement is equipped with a washer, dryer, a belt on rollers that runs to a mangle ironer. Most of the bedrooms have their own bath and shower. Being a conqueror is pretty good duty!

The demolition platoon is together, once again, those of us who are left. The 17th Airborne is now the military government of the Ruhr Valley.

Our platoon's first orders: go into the city of Essen and cut to ground level all streetcar and train tracks that were raised from the bombings so that our trucks can travel unhindered. We now have jeeps at our disposal, not stolen, for use in our work.

The German people had never felt the ravages of war before. Prior to WWII, it was always in some other country. Now they are without homes, apartments, or hotel rooms. Some have gone to the country to live in barns, others live in basements or lean-tos, put together with whatever they can salvage. They don't have to worry about utility, phone, or water bills. They do have to stand in food lines and walk for drinking water. Wrinkled brows and somber faces are prevalent except for the children who still play and laugh, pester the GIs for Kaugummi and Schokolade (chewing gum and chocolate).

We decided to cut the tracks in the center of town where tracks criss-crossed each other and had the most damage but because of the activity in the area we chose to do it at dawn. We arrived the next morning at dark and waited for the first light of day, then set our charges, took cover in a bomb crater and let her rip. The Germans, hearing a big explosion, came running out all over the place and the MPs converged on us. They all thought the war had started up again.

On another occasion, in a residential neighborhood, we had two tracks to level. We got hold of a couple of German cops and told them our plans. They were to keep everyone at a distance. There was a small park on the corner so we asked one of the cops to check for people living there. He gave me a negative answer so we set charges with a time fuse and took cover in the park.

After the explosions had settled, we checked the streets and no one was injured. Then an old German in his late 70s or early 80s came out of the park shouting,

Trooper Jim Costello, who died in June of 1991, wrote this account of the occupation and the story on page 95 about the Battle of the Bulge.

"Mein frau, Mein frau." It didn't take much thought to figure what happened. Three of us, plus the cop, followed the old man. There was a lean-to and inside an old woman on the floor. She had been hit below the hip by a piece of track, the size of an anvil iron.

I pointed my weapon at the cop and he kept saying over and over: "I didn't know they were here." I lowered the weapon. We had a young kid with us, newly arrived from the States and I guess this was the first time he'd ever seen blood. He started shaking and shouting, "Do something. Do something!"

I told him to shut up! We put sulphur powder on the wound and bandaged it, making her as comfortable as possible. Then I asked the cop if there was a doctor or hospital nearby. He said a hospital was two streets away. To get the young kid out of the way, I sent him with the cop, with orders to bring back a doctor.

Some time passed and finally they returned with a woman doctor. The kid is walking behind her with his rifle pointed at her head and she's laying in on him with every swear word in the German language.

We commandeered a horse and wagon, put the old lady, her husband, and doctor on it and sent them to the hospital. I wanted to talk to the cop who had given a negative answer but he was gone.

The kid said he had to threaten to shoot the doctor before she'd leave the hospital. I asked, "Would you have shot her?" He answered, "Yes."

"That would have been hard to do," I told him, "you don't have a clip in your rifle!" Sure glad he wasn't in combat with us. That was the last detail I brought him on.

Our next order was to take charge of all police substations throughout the city. The police would be subject to our control and our decisions would be abided by.

Four of us would cover a district called Schonebeck, on the other side of town. We drove through town past the ruins of Krupp's factories (the only thing standing is a statue of Krupp) on and on to the outskirts of town.

The police station was an old castle with a moat around it. We felt like the musketeers of old. The cops treated us royally—they wanted to keep on the good side, afraid they might lose their jobs.

We drove there twice a day, in the morning and after lunch. It was a peaceful area and we spent time driving around the countryside visiting farms. Everything went along smoothly, except once.

Three cops, all of them chattering loudly, brought a young boy with a bicycle into the station. I told my interpreter to quiet them down and only one speak. I was told the boy had stolen the bike. So comes the trial:

"Who owns the bike?"

"We don't know."

"Does it have a license?"

"No."

"How do you know he stole it?"

"He is not from here."

"Where are you from?" (asked of the boy)

"From Poland. I was brought here three years ago from my home."

"What did you do here?"

"I worked in the factory."

This kid was 16 or 17 years of age and would have been 13 or so when they took him from his parents. I knew what the answer to my next question would be, but I had to ask. "Did they pay you?"

"No."

"Why do you want the bike?"

"To ride to my home."

"Take the bike and have a good trip."

The kid was all smiles, the cops were shocked and upset when I said they were not to follow him.

The bike would never make it to Poland but it gave the kid some happiness after three years. He could go as far as it would take him and then the Allies would put him on a train or truck to Poland.

The division found a mass grave of Russians, Poles, and Jews in a small park. The Germans were made to remove the bodies and place them in individual graves. It was a messy operation.

One day I broke my front tooth on a marble windowsill. Our dentist had been killed so his assistant (a corporal), went with me to a displaced person's camp to pull it out. The drill he used had to be operated by a foot treadle.

We were lucky to have some great cooks. The mess sergeant had owned a restaurant in Oswego, New York and what he could do with powdered eggs and other ersatz food was amazing.

In mid-June, the 17th Airborne Division moved to Nancy, France to be deactivated. Those of us without enough points (85) to return home, were transferred to the 82nd Division on June 21.

On July 19, a group of us received a furlough to London (back to being tourists again). They flew us over and we were deposited in a hotel near Picadilly. The next morning I hunted for a dentist to get a new front tooth. I found one with an office three flights up.

The man who greets me is wearing pin-striped pants and a swallow-tail coat. I thought, "My God, an undertaker." He was also the dentist. He took an impression and told me the plate would be ready that afternoon. It was. I still have that plate and my daughter, Pat, will probably want it for her mantelpiece in memory of me (she likes antiques).

My next move was a photo studio to pose for pictures to be sent home. We enjoyed the week in London, except for the food.

The 82nd Airborne Division was chosen to occupy Berlin, so after another three day pass to Paris, we were taken by train around through Holland to Berlin. The GIs had named the trains in Europe 40 and 8s. The boxcars held 40 men or eight horses.

While traveling through Holland, one of the men was sitting in the open doorway. The train lurched and he fell out. We rushed over to see if he was hurt. He wasn't so we all waved to him. Later he passed us riding in a jeep and got back on at our next stop.

We arrived in Berlin on August 9. Our home was a three-story affair, right next door to the colonel's Regimental Headquarters.

The duties assigned were nil. We had absolutely nothing to do. Our time was our own and most of it was spent across the street at the Red Cross Club, playing pool, badminton, etc. and talking over coffee and donuts.

The USO did bring entertainers to Berlin. Bob Hope, among others, and Marlene Dietrich came by our Red Cross Club to sing and talk to the troopers. She was a native of Berlin and had been quite concerned about her mother, who still lived and owned a jewelry store in the city. She was happy her mother had survived the war and was in excellent health. Before leaving, she lifted her dress (she had an Airborne patch on her garter and drew tremendous applause from the troopers).

The Army issued a booklet stating: "No fraternizing!" There are over 20,000 men in this division and most went through the war and they're telling them not to show brotherly love to the Germans. It was the quickest order ever ignored in the service. There were bars open in Berlin with dance floors and music. The troopers were drawn to them like bees to the queen bee's hive. It wasn't so much brotherly love, as sisterly love. No one was ever picked up by an MP for fraternizing.

We were issued a liquor ration and everyone got stoned. Troopers were going to the second floor and jumping out windows to the grass below. The Germans thought we were lunatics, but when you came down in a parachute, the impact with the ground was the same as a two-story fall and the jumpers knew how to land.

The Black Market was the big operation in Berlin. We were issued "invasion money" (German Marks), and I don't believe it was backed up in the USA. The Germans were selling jewelry, cameras, furs, watches, heirlooms, silverware, china, crystal, etc. and the GIs were selling a carton of cigarettes, $200; five cent candy bar, $20.00; bar of soap, $10.00; pack of gum, $5.00; tube of toothpaste, $15.00; and shaving cream, $10.00.

The Russians took as much of a beating as the Germans. Russian officers would give their enlisted men money to buy watches from the Americans. A plain watch sold for $200 (with a luminous dial $300). The Russians would check to be sure they had jewels inside before they'd pay the price. Whenever troopers were going on a furlough to Switzerland, they would be given money by others to buy watches, in the two to five dollar price range and also some bottles of red nail polish. It's amazing how many watches went onto Russian wrists with Revlon jewels.

Another idea they came up with was to steam the wax paper off the cigarette cartons, fill them with paper and re-seal them. This was one of the reasons why Berliners in later years were to refer to Americans as gangsters. Even some mail clerks were getting in the act and selling money order blanks for $10.00 apiece.

In the beginning, thousands of dollars were sent home, but finally the government limited it to $300 over base pay. By the time we were ready to leave Berlin, some men with suitcases full of money ended up burning most of it. I was not a black-marketeer.

Berlin had been hammered with bombing by the Americans and the British. A German told me the Americans would fly over in the daylight and everyone would go to the park to watch. The British bombed at night, drop bombs all over the place, so the Germans would head for the shelters. The British probably retaliated for the buzz-bombs the Krauts sent to England that showed no preference for a pin-point target. Berlin was collapsed into 2.6 billion cubic feet of rubble.

The city, under occupation, was divided into four sectors: American, British, French, and Russian. There were no barriers and you could travel city wide. In 1961, the Communists started building a wall completely around the Western sector, turning it into an island (185 square miles), surrounded by the Communist government of the German Democratic Republic.

There was a canal running through the center of Berlin and alongside, an underground metro system. As the Russians were advancing, they pounded the city with artillery. The civilians took cover in the metro. The German SS ordered them to come out and bear arms for the Fatherland. They refused so the SS blew a hole from the Canal and drowned them. There were thousands in there—mostly women and children.

As the Russians entered the city, the people were terrified. They would place their wives and daughters in cellars and cover them with debris. Everywhere was rape and plunder. As I said before, "war is inhuman and vicious."

I talked to one German who was on the Western Front and because he could speak English, his commanding officer would

Troopers of the 155th examine a captured German "doodle-bug." The radio-controlled robots were used to blow-up Allied fortified positions or other hard-to-attack targets.

send him to a listening post to find out what the Americans were planning. He told me the Americans always used slang and he never knew what they were saying. He'd make up stories for his officer.

The first sergeant had acquired enough points to go home so I was railroaded into the job. Railroaded, they wouldn't give me the stripes because there were too many master sergeants in the division. I asked the company commander why he didn't use one of them. He said "they're not familiar with the job."

We received word that a combat-type jump would be coming up. There were dignitaries arriving from Russia, France, Britain, and other countries plus senators, congressmen, etc. from the United States.

The day before the jump, I broke a mirror. The men taunted me continually about that. "Hope you make it okay Sarge!" "Don't hit your head going out the door." "Play sick." "Better check your own chute," etc. They almost had me believing it was bad luck and they were almost right.

We donned our gear and chutes. The equipment bundles were attached under the belly of the plane. Except for the new faces in my stick, it was "Operation Varsity," all over again. The memory of that day, March 24, 1945 will always linger.

It seemed the C-47 would never get off the dirt runway but finally, it did, just clearing the trees. I was jumping third and had to hit button number three to release one of the equipment chutes.

We had a rocky ride towards Tempelhof Airport and circled the field about three times. I went to the pilot and asked what the delay was and he said, "There's a gale blowing out there and we are waiting to see if they cancel the jump." He received his answer and turned and said "I'm sorry Sergeant, you're jumping— we'll be coming over at 400 feet."

He made one more pass of the field and all systems were go. Prior to jumping, I hit the number three button and as I left the plane I saw my equipment bundle descend and collapse the canopy of a trooper

With the war in Europe over, the ship ride back to the States was quite relaxed. In mid-ocean the word came that Japan had also surrendered.

that the wind had carried under our plane. I had no time for remorse as the wind filled my canopy and I thought it would jerk me out of my uniform. I tried to pull on my risers for a quick descent but they wouldn't budge.

Finally I came down on the edge of the grass, stunned, and was dragged 25 yards along the tarred runway before I could collapse my chute. I ended up with a twisted knee and skinned hands—one of the lucky ones. There were troopers lying all over the place. Many of them banged into the hangers and some were carried completely out of the airfield. It was a blood bath.

There was a big outcry in the United States over the jump. Troopers had lived though a war and then gave their lives in the entertainment field. Orders came from Washington, DC—no more jumps.

On November 14, 1945, we left Berlin. We were taken by train to France and on December 12, we arrived in England. Back to a diet of hard boiled eggs, beef hash and brussel sprouts.

On December 29, we left England on the *Queen Mary* and on January 12, 1946, we paraded up 5th Avenue in New York City.

"A HERO IN PARIS"

As told by John K. Kern, 194 G

When the orders came out, my name was listed as the OIC of a 194th Glider Infantry contingent of enlisted men and officers headed for Paris for three days of R&R. On the designated day, I checked off each of the troopers as they arrived in Class "A" uniform from their encampments in Vittel, Neufchateau, and (I think) Epinal in eastern France, to board the troop train. This happened sometime in early-to-mid-summer of 1945, after the 17th Airborne had withdrawn from Germany and personnel were undergoing reassignment. The troop train was carrying contingents from other units of the 17th in addition to our own.

It wasn't long before the train arrived in Paris, and everyone was in high spirits anticipating the great time ahead. But before I released my charges, I gave them specific instructions to meet at this same spot at a specified time three days hence. And so off they went, I among them.

I'm sure some guys found their way to Place Pigalle, some saw the Eiffel Tower and did other sightseeing, some savored fine French food, and others amused themselves in other ways. For myself, I fell in love with a French girl who, by chance, came from our Nancy area of eastern France and spent the whole three days being captivated by her. When I visited her later in Luneville, her mother served me the absolute worst cup of coffee I've had in my life and that dampened my enthusiasm for subsequent visits.

Then all too soon, the three days were up, and everyone gathered as instructed at the appointed hour at the troop train. In my head a little plan came into mind and I acted on it immediately. I kept my group of returnees back away from the part of the train where embarkment by other units was taking place, in the hope that no room would be left for us. And by golly, my ploy worked! When we were unable to board the train, I happily announced to my R&R'ers that they would just have to stay in Paris another day, but to be back at this same spot the next day at the same time. They shouted with glee and rushed themselves off for another day of fun in the French capital. And so did I.

The following day at the same time and place, we assembled once again, now happy at having had an extra day in Paris and fully expecting to now be traveling back to our units. But, gutsy me, I decided that if my strategy could work one time, it might work a second time. So again I held my contingent away from the troops who were being loaded onto the train, and, "sho'nuff," there just wasn't any space left on the train for my group! So off we all went again for yet another unexpected day of pleasure in Paris.

When we gathered the following day, I could tell there was no chance that we wouldn't be accommodated on the train this time, so everyone got on, and we made it back to our destination in eastern France having miraculously stretched a three-day pass into a five-day pass. And somehow I suspect that the glidermen and paratroopers of the 194th who got off that train regarded Second Lieutenant Kern as something of a hero of a different sort.

"CAPTURED BY THE RUSSIANS!"

As told by Harold "Bill" Crehan, 517 Sig

Editor's Note: *This story, although it occurred after the two troopers concerned had been transferred from the 17th Airborne to the 82nd Airborne for occupational duty, is included because of its unusual nature. It documents what may be the only case of American Airborne troopers held prisoner by the Russians. And, it came after peace had come to Europe.*

Joe Wood and I were drafted at the same time and arrived at Camp Mackall on the same troop train. We both became radio operators in the 517th Signal Company, went all the way through the war and ended up in Berlin on occupation duty, still together. The Army was good at splitting up friends it seems, but someway we beat the averages.

The 517th Signal had a club on our street in Berlin called the "Sleepy Time Club." It was complete with bar, dance floor and live music—three German civilians who played very bad Schmaltzy music. It was nice, but that band was bad.

We had several guys in the unit who had played instruments in civilian life and we hit on the idea that we should form our own combo. The problem was the instruments which were hard to come by in post-war Berlin.

Joe contacted the owner of a music store in Berlin, a man named Mutzelberg who was about 60 years old, stood only about five feet tall and weighted a whopping 90 pounds. He said he thought if he could get to this factory in Pilsen, Czechoslovakia, where he had done some business before the war, he could get some instruments for us at a good price.

Joe went through the necessary channels and eventually got orders cut for the two of us, and Mutzelberg, to take a jeep to Czechoslovakia and get the instruments. One of our sergeants, Tap Boswell, lent us his .45 caliber sidearm as we had a lot of money and there were some shady characters on the roads during those days. On September 6, 1945, we set out on an adventure we never dreamed could happen.

Bill Crehan and the German guide Mutzelberg on the road to Czeckoslovakia and the Russian adventure.

As our orders specified, we traveled on the Autobahn the first day. The traffic was very light and we made good time. Joe kept studying the map and finally said he thought we could shave some miles off the trip if we went across some road he had found. I didn't really care, so we took Joe's short cut. We were to live to regret it.

At about nine o'clock that night, we suddenly came upon a Russian roadblock. The guards looked over our orders (which were in English) and got real excited. I don't know if they could even read them, but they got real upset and wanted to know why we were 80 miles off the route and going in the wrong direction.

They telephoned someone and eventually a truck appeared with several armed soldiers aboard. They were led by a motorcycle and an "officer-in-charge" riding in a Russian type jeep. We had certainly gotten their attention.

Joe and Mutzelberg were put into the Jeep and I had the honor of riding in the sidecar of the motorcycle. The truck followed us. It was then about 10 o'clock and as I had been driving all day, I was tired and sleepy. However, once I got in that sidecar, I woke up in a hurry as that driver was a real hot dog.

We arrived at the Russian Headquarters in Zwikow, Czechoslovakia, and were told that we were being held for questioning and investigation. Because of the German civilian with us, these idiots thought we were spies!

Our jeep was impounded in their motor pool and we were not allowed to use the radio in it. They wouldn't even allow us to call Berlin. Poor Mutzelberg was taken and put in a cell in the city jail and they wouldn't let us see or contact him.

Joe and I were given a large room in the officers' quarters with a private bath, double beds and the works. It was very comfortable. We ate with the Russian officers in their mess hall and the next morning at breakfast we had our first of a series of bad meals.

The coffee they gave us was pure black chicory. We had black bread, cabbage soup and either vodka or beer. We then knew why the Russian GIs didn't smile very often. We sure were glad we had brought along some American rations. Poor Mutzelberg told us later that he had received nothing but bread, water, and some very bad soup.

We were questioned by a couple of Russian officers and a German interpreter at least twice a day. Joe spoke excellent German and had taught me enough that I could follow a conversation fairly well. The questioning became very boring as they kept asking us the same dumb questions over and over again.

After we had been there about a week, we were awakened early one morning about one o'clock. I was feeling lousy, having picked up a flu bug or cold, but with the loud pounding on our door I got up and opened it. There stood a young Russian officer, obviously with a load of vodka under his belt, and he stated he wanted to ask us a few questions.

I thought to myself that surely they didn't plan to do it all over again! Sure enough, he started with the same dumb questions. He said he was gong to straighten this situation out once and for all. He didn't understand English and he was speaking in broken German. We were getting nowhere.

Feeling half sick, I got fed up with this routine in a few minutes. I told Joe in English that I had had enough of this drunk and that I was going to deck him and throw him out. Fortunately, Joe had a cooler head than I and he warned me that if I did, we could spend the post-war in a Russian prison.

Joe then explained that I was sick and running a temperature and that the officer had better leave before he caught my illness. He seemed to get through to him, because the guy left and we never saw him again.

A couple of days later, Joe met another officer who was a Russian parachutist. They had a few vodkas together and the officer agreed to help us. Then, doing what they should have done long ago, he called Berlin and checked us out. In no time we were released, but we couldn't get poor Mutzelberg freed.

We wasted no time in getting back to Berlin. The idea of getting the musical instruments was quickly forgotten. Joe and I took turns checking the music store each day for poor Mutzelberg, but it was another three weeks before he showed up. He looked even thinner than before and said the Russians had treated him badly.

We took Mutzelberg some American rations and some cigarettes and he surprised us by giving each of us a beautiful Swiss music box. He was a really nice guy and probably the only German I met during our stay in Europe that I ever trusted.

A few days later, the division was moved back to Calais, France in preparation for returning to the States. Joe and I have often wondered about just what the Russians were thinking when they detained us for all that time. Although we were definitely prisoners, they treated us like guests. And, you know something: they never did take the .45 away from me! I wore it all through the stupid incident!

"THE BEGINNING OF A LONG EVENING!"

As told by BGen David Schorr

When the 17th Airborne Division left Germany for France in the summer of 1945, the 513th ended up in a tent encampment near the small village of Tantonville. Shortly after our arrival, as commander, I was invited by the mayor to his home for dinner. It was suggested that I bring an interpreter along.

The lieutenant who had been doing the interpreting for the regiment had recently been transferred, but a replacement was found whom I was told could do the job. I found out that he was a sergeant who in civilian life had been a roustabout in a circus. In any event the two of us set out for the mayor's home.

I looked forward to an interesting evening. The mayor was a gentleman in his 80s. He had seen the Germans come through his village in 1870, 1914, and 1940 and I knew he would have some great tales to tell.

Since Tantonville was located in the Moselle Valley, famous for its vineyards, I started the conversation by saying I had not seen any vineyards in the immediate area and wondered why. My interpreter-sergeant put the question to the mayor who replied back to the sergeant.

The sergeant then turned to me with these memorable words, "The mayor says there used to be a hell of a lot of vineyards around here, but some G___ D___ bugs got in them and the S___O___B___s ate them all up!"

The mayor's great-granddaughter was present and I had sensed that she understood English. I knew right then that I was in for a long evening.

"WEREWOLVES AND DP'S"

As told by Walter J. Klepeis, 513 E

Some may think that my ability to speak German fluently would have been of advantage to me serving in the European Theatre. It didn't work out that way. I was put on detached duty so often, that in my company I was regarded by the first sergeant as a goof-off. All soldiers know that in the Army your company is your "family" and when you spend most of your time away from your family, it is a lonely life.

This ability to speak German was the reason that one day when our division was in the Ruhr Basin, I was ordered to report to the British Army Headquarters in Essen. The mission, I was told, was to track down German werewolves!

The retreating German troops had reportedly equipped a number of fanatic Nazis to fight as guerrillas behind the Allied lines after the regular troops had gone. From this grew the story that these guerrillas were "werewolves." The Germans loved legends and whether there was any truth or not to this one, guerrillas posed a definite threat to our forces.

When another trooper (who also spoke German) and I checked into the British Headquarters, we found the Brits were equally perplexed as to what the first move should be. Finally, someone came up with the idea to contact the German police.

This proved to be a good move as the police were anxious to cooperate. They came up with three lists. One was of known fanatic Nazis (those they knew were threats) another was a list of possible active Nazis and finally, a third list of so-called "running dogs." These were suspected sympathizers who had just recently come to Essen and about whom little was known.

We also received great cooperation from the populace. Essen had been heavily bombed and many citizens, fed up with living under the Nazi government, blamed the loyal Nazis for the bombings and prolonging the war. The occasion also became a good excuse to settle old grudges. Informing on your neighbor had become a way of life for many Germans.

The homes of all these suspects were "staked out" and the post office began opening their mail. In a few days all suspects had been taken into custody and we began questioning them. It shouldn't come as a big surprise that we found no werewolves in Essen and few if any citizens that could be connected with any guerrilla operations.

In about a week, our task was completed. About the only positive thing that came out of the whole effort was the fact I was able to take back two bottles of excellent French champagne to the members of my squad. We divided the contents and toasted the German werewolves!

My next detached duty came when I was assigned as an allied representative at a displaced person (DP) camp. This camp was located south of Wesel in the Ruhr and was called Voerde.

Because of the shortage of laborers for industries and war damage repair, the Germans had seized able-bodied workers from all over Europe and shipped them to where they were needed. When the Nazi machine collapsed, the DP problem loomed big for the conquering Allied forces.

There were three types of DPs. The first type was the concentration camp forced laborers who were treated as criminals or worse. They had been arrested for political, religious or ethnic reasons and included men, women, and children. Fortunately, at Voerde we had none of this type.

The second type were volunteer laborers, or "freiwilligr" as they called them. They came from all over Europe and consisted of family units—father, mother and children. Because of their volunteer status, they now carried the stigma of being a traitor and were trying now to cross the line and declare themselves "forced laborers." However, it was to no avail.

The third type were people who were forced to work in Germany against their will. They were conscripted slave laborers from all over Europe and most were men and single. Our camp at Voerde had about 60% of the volunteer type and 40% of the forced labor type.

When the war came to an end, all industry in Germany came to a screeching halt and all the DPs were out of work. Our first job was to feed them and get them back to their home countries as soon as possible. It was no easy task.

An American lieutenant colonel (a civil affairs type from Army level) gave me my orders which was to "go to the camp and keep peace, but don't assume management." However, on arrival I checked in with the United Nations Relief Association (UNRA) people and was told my job was going to be to guard a prisoner who was accused of being a Vaslov army soldier.

General Vaslov had formed an army of Russians who were sympathetic to Germany and fought against Stalin. That being true, this guy was in deep danger. He was branded as a traitor and anyone who could kill him would curry favor with the Soviet Secret Police and maybe even save himself and his family from a vacation in Siberia.

We took the threat seriously and when I questioned him, I found out that he had not been physically harmed, but had been verbally abused. He spoke above average German and I wondered if he wasn't a volunteer in the German Army. When I processed German POWs, I found many Russians in their ranks and this guy was well fed.

The UNRA people told me he was going to stand trial at another location. The chief gripe the man had was that his wife and children were there and they wouldn't let him see them. I slept in the cell with him for two days with my rifle loaded. I made sure he didn't get out and no one got in. I also sent his family to him and I had no problem.

The camp was managed by a committee composed of representatives of the various eastern nationalities who were residents there.

Walter Klepeis had some interesting "special duty" assignments in Europe.

These nations later became members of what we called the Iron Curtain Nations. Another one of my duties was to attend the committee meetings as an observer.

The majority of the committee spoke some German, but there was a Ukrainian girl who acted as translator. I made my position clear at the very beginning. I let them know I was only an observer, but that I would report everything to "my Colonel" and that they had better not displease him.

Numerous problems were discussed for hours, but very little was resolved. An example was the argument over the German tractor which was parked in the Polish area of the camp. The Poles couldn't get it operating, so the Russians insisted that it be rolled to their side "because it was well known that the Russian engineers were much better than Polish engineers."

Hours were consumed every day arguing about the tractor which if repaired, couldn't be used for anything. There was no diesel fuel and there was no work for the tractor.

They also spent hours arguing over the plumbing. Each of the buildings had a men's and women's toilet on each floor. The drains were non-functioning except in the Czech and Hungarian buildings because they had some skilled plumbers and they kept them working.

Many of the Soviets had never used indoor plumbing until they arrived in Germany. There were no Polish or Soviet plumbers. The Czech plumbers wouldn't fix the plumbing in the Soviet buildings because they argued they

Typical of the massive displaced person problem the 17th faced after the war are these Russian DPs being shipped back to Russia.

already had and it was plugged up again in a few days. They said the Soviets needed "toilet training."

One of the most gruesome practices in the camp was of the "boy meets girl" variety. It is almost impossible to regulate against love as it transcends everything including nationalistic lines. The problems existed only in the Polish and Soviet groups. If a Soviet girl was found to be seeing a Polish boy, the girl would be stripped of her clothes, all hair shaved off and she was paraded in the camp street and jeered by her own people.

I understand the same practice was carried out by Polish men against Polish girls that were caught seeing Soviet boys. The Ukrainian translator informed me of the practice and I moved quickly to stop it at the next committee meeting. No other cases of this were brought to my attention; however, I did hear that one girl was severely beaten in one of the buildings.

Boredom was one of the biggest problems we had, so classes in various subjects were started. The most popular being the English language classes. Footballs were plentiful and the teenage boys started games. Things began to calm down and at the committee meetings they actually reached agreements on several matters.

After I was at the camp about 10 days, the area civil affairs representative responsible for the administration of the camps decided to isolate the various nationalities in separate camps. Seems the other camps were having the same problems we were having.

Under the new setup, we became a Soviet camp and the ethnic Soviet groups couldn't agree on anything. In fact, the in-fighting was even worse. Fortunately, it was determined that my presence was no longer needed and I was ordered returned to my company.

The night before I left, they had one of those famous Russian parties with vodka made from stolen German potatoes. It lasted all night and was complete with the traditional Soviet sword dances and polkas. The next day when a Jeep came to pick me up, about 40 men and women kissed me goodbye and little girls brought me flowers. I got really choked up.

Two postscripts: The Ukrainian girl that acted as a translator refused to go back to her native land. She escaped and fled to France. And, there was the much-talked-about tractor. Before the Poles departed, they took a sledge hammer and completely smashed it so that the Soviets could not have it!

"HUNTING WEREWOLVES"

As told by Don Barone, 411 QM

When the war began to wind down, a lot of rumors began to make the rounds of the division. Some said the Germans were going to form a redoubt in Austria and wage guerrilla warfare from there. Other stories told of "werewolves" or diehard SS troopers who had been left behind to snipe at us and to sabotage our operations by organizing the German civilians.

Although there might have been some actual cases of this happening, for the most part it was only talk. It was the aftermath of a complete victory over a conquered enemy. Nevertheless, our unit was put on alert and we were very cautious as we went about our duties in post-war Germany.

In late April of 1945, we were operating in the Essen area near the village of Bottrop. I was a member of an eight-man patrol that was sent up the Ruhr Valley one

While hunting "Werewolves" in Germany, Don Barone found that his ability to speak Italian came in handy!

day to hunt down some "werewolf" snipers that had been reported to be in the area.

We had about reached the conclusion that it was another wild goose chase when just before twilight, I heard some voices coming from a wooded ravine. Quietly, I closed in on the location and finally got close enough to realize they were speaking Italian!

There, taking a break were about a half dozen civilians, all jabbering in Italian. They had no idea we were in the area and we were able to surprise them. After searching them, we took them into custody and returned them to our headquarters. There, Charlie, one of our cooks, and I, being able to speak Italian, interrogated them.

When the truth came out, they were Italian Displaced Persons (DPs) and had been brought to this area by the Germans to work as slave laborers. Furthermore, they were delighted that we had picked them up and volunteered that there were many more hiding back there in the forest.

They seemed very grateful to be under our control and to know that they were free from any danger from the Germans. They really did have it pretty good—no more fear, someone was going to feed them, and best of all, they saw we were making arrangements to return them to their homes.

From this time on, while they were with us, life in our compound changed markedly. There was singing and dancing every night and we all enjoyed their laughing and happy music. Several of them took over all the cooking chores and others took care of our laundry and ironing. We were living like kings!

During the period they were with us, I guess I fell for one of the young ladies. She was a red-headed, green-eyed girl from Bologna, Italy. I think her name was Ann. I also had the feeling that our colonel was intrigued with her beauty!

Several weeks later after the war had ended, arrangements were completed to send them back to their homes via Army convoy. It was a sad time and there were many teary eyes as we said our goodbyes and the trucks pulled out. We knew we would never see each other again.

I kissed my young friend goodbye and she waved as the truck disappeared down the road. I was sorry to see them go, but I have always felt good about being able to send those people back to their homes. It was like I had been able to help "right one of the many wrongs" that Hitler had inflicted on Italy, the native home of my ancestors.

"DAYS OF HIGH EXCITEMENT"

As told by Michael Umhofer, 194 D/G

I was assigned to Company "D" of the 194th in November of 1944. I had just graduated from Jump School and arrived just before the 17th left for the Bulge. I served as a rifleman, platoon runner and a court interpreter and investigator during the occupation.

When the war was over, I returned to college and received my degree and a commission through the ROTC program. This got me a front row seat in the Korean War and later, a ticket to Vietnam and eventually, retirement as a colonel. Nevertheless, as I look back over my career, my experiences as a private in the 17th Airborne loom as the best of times. Let me tell you a few of my experiences.

I sailed to England aboard the *Queen Mary* along with 500 other brand new paratroopers. We joined the various units of the 17th Airborne in one of those many Table of Organization and Equipment (TO&E) changes the division underwent in those days.

Upon our arrival in Tidworth, we were directed to a fenced-in area and warned by a fat, rear echelon major standing on a tree stump, that we faced a week of processing. He added that we would be confined to the area until given our unit assignment. There was about three seconds of deafening silence before some one in the crowd shouted an obscenity at the major and 500 paratroopers stampeded for the fence.

Clamoring over the fence with not the slightest idea of where they were going, the men were determined not to be confined another week after the long ocean voyage. Although the major screamed at the top of his voice to stop, his efforts met with little success.

Outside the fence, the road to the right led to Andover and to the left to Salisbury. Most of the troops ended up going to Salisbury and that was where the "French leave" ended. A fight started there between British and Canadian troops and our guys threw in with the Canadians. The mini-riot that followed completely destroyed a beautiful Salvation Army Club in the city.

MPs swarmed all over the area and the troopers were quickly rounded up and returned to Tidworth. The lengthy processing procedure the major had predicted was completed in two days and we were out of there!

When we entered combat in the Bulge, we often found ourselves fighting the cold 1945 winter as much as we did the Germans. I recall one night in Luxembourg when we were able to take shelter in a farmhouse. Our squad had "liberated" some excellent wine earlier in the day and that night when we returned to the house after pulling guard duty, we were all eager for a long, healthy drink before bedding down.

One of our guys saw a half-full bottle on the table, grabbed it and began to gulp it down. The rest of us awaited our turn. Suddenly, he stopped, his eyes popped out and he began to gag and choke. He bolted through the door and plunged head first into the snow and began to retch.

Seems the guys sleeping in the room had already polished off the wine and they had been using the empty wine bottles for a latrine to avoid having to go outside in the cold! Needless to say, this incident made all of us quite cautious about drinking anything found in a bottle from then on!

I guess I am a slow learner, however, as I had a bad experience along these lines later on as we were in the Ruhr Valley. Each day we would march some 15 to 20 miles, have a short fire fight and then bed down in a house before repeating the process the next day. It was a hot, dusty job.

One night after such a day, I retired to the house where my squad was staying. All the guys were sitting around a large oak dining room table cleaning their weapons. They seemed to be drinking tea out of some fine china cups.

Needing a cooling drink after my efforts that day, I grabbed up one of the cups and took a big swallow. Everyone burst out with a roar of laughter as I spluttered and wheezed. I had gulped down a mouthful of rifle bore cleaner!

The bane of any combat infantryman is that he is his own pack mule. This is especially true of the Airborne soldier whose vehicle support is greatly limited. As the fighting gradually wound down, instead of getting lighter, his load usually increased. This was due to the personal loot he acquired such as pistols, daggers, cameras, etc.

Shortly before our last major fire fight at Soest, in addition to my walkie talkie and M-3, I also carried on my person, five pistols, an SS dagger, a plate camera and my most prized possession: an encased silver barrelled shotgun engraved with the name "Herman Goring." It was given to me by a German forest ranger who didn't have the heart to destroy it as he had been ordered.

Worn down by long marches, I decided to put some of my loot on one of our company's ammo trailers as had many of the other members of the company. The very next day the battle for Soest became heated. Both ammo carriers were rushed back to the ammo point. You can probably guess what happened.

Back at the ammo point all the baggage on the trailers was dumped by the side of the road to make room for the ammo. That was the last any of us ever saw of our treasures. It was rumored that one of the other companies of the battalion helped themselves to our goodies. True or not, our relationship with that company was never the same!

I recall another time in my career. This one took place in the Bulge. My "foxhole buddy" and I made the mistake of digging in under what we assumed to be a frozen haystack. It turned out to be a manure pile the farmer had prepared for the next planting season.

It was a warm spot okay, but the heat from our bodies caused a continuous dripping of the manure. As luck would have it, we sustained a prolonged enemy shelling and were unable to change our positions. Needless to say we were a total mess.

Mike Umhofer one week after the Rhine jump at Bad Sassendorf near the site of the "Soest" battle.

We were also declared unfit for patrol duty—the enemy could smell us a mile away!

When we occupied positions along the Our River in early February of 1945, we were involved in extensive patrolling activities. This also afforded us the opportunity to refit the companies. I joined a party led by Sergeant Nick "Duke" DeSentis headed for Chalons, France to pick up the stored duffels of the unit.

The vehicles got as far as Verdun where they were stopped by an MP who reported that a quick thaw had flooded the roads and it would be necessary to turn back. Once the vehicles were no longer in view of the MP, Duke ordered them parked in an alley. He reasoned that it was dark and maybe too dangerous to continue back to Luxembourg that night. Besides, what good Airborne trooper could miss this opportunity to relax a little for the first time in over a month of combat?

His scheme was to find an isolated small bar somewhere away from the larger cafes frequented by the soldiers who were on pass or R&R. Accordingly, he led us down a dark alley until we came upon a thick door that had a little sliver of light at the bottom that had somehow evaded the attention of those checking the blackout rules. Inside we could hear the faint sound of music.

Resorting to house-to-house fighting technique, Duke gave the door a mighty kick that swung it wide open and revealed one of the largest cafes in

Verdun. The place was crowded with infantry replacements celebrating their last night before shipping out to the front to join their new units.

You could have heard a pin drop! The band stopped playing, the singer stopped in mid-word and the patrons of the cafe froze in fright. I guess we were a pretty frightening sight: dirty, needing shaves, our clothes filthy and torn, grenades hanging from our web equipment and rifles pointing straight at them.

I'll give Duke credit. He only hesitated a second or two before waving us in and yelling at a stunned waitress in a mix of Italian and French to fill every inch of a vacant table with wine and champagne! Then he ordered the band to resume playing and for the singer to finish her number.

After a few minutes things returned to normal. The replacements, eager for information on what to expect "up front," began sending drinks to our table and ended up paying our tab. We were really kings that night!

I'm not sure when we finally got back, but it was either one day or two days late. Duke, of course, took the brunt of the chewing out. Although there was some speculation that he would be busted, instead he was sent to Paris for two weeks of officer training and came back a second lieutenant. I guess that was punishment enough!

It may be interesting to note that in June of 1950, while I was attending the tactical phase of the Associate Basic Officers Course at Ft. Benning, I was surprised to learn that historical examples involving the 17th Airborne Division were frequently cited throughout the course.

One described the teamwork between the 193rd Glider Infantry and the 11th Armored in their attack on the German "Bois Bruhl-Compogne" line. It was considered by seasoned German commanders to be the first action in which American tanks and Airborne infantry had been effectively coordinated in the attack.

The use of "reverse slope defense" by the German army against the 194th Glider Infantry on January 4, 1945 was also considered a classic. I'll never forget that one and never will most of the 2nd Battalion who moved across the top of that low-lying hill to be greeted with intense mortar and machine gun fire like we had never seen before or did afterwards.

From the prone position, I looked up at the sky that day and I could see dozens of tiny black specks hurtling toward us. One sailed over my head and as my heart nearly stopped, landed at my feet and failed to explode. I still thank God today for that dud.

All of us owe our lives to the non-coms that day who yelled and cussed us until we got to our feet and got off that killing ground. Some went on into the woods, others back into the ice-filled creek in the draw and then back up the other slope. We took heavy machine gun fire, .88s and tank fire and we took many casualties. The icy creek was later responsible for many a case of frozen feet.

We hung on until ordered back down to our old positions in the late afternoon. By that time my legs wouldn't support me and I kept falling. Four of my buddies dashed back up the hill despite the heavy small arms fire and dragged me back down. You don't soon forget comrades like that because they have given you the gift of life. I feel you have an obligation to make sure you were worth it.

At the hill's base, slit trenches were prepared for the expected counter attack. During darkness at least three attempts were made to overrun us with tanks, but our artillery kept the enemy back. Burning tanks provided both light and heat, and during the night maimed cows stumbled around stepping on men in their shallow holes.

Shortly after first light, 2nd Battalion survivors were withdrawn and marched through the snow dazed and exhausted to Hubermont, a town which was bustling with activity. There I saw a jeep parked alongside the road with a plate on it displaying three stars.

It took a few minutes for me to realize the significance, but then I saw him, General Patton, standing there with three stars on his helmet and coat collar turned up. As we walked by, you could hear him say, "Good job, good job, we'll get them yet, men!"

We were so beat, I don't think any of our guys paid any attention to him. In his eagerness to roll up the German rear guard, Patton had resorted to desperate measures that had gotten a lot of good men killed. Even a lowly private knew you don't throw lightly equipped Airborne units against tanks.

In town we were housed in the local church and it was there an incident took place that has always bothered me down through the years. As the floors were made of stone, someone started a fire in a corner of the church to get warm. Later, when it became hard to find firewood, someone chopped up one of the church pews and we burned that.

Even worse, as were getting mortar fire landing in the street and it was dangerous to venture outside, we used a corner of the church for our latrine. After being exposed to the killing and misery of combat, you lose your good judgement and do things you would never think of doing under normal conditions.

Later, the parish priest came in and when he saw what was happening, he wept. I will never forget how bad I felt about our actions. I was glad to hear that our 17th Airborne Division Association had helped to rebuild the church at Houmont, but I am sure the church we desecrated was located in the nearby town of Hubermont.

Appreciation for the concept of human treatment of Prisoners of War can be gained from the experience during the Rhine operation of "G" Company's Commander, Gorden Gatch. His glider landed in the vicinity of the enemy regimental CP and came under intense small arms and heavy weapons fire.

Captain Gatch's runner was killed and he was severely wounded himself. Taken to one of our aid stations, he was prepared for evacuation but given only a slim chance for survival.

A German doctor recently captured was tending some of the enemy wounded nearby and saw what was going on. He asked permission to try some emergency procedures on the captain and he was granted that right. Apparently, he knew what he was doing as his treatment was later attributed to saving the captain's life.

I found out about this incident when I asked Virgil Stuart, the company medic about the captain's condition. Earlier that morning, in the vicinity of the LZ, I had seen one of the squads capture the group which included the German doctor. A couple of the guys got carried away and were brutalizing the prisoners with their rifle butts. Fortunately, I was able to step in and stop them.

As the years have passed, I am afraid I have forgotten many of the experiences that happened during my military career and unfortunately, many of the wonderful friends that I have had. But, someway, those days in the 17th Airborne are etched in my memory. I was a skinny, young kid, but the people I served with were 10 feet tall.

"WHERE'S MY DAMN PANTS?"

As told by Bill Rudicel, 193 D

Since we left the barracks area in France on Christmas Day, we had been in reserve or seeing only light patrol action. On January 7, 1945, however, we set out on our first offensive action and it was a dandy.

I was the platoon leader for the 1st platoon, Company "D". We came under heavy artillery fire as we approached the woods we were to attack. We began to take casualties immediately. I caught a piece of shrapnel in my shoulder and my whole arm went numb.

As I had the platoon radio, I called Lieutenant Jim Logan, the company XO to tell him I was turning over the radio and command of the platoon to the platoon sergeant, Tech Sergeant

Bill Rudicel was wounded in the first action his company saw. For 45 years they believed him KIA.

Charles Pierre. I had the key down and was talking to Logan when another shell came in and hit a few feet from me, slicing a big chunk out of my left hip and I must have let our a big scream right into the radio. Nearby my runner, Earl Kier, was also hit, bleeding badly and was in a state of shock.

Earl and I crawled to a sugar beet storage mound nearby where Lieutenant Telesca of Company "E" bandaged our wounds. After a while, the shelling in this area decreased and by continuing to convince Earl "that he could make it," we crawled to the rear area approximately 100 yards where the medics were just arriving. Earl and I rode on the same jeep to the aid station. Soon I was evacuated to the field hospital, then to Paris by train, to LaMans for surgery, and to England for recovery.

Lieutenant Logan sadly told all that he had been on the radio talking to me when the shell hit and that I was surely KIA. So, all my men wrote me off and until I found out about the association in 1990, just in time to make the Washington reunion, they all thought I was dead.

Apparently Lieutenant Logan did too. When I returned to the division in Germany after five months in the hospitals, I was reassigned to Division Headquarters and went to Quartermaster's hunting for my duffel bag. When I found it, all was intact except my "pinks," the dress uniform pants. I was told that Lieutenant Logan had helped himself to them.

Mad as hops, I looked the good lieutenant up at his new duty post at MP Headquarters. When I found him, he was bent over a desk working on something. I waited calmly until he looked up and then I yelled, "Where's my damn pants?"

Logan turned as white as a sheet and began to stammer, "I thought you were ... I thought ... Is it you? Are you real?"

Logan looked like he had seen a ghost and he was thoroughly shaken. I got my pants okay and a thousand pardons from him. That was the last time I saw him. I just never could think too kindly of a guy who would steal your pants!

"MY LIFE AS A SHAVETAIL"

As told by J.R. Jones, 513 A

It's funny how when I think back on it, my service in the 17th Airborne seems to be brief episodes of almost impossible situations. Here's some quick ones to stimulate your memory:

1. When Captain John Spears introduced me to the other company officers in the BOQ one night, he had to interrupt a crap game. The guys were friendly enough, but it was obvious they were more interested in getting on with their game than they were in meeting me.

2. When Captain Spears introduced me to the First Sergeant, he quickly excused himself as he said he was on his way to participate in a "knuckle drill." I later learned he had a fight out behind the barracks. That's a knuckle drill.

3. We had a chronic AWOL so they handcuffed him to his bed one night. As duty officer, I was given the key in the event there was an emergency and told to check on him every hour during the night. He got a good night's sleep and I was exhausted the next day.

4. At Camp Miles Standish before we went overseas, we were taken to a secure area and shown a secret weapon. When the cover was removed, we were told it was a .57mm recoilless rifle and it was a deadly anti-tank weapon. We finally got them seven months later when we went over the Rhine.

5. During the motor movement to the front in the Bulge, our two and a half ton truck broke down due to a broken fan belt. The others went on without us and after a three hour wait, we finally begged one from a passing truck and arrived in our area. We were greeted by firing from two Germans that had been left behind.

6. A .57mm anti-tank gun (towed) crew attached to our platoon decided to pull out and said they might be back in the morning. We said no deal. They left without their gun and we were stuck trying to learn how to work it and expecting an attack any minute.

7. In Germany we were assigned the duty of administering several Russian Displaced Persons camps. Our main problem was keeping the Russians in the

camp and away from the German populace. We were instructed to use "minimum necessary force." With that in mind, one night one of the DPs attempted to sneak out of the camp and one of our troopers shot him. Before daylight the trooper is on his way back to the States. The U.S. Command is somewhat embarrassed and the Russians are amazed that we took such strong action. No formal investigation was ever conducted.

8. Another mission we had was to inventory the food supplies in the possession of the German householders. This didn't pose much of a problem as there was very little food on hand and they were anxious to show us their bare shelves in hopes we would give them some.

9. At Nancy, France, I was detailed to the Regimental Chute Patrol (CP). The primary duty of this body was really to look out for and take care of any delinquent 513 troopers before area MPs could give him a DR. On one particular night, a trooper was stopped in an "off-limits" area. He looked me straight in the eye and dared me to pull my .45 on him. With that he turned and hightailed it off into the night.

10. As I had pulled 15 months with the 37th Infantry Division in the Pacific Theatre before returning to the States to attend OCS, I suddenly found myself the high point man in the division. It was nice to learn I was to be rotated home, but I sure hated to leave the great life of a "Shavetail" in the 513th Parachute Infantry Regiment!

"TO EUROPE AND BACK"

by Col. Gabe W. Lewis, Div. HQ

Editor'sNote: *The following are excerpts from the journal of Colonel Gabe W. Lewis who served as AG of the 17th Airborne from its activation until he became the last man to officially be a member of the division. We are also indebted to Colonel Lewis R. Good, his good friend as well as our Division G1, for providing us with a copy of this narrative account.*

$\mathbf{W}$e arrived at Camp Miles Standish, a camp outside of Boston in August in the midst of a heat wave. It was miserable and we were relieved when after a couple of days we entrained to go to the docks. The entire division was loaded on two ships, even our chief of staff, Colonel Liebel, with his leg in a cast. There were two that didn't make it—one lieutenant and one private.

The lieutenant had attended a farewell drinking party the night before and decided to demonstrate his ability as a parachutist by jumping from a balcony to the dance floor of the Officer's Club (without a parachute) resulting in a broken ankle. The private, whose name I do not recall but will call Schwartz, just didn't show up at the gangplank. We presumed he stayed behind to enjoy the pleasures of Boston.

This was not the last we heard of Private Schwartz. Months later, when the division was in heavy combat, we had the rear echelon at Virton, Belgium. Utmost secrecy had been observed to keep anyone from knowing the location of any of our units—letters were censored, shoulder insignia removed, and unit designations on the vehicles painted over.

One morning the personnel officer of the engineer battalion came to my office and said, "Colonel, do you remember that guy Schwartz that missed the boat in Boston?" I replied, that I did. "Well, he is out there in the chow line right now," he told me. The personnel officer wanted to know whether to prefer charges against him for going AWOL or whatever.

"Listen," I said, "we don't have time to court-martial a resourceful soldier like that. Anyone who can hitch-hike across the Atlantic, find out where his outfit was and go to it, is too good a man to lose. Just make an entry on his record 'assigned and joined,' and send him to his unit. With millions of personnel records floating around, no one will ever know the difference." This is what we did and we did not question him as to what happened.

We docked at Liverpool and went by train to a vacated British camp near Chiseldon, Wiltshire, on the Salsbury plain. It was quite a thrill for me as I had always wanted to go to Europe, sparked somewhat by my reading a lot of English literature and studying architecture and the history of art.

General Miley, as usual, used me in England to do almost everything except what I was supposed to be doing as adjutant general. Again I was liaison officer with the Troop Carrier Command for a while. Later, along with seven or eight other officers, I was sent to coordinate activities with the RAF.

The thing I remember best about the assignment was the horrible food we had for the first several days—mostly boiled cabbage and mutton. In desperation, one of our officers went to our quartermaster depot and returned with a jeep load of sugar, butter, bacon, and other goodies—a real treat for the British. In return, they provided us with an ample supply of Scotch. Unfortunately, I didn't (and still don't) care for this popular drink.

All this duty resulted from plans that the 17th was to participate in an airborne invasion of Holland as soon as the 82nd, 101st, and the 1st British Airborne Division had established a firm hold there. As depicted in the movie, *A Bridge Too Far*, the mission was a failure and the 17th didn't participate.

Also, we were coordinating training with the 6th British Airborne, especially in radio communications. Like most paratroopers, they were a happy-go-lucky bunch. Once, with other officers I went to their area to observe a small field exercise. Afterwards, we were invited to their Officer's Mess for dinner. I noticed that the ceiling was literally covered with initials—all in red. I asked one of the British officers what this was all about. He told me that at their parties it was a custom that each female guest leave her initials on the ceiling, written in lipstick. To do this she was hoisted up by a couple of officers. They must have had a lot of fun!

My hopes for a pleasant prolonged stay in England was shattered by the massive drive of the Germans in the Ardennes, later called "The Battle of the Bulge." Immediate plans were made to fly the division to France to try to stop the drive, which had already wiped out two American divisions and threatened to capture the port of Antwerp. Twice we went to various airports to enplane, only to be told the mission was delayed as all C-47s had to be used to transport gasoline to General Patton's armored divisions. The third time we made it.

Transporting 8,000 men and their equipment, even a short distance, presents a major logistical problem. Hundreds of airplanes and dozens of airfields are required.In the plane I was in was Lew Good, the G-1, and his enlisted helpers. Also, I had my key personnel. In addition, we carried two jeeps, securely tied down.

The weather was very cold, and along with several other C-47s, we landed at a small snow-covered airfield in France about dusk. We wrestled the two jeeps off the plane and started wondering how we would spend the night. The field had recently been taken over from the British, and one of the American officers came down and told us they had quarters for the officers but no room for the enlisted men. It was Christmas Eve. Lew and I decided we would stay with the soldiers.

We located a large foxhole that had previously been used for an anti-aircraft gun crew. We dragged in a lot of kindling for a fire, and cleared out the snow as best we could. Ignoring precautions about any lights, we soon had a fire going. We ate very cold K rations and then something happened that even now seems hard to believe. One of the boys found hidden in a niche in the foxhole, two one-gallon cans of plum pudding, probably purloined and hidden by some British soldier in anticipation of a Christmas feast. We opened the cans with a bayonet, and at least we had some Christmas cheer. As it was too cold to sleep much, even shrouded in our bed rolls, we sang Christmas carols well into the night.

When daylight came we loaded into the two jeeps with our gear and headed for our assigned area, an abandoned French air base near Mourmelon-le-Grande. It had been occupied by the 101st, which had been rushed to Bastogne to defend that rail and road center. Here it was that General McAuliff gave his famous reply "Nuts" to the Germans who demanded his surrender after he was surrounded by four German Divisions.

En route to the area one of our columns was strafed by German aircraft, and we suffered our first battle casualties. A number of jeeps were stopped by MPs, still searching for infiltrating Germans in American uniforms.

Ed Messinger, our G-5, was stopped, and before he was permitted to proceed had to sing for the MP "Marzy Doats," a silly little song that was popular with Americans at that time. He also had to tell what the "Bums" were and what State Camp Hood was in. Finally he convinced the MP he was not a German saboteur.

We had Christmas dinner with the rear echelon officers of the 101st, who were billeted in the deserted French Officer's quarters that bordered the airfield. That day the weather cleared for the first time since the German offensive, and our air power was able to strike back. I saw a string of gliders pulled by C-47s fly over. They were carrying medical personnel to the isolated 101st; their medical company had been captured.

Our units started pulling out piece-meal for the front as they arrived. The rear echelon stayed behind, and I got my first taste of combat at midnight on New Year's Eve. My sister, Gladys, had sent me some home-canned chili which I had brought over from England. Colonel Lisenby had obtained several bottles of champagne, and we were eating chili and drinking champagne from canteen cups in celebration of the New Year when we were shaken by a loud explosion and gunfire—exactly at midnight. I told my fellow officers, "Those GIs are crazy wasting ammunition to celebrate New Year."

Lew Good said, "New Year, hell, we are being bombed."

This was true. Later I learned that Goering had scraped together every airplane and every gallon of gas he could find to make a unified and final bombing attack on the allied airfields throughout France.

General Miley and all our units had been gone several days and had left without leaving me any instructions or means of communication with them. I knew we must be having battle casualties and other administration problems that needed to be taken care of, and I decided I had better try to find the division. From the AG of the 101st, I learned that our division headquarters was probably at a little town in Belgium called Moret. To reach there one had to drive up the narrow corridor leading to Bastogne, which had just been opened by Patton's tank units.

John Gray and I talked over the situation and we agreed that we had to be closer to the division if we were to function at all. We picked out a town in Belgium (Virton) that was reasonably close to the front. While I was going to see General Miley, John would try to borrow some trucks from a nearby quartermaster unit and move the rear echelon to this new location.

As I entered Belgium and went further on into the corridor, the war became very real to me. First, there were the refugees, thousands of them in the snow and bitter cold, clogging the roads and trudging on foot or in carts piled high with their belongings, fleeing the German—innocent victims of the war. We passed through St. Vith, where the Germans had lined up over 150 American prisoners of war and massacred them with machine guns. Then, I heard the heavy artillery firing, and later saw our huge batteries firing in the direction of my destination.

The corridor was crowded with tanks and troops being rushed to the aid of the 101st and other American units. The battlefield hadn't been cleaned up, and dead and frozen German soldiers lined the roadside. A real shock came when I saw the first dead American GI, lying face down in the snow. The real horror of war came to me then. Also, I was somewhat concerned about my own safety. The Germans were still shelling the corridor. An airburst of a shrapnel shell would sound overhead and I would hear fragments whistling through the air. Luckily, I saw no one hit. Some of the villages we drove through were burning, and gutted houses and rubble were everywhere.

I am sure that our journey up the corridor coincided with General Patton's first visit. I heard a siren and looked back. A jeep with flashing light and Patton was speeding by on the shoulder of the road, passing the congested mass of troops and machines. That was the only time I saw Patton, though later I was to teach his grandchildren in Sunday School at the Army War College and to know one of his daughters and two of his sons-in-law.

The reason I think Patton and I went up at the same time is that he described in his book a sight that impressed him—one that impressed me also. At the left of the road was a German machine gun squad that appeared to be ready to start firing. The gunner was leaning over his weapon with his finger on the trigger. Sitting next to him was his assistant with a belt of cartridges in his hands. Other members were sitting around, one in the act of falling over. They were dead and frozen stiff, apparently all killed by an American shrapnel burst. This appeared to me, as it did to General Patton, as something one might see in a wax museum.

I arrived at the Division Command Post about dark, and went to see General Miley. They had taken over a Catholic priest's residence next to an old rock church. General Miley told me the 194th Glider Infantry had gone into the attack that morning and had "done themselves proud." (Later I found that it had been a very costly affair.)

In the midst of the tragedy of war there is frequently an amusing incident. The headquarters personnel had shoveled away snow and dug foxholes in the priest's yard. In so doing, one of the GIs uncovered a large cache of the priest's wine, which he had buried to hide from the Germans. This was distributed to everyone, and General Miley gave me two bottles to take back with me.

I didn't sleep much that night as one of our artillery battalions had four 75mm pack howitzers just outside the window where I slept that fired off and on until daybreak.

Here, I should tell what a discouraging situation our division faced. We had been air lifted from England on December 23 and 24 to numerous airfields in France, having to leave much of our equipment behind. The Germans had bypassed Bastogne and had pushed the point of the Bulge to Houffalize, Belgium. There they had concentrated their Tiger Tanks and best troops in a last desperate effort to break through and proceed to the capture of the port at Antwerp. The American Division holding the tip had been so decimated that it was no longer effective.

In this confused situation our units picked up additional ammunition and immediately started for the vicinity of Houffalize, where they were to attack the next morning, taking over from the relieved division during the night. This they did, although some units were still en route when the fight was started.

The tank destroyer units assigned to support the attack refused to offer much assistance as their vehicles and guns were so inferior to those of the enemy that it was suicidal to do so. But the weather was the worst enemy. The attack was launched in a blowing snow storm in eleven degree weather. Our men had neither white snow suits nor shoe-pacs (a loose rubber overshoe) which permitted the soldiers to wear two pairs of wool socks to prevent frost bite.

The troops tried, but German tanks rolled out and beat them back. True, our small pack howitzers knocked out a few and left them burning in the snow, but to no avail. These attacks and counter attacks went on for four days until, with the help of the Air Corps, our division finally captured Houffalize, and the back of the German force was broken.

The cost was high. In the four days we suffered 4,000 casualties—killed, wounded, captured, missing, or suffering from frozen feet. This meant that my office would have to process thousands of casualty reports, including many letters of condolence—those "I regret to inform you" letters which brought heartbreak to families at home.

Out of curiosity, I went over to a house where our interrogation team was questioning Germans captured only a half hour before. They were quite skilled, and I observed no prisoners who didn't talk. While I presume the Geneva rules were followed, it was pretty rough. Fifty or sixty prisoners were lined up outside, standing in the snow and cold. They were not allowed to urinate until after they were interrogated, and some of them were obviously very uncomfortable.

The division artillery headquarters was housed in a rock house, and only a few feet away was a dead German with a hand grenade in his hand—with the pin pulled. Apparently, he had been killed as he was about to throw it, and was frozen stiff. The artillery men, knowing they would soon move, and with no sign of a thaw in sight, just left matters as they were.

Next I drove to the division aid station located in a store in a small village with cobblestone streets. I knew this would be where most of the battle casualties would be recorded. Wounded were on stretchers on the sidewalk and in the streets. Medics were frantically dressing wounds inside. Not only medics but the veterinarians, dentists, and band members were busy taking care of the wounded and loading them in ambulances to be taken to the rear and a hospital. For the first and only time I saw blood running in the street gutters.

It was late when I started back down the corridor to Virton. The same dead German soldiers (the wax-like German machine gun squad, smashed vehicles and tanks) all were the same as the day before. Later, in the Spring when the snow began to melt I was to drive over the same road, and it was worse. Countless corpses covered and hidden under the snow were emerging, and the graves registration people were gathering them up and stacking them in piles like cord wood.

The rear echelon, when separated from the division, is hampered in several ways. There is no provision for cooks, medical personnel, supply people, transportation, or communications. At times there are several hundred people involved who must be fed, clothed, and cared for, and one has to resort to all official and unofficial devices to survive. I let each staff section set up its own mess, and they were issued daily "C" rations, which were gallon cans of food, and they cooked them as best they could.

The division, involved in combat, had no time or interest in providing support for the rear echelon. There was no communication with the division except for hunting for them by messenger, and yet we had to take care of all the red tape and administration involving the division. This was a chore, as in many cases answers to "immediate action" letters required the decision of the commanding general, who couldn't always be reached, and answers were delayed until he was located.

This is one small example of situations in which I had to stick out my neck and hope for the best. At the time we were under Patton's 3rd Army, and he had issued a directive that officer promotion recommendations would be submitted on the last day of each month, and that each letter had to be signed personally by the division commander.

When the last day of the month arrived, I had no idea where General Miley was or how to get in touch with him. I did know of several officers he wanted promoted, and that if they were not recommended, green officers newly arrived from the U.S. of the required rank would be assigned to fill the position vacancies. So, I wrote seven recommendations for promotions and forged General Miley's signature to them.

Had my indiscretion been discovered, knowing General Patton's violent temper, I am sure my military career would have been in jeopardy. The next time I saw General Miley I told him what I had done, and he just laughed—and I felt better.

One problem presented itself that I had not thought about. Replacement of GIs to compensate for our losses began to pour in by the scores, and I had no transportation to send them to their units at the front. It happened that Elliot Roosevelt had a reconnaissance squadron some miles away, and he seemed to have everything. Some of my non-coms had become quite friendly with some of his, probably in search of alcoholic refreshments and good looking female companions. When I discussed my transportation problem with one of my sergeants, he said, "Let me see what I can do about it."

That afternoon he came back and told me, "Colonel, those boys over at the squadron are dying to see what a battle front looks like. They will be glad to bring some big trucks over and haul our men to Division Forward if a few of them can go along for the ride.

Thereafter we had almost daily runs to the front. Whether General Roosevelt ever knew about this, I don't know. I had learned that a lot of necessary but unofficial details could best be taken care of by segeants rather than going through official channels. This is only one of the many things Elliot's non-coms did for us, and for which I am grateful.

The close attachment and feeling a GI has for his outfit and buddies became apparent to me during this time. Hundreds of our GIs had gone to various hospitals in Belgium and France for treatment of wounds and frostbitten feet. Daily several would show up who had gone AWOL from the hospital before the doctor released them, wanting to get back to their old outfit and buddies. They were giving up a warm bed and hot food to go back to the snow and cold and the dangers of combat.

Strictly speaking, they should have been court-martialed. I doubt if any ever were. I told the personnel officer to mark their records "Returned to Duty" and send them on their way. It was what they wanted.

We knew that much of the value of the three day rest period we were providing for our battalions on a rotating basis was largely negated by the chilling three-hour ride to and from Virton in crowded open trucks. One of our units had driven the Germans out of a mountain resort town, Clervaux, Luxembourg, although it was still receiving artillery shellings daily. General Miley asked me to go with him and his aide to this town, about an hour's drive from Division Forward, to see if we could find a facility for a new rest area.

The road was covered with snow, but a snowplow was working at clearing it. We came to a revolting sight. The plow had gone over a dead German buried in the snow, with the results one might expect. By this time, though, the sight of dead people (if they were Germans) failed to shock me.

We went to the building housing our unit headquarters. In a room, huddled around a stove for warmth were several officers and GIs. On the floor was the form of a man covered with a blanket, only his blond hair showing. "Why is that man sleeping this time of day?" General Miley asked.

"He is not sleeping; he is dead," replied one of the officers.

He was a medic who had been shot while crawling forward in an attempt to reach a wounded soldier. The thought crossed my mind, "What sorrow will come to some family when they learn of the death of this blond-haired kid."

The only building in the city that would have been large enough to meet our needs for a rest area was a Catholic orphanage run by an order of nuns. The Mother Superior met us at the door when we went to look at the place, and she was weeping. The place was in shambles. She told us that just before departure the day before, the German troops had taken machine pistols and shot up all the steam radiators, wrecked the boilers, and knocked out all the window panes. The nuns had all the children in a couple of rooms covered with blankets. There were 12 civilian corpses in the basement which the nuns were keeping until a proper Catholic burial could be made.

We then drove to the city hall, where General Miley told the burgomaster to bury all civilian dead and put as many men as necessary to work restoring water and electricity to the town. We went home.

Finally, the 17th was pulled out of the line and ordered to the Chalons-sur-Marne area to rest, recuperate, and resupply. This was the latter part of February, and the weather was still cold, but there were occasional thaws. I returned to Virton and we loaded men and equipment on trucks and started out. It was a miserable voyage. As the snow melted on the roads, countless, sharp, shrapnel fragments were uncovered, and we had 42 punctures in my small convoy.

The entire division staff was quartered in an old French Caserne which the Germans had used to imprison several thousand French Jews. It was the essence of filth, with human excrement all over the court yard, and the rooms were infested with vermin. This was a good stay, though, after we got everything cleaned up. A division mess was established, and my office had nothing to do but the usual administrative work, which was relatively light. The troops, for the most part were housed in tents.

Our next campaign was to be fought under the command of the eccentric, egotistical, but sometimes brilliant British General Montgomery. He was from the first a thorn in the side of General Eisenhower and other American generals. Many books written since the war delineate their different concepts of strategy. Basically, Montgomery was convinced that a concentrated spearhead thrust into the heart of Germany would end the war quickly, whereas the American commander favored the broad front concept. Of course the English general wanted to command the operation.

We were involved in a scheme Montgomery had talked Eisenhower into undertaking, though the American general consented grudgingly. This was to force a crossing of the Rhine at the town of Wessel. Supposedly, this was to be a limited action, but as events turned out there is no question in my mind but that Montgomery intended to circumvent his superior's directive and push rapidly to the capture of Berlin. The controversy as to which general was right continues to this day among military analysis.

The two Airborne divisions involved were the American 17th and the British 6th. In contrast to all previous Airborne assaults, the plan called for a crossing first by ground troops, followed by a drop of parachutists and glider troops 12 miles behind the lines to facilitate a rapid advance into Germany. Also at stake was to be the honor of achieving the first crossing of the Rhine by a large allied force.

To insure secrecy, the entire division was sent to a staging area some 15 miles from Chalons and completely sealed off from the outside world—no outgoing mail or contact with outsiders. Intensive planning and briefing was carried out. We were somewhat chagrinned when immediately we began hearing broadcasts from "Axis Sally" in Berlin, telling exactly where and when the operation was to be launched and promising dire results when it was attempted. There must have been numerous German agents, or perhaps French collaborators, in the area.

My small part of this operation was to take not only the rear echelon, but all of the vehicles of the division to a designated area a couple of miles from the crossing site, a hard two day's drive. I forget how many jeeps and trucks were in the convoy, but there were several hundred. We were following plans formulated by Montgomery's staff, and they were far more detailed than any prepared by Americans.

The first overnight stop was made at a Dutch army camp. My chief clerk, checking our convoy, found that we had lost one vehicle on the road.

The next morning before daylight, when we started moving the vehicles out in sequence and at designated times, all of our officers were out, shouting instructions, and there was a lot of confusion. I walked over to our neighbor's convoy, and there wasn't an officer to be found. A lone British sergeant major was in charge, aided by non-coms, and they were moving out in a quiet and orderly manner.

The area assigned us for a final bivouac before the crossing was heavily wooded, right next to the road that led to the blown bridge at Wessel, and only a couple of miles from it. What shocked me was that in our areas were thousands of German heavy artillery shells stacked like cord wood. a team of British sappers were busy defusing the shells. Although they assured us that when they finished their job there would be no danger, all of us were apprehensive.

Usually GIs have to be urged to dig foxholes unless they are being shot at. In this case, it wasn't necessary to urge them. They started digging with vigor, and some of the holes were five or more feet deep, in which they slept.

Long columns of heavy artillery, tanks and troop carriers constantly clogged the adjoining road on the way to their assigned areas. Of course the Germans knew exactly what was going on, so as soon as it got dark the biggest pyrotechnic display I ever hope to see started. I know I shall never see it equaled in any Fourth of July celebration.

German aircraft would fly over, drop a few bombs on the bridge site to prevent or delay any attempt to repair the structure, then continue down the road beside our campsite, strafing it in the hope of catching some column moving up. Brilliant pyramids were formed by searchlights, reaching to the sky, trying to focus on the raider, and anti-aircraft fire and tracer bullets added to the display. I almost held my breath wondering what would happen if a bomb fell among the stacks of artillery shells, but none did.

Only recently did I read authentic statistics as to what Montgomery had assembled by March 23, the day before the attempted crossing. There were 300,000 tons of ammunition and supplies, 5,500 pieces of artillery, and the entire 2nd British and 9th U.S. Armies, plus attached units. Altogether there were 30 Allied divisions. Opposed to him was a strong German force.

At daybreak on the morning of the 23rd of March there was a constant roar as all 5,500 pieces of artillery opened fire, and that continued all day and all night. One had to shout to carry on a conversation. To add to the confusion there was air strike after air strike against the town of Wessel.

On the morning of the 24th, my driver and I drove as far forward as permitted to watch the show. The barrage continued and our vision was obscured as smoke was laid down to shield from view the engineers as they laid prefabricated bridges across the Rhine. British Commandoes crossed the river in rubber boats and established a bridgehead with very little opposition.

There just wasn't much that survived the intense shelling and air strikes. Soon troops and tanks started crossing the bridges, and overhead the Airborne operation came into view. All told, there were 1,696 transport planes, slow-moving C-47s carrying parachutists or pulling gliders. It was an awesome sight, never to be seen again. There were 1,348 gliders, 240 bombers, and like specks in the sky, 889 fighters. The air train was 500 miles long.

While it was a relative picnic for the ground troops, the Airborne troops had problems. The smoke laid down by Montgomery and from burning buildings had partially covered the selected glider landing areas, causing landings and drops to be made more or less by guess, with resulting casualties. Too, there was a heavy concentration of hostile troops which had fallen back from the bridge area. When the transport planes made the turn to return to their bases, they ran into heavy anti-aircraft fire, and I saw a number of planes wobbling along with smoke streaming behind, with one or more engines knocked out.

I never found out how many were lost, but the number must have been considerable. For our division on that day, we had 159 killed, 552 wounded, and 240 missing.

The operation was a success, and according to what Eisenhower wrote in his book, the most successful Airborne operation of the war. Unfortunately, Montgomery lost his hoped-for glory to be added to his fame as the "Hero of Alamein." A few days before, by accident rather than planning, the bridge at Remegen fell into Allied hands, and the first breach of the Rhine was made there, the acclaim of this crossing far exceeding our larger operation.

Always there are humorous incidents arising from tragic experiences in war times. One of my young lieutenants, a Puerto Rican by the name of Claudio, wanted to jump with the troops, arguing that he could help with the battle casualty reporting the first day of combat. I didn't think he could do much in that confusion, but I told him he could go.

A piece of shrapnel caught him as he was floating to earth. It hit the front of his helmet, made a crease around it and emerged in the back, without making so much as a scratch on his head. It did knock him out for a half hour or so. He proudly continued to wear this battle-scarred helmet.

My good friend, Ed Messenger, went in on a glider. At his feet was a briefcase which contained the plans for the 17th operation. A shrapnel burst caught the glider. His briefcase was shredded. The bottom of his shoes had shrapnel fragments in them. Days afterward, he felt the lining of his jacket and worked out small pieces of metal. He didn't lose a drop of blood.

The day after the drop I crossed the repaired bridge to visit Division Forward. On the bridge at intervals of ten feet or so were riflemen. They were watching for bombs that might be floated down the river in an attempt to destroy the bridge, hoping to explode them by rifle fire before they could do any damage. I drove through the encampment of a British Ranger Regiment and they were in a festive mood after their almost unopposed crossing. At the time, a number were picking geese they had "liberated" from some farm yard.

The GIs as well as the British lived off the land when they could. Whenever we stopped in a rural village the GIs would jump off the jeeps and rush to the hen houses to gather eggs and even to milk cows. I must admit that at times I enjoyed eating the German black bread and the cured ham and sausage taken from some German farm house.

I found Division Headquarters comfortably settled in a building about ten miles from the river. The Signal people had followed the troops, laying wire and establishing telephone communications with all elements of the command. I called my office (just a tent) and was talking to John Gray when I was rudely interrupted. A German plane had flown over and strafed our building, and stitched the room I was in with a line of bullets just a few feet from where I was sitting.

Very stupidly I threw down the phone and dived under the desk. Then I jumped up and ran outside just in time to see the plane turn and start back over us at a very low altitude, so low that I could clearly see the pilot. By now the headquarters personnel were firing at the plane with carbines, but the pilot did not return the fire.

I hadn't had a chance to talk with General Miley when Colonel Liebel told us to pack up and leave immediately for a new command post about 15 miles away. The Germans were retreating as fast as they could and our people were in hot pursuit. The enemy was thoroughly defeated.

Along the way we passed numerous German soldiers who had thrown away their arms, and even one or two groups which were in marching formation, probably trying to find someone to surrender to. We had no time to fool with prisoners so we rushed on by them to our destination. I decided then I couldn't return to my outfit until things settled down as there were reports of fanatical Nazis we had by-passed ambushing our people, especially when travelling in single vehicles.

This same pattern of movement continued for days. At times we would arrive at a place and be ordered to move before we got unpacked. On one move, at a turning in the road, A German .88mm gun was looking right at us. Shells were stacked nearby, but there was not a German in sight. Shortly after we arrived at our new destination, we found that a lone British lorry was blown to bits by that gun. The crew had hidden behind a house and let us pass as there was a dozen or more vehicles in our convoy.

As it turned out, Haltern, Germany, was one of our last stops in this campaign. Our units were preparing for an all-out attack on Munster. By this time John Gray had brought up our people and we selected a site for our office.

It was a beautiful rock clubhouse with a large room completely glassed in on one side overlooking and at the edge of a large lake. There was a dead German outside the door which we had the graves registration people take away. One of the boys had picked up a large generator which they set up, giving us electric lights—quite a luxury.

Division Headquarters, about two miles away, had set up a mess in a warehouse that was full of clocks and watches. At our first meal there they gave everyone either a watch or a clock. I took a cuckoo clock and hung it on the wall of our deluxe office. Every time the bird came out and "coo coo'd" the room would be filled with laughter. There wasn't much else to laugh about. Better still, we found a room filled with old German rifles and sabers. I took one of each.

The next day I felt a little uneasy. Several shells fell in the lake a few hundred feet from our glassed in view, and I knew they were shooting at us as there was no other target around. I jeeped over to headquarters and asked our G-2, Colonel McAllister, about our situation. He told me that German patrols were crossing the river at night, and in view of our isolated situation, he advised me to move.

I didn't need much encouragement to do so. We left our beautiful home and moved into one of the two large houses, side by side, that the division staff occupied. At this stage, advancing was so easy that the troops turned the war into a sort of comic opera. Soldiers passing through on the road right in front of our headquarters were wearing top hats; some were riding in carts pulled by horses, others were in liberated German sedans, and one was in a motorized wheelchair! A tank came through with a large statue of a saint standing on top, which General Miley had removed. Obviously it had been taken from a church.

A fire fight was going on at the river bank all day, only a couple of thousand yards from our headquarters. I could step out of my door and watch it. A couple of times when things got pretty hot, the defense platoon would call for help, and my boys and other headquarters personnel would leave their paper work and go down with their carbines and participate.

A rock house on the enemy side of the river appeared to be the source of a lot of enemy rifle fire. Ed Messenger stopped a passing tank column and asked the commander to neutralize it. The gunner must have been expert. He spent a couple of minutes sighting his gun, and put a shell right through a gable window. I saw shingles flying in all directions and smoke pouring out. A score of German soldiers ran through the door and scattered like quail.

We continued to get intermittent shell bursts, but on the third night, although there was no increase in firing, we had a premonition that we had better go to the basement. I went upstairs where my driver and I were bunking. He was sleeping peacefully in his sleeping bag and was reluctant to crawl out until I insisted. We hadn't been in the basement more than ten minutes when an enemy patrol fired four concussion rockets, two hitting our house and one a barn where our jeeps were parked.

The half-windows blew out of the basement, and dust filled the air so that we couldn't see. All but three or four of us were cut by flying glass. The most serious injury was a kid from the G-4 section who must have had his mouth open because a jagged piece of glass protruded from his mouth. He was bleeding profusely. My good friend, Lew Good, was in shock, and we had to help him get out of the basement. None of the injuries was serious. I couldn't hear very well for a while, and the medics now tell me my present hearing problem might have been caused to some extent by this.

The house was a shambles. The stairway was torn loose from the wall, but I climbed over rubble far enough to look into the room in which my driver and I had been sleeping. It was just one big pile of plaster and broken furniture. Under it was my sleeping bag, all my clothes, the German rifle and saber, and the cuckoo clock. I wonder who finally got them. We just left everything where it was. A couple of the jeeps were knocked out. Mine had a big dent in one side, and my driver painted a purple heart beside it.

There was a tall, dark-haired and very quiet private, a G-2 driver, in the basement at the time. He must have felt personally insulted by the affair. The next morning, without asking his boss or telling any of his buddies, he took his carbine to the river bank, swam the river, and sneaked through the woods. By the sound of the firing, he located a battery of two of the Russian made guns.

There were seven men servicing the pieces, and with three shots he killed three of them. He made the remaining four break up the firing mechanism of one of the pieces, and for some reason he decided to "capture" the other. He ordered the men to push it to the river and dump it in. Then he made the four Germans jump in the river and start swimming to the American shore.

Some nervous GI clerk shot one of them in the river. I never made any inquiries into who it was. When this one-man patrol returned to the G-2 section his immediate reward was a bawling out by a captain assistant G-2. When General Miley learned of the escapade, however, he had me write up a recommendation for a Silver Star, which was approved.

The capture of Munster was quite easy. It was made by the 513th Parachute Infantry, commanded by a good friend of mine, Colonel Lou Coutts. Lou had received a painful shoulder wound, but he had the division medics patch him up and he refused to go to the hospital. He tapped an open telephone wire to Munster and tried to talk the Burgomaster into surrendering to avoid a lot of civilian casualties. The Burgomaster refused, saying that if the Americans attacked, the streets would run red with their blood.

It was a foolish boast as we knew they had little to defend the town with. Three air strikes were called for, and after their devastation, our troops just marched in. We stayed there one night, and the next day we were ordered to pull out immediately for the Rhur area. General Miley was quite upset about the order as we were in good shape and advancing fast with little resistance. He protested to higher headquarters, but to no avail.

When we were in Haltern one of our British tank commanders stopped by my office and showed me his secret orders issued by Montgomery. He was to proceed to a certain crossroads, turn east and proceed to Berlin. We were only about 200 miles from there, meeting little resistance and the Germans were surrendering by the tens of thousands to avoid being taken prisoner by the Russians.

Much later, I learned that not only our division, but the entire 9th American Army was pulled out from under the British General. In my own mind, I am certain that Eisenhower learned that the eccentric General Montgomery intended to circumvent his orders and take Berlin. With our troops gone, he didn't have the forces or logistic support to do it.

As usual, I sent John Gray ahead to find a new location for my office and all the unit personnel sections, and I went with the Division Headquarters convoy.

John had selected for us the former Gestapo Headquarters in Hamborn, a city adjoining Essen, which was to be our next objective. As soon as we got settled, I called the chief of staff, Colonel Liebel, and told him where we were located. He was aghast.

"Hell," he said, "you are three miles closer to the front than Division Forward! Now I am going to have to send you some troops from the 507th to protect you."

He needn't have worried. The Germans were licked and caused us no problems. Our headaches came from another source.

In the Rhur area there were 600,000 slave laborers, mostly Russians, and of these about 35,000 were assigned to us. Never have I seen such an orgy of looting, drunkeness and murder as there was here. Understandingly, I guess, they felt they were due revenge. But wholesale looting, rape, murder couldn't go on, so we had to erect barbed wire compounds, separate them by nationality, and provide food and shelter. To be imprisoned by their liberators was something they couldn't understand. As General Miley felt sorry for them he at first issued them double rations, and as they were not accustomed to eating so much many of them became ill.

One amusing, though tragic incident, I remember was the German arms and ammunition that were laying around everywhere, thrown away as the enemy left. One Russian got a German rifle, sawed off the butt so it could be held and fired like a pistol. Also, he obtained an old auto horn, the type you could make squawk by squeezing a rubber bulb. One night he went from house to house, and under a window he would sound the horn. When a German stuck his head out the window to see what was happening, the Russians would shoot him. He killed five before our troops finally stopped him.

The Russian leaders showed little interest in relieving us of our responsibility of feeding and caring for their nationals. Finally, after much prodding, they sent a commissar down with an agreement to repatriate these slave laborers, provided we would deliver them to a designated border town in Russia. This was accomplished with a big airlift. Later, we learned that these unfortunate people did not get to go home at all. The Russians sent them all to Siberia.

The small towns in our areas began to surrender without a fight. The Germans were accustomed to doing what they were told to do, and when the Civil Affairs officer ordered them to turn in all weapons of any description (field glasses, radios, etc.) they complied. I drove into one town that just capitulated, and at the city hall, where the Civil Affairs office was located, a large room was filled with shot guns, antique duelling pistols, old cross bows, radios, and other items.

At the time I was in a hurry, and the Civil Affairs officer told me to take what I wanted. My driver and I quickly grabbed up an arm load of shotguns and threw them in the jeep. I intended to return later in the day and carefully select a few valuable pieces. Back at the office I distributed the shotguns to the men, keeping one for myself.

Essen fell without firing a shot. The industrial complex there had been bombed so much it appeared that some giant in the skies had reached down and scrambled the buildings. German workmen were still building tanks and locomotives. No one had told them to stop.

The war was winding down. One of our officers captured Von Papen and took his beautiful pearl handled automatic for a souvenir. A German general surrendered his command to General Miley. He told General Miley, "My division and equipment is largely intact. I suggest you let me keep things as they are because you are going to have fight the Russians, and I can help." Of course, his offer was declined.

Americans were liberated from POW camps after months and even years behind barbed wire. They were to be evacuated in an orderly fashion and any found wandering around were to be picked up and placed in the "pipe line." This didn't please many of them who decided to return on their own. One day five of them came into my office. They had "liberated" a German car and were en route to Paris and wanted gasoline and road maps. Although it was contrary to Eisenhower's orders, I wasn't about to call the MPs.

When unconditional surrender finally came, there was one question uppermost in our minds ... What is going to happen to us? General Miley reasoned that our division would be held intact as occupation forces because this is the way it was done in World War I. After all, we hadn't been in combat nearly as long as many of the other divisions. Of course, there was a possiblity we would be sent to the Pacific to fight out the war with Japan. To keep morale up, General Miley planned an active athletic program, and told me to scan all personnel records for athletes, particularly baseball players as he wanted the best team on the continent.

For us, the war was over—but not without a high cost. With an authorized strength of about 8,000, we had 1,119 killed, 4,214 wounded, and 87 missing. What price glory?

One event happened only two days after the final surrender of Germany that made me realize how useless and silly war really is. For some reason, I have forgotten why, several of us had to fly north to coordinate some business with the 82nd Airborne Division. We landed on a German airfield, with German aircraft all around. Also at the airfield were two German infantry divisions casually going about their daily routine of camp life. Only three days before we had been shooting at each other. German MPs wearing their side arms, courteously escorted us to headquarters.

There we found a joint American-German staff, working in the same building, taking care of the logistics involved in feeding the troops. There was only one company of 82nd combat troops in the area. Perhaps this unusual association was eclipsed only during the big airdrop of fierce fighting at Arnheim, Holland. There, the 101st hospital was in one end of a building, and the German hospital in the other.

That we were designated to go home proved to be empty words as far as most of the personnel of the 17th was concerned. Eisenhower announced the "point system," which provided that those who had been overseas the longest and who had the most decorations would go home first. This completely wrecked the organization of the U.S. Army, the most powerful military organization in the world. Coupled with this, Drew Pearson, the columnist, was writing daily about the gripes of individual GIs and criticizing the stupidity of officers, urging speedy return to the U.S. of the soldiers.

To undergo this ordeal of reshuffling personnel, we were sent to an area near Vittel, France. Soon we had lost most of our personnel to the 101st, which was to occupy Berlin, and we got about 8,000 people from that division and the 82nd. It was amazing to see how magnificent and disciplined fighting men could change, almost overnight, into an undisciplined rabble. They were organized into units, of course, but the officers didn't know the men and the men didn't know the officers, and neither group cared much about anything but getting back to the U.S.

To show the inconsistency of Army red tape, there were two cases that came up at this time. One involved a lieutenant colonel of artillery from the 101st. He had picked up two fine, pure bred horses that he claimed a German general had given him. There was no question in my mind but that he had stolen them. He came to me and wanted me to cut orders authorizing him to ship them home commercially and to detail a sergeant to accompany them. The whole thing appeared so ridiculous that I said, "No."

He left in a huff and went to the chief of staff, Colonel Liebel. After a while I was called in and they had a book of Army Regulations open. Left over from the old days and never rescinded, was a regulation stating that an officer could ship two of his personal mounts to his next station and that the Army would provide an enlisted escort. The chief of staff told me to cut the orders, and I did. The sergeant accompanying the horses was the first person of the 17th to arrive in the U.S.

On the other hand, I had a kid that was a hard and willing worker sent to me. The correspondence with his orders indicated he had shipped home through the mails a fleece-lined Air Corps jacket that was government property; that the package was intercepted, and that we were to turn him over on arrival to a designated MP unit for trial for theft. This was inconsequential in comparison to the two stolen horses and all the "liberated" stuff I knew most of the officers had in their foot lockers.

Marseilles at that time was a hotbed of smugglers, black marketeers, con men, and prostitutes. General Miley assembled the men and explained to them the situation and told them they were restricted to the area until we boarded ship. "If I permit you to go into town," he said, "some of you will not get home."

The troopers soon found local entertainment. Because of the confusion of personnel shuffling, the men had not been paid for three months. When they were paid, there were the wildest crap games I have ever seen all over the area. Most of the pay was in ten dollar bills, and when a player said, "I'll shoot five," he didn't mean five dollars, he meant five, ten dollar bills. Fortunes changed hands hourly. After months overseas, with nothing much to buy, all sense of the value of money was lost.

We came home on the old luxury liner, the *Mariposa*, which had been converted austerely into a troop ship. The voyage was a nightmare, and only added to my determination to get out of the Army as quickly as possible, and to get back to my family. We had 8,500 troops aboard, with bunks for only a third of them. All signs of discipline disappeared, and the men, for the most part, were uncooperative in our efforts to get them safely home.

The ship was crewed by civilian merchant marine people, whom the soldiers despised because they felt, rightly or wrongly, they had avoided the war while drawing high pay, eating well, and sleeping between clean white sheets. There were numerous fights between crew and soldiers, and almost daily we had to placate an angry ship's captain.

Feeding was a problem, and to provide two meals a day the galley was operated 24 hours a day. We were supposed to provide KPs, but when we picked 20 or so men for the job, they would frequently disappear before they even reached the kitchen. Finally, we made a deal with the steward, whereby KPs would be rewarded with a big steak at the end of their tour, and this helped.

The ship's captain had ruled that all men would wear life jackets at all times, except when they were in bed. This was practically impossible to enforce, and we decreed that any man not wearing a life jacket would not be fed. This didn't help much either, because as soon as a soldier got his chow he would throw off his jacket. In a short time a mountain of jackets would cause the chow line to be halted until they were removed. These are examples of the many problems we encountered at sea.

All this time I worried about the youngster I had grown to like very much—the one who wouldn't be allowed to go home on arrival because he had been caught shipping home a government jacket. With General Miley's approval, I decided to do something about it. I called the boy into our cabin and explained to him that his records had been tagged and that there was no way we could avoid the order to turn him over to the MPs.

"However," I said, "if you are willing, I can try you right now for this offense by Summary Court. That way, only I will be the judge, and I will fine you $25.00. Otherwise, you will be thrown in the guardhouse, and when you are tried by a Special or General Court you can be given a prison sentence. Which do you prefer?"

Naturally, he was glad to have me try him. I completed the trial papers and explained to him about "double jeopardy" and advised him to show the papers to some officer as soon as he was delivered to the MPs. That was the last I heard of him.

Finally, we landed in Boston, the port from which we had sailed months and months ago. Within one day after our debarkation, all the troops were gone. In another day, only Colonel Liebel and I remained of the 17th.

Soon, Colonel Liebel left and only I remained. I had to turn in the division's records and tend to a few last minute details. That left me, one of the original names on the 17th activation order, as the last member of the 17th Airborne Division.

Index

334